The Best American Travel Writing 2009

GUEST EDITORS OF
THE BEST AMERICAN TRAVEL WRITING

2000   BILL BRYSON
2001   PAUL THEROUX
2002   FRANCES MEYERS
2003   IAN FRAZIER
2004   PICO IYER
2005   JAMAICA KINCAID
2006   TIM CAHILL
2007   SUSAN ORLEAN
2008   ANTHONY BOURDAIN
2009   SIMON WINCHESTER

The Best American Travel Writing™ 2009

Edited and with an Introduction
by Simon Winchester

Jason Wilson, Series Editor

A Mariner Original
HOUGHTON MIFFLIN HARCOURT
BOSTON · NEW YORK   2009

www.hmhbooks.com

ISSN 1530-1516
ISBN 978-0-618-85866-8

Printed in the United States of America
DOC 10 9 8 7 6 5 4 3 2 1

Contents

Foreword

"GO TO A PLACE, report on its cultures, foibles, distractions, and bring it back to entertain your readers . . . it's not enough just to say what happened — you have to make people understand what it felt like to be there when it happened." This seems like a pretty good description of travel writing, right? It wouldn't seem out of place as advice given by an editor to a first-time travel writer. But actually, this quote is by a video game journalist named Kieron Gillen, taken from a manifesto he wrote not too long ago on what he calls "The New Games Journalism" (after Tom Wolfe's famous term "The New Journalism"). In his manifesto, Gillen exhorts his video gaming colleagues to become "Travel Journalists to Imaginary Places."

"The thing with travel journalism or reportage is that it's interesting even if you have absolutely no inclination of going there," he writes. A key difference between travel writing and video game writing, according to Gillen: "Our job is to describe what it's like to visit a place that doesn't exist outside of the gamer's head . . . The worth of gaming lies in the gamer not the game."

I was recently struck by how similar this is to Paul Theroux's memorable assertion about travel writing: "The misperception is that the travel book is about a country. It's really about the person who's traveling."

An old girlfriend also once insisted that travel writing was a lot like playing video games — though it was not a compliment. This girlfriend fancied herself an intellectual and a literary person and looked down on travel writing as well as video games, and her comment was an attempt to dissuade me from both activities, which she believed were keeping me from finishing the Great American Novel. This was probably true, but it didn't bode well for our long-term prospects. We were in a dive college bar in Boston when she sternly pointed a French fry at me and said, "You know, I read an essay recently by these scholars from MIT. And they put forth this thesis that the simplistic narratives of many video games have their parallels in travel writing narratives."

This was around fifteen years ago, when it was not uncommon to find myself in a certain type of ridiculous-but-supposedly-deep conversation, debates about whether or not the Smurfs were actually Communists or whether Ho Chi Minh had once worked as a pastry chef for Escoffier or whether Mikey from the Life cereal ads had truly died from mixing Pop Rocks and soda. During that period, for instance, I once used the plot of Scooby Doo to teach a freshman writing class about narrative.

Nintendo's *Street Fighter II* was the video game she used as an example. "You know how in *Street Fighter,* the two characters fight in all these different exotic global spaces? In one fight, they're in a Chinese street market. Then they're in a Japanese temple. Then they're on a dock in the Amazon. Then they're in a Soviet-style factory. Then they're in a Vegas casino. In some scenes, they have flamenco dancers behind them. In others, they have Indian men riding elephants. Anyway, the scholars' point was this: all of the worlds that the fighters enter are really just eye candy, simply ornamental local color. All these new places are consumed by the game player one after another, and the video game makers understand that they need to keep changing the scenes, with all new local color, or else the game will become boring. But while all the eye candy always changes, the same basic plot and the same basic narration — in this case, two street fighters kicking the crap out of one another — never changes."

"I see," I said, with a raised eyebrow.

"Well," she said, growing more argumentative, "don't you agree that travel writing, or even just the travel stories most people tell, present a similar worldview? That people basically play out their same personal dramas no matter where they go. That only the eye candy changes."

"Um, no," I said. "Actually, that sort of sounds insane." This led quickly into one of the stupider arguments in a long line of very stupid arguments.

Not too long after we'd broken up, I came across the essay she'd referenced, "Nintendo and New World Travel Writing: A Dialogue," by Mary Fuller and Henry Jenkins. Fuller and Jenkins likened Nintendo's Mario Brothers' adventures in rescuing Princess Toadstool to the nonfictional New World travel narratives of John Smith, Virginia Dare, and Pocahontas in the lost colony of Roanoke. Both are "forms of narrative that privilege space over characterization or plot development" and "a different way of organizing narratives" that they call "spatial stories." At the time, it seemed the sort of loopy scholarship that got debated over a bong in someone's dorm room. But now I'm not so sure.

I thought seriously about travel writing and video games this past year — when I wasn't reading nominations for *The Best American Travel Writing*, I spent some time playing Wii with my two sons. We enjoyed a game called *Endless Ocean,* in which you play the role of a deep-sea diver who, along with a somewhat irritating companion, a marine biologist named Katherine, explores the fictional Manoa Lai Sea in a fictional South Pacific. The graphics are amazingly lifelike, and over time a whole world with a diverse underwater ecosystem — full of whales, tropical fish, stingrays, sharks, and other sea life — slowly, gently emerges. In fact, calling *Endless Ocean* a "game" at all is stretching the definition. The challenges aren't very taxing — it's almost impossible to run out of air, and not even the sharks bite. There's only a light plot involving the legends of the native peoples of fictional Pelago. Most of the time, you just sort of swim around, unscripted, collecting new species of sea creatures and exploring coral reefs, sea caves, and sunken ruins. But after hours of leisurely navigating, a strange emotional experience begins to take hold. Suddenly, the discovery of a simple seahorse or a bit of an artifact is a cause for joy. Upon uncovering an ancient, fossilized whale whisker, I found myself looking forward to surfacing and celebrating with my kooky shipmate, whom I now called Kat. Virtual as it was, *Endless Ocean* was beginning to take on the recognizable rhythms of travel.

All of which meant that *Endless Ocean* was becoming a little scary. I wondered if someday in the not-so-distant future, fake gaming worlds like Manoa Lai might replace, say, the real South Pacific as an actual destination. If the current economic and energy crises continue, perhaps my boys will have to skip the old backpacking trip to Europe and instead experience that formative travel through some type of gaming. I guess if that unfortunate outcome truly does come to pass, at least I take solace that some form of travel narrative might still possibly thrive.

I realized this kind of techno-futurist thinking meant it was time to return to my reading of the wonderful travel writing you'll find in this anthology. When I did, I breathed a sigh of relief. The writers collected here have gone out into the world, the *real* world, and brought back stories that give us not only what happened, but also an understanding of what it felt like to be there — a deft intertwining of both the personal and the universal. All of them are giving us much more than just eye candy.

This is our tenth edition of *The Best American Travel Writing*. The stories included here are, as always, selected from among hundreds of pieces in hundreds of diverse publications — from mainstream and specialty magazines to Sunday newspaper travel sections to literary journals to travel websites. I've done my best to be fair and representative, and the best travel stories from 2008 in my opinion were forwarded to Simon Winchester, who made the final selections.

I now begin anew by reading the hundreds of stories published in 2009. I am once again asking editors and writers to submit the best of whatever it is they define as travel writing. These submissions must be nonfiction and published in the United States during the 2009 calendar year. They must not be reprints or excerpts from published books. They must include the author's name, date of publication, and publication name, and must be tear sheets, the complete publication, or a clear photocopy of the piece as it originally appeared. I must receive all submissions by January 1, 2010, in order to ensure full consideration for the next collection.

Further, publications that want to make certain their contributions will be considered for the next edition should make sure to include this anthology on their subscription list. Submissions or subscriptions should be sent to Jason Wilson, The Best American Travel Writing, P.O. Box 260, Haddonfield, NJ 08033.

I very much enjoyed working with Simon Winchester, who even

did a large part of his work on the book during a very long boat trip that took him across the South Atlantic from the South Georgia Islands to South Africa, via the remote Tristan da Cunha. I am also grateful to Nicole Angeloro and Jesse Smith for their help. Here's to ten more years!

JASON WILSON

Introduction

I COME FROM BRITAIN, and chauvinism has long led me to believe — wrongly, I now happily admit — that the best of all travel literature comes from my own country. In the British Isles, the concept of connection with the outside world is unique, and a positive fascination for things foreign seems bred to the bone.

There are a host of reasons for this. Five hundred years of empire, for example, left an indelible legacy — familial, spiritual, commercial — of an abiding intimacy with our overseas possessions. My own experience as a child is typical: my father soldiered in Egypt and Palestine, there was an uncle who policed in Burma, another in Bechuanaland. All kept picture albums, which were taken down and dusted off to be shown to *the boy* at regular intervals.

Along the nave of our local village church were lines of well-shined brass plaques, memorials to locals who died — from malaria, tigers, accidents, unruly natives — in every corner of the empire, from Newfoundland to Namaqualand, from Sierra Leone to Singapore. And our High Street shops — the Home & Colonial being the best example — brought us goods that made us entirely familiar with words and places from the faraway: my mother's expeditions to buy Kia-Ora orange squash from New Zealand and Outspan grapefruit from South Africa spring first to mind.

Propinquity is another. As with Russia from Sarah Palin's back porch, so with France, which can be seen (and certainly heard, when there is a war on) from England's White Cliffs. It cost a pittance to board the packet-boat from Dover and get oneself onto the edge of a landmass that stretched as far as Vladivostok. So there was seldom much by way of fear or intimidation when it came to considering the concept of abroad: it was always there, next door, easily and inexpensively attainable.

I once traveled from London to Hong Kong by train, and thought I'd show off by buying my through ticket from the clerk at Liverpool Street Station. After the man in front of me had bought his monthly season ticket to Chelmsford or some such suburb, I stepped forward and asked the man in the *guichet* for a single, first-class ticket to Kowloon Station. He didn't even look up: *You wishing to go by way of Khabarovsk or Irkutsk?* he asked in a tone of boredom and casual irritation. And when I mumbled that I didn't know, he asked me to step aside so he could sell a ticket to the man behind, a vicar wanting a day-return to Saffron Walden. To an English railway official, the notion that a customer might wish to buy a ticket good for eight thousand miles of eastbound travel was perfectly normal, almost routine.

School geography lessons, too, leave a permanent legacy — something I would argue to my last breath to any curriculum philistine who would dare, as increasing numbers are now daring, to abandon teachings about the nature of the Levantine, the rain shadow of the Atacama Desert, or the social significance of karst topography. To this day I remember the essay I was asked to write, at age twelve, on *The Significance in American History of the Hudson-Mohawk Gap.* It left an indelible impression — if for no other reason than by allowing me to understand just why New York City, where I now choose to live, is so very rich and important.

And geographical schooling in Britain goes on long after the classes have been dismissed. Almost all students now take what is known as a "gap year" before going on to university — and almost all gap years are spent traveling overseas. The idea in fact originated in New Zealand, where it was called "overseas experience," or OE — and it embodied the recognition that with New Zealand being so far from almost everywhere, it would be unlikely that more than a very few would ever be able to afford the time or the funds to go traveling — except in this one year before entering full-time study and the job market.

The OE idea then spread to Australia, where it became a habit among students to get themselves to nearby Singapore and then

drive overland to London, finally selling their road-stained cars —
most of them Volkswagen Combis — in the roadway outside the
BBC World Service headquarters off the Strand. British students
took up the idea promptly, often driving the same cars back to Australia — with the result that Britons, Kiwis, and Aussies became preternaturally knowledgeable about the finer details of long-distance
traveling. (One such pair, Tony and Maureen Wheeler, founded
the Lonely Planet empire initially to cater to them.)

Then again, almost all good British universities have an Exploration Club, and all send, during each summer vacation, full-fledged
expeditions to some of the most weird and wonderful corners of
the globe, with the students deciding on a genuine scientific purpose for the adventure and raising the funds to make the trip.
When I was an eighteen-year-old undergraduate, I went with five
others on a three-month geological expedition to East Greenland;
a friend the same year went with two colleagues to look for relics of
the Ark on Mount Ararat. The Royal Geographical Society in London is central to these university endeavors: to raise funds, the RGS
has to approve the venture, and so planning has to be rigorous, attention to detail scrupulous, and the results written up afterward in
the geographical literature.

And travel writing has not surprisingly long played a vital part in
this wander-soaked culture. In my schooldays such ripping yarns as
Eric Newby's *A Short Walk in the Hindu Kush* and James Morris's *Cor-
onation Everest* were hugely popular, while necessary classics like Alexander Kinglake's *Eothen* and Robert Byron's *The Road to Oxiana*
were set texts in class. We soon graduated to writers like Geoffrey
Moorhouse, Dervla Murphy, Bruce Chatwin, Patrick Leigh Fermor,
and Jonathan Raban. The genre has quieted somewhat, the pub-
lishing moguls say, but there are still tables galore in all the great
English bookstores today devoted simply to travel, and still there
exist bookstores that sell little other than books about the great
outside — Stanford's in Covent Garden, where one always went
for the best and most obscure maps, and Daunt's on London's
Marylebone High Street, where the edgiest of travel literature is
eternally piled up like autumn leaves, endlessly tempting.

It is all rather different here in America. The background, the wan-
derlust-rich marinade, is in one sense simply not there. There was

essentially no empire (the Philippines, Puerto Rico, and a scattering of Pacific islands excepted), and hence little by way of imperial
legacy. The country is formidably isolated by thousands of miles of
ocean from almost anywhere truly foreign, and getting abroad is
very much more costly. Americans seldom went to seek their fortunes overseas, as Britons so often did: the country is so vast and
crammed with treasure and ideas, there was rarely a need to venture beyond its coasts — one of the many reasons, no doubt, that
geography is nowadays taught virtually nowhere: there is no perceived need. There is also these days little tradition of American exploration (aside from exploration-as-entertainment put on for the
benefit of a number of some rather dubious but fashionable clubs
and societies).

And there is what I can only describe as a pervasively dismissive
attitude among many to the very notion of overseas travel. The
State Department says fewer than one in four Americans have pass-
ports, and when I asked a group of twenty-eight students at a university in northern Nevada recently how many had traveled abroad,
only three raised their hands. (By contrast, when I asked a group of
twenty students at a university in Sydney how many had *not* traveled
abroad, not a single hand went up.)

One especially egregious example will serve to illustrate. I have
friends who live close by me in New York, an intelligent couple of
considerable wealth and sophistication, who have a daughter of fifteen. The child attends the United Nations International School in
Manhattan, at a very significant annual cost to her parents, and is
according to all who know her an achiever, both academically and
physically; she is popular and wildly pretty, and seems destined for
goodness, a preeminently electable member of the *jeunesse dorée*.

When I saw her last, however, there occurred a faintly troubling
incident. I was in the family's large and sprawling penthouse loft,
where there happened to be on the coffee table (as there should
be on all coffee tables) a copy of the *Times Atlas, Comprehensive Edition,* the Godzilla of good atlases. The volume happened to be
open at its front endpaper — which as any close reader will know
displays a Miller-modified Mercator projection index map of the
entire world.

For no better reason than to satisfy a mild curiosity, and because
I had read one of those distressing recent polls about Americans'
geographical ignorance, I asked the girl if she could possibly point

out on the map the location of Israel. For a student at the United Nations school, such should be child's play.

But no. The youngster grinned sheepishly, glanced nervously at her parents, who seemed to have suddenly turned white with nervous anxiety, waved her hand in the air as though blindly pinning the tail on a donkey, and then finally, with an exultant cry of *Eureka!* jabbed her index finger firmly and unequivocally down — in the middle of Cameroon.

The school's website, which we visited within moments, offered something of an explanation for the poor girl's lapse, and gave perhaps some small comfort to her stupefied and humiliated parents. The curriculum, we noted glumly and without surprise, includes the teaching of information and communication technology, naturally; of the history of the UN, reasonably; of art, mathematics, and English, of course. But what it does not teach as a single subject is that topic which might have prevented this poor teenager from placing Zion in West Africa: geography.

True, the word *geography* is to be found, by close scrutiny of the class schedules. But it is buried in a shallow grave within that vague and omnipresent catch-all cop-out known as the social studies and humanities programs. It has been stripped both of its symbolic importance and of its academic rigor — even at the UN school, which one might have hoped would have known better. And yet what has befallen geography in New York is a simple reflection of its fate throughout the nation: it is a subject that now suffers the same popular ignominy that has befallen geology, ever since some wiseacre coined the phrase "rocks for jocks," a field only Steinbeck's Lenny would be dense enough to want to know about it. The two disciplines have thus lately become nonsubjects, essentially, and the consequences are dire.

We all know the statistics — 73 percent of American children can't find France on a map, 50 percent don't know the oceans on either side of the Americas, 60 percent think the Vietnam War was fought against Germany. Some of us rail against the education system that produces such cud-chewing stupidity; but no one, and thus far not even the brightest savants of the Obama administration, seems to have a plan or even the will to restore geography to any meaningful place in American student life.

Brave individual efforts are still being made: I was recently sent a five-hundred-page, highly elaborated comic book published by a firm in Dubuque, which stars a *manga* character called the Plaid Avenger *("We will see the world in plaid: a mystical weaving of facts, figures, cultures, and viewpoints . . ."),* by which it is hoped to soft-sell some degree of world knowledge into teenage brains. I admire the author; I feel the pain of his desperation. But I fear that his plan, like almost every other well-intentioned attempt to do likewise, just isn't going to work — for the simple reason that among the young in America these days, to want to know in any detail about the enginework of abroad (other than the location of the hottest spring break hotspots in Cancun) is for most simply and tediously *uncool.*

Yet all may not be lost — not even to this benighted generation. Although it probably has to be acknowledged that it is going to be a very long while before any more geographic force-feeding is going to be allowed in even the best schools, it is perhaps not too late to look for other ways to try to alter the American cultural landscape, so as to transform the concept of overseas, and of overseas people, things, and places, into objects of popular desire once again.

And it is here that geography as theory and travel as practice become firmly connected — for though few whose essays appear in these pages may have ever considered this, I have come to feel that good travel writing may have an unexpected and influential role to play in changing this country's cultural landscape.

Good travel writing, long vaunted for its literary nobility, may come to play a didactic role as well. It could be employed to lure readers — the young especially, perhaps — toward a fondness for the faraway. And in this respect, America seems to be unexpectedly blessed: for despite all the reasons I have cited, reasons that make the notion quite counterintuitive, American travel writing of a certain kind is better and more stimulating than anywhere else in the world.

Of the relatively few Americans who do travel, who are afflicted by the yearning to move, the "restless goading" of Robert Louis Stevenson, and who choose to write, a remarkable number do so very, very well indeed. I would go further: it seems to me that in America there has developed a tradition of long-form literary journalism devoted to travel that for reasons I cannot properly discern is far superior to anything elsewhere.

Part of the reason — but only part — is, I suspect, due to the vastly greater space available in which to have such journalism published. Vastly greater than has ever existed in the United Kingdom, say. Consider, for instance, the different range of possibilities that confronts a wandering writer in Britain and in America.

In Britain, steeped in the travel tradition though her people may be, there are precious few magazines and journals available to publish the longer and more thoughtful travel essays of the kind that appear here. True, there is a local version of *Condé Nast Traveler,* devoted mainly to proposing grand-luxe locations for high-worth readers; and the RGS publishes *The Geographical,* for the grittier kinds of wandering. The better daily newspapers — and of London's daily eleven, six can be so described — give much space to travel, too, but also of the holiday-planning kind (which I don't think of as travel writing, *sensu stricto*). And there are a tiny number of vanishingly small-circulation magazines in which one can find essays on the remote and the obscure. But little else besides. Besides books, of course — and no one would doubt that British travel authors are numerous, and in a class of their own.

By contrast, in America the newsstands are thick with publications that offer acres of pages across which the writer can roam at will. To the delight of all writers, these magazines are staffed in the main by small armies of sensible and understanding editors, men and women willing to give writers their head, and who have commissioning mindsets of imagination and flair. The world of American magazines is a writers' paradise; for travel writers — since almost every magazine seems to have a niche for them, too — it is a paradise also.

Only look at the journals in the selection here: *Travel* + *Leisure* and *Condé Nast Traveler,* of course; *National Geographic* (currently enjoying a literary rebirth, here represented by engaging essays on Bolivian women wrestlers and the dire straits of the Sahel), the *New York Times Magazine, Outside* (with one piece in particular, Patrick Symmes's essay on Burma's new capital city of Naypyidaw, destined to be ranked among all-time great magazine essays), *Esquire, Ski* (on the slopes and surrounds frequented by James Bond — a brilliant idea), the entirely unanticipated *Virginia Quarterly Review* (from which I have chosen no fewer than *three* wonderful essays, on Lebanon, Syria, and the Roma of the Balkans), *GQ,* the always superb *Harper's Magazine, The New Yorker* (currently better than it has ever been, most especially here with Lynne Cox's extraordinary peroration on the joys and rigors of ultra-cold-water swimming), and the *American Scholar*— and with additionally just one online journal, *Slate* (to be joined in later years by many others, for sure — not least because so many more magazines will become electronic-only, one suspects). That is a dozen publications, all of them able to publish at length — and there are scores more, unrepresented here this year: *The Atlantic Monthly, Smithsonian, National Geographic Adventure* . . . Small wonder good writers flock to America to be published; small wonder the difficulties of selection are prodigious.

A book like this could probably not be published in Britain — or if made would be watery gruel indeed. One might discern a paradox here — that an abundance of geographical education in Britain results in a litany of comparatively ordinary journalism, while a want of geographical education in America is inexplicably linked to an immense and unceasing production of exceptionally good journalism.

But paradox aside — how does this all relate to our fifteen-year-old and her cud-chewing topographical ennui?

The challenge of which her case is just a symptom relates to the need, as I will say again, to change the cultural landscape of America, so to make the highly uncool concept of *abroad* into an object of popular fascination. To make the Hudson-Mohawk Gap and the dryness of the Atacama and the modern history of the Levant possibly, if I dare say it, *exciting.*

There is probably not much point in hoping such acculturation could trickle down from some higher source: there is no higher source, or certainly not one that currently has the interest or the background to act as an authority anymore. But there is, on the other hand, so much evident literary richness on the ground, in the writings that fill the newsstands of every American train station and bookshop and drugstore and Greyhound depot — some of the best of which are extracted here — that a forthright suggestion comes to mind: that a campaign should be started to ensure that brilliant travel writing is matched by *energetic travel reading.* The hope should be fostered that by simply encouraging travel magazine reading among the young, and by tempting the lost generation to find itself by reading about such diversities as swimming off Ellesmere Island, or skiing where 007 skied, or understanding life for a Roma, or investigating the madness of the Tatmadaw in Rangoon, it might be possible that a popular desire for abroad, for overseas, for things foreign, could be allowed and encouraged to do what it has never done before in this country, and that is quite simply to *trickle up.*

I found that by reading all of these pieces, I wanted to go and see and feel and know for myself — I was drawn, I was seduced, I was fascinated. And even though some might argue that is because I'm older, and I'm British, and that therefore wanderlust runs in my veins, I'm not so sure that it is only to the likes of me that these pieces will appeal. The articles I have chosen are just so vivid, so powerful, so plaintive in their siren song, that I venture to say that anyone — even my fifteen-year-old friend in Manhattan — might say on reading them, My word, *how cool.* If, that is, they are encouraged to do so.

But she has to be shown the way. So my message is simple: that all of you readers should do what I now fully intend to do. I will send to my fifteen-year-old a copy of this book, and I will urge her to read it, cover to cover. And then maybe if she likes it, I will follow up by giving her a subscription to *Outside,* or to *The New Yorker,* or even to *The Virginia Quarterly Review.*

My hope is then that she will read such essays as are found in these pages, will be surprised, and will enjoy, and that she may in consequence do one of two things, or, best of all, do both. She may turn to the Miller-modified Mercator index map of the world in her parents' atlas to find out more. And — *mirabile dictu,* perhaps — she may then demand of her parents that after she graduates from the United Nations school, and before she goes on to whatever university is fortunate enough to take care of her, she takes a full year off, stays her entry into the grim realities of the real world of wage-slavery, and *goes traveling.*

By doing so, this young woman will be presented, as all Britons, Europeans, and Antipodeans have long been presented before her, with an opportunity to find out what *abroad, overseas,* and *foreign* are

really all about. And just as important, she may find that by going
wandering, and by coming to understand that the outside world is
truly a great deal cooler than she ever supposed, she will eventually
be able to discern exactly why it is that Israel is not, never was, and
never will be anywhere near Cameroon.

SIMON WINCHESTER

The Best American
Travel Writing 2009

PATRICK SYMMES

The Generals in Their Labyrinth

FROM *Outside*

THERE NEVER WAS A MAN on the ferry to Pakokku, and he didn't say what he said. I didn't meet Western diplomats from three nations. Not for coffee. Not for drinks. Not in the official residence, with rain and palm fronds pelting down, just hours before the storm hit.

I didn't talk with the country's most distinguished astrologer or its worst comedians. Nobody from any NGOs helped me, either. If I had tea with a prominent intellectual or lunch with a noted businessman, nothing happened. I was just in Burma — sorry, I mean Myanmar — to play golf and look at the ruins.

The boy monks never cried and begged me to conceal their names. At the monastery in Pakokku, they never told me anything at all.

I wasn't there when the storm hit. There was no cyclone. I didn't see anything.

But of course it did hit. I flew out on the last plane out of Burma, on the evening of May 1. On May 2, at 6:30 P.M., Cyclone Nargis came ashore near Labutta, in the southwestern corner of this poor and unlucky country, at speeds of up to 121 miles per hour. Howling in from the Bay of Bengal, the winds shoved a twelve-foot wall of storm surge up the delta of the Irrawaddy River. Perhaps 134,000 people died in this initial rampage up the low and braided coastal channels. By dawn, the storm center was in Rangoon, blowing eighty-one miles per hour, taking more roofs than lives. Then it dissipated inland, leaving some 2.4 million survivors in ruinous condition, without shelter or food or safe drinking water. In some areas, up to 95 percent of homes were destroyed.

In the weeks after the cyclone, as the waterways went putrid with the bodies of people and some two hundred thousand water buffalo and cattle, as flooded rice fields were poisoned by saltwater, the paralytic failure of the Burmese military government to do anything for the victims of Nargis became an international scandal. For weeks the junta's generals turned away aid from U.S. and French ships waiting offshore, harassed journalists, stonewalled the UN, started and stopped relief efforts, confiscated food donations, finally admitted some international workers, and then denounced them, saying that the Burmese needed no "chocolate bars" from foreigners. Meanwhile, the 40 percent of children in the Irrawaddy Delta who were already malnourished faced months of starvation.

The Burmese were never warned that a cyclone was coming. I was. On the last afternoon of my trip, I waded through knee-deep storm floods to visit one of those Western diplomats you hear from, anonymously, in reports about Burma. We met in her official residence; she was barefoot, in shorts and a red Hawaiian shirt. As we talked, a windy new order was already rattling the patio doors. Palm fronds were spinning through the air like knives. It had been raining for two days. The water was above the grass.

My departure was in five hours. As I left, I asked the same question I'd been asking everybody: why was there a monsoon in the dry season? I thought it never rained this early.

"This isn't the monsoon," the diplomat said, stopping me. "We're going to get hit by a cyclone. Didn't you hear?"

No. She'd been notified by her own government and CNN. I, like the vast majority in this country of fifty-three million, was totally clueless.

I put on my poncho and rolled up my pants, and another diplomat led me down the driveway to the security gate. The Burmese embassy guards pressed a button and then went back to eyeing the sky. Out front, the avenue was flooded, cars throwing up cascades.

"It's good you are leaving," this diplomat said as dirty water flushed over his Tevas.

So I got out. I didn't see the center of Nargis, which was closing in on the coast. But before the storm, I saw the center of something else: the bigger, slower, even deadlier disaster that long ago started washing over Burma. I saw how its rulers — through their fear, ignorance, and greed — would end up converting the natural disaster coming down on our heads into a shameful man-made catastrophe, an epic of incompetence and indifference. Let's call what I saw by its name: evil.

Like an Asian Havana, Rangoon is filled with rounded and rusting cars older than I am, and billboards denouncing foreigners. It is a low, humid dump, more Shanghai than Shanghai, stained with mold, clouded overhead by knots of electrical wires, and stuttering and sputtering from the private generators crowded everywhere. (The electric grid can black out half a dozen times a day.) Bicycle rickshaws are loaded up like SUVs, monks and palm readers rule the streets, and laborers sweat all day for pennies. Authenticity is in oversupply here. It's Asia before the microchip.

I spent my first morning, April 17, at the nation's most important temple, Shwedagon, a 320-foot-high gold-leafed pagoda that dates back more than a thousand years. It was packed with Buddhist pilgrims for the Thingyan festival, held during the hottest, driest time of year, when people appease the Naga water spirits by shooting squirt guns and launching water balloons in all directions. It was a holiday, and the weeks ahead looked soporific. The forecast was for scorching, humid days with a bit of isolated rain, or what the government newspaper, *The New Light of Myanmar,* called "generally fair." The only event on the horizon was a vote on May 10, what Human Rights Watch called a "sham referendum" to enshrine military rule. *The New Light* urged everyone to vote yes.

Amid thousands at Shwedagon that morning, I saw just one other foreigner. Thailand received almost fourteen million visitors in 2006; Burma had just under three hundred thousand. There is a nominal boycott on tourism here, but the real problem is the lack of infrastructure, the limited beaches, and the high costs that scare off many backpackers. The most frequent visitors, other Asians and European retirees, make a circuit through the "Land of Gold," as Burma is known, from Shwedagon to the ruins of Bagan, a complex of ancient shrines and pagodas grander than Cambodia's Angkor Wat. They pass through the palaces of Mandalay, the last royal capital, and then head into hill country to take in lakes, forests, and minority ethnic cultures — Chins and Kachins, Karens and Karennis — whose homelands touch on the frontiers of India, China, and Thailand. This Burma is as fetching as it is poor, a backward land that is therefore picturesque and old-fashioned, amid a barefoot poverty that remains nevertheless communal and dignified.

I was equipped with a two-week ticket and a tourist visa that allowed me to slip into this rivulet of foreigners circling through Burma. But I had a very different itinerary, through a different country. I was headed north, to the mysterious new capital, Naypyidaw, a place unmentioned by Lonely Planet. In 2006, the junta — led by General Than Shwe and his forty-seven cabinet members and "chiefs of state" — announced that all the government ministries of Rangoon were decamping to a location 250 miles north, where a city had been built, from scratch, in the middle of nothing, without warning. I wanted to see the generals' lair.

It is the military that has trapped this nation in a regressive time sink. A kleptocratic clique of officers presides over 428,000 greenclad soldiers, the second-largest army in Southeast Asia after Vietnam's. The Tatmadaw, as the army is known, is a cult, really. It was founded by Burma's independence leader, General Aung San, who fought the British, danced with the Japanese, and was murdered in a hail of bullets by his own officers in 1947, just months before British colonial rule ended, leaving behind a two-year-old daughter, Aung San Suu Kyi. A military coup in 1962 led to decades of isolation and xenophobia; since 1992, the dictatorship has been in the hands of General Shwe, a reclusive, frog-faced seventy-five-year-old with a chest full of medals and an astrologer at his right hand.

The junta has tried to erase history. In 1989, they changed the capital's name to Yangon and the country's to the Union of Myanmar, though I've found that most people continue to say Burma, either because it implies opposition or it's quicker. They rebranded themselves as the State Peace and Development Council. Burma's clocks run half an hour out of step with its neighbors, there are eight days in the week, and, according to *The New Light*, we're living in both 2008 and the year 1370 of an ancient Burmese dynasty.

Meanwhile, Aung San Suu Kyi grew up, went to Oxford, married, and returned permanently to Burma in 1988. Now sixty-three, she is an apostle of nonviolence and democracy, known within her country simply as "the Lady." In 1990, her pro-democracy party won the only free elections in Burmese history; she won the 1991 Nobel Peace Prize for her efforts, but the junta locked her inside her elegant lakeside house in Rangoon. After eighteen years of intermittent imprisonment and release, she is still there — on May 27, the junta extended her house arrest for another year.

Sometimes it feels like all of Burma has been locked in with her. A censorship board controls radio, books, magazines, and television; cellular phones cost $2,500; and the Internet is simply turned off during a crisis. Even in calm times, most e-mail accounts are blocked by a firewall (although bright kids in cybercafés proxy-tunnel to servers in Germany). The day before Nargis struck, as the storm began to nip at Rangoon's roofs, starlets paraded across the screen of my hotel room's TV set, lip-syncing progovernment ballads.

There is room for only good news in this official Burma. Even disaster reports from a cyclone barely reach the ears of top leaders. "In Burmese culture, you don't tell each other truth if it will hurt," Ma Thanegi, a noted Rangoon painter and former assistant to Aung San Suu Kyi, told me. "That is the worst part of our culture. No argument if it hurts feelings. Objective criticism does not exist. Any criticism must be based on hatred or jealousy."

Thanegi did a year in jail herself for opposing the government. As recently as 2004, Than Shwe conducted a messy purge of the military ranks, arresting hundreds of his own men. Even the country's cadre of perhaps four hundred thousand Theravada Buddhist monks is not immune. Last September, during what became known as the Saffron Revolution, thousands of them led pro-democracy protests across Burma, beginning in the town of Pakokku. By the time the military snuffed out the unrest, on September 27 in Rangoon, at least thirty-one people had died. I was headed to Pakokku, too.

Back in the days of the British Raj, Burma was considered such a hardship post — so hot, so remote, so difficult, and so lawless — that Rudyard Kipling called it "unlike any land you know about." Even George Orwell, who spent five years here as a colonial policeman in the 1920s, found it tough enough for his liking. Some intellectuals here see their crazy government prophesied in Orwell's later books, *Animal Farm* and *1984*. But his 1934 novel, *Burmese*

Days, offers a more direct portrait — a deeply superstitious society in which the strong prey on the weak, and conspiracies are made with witchcraft, magic amulets, and knives in the back.

Astrology *is* Burma, Ma Thanegi told me. People look for a short-cut, a way to predict their Buddhist karma before it comes back to them. "It's cheaper than a shrink or a marriage counselor," she said. "We don't have any neurotic people, thanks to astrologers. If you are failing in your profession or your life, it's not your fault. It's because of your stars."

The generals have taken this national obsession to new heights. U Ne Win, the dictator who completely isolated the country from 1962 to 1988, issued currency in unusual denominations — forty-five and ninety — that added up to his lucky number. In 1970, the story goes, an astrologer said he would be killed from the right, so he decreed an overnight shift from left-hand to right-hand driving on Burmese roads. Than Shwe has continued this prudence, dispatching whole caravans of bureaucrats, and even hundreds of animals from Rangoon's zoo, to the new capital at auspicious moments. One convoy of eleven battalions and eleven ministries, I was told, left for Naypyidaw in 1,100 trucks at the eleventh minute of the eleventh hour of the eleventh day of the eleventh month.

I wondered how my own karma was going to play out. My visa application specifically threatened "legal measures" for snoops who "interfere in the internal affairs" of the country. In addition to Naypyidaw and Pakokku, my dicey agenda included jumping the fence to see Aung San Suu Kyi — something I figured I'd do on my last day in Burma, just before beating a hasty retreat out of the country. So one muggy morning, I joined a queue of upper-class Rangoon women outside the office of San-Zarni Bo, said to be one of the best fortune tellers in the land. As his sign read:

MODERN PROGNOSTICATOR SAN-ZARNI BO
B.SC (CHEM)
1ST. DEGREE (SORBONNE PARIS)

He proved to be a brown, bald, and commanding man, with a milky right eye hinting at second sight. As soon as I handed over thirty dollars, an assistant inked my hands and pressed them onto gray paper. San-Zarni Bo spent several minutes in a frenzied silence, applying a tape measure, compass, and ruler to the palm prints, making rapid calculations, and filling out charts. Finally, he looked up and delivered a thirty-minute monologue in English that boiled down to this: my lucky dates are 1, 3, 9, 10, 17, 19, 21, 27, and 30, and my auspicious letters are *A, M, S, T,* and *J.* Any day of the month in that list is auspicious for me; any place name beginning with those letters is good, too. The past five months, he told me, had been full of "annoyances and disturbances." In two years, I would get married.

"Any questions?" he said.

A few. I was already married, and I had a nine-month-old baby boy at home; you don't get a better five months than that. But I told him only that I was planning something for my last day here. Something dangerous. Was May 1 an auspicious day? "Yes," he said. "The first is a good day for you. Go ahead."

Blessings secured, I set about plotting my immediate itinerary. During the hottest part of the afternoon, I went to the Savoy Hotel, an outrageously expensive relic of British rule, where I ran into another Western diplomat. He suggested the rosé ("made by two Germans up in Shan state"), and I asked about a rumor that all embassies would be moved up to Naypyidaw, far from the bars and markets of Rangoon. He didn't believe it. "Isn't that why they built the place?" he asked. "To get away from foreigners and monks?"

When it was first sprung on the world, Naypyidaw was closed to outsiders. In 2006, the American biologist Alan Rabinowitz became one of the first foreigners to visit, on a Wildlife Conservation Society mission to coordinate a tiger reserve in Hukawng Valley. (The generals love tigers more than they dislike foreigners.) Rabinowitz told me I'd never get on the plane to Naypyidaw without special permission, but that the capital did have a "hotel zone." Meanwhile, I'd heard vague reports of vast golf courses, and read a blog by a Canadian who'd made it in by bus, although he'd been followed and made to stay in the hotel zone. In 2007, foreign press had been flown to Naypyidaw for Armed Forces Day celebrations, always closely minded, but few other journalists had ever gone. Now the diplomat was suggesting I could just get on a plane and go. "You'll never get into the civil-admin part, or the military part, though," he predicted.

The locals were dismissive of the place. The generals had moved to Naypyidaw "because of the stars," a Rangoon gem trader told me

with a wry smile. "They spend all our money on this new capital. It
is very nice. So nice."
    He was being sarcastic. Naypyidaw was a barren place, he said.
"Worst place in Burma. Terrible weather. They can change everything there but the weather."

Building a new capital in the middle of nowhere is actually a fairly
normal idea. Brasilia and Washington, D.C., were laid out that way;
Kazakhstan is finishing Astana now. But Naypyidaw is anything but
normal.
    Getting there was the easy part. A Rangoon travel agent looked
at me funny but sold me a plane ticket, and no one asked any questions when I boarded a late-afternoon Air Mandalay flight full
of colonels and businessmen. At the small Naypyidaw airport, I
glommed on to some surprised Thai businessmen, sharing a taxi to
their hotel. The hotel zone consisted of a handful of sprawling lux-
ury-bungalow compounds along the airport road, near nothing.
All night, I kept jumping out of bed, startled. The geckos on the
walls made a sound just like keys tapping on glass.
    In the morning, I took the Naypyidaw visitor's tour — meaning I
hired a taxi. No tourists come here, and the few Burmese businessmen who have to visit the capital leave as fast as they can. Among
foreigners, only diplomats and people like Alan Rabinowitz have a
reason to go. Almost nothing was as rumor had it. In 2007, *The
Economist* posited a "remote mountain fastness"; *Time* and the *Washington Post* described a "jungle." Instead, daylight revealed a flat
plain covered with rice paddies. Only half finished, Naypyidaw
was a brown, barren, and superheated Lego city, a cross between
Pyongyang and a gated community outside Phoenix. Rebar poked
out everywhere, and women carried firewood on their heads past
just-finished office parks. Spread across miles of empty landscape,
it was a field of pre-ruins, a folly as ambitious in its way as the pagodas at Bagan.
    There was no traffic. I saw one restaurant in the entire city. There
were no crowds, no history, no neighborhoods, and so few schools
and shops that many bureaucrats have left their families behind in
Rangoon. (Even some top leaders have quietly moved back to Rangoon or to the cooler British hill station near Mandalay, Pyin-U-
Lwin.) The population — which the junta claims numbers a million — is almost all government workers, sorted by their ministries

into housing blocks and carried to work each morning together in the backs of army trucks.

Naypyidaw is really an open-air prison, where functionaries twirl their fingers at make-work jobs and generals loot the budget. Although U.S. and EU economic sanctions have driven out many international companies, Chevron still does business here, and Naypyidaw is buzzing with deals on oil, natural gas, gems, timber, and hydropower — deals made largely with Burma's needy neighbors, China, India, and Thailand. In my hotel, the Thai businessmen had been discussing drilling technology. No wonder: many of the lights in Bangkok are powered by natural gas from Burma, and according to the *New York Times,* the Thais pour $1.2 billion into Burmese accounts each year. As yet another Western diplomat explained it, the revenues from oil and gas exports are paid in dollars, which the junta converts to Burmese kyat at an official rate of six to the dollar. In Rangoon, I was routinely getting 1,100 kyat to the dollar. So where did the other 99 percent of the oil and gas billions go? Take a guess.

After a while my driver turned around and looked at me pointedly. "Want see?" he said.

He didn't wait for an answer, veering down a broad avenue through rolling country. This was the civil-admin section, the zone that the Savoy diplomat had claimed I would never enter. One by one came the gleaming ministries, mile after mile of countryside dotted with occasional buildings, all new, all labeled, with color-coded roofs. The Ministry of Progress of Border Areas (black roof) is in charge of the military's endless war on the tribal people. The Ministry of Health (blue) oversees the worst health system in Southeast Asia. The Ministry of Home Affairs (pink) is in charge of catching journalists on tourist visas. I didn't see an education ministry or a ministry of justice: the junta does not bother to operate a court system.

The one thing they did have in Naypyidaw was emergency services. In the middle of wilderness, I saw a brand-new fire station. Miles away, amid more emptiness, a police station, bearing the Orwellian slogan MAY WE HELP YOU? One of the tallest buildings in Naypyidaw is an eight-bay firehouse with a watchtower. With its strong concrete and inland location, Naypyidaw never felt the cyclone's winds. Three hundred miles down in the Irrawaddy Delta, however, where damage was worst, the generals had not bothered to build rescue squads or sheltering police stations. *No, we will not help you*. When Nargis hit, the military put its head in the sand.

It is said the generals live in a bubble when they're outside Naypyidaw, and a bunker when they're in. I found the bunker. "Want see?" my driver asked again. I nodded, and he detoured far into the east of the city. He showed me a simple gate in the middle of trees, which led to an invisible nightclub for the Tatmadaw. On a roundabout, there was a closed exit that led to the "top man restaurant," the cabbie said. A gate, glowing with red warning lights, led to a park and playground for the junta's families. What looked like a partial stadium turned out to be a multistory driving range. Where Rangoon had blackouts, Naypyidaw had penguins, living on ice, their habitats cooled by twenty-four-hour power.

Finally we came to a vast intersection cordoned with razor wire and watched by police. "Than Shwe house," my guide said, pointing discreetly. There was an eight-lane road of white concrete, leading thousands of feet down to a triumphal arch and, beyond that, the houses of Dictator No. 1 and the other cronies.

"No photo!" the driver screamed, too late.

But you don't need a camera to get a peek at the weird world of the junta: on YouTube, just type in "wedding of Than Shwe's daughter." As the resulting video shows, the generals are not in isolation. "There are hundreds of rich people around them, flattering them," said Ma Thanegi, the painter. "A nouveau riche, kitschy society, unbelievably luxurious and conformist."

Than Shwe may have "lots of old-man diseases," as the barefoot diplomat had told me, but he plays golf, and I hit Naypyidaw's City Golf Course, hoping to crash his foursome. No such luck: a manager standing beneath a portrait of Than Shwe said they wouldn't let me play (twenty dollars), I wasn't a member (twenty dollars), there weren't any caddies (twenty dollars), and I had to buy a City Golf Course shirt in red (six dollars).

I balked at the shirt. Five days ago, *The New Light of Myanmar* contained pictures of regime cronies playing golf in Naypyidaw. A general named Thiha Thura Tin Aung Myint Oo (identified as "Secretary-1") had inaugurated a tournament on April 16. In the photos, which I held up, Secretary-1 was not wearing an official shirt.

I had to buy the shirt. Equipped with a hugely optimistic two balls, I grabbed a caddy and hit the links as the temperature reached 104 degrees. The nice thing about being dictator is that nobody denies you a mulligan. My first pair of tee shots went a total of ten yards, so I took a third, like Than Shwe would. On the second hole, I had a couple of good drives and two-putted; on the third, I sliced into the barbed wire and lost the ball. On five, I hit a sweet drive of 175 yards ("Three hundred!" my caddy insisted). Six, which looked onto a construction site, saw my best drive yet, but I three-putted. On seven, I discovered that the official shirt had dyed my belly a sweaty pink. On eight, I took a penalty rather than play my ball off a mound of snake holes. On nine, I hit into a water hazard, twice, which the caddy forgot while scoring me a decent fifty. A lie. Here was the general's ideal country, a back nine of yes-men to carry the bags and ask no questions.

M is auspicious for me, so on April 23 I flew out of Naypyidaw to Mandalay, the last royal capital. For two days, there were heavy rains here, which plunged the city into darkness and left the Burmese grinning: rain, in the dry season! But when I hired a taxi and drove southwest, across the paddy-flat plains of central Burma's "dry zone," the fields were powdery again with dust. The temperature climbed over a hundred and then kept rising during a long day of rumbling down increasingly desperate roads, impoverished children chasing after the car.

I was headed for the town of Pakokku, the place where the Saffron Revolution had begun. The Burmese were once allotted two gallons of gasoline a day, at subsidized prices. Last August, the junta — having sold Burma's own hydrocarbons abroad — eliminated the subsidy. The cost of bus rides, running a generator, even eating a bowl of rice, jumped as much as 500 percent. The unrest, which started as a protest about the price of gas and exploded into nationwide demonstrations, was sparked at one monastery, in Pakokku.

The town is on the west bank of the great Irrawaddy, which cleaves and defines Burma. To get there, I had to catch a riverboat at Bagan, where thousands of ancient temples squat on the river's east bank. There are more than four thousand Buddhist structures here, built between the eleventh and thirteenth centuries; more than two thousand still stand, from tiny shrines to eighteen-story numbers rivaling the tallest of the Maya pyramids at Tikal. In the off-season of an off-country, with the temperature hover-

ing somewhere near 110 degrees, even the trinket vendors had retired. There were a few Spaniards and Germans about, but at one
of the world's greatest archaeological sites, I had a temple — a
dozen temples — to myself at sunset. If the government were less
charmingly North Korean, less reeking of Cambodia in 1978, Bagan and Burma could mean a great deal to the world.

Early the next morning, I boarded the slim, crowded ferry to
Pakokku. The passengers included market women, giggling students, and an English-speaking professional, who at first talked
freely about the Saffron Revolution and what he'd seen. Eventually
he realized that I was a journalist and recoiled. The docks were full
of informers, he warned me. Spies were everywhere. "I'm sorry," he
said, "I can't get involved in politics." He stared into the dirty bilge
water for the rest of the trip.

No one was waiting on the dock to arrest me. I visited Pakokku's
garish pagoda, filled with glass tiles, gold paint, and real birds
flitting past murals of bodhi trees. I hired a rickshaw and went
to the particular monastery where the Saffron Revolution began.
There, the giggling young monks gave me lumps of palm sugar
and showed me their teak longhouse, with its dusty library full of
tripitaka scriptures and colonial-era British encyclopedias and a
Bengal tiger pelt on their teacher's throne.

But now there was no teacher. Roughly 150 of the monastery's
older monks had been "sent home" — a form of house arrest — by
the junta in the wake of the rebellion. The unrest started on September 5, when several hundred monks began a march for the
poor, chanting, "Release from suffering" — their way of asking for
lower gas prices. On the town's only bridge, their moral force met
the junta's plain old force: warning shots, beatings, and arrests.
That kind of repression is normal for Burma, but then the army,
people in Pakokku told me, tied up one of the monks and left him,
bound in the street, for a whole day, roasting in the sun.

You do not humiliate monks in Burma. The next day, when a
government delegation came to the monastery to apologize, a mob
burned their squad car and then smashed up the business of the
town's biggest snitch. Inside a week, word of the beating of several
monks had spread, and tens of thousands of his colleagues took to
the streets. Almost every town in Burma saw demonstrations, led by
the red-robed clerics and followed by angry students and just about
everyone else. But in Rangoon it ended. On September 27, at the

Sule Pagoda, a miraculous gilded landmark that sits inside a traffic circle, the army lashed back, shooting into crowds. Officially, thirty-one died over the course of the unrest, but human-rights groups say it was hundreds. The revolution was put back in a bottle, for now at least.

Not that anyone told me any of this in Pakokku. Later during that burning afternoon, at the well in their monastery courtyard, the monks never warned me that we were under surveillance or said that they were just young initiates, left behind, afraid.

They never cried and asked me to forget their words, their names, and their faces.

The whole way back down to Bagan, the wind was blowing so hard that the boatman wrapped his head in a checked *longyi,* a kind of sarong, against the stinging sand. The Irrawaddy was enormous even in the dry season, light brown and dotted with overloaded sailing canoes. We sputtered through back channels lined with reeds, eroding sandbanks, and impoverished hamlets on stilts. These shacks were mostly made of bamboo and woven grass and stood only a couple of feet off the ground. The cyclone would only brush through this area, but downriver it would hit with full force on more than a million people living like this — fishing with nets or lines, crabbing, and cutting down the mangroves that would normally protect them from a storm surge. Nargis would smash their houses and boats to pulp, like Hurricane Katrina hitting a New Orleans made of cardboard. The storm surge flooded about 30 percent of Burma's best rice paddies with saltwater and rotting bodies. In a disaster, the timeless qualities of Burma turned out to have sixteenth-century consequences.

It started to rain hard on the approach to Rangoon, my Yangon Airways flight pitching violently up and down. The Burmese being fatalists, the pilot skidded us right in. Before I reached the hotel, the rain had doubled in weight. It was April 30.

That afternoon, in a crushing and continuous downpour, the downtown business district was the first to go. Indian and Chinese shops backfilled with water. Intersections became lakes, sewers spilled over, trash spun in the wakes of cars. Then the side streets began to back up. The huge generators on the sidewalks snuffed out, one by one.

The next morning, May 1, a taxi took me to an interview with a final Western diplomat. She'd just returned from Mandalay and had a patch of sunburn on her nose. Over coffee in an old colonial hotel, she confessed to being in love with the country, the desperate strength of the people, the dignity of an ancient culture undiluted by mass tourism, unbroken by repression. But the frightened and clumsy regime was getting more brutal by the month. The most recent development, she said, was the appearance of organized progovernment mobs, called Swan Arr Shin, or "Capable Strongmen," who had attacked followers of the Lady. People had been arrested for blogging about politics, forwarding e-mail attachments of antigovernment posters, and even writing a Valentine's Day poem that included the words "crazy with power."

She hadn't heard anything about the baffling weather — it used to rain this way "in the old days," her Burmese staff had told her.

Leaving the hotel, I made the mistake of heading for the post office. Moving north as the rain came pelting down, I hitched up my trousers and joined a ragged column of wet Burmese wading along. At General Aung San Road, there was only a river. Rolling up my pants was useless — even with a poncho I was streaming wet. Out in the avenue, poked by umbrellas, dodging pushed rickshaws and the SUVs of the rich, feeling my way knee-deep in rushing brown water for the broken asphalt underneath, I gave up and turned around. I went back, to a drier part of town, hunted for a taxi, and began leaving Burma.

When I asked the driver why it was raining so hard, he said the Thingyan water festival must have been "auspicious." We were getting our forecasts from the wrong sources. We passed the forlorn zoo, many of its animals deported to Naypyidaw, and the empty ministry buildings whose people had gone the same way. There was a tree blown down in Pyay Road and cars stalled in the floods. On the balcony of my hotel, I watched the rain bucket down, harder than ever, and the wind smash a thousand palm trees together on the fringes of Inya Lake.

Aung San Suu Kyi's house-prison was over there, hidden. I'd studied Google Earth views, to see if there was a way to get around the lakeshore to see the Lady; I'd walked the edges of the frozen area around her house, staring up at high walls, topped with both

barbed wire and razor wire. Jumping the wall here was the dangerous thing the astrologer had green-lighted for May 1. But the Lady
remained out of reach.

There were reports later that she'd lost part of her roof in the cyclone but, without a choice, had simply ridden Nargis out. Sometimes there is nothing to do but survive.

There's a joke that Mandalay comedy troupe the Moustache
Brothers tell about the tsunami of 2004. For once, Burma was
spared, and the joke is about why. Three corrupt Burmese generals
die and for their crimes are reborn as lowly fish. When they see the
deadly wave coming, they tell it to turn back from Burma: "We already ruined it."

Two weeks after the cyclone, I got an e-mail from the sunburned
diplomat. "Somewhere between one hundred thousand and two
hundred thousand" had died, she wrote. She'd spent fifteen days
trying to organize relief efforts. There were more than two hundred thousand survivors at that point still in dire need of aid, and
maybe 1.5 million more were affected — numbers that would swell
to more than two million. Plagues were coming.

In another country, like Thailand, there would have been deaths
as well. But there would also have been roads, bridges, emergency
services, houses of cement, a measure of accountability, and information about the coming storm. In Burma, the generals guaranteed that there was virtually none of that.

Burmese citizens who tried to distribute aid had their cars im-
pounded; refugees waiting for help along the few roads were
scolded by the army for daring to beg. It took UN Secretary-Gen-
eral Ban Ki-moon two weeks to get *any* Burmese leader on the
phone. Weeks into the disaster, the junta finally allowed him to visit
Naypyidaw; he returned with clenched teeth to announce "progress." Aid flights did eventually begin to flow in large numbers —
the United States delivered water containers for some 187,000
people and plastic sheeting for almost two million, purification
equipment and medical supplies, ten Zodiacs for navigating the
delta, and seventy-five thousand mosquito nets. But at first, most
aid went no farther than the Rangoon region, and NGOs claimed
that the military stole some of the best supplies for itself. Many people were forced to go back to their destroyed villages with only a

piece of that American plastic sheeting and a stick to hold up their new "tent." The government told people to be "self-reliant" and eat frogs.

The people I met in Burma all survived, it seems. The barefoot diplomat talked to newspapers worldwide under her own name. The Moustache Brothers tried to hold a fundraising concert for victims but were rebuffed for their cracks about the generals; another comedian, called Zarganar, was arrested for distributing aid. Ma Thanegi e-mailed that even the generals could not keep the crescendo of bad news at bay.

She underestimated them. After weeks of hiding, Than Shwe finally appeared, once, to stroll through a "show camp" for refugees near Rangoon, where he announced that relief efforts were now over. When foreign donors produced $150 million in funding for relief projects, Than Shwe demanded $11 billion. It would be farce if it were not so cruel.

The Burmese merely suffered. An NGO contact wrote that the generals have "holes where their hearts should be" and described a Rangoon taxi driver angrily demanding an invasion by "Britain or Germany," since the UN would do nothing. A Burmese contact said that Britain and the United States should arm the ethnic insurgents in remote corners of Burma so they could blast the generals out of power. The French foreign minister Bernard Kouchner, a founder of Doctors Without Borders, briefly called for a forced entry to deliver relief supplies, but realpolitik soon asserted itself and the U.S. and French warships sailed away. For their own reasons, China and the nations of Southeast Asia insisted on "noninterference" in Burma's internal affairs. The junta went ahead with the May 10 election in most parts of the country, evicting refugees from schools and temples to create polling stations. And as I write, a month after the cyclone, the generals have announced the one statistic they care about: exactly 92.48 percent of Burma's cowed and beaten voters chose to keep the iron fist.

The cyclone should have blown down this house of tarot cards. Maybe it still will. The only effective internal relief force in Burma was the monks, who led truck convoys into the delta and sheltered, fed, and consoled the victims of Nargis at village temples all over the devastated area, claiming their unambiguous position as the real leadership of Burma. Another attempt at a Saffron Revolution, a louder, angrier, and more desperate uprising, seems inevitable in time.

For today, the generals are getting away with it, again. As Alan Rabinowitz told me before the storm, "They couldn't care less what the U.S. or the West does or doesn't do."

In that sense, San-Zarni Bo was right. I got out of Hell on the first of May. It must have been my lucky day.

FRANK BURES

A Mind Dismembered

FROM *Harper's Magazine*

No one is entirely sure when magical penis loss first came to Africa. One early incident was recounted by Dr. Sunday Ilechukwu, a psychiatrist, in a letter some years ago to the *Transcultural Psychiatric Review*. In 1975, while posted in Kaduna, in the north of Nigeria, Dr. Ilechukwu was sitting in his office when a policeman escorted in two men and asked for a medical assessment. One of the men had accused the other of making his penis disappear. This had caused a major disturbance in the street. As Ilechukwu tells it, the victim stared straight ahead during the examination, after which the doctor pronounced him normal. "Exclaiming," Ilechukwu wrote, "the patient looked down at his groin for the first time, suggesting that the genitals had just reappeared."

According to Ilechukwu, an epidemic of penis theft swept Nigeria between 1975 and 1977. Then there seemed to be a lull until 1990, when the stealing resurged. "Men could be seen in the streets of Lagos holding on to their genitalia either openly or discreetly with their hand in their pockets," Ilechukwu wrote. "Women were also seen holding on to their breasts directly or discreetly, by crossing the hands across the chest . . . Vigilance and anticipatory aggression were thought to be good prophylaxes. This led to further breakdown of law and order." In a typical incident, someone would suddenly yell: *Thief! My genitals are gone!* Then a culprit would be identified, apprehended, and, often, killed.

During the past decade and a half, the thievery seems not to have abated. In April 2001, mobs in Nigeria lynched at least twelve suspected penis thieves. In November of that same year, there were at least five similar deaths in neighboring Benin. One survey counted fifty-six "separate cases of genital shrinking, disappearance, and snatching" in West Africa between 1997 and 2003, with at least thirty-six suspected penis thieves killed at the hands of angry mobs during that period. These incidents have been reported in local newspapers but are little known outside the region.

For years I followed this trend from afar. I had lived in East Africa, in Italy, in Thailand, and other places, too, absorbing their languages, their histories, their minutiae. I had tried to piece together what it might be like not just to live in those places but really to *be* in them, to jump in and sink all the way to the bottom of the pool. But through these sporadic news stories, I was forced to contemplate a land more foreign than any I had ever seen, a place where one's penis could be magically blinked away. I wanted to see for myself, but no magazine would send me. It was too much money, too far, and too strange. Finally, when my wife became pregnant, I realized that it might be my one last reckless chance to go, and so I shouldered the expenses myself and went.

On my first morning in the Mainland Hotel, a rundown place with falling ceiling tiles and broken locks, I awoke to a din, and I realized it was simply the city: the clatter of the seventeen million people of Lagos. It was louder than any metropolis I had ever heard. My windows were closed, but it sounded as if they were wide open. For the next few days, I wandered around the city not quite sure where to begin. I went to bookstores and took motorcycle taxis and asked people I met, friends of friends, but without much insight or luck.

Eventually I found my way to Jankara Market, a collection of cramped stands under a patchwork of corrugated-tin sheets that protect the proffered branches, leaves, seeds, shells, skins, bones, skulls, and dead lizards and toads from the elements. All these items are held to contain properties that heal, help, or harm, depending on what one needs them to do. The market is better known for the even darker things one can buy. At Jankara, one can buy *juju:* magic. On my first trip to Jankara, to look around, I met a woman who loved me, she said, and wanted to marry me. When I told her I was already married, she threatened to bind me to her magically with two wooden figures so that I would not sleep at night until I saw her. But she said it with a glint in her eye, so I didn't worry.

A few days later, I returned to Jankara to ask her some questions. As soon as I walked into the dark, covered grounds of the market, she saw me.

"Ah," she said. "You have come back!"

"Yes," I said.

"Sit here," she said, and pointed to a bench. She sat down across from me. "What did you bring me?"

I showed her some fruit I had brought.

"Ah, very nice," she said, and started to eat, even though it was daytime in the middle of Ramadan and she was Muslim. "How is your wife?"

"She is good."

"And what about your other wife?"

"Who is that?"

"'Who is that?'" she said in mock surprise. "I think you know who that is. That is me."

"That is nice," I said. "But in America it's not possible."

A man came up to her and handed her a crumpled piece of paper with a list of ingredients on it. She peered at the list, then got up and went around collecting sticks and leaves and seeds and plants. She chopped them all up and put them in a bag. While she was doing this, the man sat next to me on a bench.

"Is that for you?" I asked.

"Yes," he said. "It makes you very strong."

Then another man came up and put in his order. It was something for the appendix, he said. When he was gone, the woman sat down next to me.

"I have a question," I said.

"Yes."

"In my country, we don't have *juju*."

"Yes."

"But I was reading in the paper about penis snatchers —"

"Ah," she interrupted me. "Don't listen to them. That is not true. If I touch your thing like this" — and here she touched my leg — "is your penis gone?"

"No," I said, uneasily. "But what if I come to you and ask you for protection? Can you do it?"

"Yes, I can."

"How much?"

"One thousand naira. Two thousand. Even up from there." This was a large sum by Nigerian standards — more than fifteen dollars.

"Do you have many people come and ask for this?"

"Yes," she said in a low voice. She looked around. "Many."

Nigeria was not the first site of mysterious genital disappearance. As with so many other things, its invention can be claimed by the Chinese. The first known reports of "genital retraction" date to around 300 B.C., when the mortal dangers of *suo-yang*, or "shrinking penis," were briefly sketched in the *Nei Ching*, the *Yellow Emperor's Classic Text of Internal Medicine*. Also in China, the first full description of the condition was recorded in 1835, in Pao Siaw-Ow's collection of medical remedies, which describes *suo-yang* as a "ying type of fever" (meaning it arises from too much cold) and recommends that the patient get a little "heaty" yang for balance.

Fears of magical penis loss were not limited to the Orient. The *Malleus Maleficarum*, medieval Europeans' primary guidebook to witches and their ways, warned that witches could cause one's *membrum virile* to vanish, and indeed several chapters were dedicated to this topic. Likewise the *Compendium Maleficarum* warned that witches had many ways to affect one's potency, the seventh of which included "a retraction, hiding, or actual removal of the male genitals." (This could be either a temporary or a permanent condition.) Even in the 1960s, there were reports of Italian migrant workers in Switzerland panicking over a loss of virility caused by witchcraft.

These fears, however, seem to have been largely isolated; mass panics over genital retraction were not recorded until 1874. This was the year that, on the island of Sulawesi, a certain Benjamin Matthes was compiling a dictionary of Buginese when he came across a strange term, *lasa koro*, which meant "shrinking of the penis," a disease that Matthes said was not uncommon among the locals and "must be very dangerous." Sporadic reports of *koro*, as it came to be known, recurred over the years, and during the late twentieth century the panics proliferated. In 1967, an epidemic of *koro* raced through Singapore, affecting some five hundred men. In 1976, in northern Thailand, at least two thousand people were afflicted with *rokjoo*, in which men *and* women complained that their genitals were being sucked into their bodies. In 1982, there were major *koro* epidemics in India and again in Thailand, while in 1984 and 1985, some five thousand Chinese villagers in Guangdong province tried desperately to keep their penises outside their bodies using whatever they had handy: string, chopsticks, relatives' assistance, jewelers' clamps, and safety pins. But the phenomenon was given little notice by Western scientists, who considered such strange mental conditions to be "ethnic hysterias" or "exotic psychoses."

This way of thinking has changed, thanks largely to the work of a Hong Kong–based psychiatrist named Pow Meng Yap. In the early 1950s, Yap noticed a strange thing: a trickle of young men coming into his office, complaining that their penises were disappearing into their bodies and that when this happened they would die. After seeing nineteen such cases, Yap published a paper in the *British Journal of Psychiatry* entitled "*Koro* — A Culture-Bound Depersonalization Syndrome." For years, Yap had been interested in the interplay among culture, mind, and disease. In an earlier paper, "Mental Diseases Peculiar to Certain Cultures," Yap had discussed other similar conditions: *latah,* a trance/fright neurosis in which the victim obeys commands from anyone nearby; *amok,* unrestrained outbursts of violence (as in "running amok"); and *thanatomania,* or self-induced "magical" death. *Koro* fit quite well among these other exotic maladies. In fact, it was perhaps the best example of a phenomenon that can arise only in a specific culture, a condition that occurs in a sense *because of* that culture. Yap saw that these ailments had this one feature in common, grouped them together, and gave them a name that, in spite of all the controversy to follow, would stick. They were "culture-bound syndromes."

Under this rubric, *koro* and the other culture-bound syndromes are now treated with more respect, if not total acceptance. Science is, after all, the quest for universality. In psychiatry, this means all minds are treated the same, and all conditions should exist equally across the world. Some thought that calling *koro* "culture-bound" was an end-run around the need for universality, a relativistic copout. Were these syndromes really caused by different cultures? Or were they just alternate names for afflictions that plagued, or could plague, every culture? This was precisely what I had come to Nigeria to find out, though so far with little success.

*

A few days after I arrived in Lagos, an article appeared in the newspaper. The headline read: COURT REMANDS MAN OVER FALSE ALARM ON GENITAL ORGAN DISAPPEARANCE. According to the paper, a young man named Wasiu Karimu was on a bus when he "was said to have let out a strident cry, claiming that his genital organ had disappeared. He immediately grabbed [Funmi] Bello, who was seated next to him, and shouted that the woman should restore his 'stolen' organ." They got off the bus, and a crowd of "miscreants" swarmed around the woman, ready to kill her. But a passing police patrol intervened, stopped her from being lynched, and escorted them both to the police station, where Karimu told the commissioner "his organ was returning gradually." The paper gave the exact address where Wasiu Karimu lived, so I decided to try and find out what exactly had transpired in his pants.

The day was already hot when a friend of a friend named Akeem and I rolled into Alagbado, the dusty, rundown town on the far edge of Lagos where Wasiu Karimu lived. We drove past clapboard shacks and little restaurants, through huge muddy pools, past people watching us from doorways, until we came to the address given in the paper. Chickens and goats scattered in front of our car, which we had borrowed from a journalist and which said PRESS on the windshield. The house was an ample two-story affair with a little shop next to it. We got out and asked a girl if Wasiu lived there.

"Yes," she said, "but he is not around."

Akeem went into the yard in front of Wasiu Karimu's house, and a woman jumped in front of him. She said she was Wasiu's mother and began yelling at him to get out of the yard. Akeem retreated to the car, and we stood there in the middle of the road, in the sun. Wasiu Karimu was nowhere to be found, so we decided to wait for him to show up. But after about twenty minutes, several men came around the corner and took up posts around Wasiu's house. A couple of them were holding long sticks.

Akeem turned to me and said, "Local Area Boys."

In Lagos, the Area Boys are thugs — a law unto themselves. They have multiplied since the military dictatorship fell in 1998, seeding a new kind of terror throughout the city. These young men had an ugly swagger, and they looked as if they had run to get there. I could see sweat start to drip down Akeem's head.

"Let us go," he said.

"Wait a minute," I said. We had come a long way — in fact, I had come all the way from America for this and did not know how many chances I would get to speak to someone whose penis had actually been stolen. So I made us wait. I don't know why. I suppose I figured we weren't doing any harm. I only wanted to ask a few questions. I walked to the shop next to Wasiu Karimu's house and bought something to drink.

The young girl at the shop said, "Sir, are you looking for someone?"

"Yes," I said. "Wasiu Karimu."

"Sir," she said, "maybe you should just go now, before there are problems. It will be easier for everyone."

I walked back to the car. "Okay," I said to Akeem. Now I had a sick feeling. My own back was drenched with sweat. "Let's go."

Akeem shook his head and looked down the road. It had been cut off with two large wooden blocks and a car. There was no way out.

One of the local Area Boys looked particularly eager to deliver some punishment. He ran into the street with his cane and whacked it on the ground. "We will *beat* the press," he yelled. "We will *beat* the press."

The young men huddled together in front of Wasiu Karimu's house. After a long delay, they called Akeem over. He talked to them for a little bit. Then they called me over. They wanted to see the article about Wasiu. I pulled the wrinkled photocopy out of my pocket and handed it over.

A quiet man in a 50 Cent T-shirt was clearly the leader. He took the article, unfolded it, and read through it.

"Let us see your ID," he said. I hadn't brought my passport, for exactly this reason, and my driver's license had disappeared from my hotel room. All I had with me was an expired YMCA membership card, which I handed over.

The leader, whose name was Ade, took it and turned it over. He handed it to a lanky man with crooked teeth, who looked at it briefly, then handed it back.

"Do you know who we are?" asked Ade.

I did not.

"We are OPC. You know OPC?"

The OPC was the O'odua People's Congress, a quasi-political organization that was halfway between the Area Boys and a militia. They were violent and arbitrary. Recently, they had killed several policemen in Lagos, and in some parts of the city they were being hunted by the government.

"We have to make sure," Ade said, "you are not coming here to do some harm. Maybe you were sent here by that woman." The woman, he meant, who stole Wasiu Karimu's penis.

There was a crash, as a glass bottle exploded against one of the tires on our car. Both Akeem and I jumped.

"No," I said trying to be calm. "I just want to ask some questions. Is he around?"

"He is not around."

They talked among themselves in Yoruba, then Ade's henchman with the bad teeth told the story. Unbeknown to me at the time, Wasiu Karimu himself was apparently there, listening from a distance. Akeem told me later he was sure he had seen him — a little guy standing at the back, young and nervous.

Wasiu, Bad Teeth told me, had gotten on the bus and sat down next to this woman. He didn't have a watch, so he asked her what time it was. She didn't know. Then the conductor came around and asked her for her fare. She didn't have that either. As she stood up to get out of the bus, she bumped into Wasiu.

"Then," he said, "Wasiu Karimu felt something happen in his body. Something not right. And he checked and his thing was gone."

"Was it gone," I asked, "or was it shrinking?"

"Shrinking! Shrinking! It was getting smaller."

And as he felt his penis shrink, Wasiu Karimu screamed and demanded the woman put his penis back. The conductor told them both to get off the bus, and a crowd closed in on the accused, not doubting for an instant that the woman could do such a thing. But as soon as she saw trouble coming, Bad Teeth said, she replaced Wasiu's manhood, so when the police took him down to the station, they thought he was lying and arrested him instead.

"What did she want the penis for?" I asked Bad Teeth.

"For *juju*," he said, "or maybe to make some money."

Behind us, from the corner of my eye, I could see that the roadblocks had been removed.

"Do you have anything else you want to ask?"

"No," I said. "I don't think so."
"Okay," he said. "You are free to go."
"Thank you."
I nodded to Akeem. We got in the car and drove away.

The debate over the term "culture-bound syndrome" seems to have simmered down as our understanding of "culture" has evolved. These days the terms "culture-bound" and, more often, "culture-related" have been grudgingly accepted; after all, how is Western medicine supposed to categorize such ailments as *hikikomori,* in which Japanese children refuse to leave their rooms for years on end, or *dhat,* in which Indians and Sri Lankans become ill with anxiety over semen loss, or *zar,* in which some Middle Easterners and North Africans are possessed by a spirit, or *hwa-byung,* the "fire illness" of Korean women in which anger is said to be manifesting itself in physical symptoms including "palpitations" and "a feeling of mass in the epigastrium"? How can we fit these, and a dozen other ailments, neatly into the pages of the *DSM-IV,* the *Diagnostic and Statistical Manual of Mental Disorders,* the Western bible of maladies of the mind? The fact is that there was no good place until Pow Meng Yap created one — ill-fitting as it may be — for these unruly members of the family of mental conditions whose causes cannot be found just in one mind but instead must be sought in the social. These conditions are not purely psychogenic, as psychiatry's universalists once held all things must be. They are also sociogenic, or emerging from the social fabric.

This debate has mirrored a larger debate that took place in the twentieth century over whether culture was something pure, something existing independently of the people who lived in it — something with an almost supernatural ability to shape those people into fundamentally different beings — or merely accumulated wisdom, the chance collection of the behavior of a group of individuals. Was culture a quasi-independent superorganism that shaped people? Or was it just a collection of human organisms? Did it produce us, or did we produce it?

Lately, a more nuanced conception of culture has emerged, as evolutionary psychology begins to shed some light on what exactly culture is. It is neither nature nor nurture. It is both at the same time, a positive feedback loop of tendencies and behaviors and knowledge and beliefs. It is, as the science writer Matt Ridley has called it, nature via nurture, or as the primatologist Frans de Waal put it in his book *The Ape and the Sushi Master,* "an extremely powerful modifier — affecting everything we do and are, penetrating to the core of human existence."

In 1998, Charles Hughes, coeditor of *Culture-Bound Syndromes: Folk Illnesses of Psychiatric and Anthropological Interest,* one of the few books on the phenomenon, wrote a scathing critique of the *DSM-IV*'s treatment of culture-bound syndromes, which had been gathered together in the back of the book in an appendix as if they were still under glass, a museum of exotica where nothing had changed since these ills were considered "ethnic psychoses" that affected primitive people but not us. Hughes argued that the borders around culture-bound syndromes are inherently fuzzy and that to rope them off at the back of the *DSM-IV* is a farce. He lamented the lack of a "short course in sophisticated cultural awareness" for psychiatrists and said that "to use the class-designated term 'culture-bound [psychiatric] syndromes' is comparable to using the terms 'culture-bound religion,' 'culture-bound language,' or 'culture-bound technology,' for each of these institutional areas is shaped by, and in its specific details is unique to, its cultural setting."

In other words, everything else in the *DSM-IV,* and in life, is culture-bound, too. While *koro* and its culture-bound kin languish at the back, other conditions such as multiple personality disorder, bulimia nervosa, type A personality, muscle dysmorphia, belief in government-implanted computer chips, and pet hoarding are given universal status because Western psychiatrists cannot see beyond their own cultural horizons.

Starrys Obazi sat across the table from me at Mr. Bigg's, a cheap fast-food place on the north side of Lagos where we had agreed to meet. Around us, other Nigerians walked past with their trays and sat down to eat their burgers and watch rap videos on the television behind us. Starrys dug into his chicken. A wiry little man with a nasal voice, he had been an editor for fourteen years at *FAME,* a Nigerian celebrity tabloid, until the publisher mysteriously stopped paying him. Jobs, even low-paying editorial jobs, were tough to come by in Lagos, and it had been several years since Starrys had held one.

Here, in the flesh, finally, was a man whose penis had been stolen. It happened one day in 1990, when Starrys was a reporter at the *Evening Times*. While he was waiting for a bus to take him to work, a man approached him and held out a piece of paper with a street name on it.

"Do you know where this is?" the man asked, without saying the name. Starrys did not know the street, and he thought this was strange. He didn't believe the street existed. Then another man behind Starrys, without seeing the paper, said where the street was. This was even stranger.

The two men walked away, and Starrys started to feel something he had never felt before.

"At that moment," Starrys told me, leaning forward, "I felt something depart my body. I began to feel empty inside. I put my hand into my pants, and touched my thing. It was unusually small — smaller than the normal size. And the scrotum was flat. I put my fingers into the sockets, and they were not there. The testes were gone. And I was just feeling empty!" His voice strained as he recalled the panic of that day.

Starrys ran after the men and confronted them. "Something happened to my penis!" he told the man who had asked for directions. The man said he had no idea what Starrys was talking about.

"Something told me inside not to shout," he said. "Because as soon as I shouted, he would have been lynched. And if he was lynched, how could I get my penis back?"

I watched as Starrys finished his chicken and wiped his hands. *"It was one-quarter of its normal size,"* he said emphatically, as if, even now, even he could not believe it had happened. But Starrys, a journalist and a worldly man, did believe it. And as I listened to him tell his story, I almost believed it, too. I could feel the intensity, the fear. It made a kind of sense, even if it didn't make sense at all. I could start to see the world that his fear came from. I could see what it was built on, and for a few minutes I could imagine standing there with Starrys on a street corner, alone in the world, helpless and missing my most cherished possession. I let go of my doubts and gave in to the panic in Starrys's voice, and it was real, utterly. And I was afraid. This was how *koro* could be caught.

Starrys continued with his story. Despite the men's denials, one of them agreed to accompany Starrys to a nearby hospital to document the theft. But just as they arrived at the hospital, the man grabbed Starrys and bellowed, "LET'S GO IIIIN!" And at that moment something happened.

"When he grabbed me," Starrys said, "I felt calm again. I felt an inner calm. I checked my testes, and they were there." He checked his penis as well, and the missing three-quarters had returned. The doctor examined Starrys and pronounced him fine. On hearing Starrys's story, though, the doctor admonished the penis thief to quit causing trouble on the street.

I thought about Starrys. He had been a skeptic before his encounter; but on that day, his inner world shifted, and he became afraid. He stopped giving directions. He stopped trusting strangers. He *knew* that magical penis loss was a real and terrifying possibility. He had, in a sense, been drawn into the culture, into its beliefs, so far that he had caught this culture-bound syndrome.

We all go through a similar process of being formed by the culture around us. It is something described well in Bruce Wexler's book *Brain and Culture: Neuroscience, Ideology, and Social Change,* in which Wexler argues that much of human conflict arises from our efforts to reconcile the world as we believe it to exist (our internal structures) with the world we live in. According to Wexler, we develop an inner world, a neuropsychological framework of values, cause and effect, expectations, and a general understanding of how things work. This inner world, which underpins our culture, forms through early adulthood, after which we strive to ensure it exists, or continues to exist, in the world outside. Those inner structures can change in adulthood, but it is more difficult given our decreased brain plasticity.

That different internal structures exert different pressures on the mind (and body) should not be surprising. Every culture has its own logic, its own beliefs, its own stresses. Once one buys into its assumptions, one becomes a prisoner to the logic. For some people, that means a march toward its more tragic conclusions.

Not long ago, medical researchers noticed a strange phenomenon: Turks in Germany, Vietnamese in England, and Mexicans in America all registered better health than native residents. This phenomenon has come to be called the "healthy migrant effect." Although most of the research has focused on physical indicators (cancer, heart disease, diabetes, etc.), recent studies have started to look at the mental health of immigrants, which seems to show a similar pattern. In 2000, one study concluded that first-generation Mexican immigrants have better mental health than their children born in the United States, despite the latter group's significant socioeconomic advantages — a finding, it noted, that was "inconsistent with traditional tenets on the relationship among immigration, acculturation, and psychopathology." The stress of immigration is assumed to have major mental-health costs, but here the opposite seemed to be true: the longer immigrants remained in a developed country, the worse their mental health became.

For this reason, the healthy-migrant effect is also called the "acculturation paradox": the more acculturated one is, the less healthy one becomes. One study of Turkish immigrants to Germany showed the effect to last for at least a generation. A subsequent 2004 study of Mexican immigrants to the United States showed that "with few exceptions, foreign-born Mexican Americans and foreign-born non-Hispanic whites were at significantly lower risk of *DSM-IV* substance-use and mood-anxiety disorders compared with their U.S.-born counterparts." These included alcohol and drug abuse, major depression, dysthymia, mania, hypomania, panic disorder, social and specific phobia, and generalized anxiety disorder. The longer they lived in the United States, the more they showed the particular damage to the mind that our particular culture wreaks. People who come to America eventually find themselves subject to our own culture-related syndromes, which the *DSM-IV* can easily recognize and categorize, as acculturation forces their internal worlds to conform to the external world, i.e., the American culture that the *DSM-IV* knows best.

I could feel something similar happening to me in Nigeria. I could feel plates shifting. I did not try to hold them back. As I listened to the tales of friends of friends, as I read the horror stories in newspapers, as I watched the angry crowds on television, as I saw the fear and hatred in the eyes of the young OPC men, and as I sat across from Starrys Obazi and heard the panic in his voice, I could feel my own mind opening to this world where such things were possible. I could see the logic. I could feel the edge of belief. Something was starting to make sense. Now and then I would catch myself feeling strangely vulnerable between my legs.

I was almost there, and it was time to see if I could get in just a little further.

The winding streets of Lagos were packed with people. Tens of thousands, coming and going, moving along sidewalks, jamming the streets so thickly that cars had to push through them at a crawl, blaring their horns and parting crowds like a snowplow.

I was far from Jankara Market when I started out and headed southwest toward Idumota, to walk through some of the most crowded streets in the world, where I hoped to brush up against the boundary of this culture. I wanted to look back and see someone checking if his manhood was still in place.

I climbed some stairs near a bank and stopped to watch the city flow by. I walked back down the stairs and jumped into the onrush. I moved with it. Together we were packed tightly, but we rarely touched. The winding streams of people ran easily along next to one another. I moved farther into the city, and as I did, I watched the people pass within inches of me, then feint, slip by, barely brushing me. At first I tried to nudge a few people with my shoulder, but most were too fast, too alert, too leery.

Walking along, I caught one man on the shoulder with mine. But when I looked back, it seemed like he hadn't even noticed. Then I clipped another man a little harder, but when I looked back, it was like I wasn't even there. I bumped a few more people lightly, until finally I caught one man enough that I'm sure he knew it was purposeful.

But the magic failed. He didn't reach down and grab himself, didn't point to me, didn't accuse. He didn't even give me a dirty look. I was swimming in the water, but I could not get all the way in, no matter how deep I dove. And so I let go, walked on, and allowed the current to carry me wherever it would.

BRONWEN DICKEY

The Last Wild River

FROM *The Oxford American*

> One need not weep romantic tears for them,
> But when the last moonshiner buys his radio,
> And the last, lost wild-rabbit of a girl
> Is civilized with a mail-order dress,
> Something will pass that was American,
> And all the movies will not bring it back.
> — Stephen Vincent Benét, *John Brown's Body*

THICK STROKES of early evening crimson smeared across the rolling mountains of Rabun County as I drove up Highway 23 from Atlanta toward Clayton. The whole world looked like it was burning up right behind the horizon line. It was the nine-degree, molar-rattling middle of January in North Georgia, and I was on my way to visit the Chattooga River, fifty-seven miles of fierce backcountry water and etched stone where the film of my father's first novel, *Deliverance,* was shot in the summer of 1971.

When I read some months back that a lawsuit brought by a boating organization called American Whitewater had prompted the Forest Service to consider opening the river's headwaters to boaters, an unexpected sadness came over me. It was a variant of what I felt years ago when I learned that my childhood home had been torn down and rebuilt into something I couldn't recognize. The Chattooga River is generally recognized as the wildest, most unforgiving in Southern Appalachia; its headwaters flow through some of the toughest terrain in the region. It's a twenty-one-mile stretch of swirling water where the battalions of rafters, kayakers, and canoeists who float the rest of the river every year can't go, or at least not legally. According to American Whitewater, it's the only piece of river in the entire National Forest system, in fact, where boaters aren't allowed. For reasons that differ according to whom you ask, the Forest Service banned boating on the upper third of the river in 1976, two years after the Chattooga was designated a Wild and Scenic River by Congress in order to prevent boaters and fishermen from getting in one another's way. That laws and lawsuits and controversy could extend even into the North Georgia backcountry was a reminder for me that the outside world was always pressing in on the Chattooga and on the people who lived around it.

Really, though, the outside world has been pressing in for over a century — the devastating logging period after the Civil War, the TVA dams following the Great Depression, the ever-increasing numbers of vacation homes going up — but it started pressing a lot harder when *Deliverance* hit theaters in 1972, and with that fact comes, for me, a twinge of guilt.

I wasn't born until ten years after *Deliverance* was filmed. What I knew of the river — and by extension, what I knew of Southern Appalachia — I knew only from the film and from memories of my father: the stories he told me and the bluegrass ballads he picked out on his guitar every morning before he worked on his writing. Both of my parents' families had at one point come down from the hills, from North Georgia on my father's side and East Tennessee on my mother's. They used to say that the mountains are something you carry in your blood. If that was true for me, I couldn't feel it.

But the Chattooga I did carry with me. Ever since I was old enough to watch *Deliverance,* the river — called the Cahulawassee in the story — thundered through my imagination and, perhaps more importantly, pooled in a certain corner of my heart. It was where my father's work came alive for millions of people and lodged itself permanently in the American brain, for better and for worse. Every time I watch the film and I see the Aintry sheriff, my father at a healthy forty-eight years old, standing on the banks of the river, I want to reach right through the screen. And when I hear some version of the old spiritual "Shall We Gather at the River," I remember him playing it on his twelve-string, and I imagine the river in the song is the Chattooga. The two are forever fused in my mind. That I can't help.

I wanted to see the river while it remained, as it was called in the movie, "the last wild . . . river in the South." I wanted the place that lived for me only in film and photographs and secondhand stories to live for me in a real way, in the winter, after the tourists had gone.

The free-flowing waters of the Chattooga are the color of faded denim, so wide and flat in places that it looks like you could walk right out on them and so boulder-strewn in others that it looks like a bruise-colored sculpture garden, half-submerged. The river begins near Cashiers, North Carolina, then stretches along to form a good bit of the Georgia–South Carolina border before it turns back into Georgia, joins with the Tallulah River, and surrenders to Lake Tugaloo about seven miles south of Clayton. Its boiling rapids say as much about the people who named them as they do about the treacherous topography of the river itself: Warwoman, Bull Sluice, Sock 'em Dog, Rock Jumble, Raven Chute, Jawbone, Dead Man's Pool.

"It is," Buzz Williams, one of the principal founders of the Chattooga Conservancy, kept reminding me when he took me up into the headwaters, "a killer river." He meant that thirty-nine people have drowned in it since the Forest Service started keeping records on river fatalities in the '70s. Several rapids are considered "certain death" if you are unlucky enough to fall into them. Some of the people who fell out of their boats or fell in trying to cross the river were sucked into hydraulics or "strainers" (a piece of wood jammed into a rapid) so dangerous that their bodies couldn't be recovered.

Before *Deliverance* was released, only a few hundred people traveled down the river every year; after, that number jumped into the thousands and then the tens of thousands, and when a drowning occurred, it was attributed to "*Deliverance* fever." Despite the river's dangers — or maybe because of them — the lower Chattooga quickly became one of the most popular whitewater destinations in the country; in the past two decades, over a million people have floated it. The fever may be gone, but there's no question that the mystique of the *Deliverance* river endures.

Many of the locals were none too pleased with the flood of outsiders that arrived during the making of the film, and for years following its release, especially when they began to see that the rest of

America viewed them as violent, inbred rednecks. In much the same way as *Jaws* tapped into a primal fear of what lies under water, *Deliverance* tapped into a collective, perhaps unconscious, fear of the watcher in the woods that is as old as American literature itself. A person is most afraid when he is the most vulnerable, and never is he more vulnerable than when he is at the mercy of the wild.

The sadistic mountain men in *Deliverance* were, of course, fictional, as were the town of Aintry and the Cahulawassee River, but the residents of Rabun County were left to contend with the peculiar legacy of the film long after the cameras stopped rolling. The theme music from the movie, "Dueling Banjos," is used in commercials to sell everything from dish detergent to SUVs. PADDLE FASTER, I HEAR BANJO MUSIC is printed on T-shirts and bumper stickers all over the South. The character actor Bill McKinney, who uttered the improvised line "squeal like a pig" (the line does not appear in either the novel or original screenplay), now maintains his official website at www.squeallikeapig.com. It's hard to get away from.

When Congress designated the Chattooga a Wild and Scenic River — the only one in Georgia — that brought its own tensions. The designation protected the river watershed from industrial and commercial development, but also placed it under the control of the Forest Service, making some of the locals feel that the river had been taken from them and given to the federal government. New regulations on how the river could be used chafed against old mountain traditions. No cars were allowed within a quarter mile of the water, for example, which discouraged large family gatherings like baptisms. "With that government corridor they've created a desert," one local resident told John Lane when he was working on his book, *Chattooga: Descending into the Myth of Deliverance River,* "and nobody can make a living out there but a bunch of rich kids with colorful boats."

Most of the paddlers who flocked to the river were from elsewhere, and they soon became the lightning rod for local resentment. People told me stories of boaters who left their cars in parking areas near river put-ins and came back to smashed windows and slashed tires. Even as late as the mid-'80s, they said, arson was a problem. So was theft. Backwoods roughnecks trying to scare off paddlers sometimes fired warning shots from the bank, strung

barbed wire across the river to slash up rafts, or even hauled boats
right out of the water.

Buzz drove me up to where the headwaters ended and the rest of
the river began, at the Highway 28 bridge, the dividing line between where boaters are allowed and where they aren't. The bridge
isn't far from Chattooga Old Town, the site of the former Cherokee village for which the river was named. No one is completely
certain, but most believe that the word *Chattooga* is related to a
Cherokee word for crossing, *tsatugi,* meaning either "we have
crossed here" or "he has crossed the river and come out upon the
other side." European disease and forced displacement wiped out
the Old Town's ninety or so inhabitants by 1775. All that is left is a
flattened patch of grass, hardly bigger than a high-school football
field, a place where something used to be.

Originally from nearby Pendleton, Buzz has been coming to the
river "since he could stick his thumb out," and worked on it as both
a raft guide and a Forest Service employee before he focused on
conservation. There's a saying down on Cumberland Island that
the devil has his tail wrapped around the place, and that's sort of
how Buzz feels about the Chattooga. "There's always something
threatening it," he said. He has a deep respect for the people who
live near the river and a stronger understanding than most of the
circumstances affecting their lives: skyrocketing property taxes, for
example, force many to pick up and move from the land their families farmed before the mountains represented the luxury of weekend getaways. When rich folks build million-dollar vacation homes
on similarly expensive lots, land values and property taxes for everyone go up, and that happens with more frequency every year. "If
you're a farmer and your land is worth two million dollars," Buzz
said, "how are you gonna grow enough to compete with that?"

As we drove from place to place in his pickup, Buzz pointed out
who lived where and how long they'd been there, whose barn he
helped build, who spent a third of his life in the pen, who had a still
out back, whose moonshine was better than whose. One woman
kept a deer in her fenced yard.

We talked some about a story I'd read about a Forest Service employee who claimed to have been chased into the Chattooga by a
cougar last fall. I'd heard several people in Clayton joking around
about the sighting, playfully warning each other to "watch out for

the cougar." The eastern cougar is believed to be extinct in the South; no one has seen any proof of one for decades. Buzz didn't think there was any chance that a big cat was prowling around the backcountry of North Georgia. "Probably just a bobcat," he said.

Small ranch-style and A-frame houses with dusty pickups out front intermittently dotted the snow-dusted hillsides, smoke curling from their brick chimneys. Barns with rusted tin roofs listed at precarious angles. A power line near the road sagged under the weight of two hefty red-tailed hawks.

You can feel it when you leave the pavement in North Georgia. Even in the dead of winter, the air wraps around you with the smell of mountain laurel, hemlock, and rhododendron, a smell just a notch sweeter than that of fresh-cut grass. The world unfolds in sheaves of green and gray and blue and brown, then folds back up in layers of shadow. The dirt road drops off steeply to either side, without the added security of guardrails. Radio stations come in infrequently, if at all. Walk half an hour into the woods, and you're away from 90 percent of the population. Walk an hour into it, and you leave behind 99 percent. It's just you and the limitless indifference of a vast, tangled country.

I was in the South, certainly, but it was not the suburban South I grew up in or even a South I recognized. It was a place where people accepted the dictates of the land they were living on and understood its character, a place free — at least for now — of the gated communities and department stores, happy hours and hustle that make so many cities interchangeable. There is a sense in the hills that things are built to last.

We stopped for lunch in the town of Highlands, about ten miles from where the river actually begins, and I saw for a moment what could be on the horizon for Rabun County. Heavy gates and thick walls began appearing around large, lavish houses, some with FOR SALE signs from "Country Club Properties" staked into their yards. The shops downtown boasted faux-Tudor storefronts. At Buck's Café, I ate a mozzarella and basil sandwich while the lilting horns of loungey jazz played on the stereo. In the corner, heavily accessorized blond women with glossy polished nails picked at scones and nursed cappuccinos. The mounted deer head on the wall looked, if anything, like an ironic touch. There was no doubt that we were in high-dollar country.

*

On the way back to Clayton, we passed an old sign, so faded that I struggled to read it: AMUSEMENTS, PICNICS, COLD BEER, USED CARS. Buzz told me it was the sign for Burrell's Place, a small bar where everyone used to sit out on the front porch and drink beer while a guy named Junior Crow played the banjo. Before it closed years ago, all kinds of people gathered at Burrell's: rich kids from Highlands, hippie river guides, old-timers, and farmers from the mountains. It was the sort of place that doesn't exist in Chattooga country anymore.

"It's magic out there," Dave Perrin said of the headwaters when I met up with him at his office one afternoon, speaking of it with the tenderness one usually reserves for a first love. Perrin is the Chattooga Outpost Manager of the Nantahala Outdoor Center, one of three commercial rafting companies that are allowed to run trips on the river. Just like Buzz and most of the other people I met who have dedicated their lives to the Chattooga, Dave started out decades back as a long-haired raft guide, and like them, the river got under his skin.

Even though there had been no talk of allowing commercial outfitters to run trips on the headwaters, Dave felt that private boaters (whose interests American Whitewater represents) should be allowed access to it. "How can anyone want to protect what they can't even see?" he asked. Moreover, in his view, floating a river in a boat was the most low-impact vantage point from which to explore it. "Boating," he remarked, "is not evil. You take people out on the Chattooga, and you can see the river affect them. You can see the light bulbs go on. Most people come from a computer-driven world, and this is something that isn't virtual. It's not a computer game. If I'm taking kids out of their urban environment and they go home and they appreciate [nature] differently, that's a win."

I remembered how exhilarating and edifying my own white-water trips had been, on rivers in North Carolina and Oregon, and how much they informed my feelings about the outdoors, and I couldn't disagree with him. Could I really blame anyone in techno-heavy 2008 who longed to "get back to nature"? I'd do it more if I could. But I also thought about the Nantahala and Ocoee Rivers near the Chattooga, two once-wild rivers that are now essentially water parks, clogged with tourists looking for "wilderness adventures."

It was true: no one was trying to dam up the Chattooga or build a shopping mall on it. And it was also true that the Forest Service restricted how many people could or could not travel down it in a given year. But the headwaters controversy struck me as an issue of supply and demand that goes on in all the unkempt corners of America: the demand is getting stronger while the supply is getting smaller. Once the land is fought over like it's private property, like it's just another view lot, who draws the lines and where do they draw them?

Sometimes the only way to keep something wild, I thought, is to keep as many people out of it as you can. There was no doubt that everyone I talked to loved the Chattooga. But I began to worry that some of them, in a phrase I heard many times that week, would love it to death.

Driving through the backcountry reminded me of the first scene in the novel of *Deliverance,* where the four main characters, Atlanta suburbanites, are sitting in a bar planning a canoe trip in the mountains. Lewis, the hard-edged survivalist of the group who lacks the pure instinct for actual survival, points to the Cahulawassee on his map, set to be dammed up and turned into a lake for hydroelectric power (as so many rivers were back then) and explains to the others that "right now it's wild. And I *mean* wild. It looks like something up in Alaska. We really ought to go up there before the real estate people get hold of it and make it over into one of their heavens." Famously, this is a trip that throws the men into a horrifying struggle for their lives: one is raped, another shatters his leg, another is killed on the river.

My father didn't talk much about wilderness, it was "wildness" he was interested in. Wilderness, to him, was just an idea, a romantic falsification of nature rather than the untamed, untamable thing itself. *Wildness* was a place where man risked everything; it wasn't a theme park or a toy you played around with or a place you ventured into for thrills. It could kill you. The characters in *Deliverance* were prepared only for wilderness, and they found wildness. Wildness bites back.

"I think a river is the most beautiful thing in nature," my father wrote in one of his journals, right before the novel was published in 1970. "*Any* river is more beautiful than anything else I know." He was drawn to writers who felt similarly inspired by water, like Melville and Conrad. Heraclitus's philosophy of universal flux and his famous dictum, "You cannot step into the same river twice," particularly moved him. But there were few things that terrified my father as much as man's ever-growing intrusion into the natural world. "We're never going to be able to get out of the 'man world,'" he said in a documentary back in the '70s, "if we don't have any place to go to *from* the man world. That's why we need these rivers and streams and creeks and woods and mountains. You need to be in contact with nature as it was made by something else than men." As much as *Deliverance* was a story of survival, or, as so many define it, a story of "man against nature," it was a story about the commercial destruction of a rugged, primordial landscape and a part of the South that was slipping away, even back then.

Right across the river from Clayton, the Long Creek Bar is a plain white box of a building that looks like it might have been converted from something else, like a warehouse for three-wheelers. Inside, the place has concrete floors and the ratty shine of exposed ductwork on the ceiling. The weak lamps above the two pool tables give off the only light in the room, and, on the night I stopped in with Buzz to grab a beer, leftover Christmas garland sagged off tables in the back, waves of cigarette smoke stung my eyes, and two guys in trucker caps shot pool while AC/DC's "Shoot to Thrill" played feebly on the jukebox.

Buzz ordered a Budweiser and sat down at the bar next to a sixtysomething-year-old man with a bushy beard and camo cap whom he knew from the old days at Burrell's Place. The man had clearly had a few, and when the subject turned to the fight over the upper Chattooga (which he pronounced *Chatt*-ooga), he took a long drag from his Winston and became agitated, like he couldn't stand to hear another word about it. "All I wanna know is," he said, "if they open up that upper river, who's gonna pay to get the bodies out?"

Buzz asked him what some of the old-timers from Burrell's might have thought about all the controversy, and the guy shook his head and rested his hands on his pack of cigarettes. "I don't know about that, but I *do* know that the worst thing that ever happened to this area was that" — I knew what was coming — "that *Deliverance.*"

I was silently grateful that he didn't know who I was. Half of me wanted to apologize to him for something, and half of me didn't feel there was anything to apologize for. That was a feeling that I walked around with my entire time in Chattooga country: a shadow of guilt about the lasting legacy of *Deliverance* doing battle with the pride of my father's work. I've often wondered what it must be like to have grown up in North Georgia and to see your life, your town, your way of living flattened out for someone else's purposes and eventually turned into a national punch line. Hollywood has not been kind to Southern Appalachia in this sense. Even before *Deliverance*, there were the Kettle clan from the '40s and the Clampetts, but the shocking violence of *Deliverance*, in the imagination of so many, ratcheted up the stereotype.

It's hard for me to read much of what is written about Appalachia in popular media, because it tends to be written in a cartoonish "them-thar-hills" vernacular, always something about a "feisty, clannish" people who sit around a-drinkin' and a-stompin' and a-pickin' on the banjo. Some of that's true, sure, but some of it isn't. It's as though Southern Appalachia is the corner of America that America forgot, and the virtues that are generally lauded as defining the American frontier identity — self-reliance, resourcefulness, hard work — are now ripe material for ridicule. If the people around the Chattooga River had no particular love for the rest of the world, I couldn't really blame them.

More than the guilt/pride, though, I had to contend with the sharp pangs of loneliness that were setting in. As enraptured as I was by the Chattooga, I couldn't know it the way the locals, the paddlers, the fishermen, and the activists knew it, because they knew it like they knew a person: its moods, its temper. This is a part of the world that I always thought would feel familiar to me, but it didn't. That stuff my parents told me about the mountains being in the blood didn't feel true. I realized, slowly, that everything I did — from the clothing I wore to how I put my hair up to the way I spoke — marked me as a person who wasn't from here, and I was in a place where being "from here" mattered.

On my last day in North Georgia, I drove over to Mountain Rest, South Carolina, to meet up with Butch Clay, who wrote a guide-

book on the river and possesses an intimate knowledge of the headwaters area. He was fighting off strep throat, but felt so strongly
while talking with me about preserving the wildness up there that
he filled a thermos with lime juice, honey, and a bit of Jack Daniels
and insisted we hike down into a place called the Rock Gorge.
"You're lucky," he said, "that I have to save my voice."

He and I drove to a small parking area near the Chattooga River
Trailhead, packed up two sets of hip waders and some lunch, and
started our hike to the gorge, some of the most intractable wilderness on the entire river. It was not far from the Rock Gorge, incidentally, where the Forest Service employee claimed he had seen
the cougar. "If there is one around, it'd be up here," Butch said, the
naturalist in him sounding hopeful. "Lots of overhanging cliffs for
it to drag food into."

The hike was a sweaty, slippery, merciless hour-long descent, with
all the potential to be twice that coming back up. "There are no
roads in it, and no roads to it," Butch kept saying of the gorge,
speaking more philosophically than to me. "If you want to see it
then you have to earn it." In the words of Dwight Yoakam, we were
a thousand miles from nowhere, a fact that sank in when Butch
told me that if I broke an ankle, he'd build me a fire and leave me
his gun.

The gorge looked like a hulking rock coliseum, with the pine-
covered mountains forming a steep V on either side that the noon-
day sun blanketed with light. The wind galloped straight through
with as much purpose as the river did, chilling my skin under all
the layers of sweat-soaked clothes. Once we picked our way down to
the water, we saw that there were thin sheets of ice all over it, looking like someone had encased the scene in glass. "Rime ice," Butch
said, as he broke off some of it with his boot. Ever so often a huge
sheet of ice would break off a ledge somewhere in the gorge and
crash into the water, and I would wheel around, thinking it was a
bear or a wild hog.

The water was about two and a half to three feet deep and, from
the bank, didn't seem to be moving too fast. Butch and I pulled on
our hip waders and slowly stepped out into the river. The carpet of
rounded rocks on the riverbed was too slick for the traction on my
waders to grip, and the current so strong it felt like someone had a
rope around my waist and was pulling at it, hard. I tilted and stumbled. My arms reached out, though there was nothing to grab onto.

The water spilled over the tops of my waders and was so cold that my body didn't register it as cold but as scorching heat; it burned the tops of my legs and painted my skin bright red. If the river wanted to take me, it could have.

Eventually, we made the crossing, climbed onto an imposing boulder, and talked, while we ate lunch, about the people who wanted to bring boats to the upper river. The tide of tourism seemed inevitable: the three major cities nearby — Atlanta, Asheville, Chattanooga — are growing all the time, as are the popularity of whitewater sports and the technology with which those sports can be enjoyed. Rapids that were unrunnable thirty years ago are easy to navigate in today's smaller boats. Really, there was no empirical evidence to make a convincing case against boaters using the headwaters. Aside from the possibility for the sort of pollution that comes with every outdoor activity, I didn't feel that boaters represented more of a threat to the landscape than, say, the hunters and campers in the headwaters did. It all came down to gut feeling, not reasoning: either you wanted people up there or you wanted people to stay away; either you wanted things to change or you wanted things to stay the same.

"Everyone is asking, 'What's in it for me?'" Butch said. "No one is saying 'What can I give up?'" Perhaps thinking of his young son, he continued, "Where else are we gonna teach our children about this kind of wilderness? There *is* nowhere else." I asked him if he thought there was anything that could be done about it. He paused, looking out onto the water. "I believe someone with deep pockets and a stout heart could hold 'em off for a while, and I'll stick right there with 'em." He sliced off a piece of cheese and some sausage. "But I ain't got the deep pockets."

The last time my father saw the river was in 1987, when he visited it on a snowy winter weekend to participate in a short film about his career. Buzz Williams showed him around, and some months later, after the documentary aired in Columbia, Buzz told me that my father shook his hand at the screening and said, "Say goodbye to the river for me." In a dark twist on that line from Heraclitus, he knew that he could never step into the same river twice, and the Chattooga that existed as a site for *Deliverance* tourism wasn't the same river he stepped into back in 1971.

Sitting in the Rock Gorge, I looked around at the ice-sheathed cliffs and fallen trees spanning the water and wanted everything I could see to stay right as it was, as my father had once seen it. I wanted to lock the wildness of the river into the sandstone somehow so that it couldn't be touched by men, and climb back out — straight up — through the mud and undergrowth, crawling over decayed logs, tripping over vines, my lungs burning from the effort because there weren't any roads. In my heart, if not my head, I wanted the glittering, jade eyes of the last cougar in the South to study me from under a ledge. I wanted to feel that cold fear that sluices through your veins when you realize you're truly alone out in the wild — or that you aren't. Emerging from the woods at dark-thirty (the Appalachian term for half past sunset), looking rougher, as my dad used to say, than a night in jail, I wanted to drive back down out of the mountains knowing that the people who had been living there for generations weren't in any danger of being forced out, because I didn't want to walk around in fifty years and see flattened patches of grass where the farmers and moonshiners and hell-raisers used to live. And, before I arrived home, I wanted to stop at Burrell's Place and drink a beer out on the porch while Junior Crow played songs that sounded familiar to me. "Shall We Gather at the River," maybe. That's one I know.

ANDRÉ ACIMAN

Intimacy

FROM *The American Scholar*

I FINALLY WENT BACK to Via Clelia. I had passed by the first time I returned to Rome almost forty years ago, then a second time fifteen years later, and still another three years after that. But for reasons that had more to do with my reluctance to come back here, these visits either occurred by night, when I couldn't see a thing, or when I didn't dare ask our cabby to make a right and stall a while to let me see our old home again. From Via Appia Nuova, a bustling working-class artery, all I ever caught was a distant glimpse of Via Clelia. After that third time, I stopped trying. In Rome, whenever I come back, I never venture beyond the center.

Summer before last, though, with my wife and sons, I took the Metro and got off at the Furio Camillo stop, two blocks north of Via Clelia, exactly as I'd always envisaged the visit. Two blocks would give me plenty of time to settle into the experience, gather my impressions, and unlock memory's sluice gates, one by one — without effort, caution, or ceremony. Two blocks, however, would also allow me to put up whatever barriers needed to come up between me and this lower-middle-class street whose grimy, ill-tempered welcome, when we landed in Italy as refugees more than four decades ago, I've never managed to forget.

I had meant to enter Via Clelia precisely where it crosses Via Appia Nuova and take my time recognizing the streets, whose names are drawn from Virgil mostly — Via Enea, Via Camilla, Via Eurialo, Via Turno — and confer far-fetched echoes of imperial grandeur on this rinky-dink quarter. I had meant to touch minor signposts along the way: the printer's shop — still there — the makeshift grocer-pizzaiolo, the one or two corner bars, the plumber — gone — the barbershop across the street — gone too — the tobacconist, the tiny brothel where you didn't dare look in when the two old frumps left their door ajar, the spot where a frail street singer would stand every afternoon and bellow out bronchial arias you strained to recognize, only to hear, when his dirge was done, a scatter of coins rain upon the sidewalk.

Home was right above his spot.

As I began walking down Via Clelia with my wife and sons, pointing out aspects of a street I'd known so well during the three years I'd lived there with my parents while we waited for visas to America, I caught myself hoping that no one I knew back then would be alive today, or, if they were, that none might recognize me. I wanted to give no explanations, answer no questions, embrace no one, touch or get close to nobody. I had always been ashamed of Via Clelia, ashamed of its good people, ashamed of having lived among them, ashamed of myself now for feeling this way, ashamed, as I told my sons, of how I'd always misled my private-school classmates into thinking I lived "around" the affluent Appia Antica and not in the heart of the blue-collar Appia Nuova. That shame had never gone away; shame never does, it was there on every corner of the street. Shame, which is the reluctance to be who we're not even sure we are, could end up being the deepest thing about us, deeper even than who we are, as though beyond identity were buried reefs and sunken cities teeming with creatures we couldn't begin to name because they came long before us. All I really wanted, as we began walking to the other end of Via Clelia, was to put the experience behind me now — *We've done Via Clelia,* I'd say — knowing all along that I wouldn't mind a sudden flare-up of memory to make good the visit.

Torn between wanting the whole thing over and done with and wanting perhaps to feel something, I began to make light of our visit with my sons. Fancy spending three years in this dump. And the stench on hot summer days. On this corner I saw a dead dog once; he'd been run over and was bleeding from both ears. And here, every afternoon, sitting cross-legged on the sidewalk by the tramway stop, a young gypsy used to beg, her bare, dark knee flaunted boldly over her printed skirt — savage, dauntless, shameless. On Sunday afternoons, Via Clelia was a morgue. In the summer, the heat unbearable. In the fall, coming back after school on the number 85 bus, I'd run errands for Mother, always rushing back out of the apartment before the shops closed, and by early twilight, watch the salesgirls head home, and always think of Joyce's "Araby." The girl at the tiny supermarket down the street, the salesgirls of the tiny local department store, the girl at the butcher's who always extended credit when money was tight toward the end of every month.

There was a girl who came every day for vitamin B_{12} shots. My mother, once a volunteer nurse during World War II, was only too glad to administer the injections; it gave her something to do. Afterward, the girl and I would sit and talk in the kitchen till it was time for dinner. Then she disappeared down the staircase. Pina. The landlady's daughter. I never felt the slightest desire for Pina, but it was kinder to conceal what I couldn't feel behind a veil of feigned timidity and inexperience. Neither timidity nor inexperience were feigned in the slightest, of course, but I exaggerated the performance to suggest a dissembled feint somewhere and that behind it lurked a waggish side capable of great mischief if given the go-ahead. I feigned an earnest, bashful gaze, the better to hide the writhing diffidence underneath.

With the girl in the supermarket, it was the other way around. I couldn't hold her gaze and was compelled each time to affect the arrogance of someone who might have stared one day but had forgotten to the next.

I hated my shyness. I wanted to hide it, but there was nothing to hide it with. Even trying to cover it up brought out more blushes and made me more flustered yet. I learned to hate my eyes, my height, my accent. To speak to a stranger, or to the girl at the supermarket, or to anyone for that matter, I needed to shut down everything about me, weigh my words, plan my words, affect a makeshift *Romanaccio* to cover up my foreign accent, and, to avoid making any grammar mistakes in Italian, start undoing every sentence before I'd even finished speaking it and, because of this, end up making worse mistakes, the way some writers change the course of a sentence while still writing it but forget to remove all traces of where it was originally headed, thereby speaking with more voices than one. I dissembled with everyone — with those I wanted nothing from, with those I wanted anything they could give if only they

could help me ask. I dissembled what I thought, what I feared, who
I was, who I wasn't even sure I was.

Wednesday evenings, I remember, were earmarked for running
errands and redeeming bottles at the tiny supermarket at the end
of Via Clelia. The girl in charge of stacking the shelves would come
to the back counter and help me with the bottles. I was scared each
time I watched her empty the bag of bottles fast, feeling that time
was flitting by sooner than I'd hoped. My gaze seemed to upset her,
because she always lost her smile when she stared at me. Hers was
the dark, ill-tempered stare of someone who was trying not to be
rude. With other men, she was all smiles and bawdy jokes. With me,
just the glare.

We arrived at the Furio Camillo Metro station at ten in the morning. At 10 A.M. in late July I'd be in my room upstairs, probably
reading. On occasion, we'd go to the beach before it grew too hot.
But past the third week of the month, the money ran out and we'd
stay indoors, listening to the radio, saving the money for an occasional movie on weekday evenings, when tickets at the seedy and
deserted, third-to-last-run movie theater around the corner were
cheaper than on Sundays. There were two movie theaters. One had
disappeared, the other, all gussied up now, stands on Via Muzio
Scevola, named after the early Roman hero who burned his right
hand on realizing he'd murdered the wrong man. One night, in
that theater, a man put his hand on my wrist. I asked him what was
the matter with him, and soon enough he moved to another seat.
In those days, I told my sons, you also learned to avoid the bath-
rooms in movie theaters.

One more block and scarcely five minutes after arriving, our visit
was over. This always happens when I go back to places. Either
buildings shrink over time, or the time it takes to revisit them
shrinks to less than five minutes. We had walked from one end of
the street to the other. There was nothing more to do now but walk
back the way we came. I sensed, from the way my wife and sons were
waiting for me to tell them what to do next, that they were glad the
visit was over. On our way back up the street, I did spend a few more
seconds standing before the building, not just to take the moment
in and never say I'd rushed or bungled the experience, but because I still hoped that an undisclosed something might rush out

and tug me, exclaiming, as some people do when they suddenly show up at your door after many years, "Remember me?" But nothing happened. I was, as I always am during such moments, numb to the experience.

Writing about it — after the fact, as I did later that day — might eventually un-numb me. Writing, I was sure, would dust off things that were not there at the time of my visit, or that were there but that I wasn't quite seeing and needed time and paper to sort out, so that, once written about, they'd confer on my visit the retrospective resonance that part of me had hoped to find here on Via Clelia. Writing might even bring me closer to this street than I'd been while living there. Writing wouldn't alter or exaggerate anything; it would simply excavate, rearrange, lace a narrative, recollect in tranquility, where ordinary life is perfectly happy to nod and move on. Writing sees figures where life sees things; things we leave behind, figures we keep. Even the experience of numbness, when traced on paper, acquires a resigned and disenchanted grace, a melancholy cadence that seems at once intimate and aroused compared to the original blah. Write about numbness, and numbness turns into something. Upset flat surfaces, dig out their shadows, and you've got dream-making.

Does writing, as I did later that day, seek out words the better to stir and un-numb us to life — or does writing provide surrogate pleasures the better to numb us to experience?

Three years in Rome and I had never touched this street. It would be just like me scarcely to touch anything, or to have grazed this city all but unintentionally, the way, in the three years I saw the gypsy girl seated on her corrugated piece of cardboard next to the tramway stop, I never made a dent into her sealed, impenetrable, surly gaze. I called her the dirty girl to hide arousal and disturbance whenever I spoke of her to my friends at school.

Was I disappointed? It seemed a crime not to stumble on at least one quivering leftover from the past. Did numbness mean that even the memory of hating this street had gone away? Could parts of us just die to the past so that returning brings nothing back?

Or was I relieved? The romance of time had fallen flat. There was no past to dig up here — never been any. I might as well never have lived here at all.

I felt like someone trying to step on his own shadow, or like a

reader who failed to underline a book as a teenager and now, decades later, is totally unable to recover the young reader he'd once
been.

But then, coming back from the West, perhaps it was I who was
the shadow, not this street, not my books, not who I once was.

For a second, as I stood and looked at our tiny rounded balcony,
I felt an urge to call myself to the window, the way Italians always
shout your name from downstairs on the sidewalk and ask you to
come to the window. But I wasn't calling myself. I was just trying to
picture what I'd be doing behind that window so many years ago.
It's past mid-July, there's no beach, no friends, I'm more or less
locked up in my room, reading, and as always shielding myself from
the outside world behind drawn shutters, desperately using books
to put an imaginary screen between me and Via Clelia.

Anything but Via Clelia.

In that room on Via Clelia, I managed to create a world that cor-
responded to nothing outside it. My books, my city, myself. All I
had to do then was let the novels I was reading lend their aura
to this street and drop an illusory film over its buildings, a film
that washed down Via Clelia like a sheet of rainwater, casting a
shimmering spell on this hard, humdrum, here-and-now area of
lower-middle-class Rome. On rainy days when the emptied street
gleamed in the early evening, I might have been very much alone
in my room upstairs, but I was alone in D. H. Lawrence's "faintly
humming, glowing town" — by far the better. Dying winter light
took me straightaway to the solitary embankments of Dostoyevsky's
white nights in Saint Petersburg. And on sunny mornings when
shouts from the marketplace a block down couldn't have sounded
more truculent, I was in Baudelaire's splenetic, rain-washed Paris,
and because there were echoes of Baudelaire's Paris around me,
suddenly the loutish *Romanaccio,* which I learned to love only after
leaving Rome, began to acquire an earthy, Gallic coarseness that
made it almost tolerable, vibrant, authentic. Earlier in the morning, when I opened the windows, I was suddenly in Wordsworth's
England where "domes, theatres, and temples . . . glitter in the
smokeless air" "beneath the blue suburban skies." And when I
finally put down Lampedusa's *The Leopard* and began to see aging,
patrician Sicilians everywhere, each more lost than the other in a

scowling new world that none of them could begin to fathom, much less belong to, I knew I was not alone. All that these Sicilians had left was their roughshod arrogance, their ancient, beaten-down palace with its many, many rooms and rickety balconies that looked over the shoulders of history back to the Norman invasion of Sicily. One could step out onto Via Clelia and enter a tiny park where scrawny trees and scorched growth told me I'd stepped into the abandoned hunting grounds of Frederick II of Hohenstaufen.

Anything but Via Clelia.

So, why shouldn't Via Clelia feel dead now? It had never been alive. I had hated it from my very first day and had almost managed to hate Rome because of it.

And yet, as though to punish me now for calquing my own images over these sidewalks long ago, Via Clelia was giving them all back — but not a thing more. Here, Baudelaire's vendors, take them back; here's Raskolnikov's hat, *you* wear it; over there, Akaky's overcoat, *yours;* and if you looked over across the Appia Nuova through Oblomov's smoky windows, you'll find Lampedusa's declining mansion, and farther out, D. H. Lawrence's town — all, all yours now. I had lined the world with books; now the city was giving them back to me, one by one, as one returns a tool, unused, or a necktie, unworn, or money that should never have been borrowed, or a book one had no intention of reading. The snow of Joyce's "The Dead," which had mantled Via Celia after midnight one evening and given it a luster that would never have existed outside of books, was being returned to me with a curt inscription: "It never snows on Via Clelia, didn't you know?" De Quincey's London, Browning's Florence, Camus's Oran, Whitman's New York had been waiting in escrow year after mildewed year. "Truth wasn't good enough for you, was it?" asked the street, irony flecking each of its features.

The illusory film, the shadow of my three years here, was all I had. And as I walked back from one end of Via Clelia to the other with my wife and sons, I realized that all I'd be able to cull here were the fictions, the lies I'd laid down upon this street to make it habitable. Dream-making and dissemblance, then as now.

It dawned on me much later that evening that our truest, most private moments, like our truest, most private memories, are made of just such unreal, flimsy stuff. Fictions.

Via Clelia was my street of lies. Some lies, like impacted chewing gum, were so thoroughly stepped over each day that there was no undoing or erasing them. Look at this corner, that store, this printer's shop, and all you'll see is Stendhal, Nerval, Flaubert. Underneath, nothing. Just the memory of three years waiting for our visas to the States to come through.

We had no television in those days, no money, no shopping to take our minds off anything, no friends, hardly any relatives, no point in even discussing a weekly allowance. All my mother gave me was enough money to buy one paperback a week. This I did for three years. Buying a book was simply my way of running away from Via Clelia, taking the number 85 bus on Saturdays, and spending the rest of the day burrowed in Rome's many foreign-language bookstores. The walk from one bookstore to the other without paying attention to the city itself became my way of being in Rome, of knowing Rome — a Rome, which, for all my reclusive bookishness, was no less real to me than was the Rome of everyday Romans or the Rome tourists came looking for. My centers were bookshops and, between them, a network of cobbled, narrow lanes lined by ochre walls and refuse. The piazzas with their centered obelisks, the museums, the churches, the glorious remnants were for other people.

On Saturday mornings, I would get off at San Silvestro and wander downtown, hoping to get lost, because I loved nothing better than stumbling on one of my bookstores. I grew to like the old city: Campo Marzio, Campo de' Fiori, Piazza Rotonda. I liked the muted affluence of rundown buildings I knew were palatial inside. I liked them on Saturday mornings, at noon, and on weekday evenings. Via Del Babuino was my Faubourg Saint-German, Via Frattina my Nevsky Prospect, streets where people crowded dim-lit sidewalks that could, within seconds, seem studded by turn-of-the-century gas lamps flickering in the evening's spellbound afterglow.

I even liked the people who suddenly popped out of seventeenth-century buildings, leading flashy, extravagant, dream-made lives where love, movies, and fast cars took you to places the number 85 bus knew not a thing about. I liked hanging around a while after the bookstores had closed and the streets had begun to empty, and amble about on this magical part of the city whose narrow cobbled lanes and spotty lights seemed to know, long before I did, where my footsteps were aching to turn. I began to think that over and above Via Clelia and the books I'd come looking for, something else was keeping me from heading back home now, and that if books had given me a destination that was a good enough alibi for my parents and for myself, my staying in old Rome now had a different purpose. I'd grown to love this Rome, a Rome that seemed more in me than it was out in Rome itself, because, in this very Rome I'd grown to love, there was perhaps more of me in it than there was of Rome, so that I was never sure if my love was genuine or simply a product of my own yearnings thrown at the first old lane that crossed my path.

It would take decades to realize that this strange, shadow Rome of my own invention was everyone else's as well. Who would have guessed . . . I'd been hiding my shamefaced, lonely-adolescence Rome from everyone, yet all I had to do was share one picture, and everyone, young or old, knew exactly . . . Emerson: "To believe that what is true for you in your private heart is true for all men — that is genius. Speak your latent conviction, and it shall be the universal sense."

It wasn't Rome itself I was seeing; it was the film, the filter I'd placed on the old city that finally made me love it, the film I went to seek each time I'd go to a bookstore and would come out late in the evening to stroll down my Nevsky Prospect in search of vague smiles and fellowship in a city I wasn't even sure existed on the sidewalks. It is the film I can no longer lift off the many books I read back then, the film that reverberates over time and continues to make Rome mine long after I've lost it. And perhaps it is the film I go in search of each time I'm back in Rome — not Rome. We seldom ever see, or read, or love things as they in themselves really are, nor, for that matter, do we even know our impressions of them as they really are. What matters is knowing what we see when we see other than what lies before us. It is the film we see, the film that breathes essence into otherwise lifeless objects, the film we crave to share with others. What we reach for and what ultimately touches us is the radiance we've projected on things, not the things themselves — the envelope, not the letter, the wrapping, not the gift.

Lucretius says somewhere that all objects release films, or "peeled skins" of themselves. These intimations travel from the objects and beings around us and eventually reach our senses. But the opposite is also true: we radiate films of what we have within us and project them on everything we see — which is how we become aware of the world and, ultimately, why we come to love it. Without these films, these fictions, which are both our alibis and the archive of our innermost life, we have no way to connect to or touch anything.

I learned to read and to love books much as I learned to know and to love Rome: not only by intuiting undisclosed passageways everywhere, but by seeing more of me in books than there probably was, because everything I read seemed more in me already than on the pages themselves. I knew that my way of reading books might be aberrant, just as I knew that figuring my way around Rome as I did would shock the fussiest of tourists.

I was after something intimate and I learned to spot it in the first alley, in the first verse of a poem, on the first glance of a stranger. Great books, like great cities, always let us find things we think are only in us and couldn't possibly belong elsewhere but that turn out to be broadcast everywhere we look. Great artists are those who give us what we think was already ours. Never mind that we've never seen, felt, or lived through anything remotely similar. The artist converts us; he steals and refashions our past, and like songs from our adolescence, gives us the picture of our youth as we wished it to be back then — never as it really was. He gives us our secret wishfilm back.

Suddenly, the insights nursed by strangers belong, against all odds, to us as well. We know what an author desires, what he dissembles; we even know why. The better a writer, the better he erases his footprints — yet the better the writer, the more he wants us to intuit and put back those parts he chose to hide. With the right hunch, you could read the inflection of an author's soul on a single comma, in one sentence, and from that one sentence seize the whole book, his life work.

With the right hunch. Pascal: *"Il faut deviner, mais bien deviner."* (You have to guess — and guess right.)

What I found in the authors I grew to love was precisely the right to assume that I hadn't misread them at all, that I wasn't making up what I was seeing, and that I was getting the obvious meaning as well as the one they were not too keen to proclaim and might gainsay if confronted, perhaps because they themselves were not seeing it as clearly as they should, or were pretending not to. I was intuiting something for which there was no proof but that I knew was essential, because without this one unstated thing, their work wouldn't hold.

It never occurred to me then that insight and intuition, which are the essence, the genius of all criticism, are born from this intimate fusion of self with something or someone else. To everything — books, places, people — I brought a desire to *steal into* and intuit something undisclosed, perhaps because I mistrusted all appearances, or because I was so withdrawn that I needed to believe others were as dissembled and withdrawn as I feared I was. Perhaps I loved prying. Perhaps insight was like touching — but without asking, without risk. Perhaps spying was my way of reaching out to the Roman life that was all around me. In the words of Emanuele Tesauro: "We enjoy seeing our own thoughts blossom in someone's mind, while that someone is equally pleased to spy what our own mind furtively conceals." I was a cipher. But, like me, everyone was a cipher as well. Ultimately, I wanted to peer into books, places, and people because wherever I looked I was always looking for myself, or for traces of myself, or better yet, for a world out there filled with people and characters who could be made to be like me, because being like me and being me and liking the things I liked was nothing more than their roundabout way of being as close to, as open to, and as bound to me as I wished to be to them. The world in my image. All I cared for were streets that bore my name and the trace of my passage there; and all I cared for were novels in which everyone's soul was laid bare and *anatomized,* because nothing interested me more than the nether, undisclosed aspects of people and things that were identical to mine. Exposed, everyone would turn out to be just like me. They understood me, I understood them, we were no longer strangers. I dissembled, they dissembled. The more they were like me, the more I'd learn to accept and perhaps grow to like who I was. My hunches, my insights were nothing more than furtive ways of bridging the insuperable distance between me and the world.

In the end, my solitude, my disaffection, my shame on Via Clelia, and my wish to withdraw into an imaginary nineteenth-century bubble were not incidental to the books I was reading. My disaffection was part of what I saw in these books and was essential to my reading of them, just as what I read in Ovid was not unrelated to my tremulous yearnings for the swarthy knees of the gypsy girl. But they were essential in an altogether strange and undisclosed manner. I wasn't identifying with Dostoyevsky's characters because I too was poor or withdrawn, anymore than I was identifying with the lust of Byblis and Salmacis because I would have given anything to undress the gypsy girl in my bedroom. What my favorite authors were asking of me was that I read them intimately — not an invitation to read my own pulse on someone else's work, but to read an author's pulse as though it were my own, the height of presumption, because it presupposed that by trusting my deepest, most intimate thoughts about a book, I was in fact tapping on, or rather divining, the author's own. It was an invitation to read not what others had taught me to read, but to see what I, by virtue of the films I brought to everything, was seeing, yet to see things in such a way that the very few who heard me report what I'd seen would agree that they too had always seen things in exactly the same way. The more solipsistic and idiosyncratic my insights were, the more people said they nursed the very same ones themselves.

Maybe this is why I liked every French *roman d'analyse*. Everyone was after intimacy in those novels, yet everyone dissembled and knew that everyone else did so as well. Over and above every plot their authors spun and every grand idea they jiggled before their readers, the one thrilling moment in these novels always came when their authors bored through that amorphous landfill of inhibition called the psyche and wrote something like: *Her lover knew, by the way she showed every conceivable proof of love for him, that she was determined to say no to him.* Or: *Her future husband could tell, by the way she blushed whenever they were alone together, that she felt neither love, nor passion, nor desire for him; her blushes came from exaggerated modesty, which in her coy, girlish way she was pleased to mistake for love. The very means meant to conceal her blushes is precisely what gave them away. Her husband guessed by how happy his wife was when she heard that their friend was not going to join them on their trip to Spain that he was the one with whom she'd have betrayed him if only she had the courage.* Or: *The frown with which she seemed to dismiss the man she wished she didn't love told him everything he longed to know. Even the abrupt, rude manner with which she snapped at him as soon as they were alone was a good sign: she was more in love with him than he had ever hoped.*

*

Then, one summer evening, a sentence suddenly pops up and
seems to determine the course of my life.

*Je crus que, si quelque chose pouvait rallumer les sentiments que vous aviez eus
pour moi, c'était de vous faire voir que les miens étaient changés, mais de vous le
faire voir en feignant de vous le cacher, et comme si je n'eusse pas eu la force de
vous l'avouer.*
(I thought that if anything could rekindle your feelings for me, it was to
let you see that mine too had changed, but to let you see this by feigning
to wish to conceal it from you, as if I lacked the courage to acknowledge
it to you.)

This sentence was me. I reread this sentence from *La Princesse de
Clèves* many times over. The letter of a woman who wins back the
man who jilted her was no less intimate and dissembled than I was
in my days and nights. If she succeeds in rekindling his love, it's not
by feigning indifference for him — he would have seen through
this feint easily enough — but merely by pretending to want to conceal a budding indifference that seizes her almost against her will.
There was so much guile and so much insight in her letter that for
the first time in my life I knew that what I needed to navigate the
multiple removes of La Fayette's prose was nothing more than the
courage to think that I had lived this sentence, that I was this sentence more than this sentence was La Fayette's.

By coincidence — and if it wasn't a coincidence, what was it? —
the evening I discovered this sentence fell on a Wednesday on the
85 bus. As I walked with my *Princesse de Clèves* on my way home, the
girl at the small supermarket was sweeping the floor by the sidewalk wearing her light blue tunic. She caught me walking by and
gave me her usual ill-tempered stare. I looked away. When, fifteen
minutes later, I came to redeem our bottles, she emptied the bag,
lined the bottles on the glass counter as she always did, and, after
dropping the coins into the change plate, leaned over toward me
and extending her right hand, elbow touching elbow, rubbed her
index finger the length of my bare forearm, quietly, softly, slowly. I
felt my lungs choke, as I fought the impulse to withdraw my arm,
something at once spellbound and illicit racing through my chest.
Her touch might have been a sibling's sympathy caress, or anything ranging from a don't-forget-your-change-now, to a let's-test-if-
you're-ticklish, or a you're-sweet, I-like-you, relax!, or just simply

stay-well, be-happy. Then, for the first time, and perhaps because she seemed less busy than usual, she smiled. I smiled back, diffidently, barely hearing what she said. We'd exchanged no more than four sentences.

I had wanted smiles and fellowship. And smiles and fellowship I'd gotten. Someone, a stranger, had read me through and through — down to my jitters, my wants, my second thoughts. She knew I knew she knew. Was it possible that I spoke the same language as everybody else?

It took weeks to screw up the courage to pass by the store again. Trying not to look nervous, trying to seem mildly distracted as well, trying to show that I was capable of bandying a joke or two if prompted, trying to find safe ways to retreat in case she stared me down again — with all these feelings sparring in my mind, I heard her remember my name while I had all but forgotten hers.

I tried to cover up my mistake. Blushes, shortness of breath, more blushes. How paradoxical, that I, the most innocent boy on Via Clelia, should turn out to seem no better than a cad who forgets names — and should be tormented both for being so hopelessly enamored and for suggesting the very opposite. I decided to milk this newfound roguery by overdoing and showing I was overdoing my apologies, hoping she'd disbelieve them. "One of these days we should go to the movies," she said. I nodded a breathless and sheepish "Yes." It took me forever to realize that "one of these days" meant this very evening — last row, dark, empty weekday movie theater. "I can't," I said, trying to sound abstract, meaning never. It didn't seem to faze her at all. "Whenever you want, then."

That same Saturday evening, while coming back from bookstores downtown, I saw her standing with her beau at the bus stop across the way. They were headed downtown. They weren't even touching, but you could tell they were together. He was older. Figures. She had washed her hair and was wearing flashy party clothes. Why wasn't I surprised? I felt rage coursing up my body, around my temples. I hated everything — the street, her, me.

I put off going to the small supermarket. With the visa approaching, part of me had left that store behind long before I stopped going there. Soon, I'd be in New York, where another me, who wasn't even born yet, might never remember any of this. By next winter when it snows there, I'd never think back on this corner.

It would never have occurred to me that this other me one day would give anything to run into the shadow me trapped under Via Clelia.

So on my return visit with my family, I looked for the tiny supermarket, hoping not to find it, or, rather, saving it for last. When we reached the end of Via Clelia, I realized that the store was gone. Perhaps I'd forgotten where it was. But a second look, and another across the street even — as though the shop might have shifted to the other side, or had always been across the way — told me there was no doubt about it. It was gone. All I'd hoped was to recapture the thrill, the fear, the thumping in my chest each time I caught her eyes on those evenings when I'd go to redeem our bottles. Perhaps I longed to walk back into that same store and see for myself — my way of closing the circle, settling the score, having the last word. I'd have walked in, leaned against the glass counter, and just waited a while, just waited, see what comes up, who turns up, see if the ritual had changed, see if I'd be the same person on the same errand on the same street.

To make light of my disappointment and draw their laughter, I told my sons all that happened in the tiny supermarket: woman rubbing her finger on Dad's forearm, body touching body — was ever a come-on more explicit? — Dad running for cover under Grandma's kitchen apron, and as always scampering back to his books, never daring to go back, while skulking and prowling the streets for days and weeks afterward — for years, I should have said — for decades and a lifetime. "Were you in love with her?" one of my sons finally asked. I didn't think so; love had nothing to do with it. "So you never spoke again," said another. No, we never did.

But I hadn't told them the truth, not the whole truth. I might as well have been lying. Would they know? Would they dust for the footprints I had erased in the hope they'd ask the right question, knowing that, if they asked the right question, they'd have guessed the answer already, and that if they'd guessed it, they'd be reading my pulse as if it were their own?

Writing — as I did later that day — is intended to dig out the fault lines where truth and dissembling shift places. Or is it meant to bury them even deeper?

Before leaving, I took one last look at Via Clelia. All those rides

on the bus, the walks through Rome, the books, the faces, the waiting for visas that I sometimes wished might never come because I
had grown to like this place, the vitamin shots, the conversations at
the kitchen table, Pina, who almost seemed to rush out in tears
sometimes, and the dream launched like a desperate call on a winter night when I finished reading "The Dead" and thought to myself, I must head West and leave this town and seek a world where
snow falls "softly into the dark mutinous Shannon waves" — all, all
of it no more than a film, the aura of my love for Rome that was perhaps no more than my love for a might-be life born from a story
Joyce had penned during his hapless stay in Rome, thinking of his
half-real, half-remembered Dublin. The cold nights staring out my
window as rain fell obliquely against the lamplight; the evening I
came so close to another body that I knew I could no longer live
like this; the sense that life could have started or just turned on this
improbable three-block stretch — all of it a film, perhaps the best
and most enduring part of me, but a film all the same. All I'd encountered here were half-truths. Rome, a half-truth, Via Clelia, a
half-truth, the adolescent who ran errands after school, his books,
the gypsy girl, the girl from the supermarket, half-truths as well,
even my return trip now, a muddle of half-truths veiling the numbing thought that, if I never really wanted to come back here and
had been putting it off for years, it was also because, much as I
thought I hated it, I wished I'd never left at all.

Did I know what this numbness was? I blamed it on my fictions,
my films, my impulse to deflect the here and now by proposing
elsewheres and otherwises. But perhaps numbness had a more
troubling side. And as I neared the Furio Camillo Metro station
and could no longer see Via Clelia, something did begin to come
to me, distantly at first, then, as we were about to enter the station,
with a fierceness I'd never expected: Via Clelia was not just littered
with the many books I'd read there, but what it harbored un-
changed, untouched after forty years, were chilling premonitions
of the city across the Atlantic for which I knew I'd have to abandon
Rome some day soon, a city that terrified me and which I hadn't
seen yet and feared I might never learn to fathom, much less love.
That city had been dogging me during my three years in Rome. I'd
have to learn to like another city all over again — wouldn't I? —
learn to put new books on the face of yet another place, learn to
unlove this one, learn to forget, learn not to look back, learn new

habits, learn a new idiom, learn a new me all over again. I remember exactly the spot where this discovery had filled me with disquieting premonitions: in a used bookstore on Via Camilla where I'd found by pure chance a tattered old copy of *Miss Lonelyhearts* and simply hated it, hated the thought of moving to a country where people liked and read such books. And on that spot it had finally dawned on me that if I had never wanted to live in Rome, still I would have given everything to stay here, on this street, with these people, with their language, their yelps, their seedy movie theaters, the girl from the supermarket, and eventually become as surly and kindhearted as each and every one of them had been to me.

Outside of that bookstore, the uncanny question had bubbled up before I could quell it: What was Rome without me? What would happen to Rome once I no longer lived there? Would it go on without me, Baudelaire, Lawrence, Lampedusa, and Joyce? One might as well ask what happens to life when we're no longer there to live it.

I was like someone who comes back to life after being dead and finds traces everywhere of how naively he'd imagined death. For a moment, it was as if I had never been to America at all yet, as if all those years away from Rome had never happened. But I also felt like someone who comes back to life and has no recollection of death. I didn't know whether I was here or there. I knew nothing. The pitch-dark center of hell is a cloud of unknowing where words are tongue-tied and where writing, as I did that evening, is useless. I'd settled absolutely nothing, and the work that remained to be done here hadn't even started, might never start, was never meant to be.

I was never coming back again. Or if I were to one day, I'd come back on the 85 bus — alone. And remember, among other things, coming here with my family.

I told my wife and sons I was happy they had come with me. I told them it was good to come back, good to be heading back soon, good they didn't let me come back alone.

But I spoke these words without conviction, and would have thought I hadn't meant them had I not grown used to the notion that speaking without conviction is how I hope to be honest. What roundabouts, though, for what others feel so easily. Roundabout love, roundabout intimacy, roundabout truths. In this, at least, I had stayed the same.

Who Is America?

FROM *Esquire*

DUE TO A COLLISION of seemingly unrelated events, I now live in the former republic of East Germany. Were I so inclined, I could use this column to explain how this happened, but that process does not interest me and would not interest you. I suppose I could also write eleven thousand words about why the rotisserie chicken is substantially more delicious over here (!), or why everyone in Germany is convinced John McCain has no chance in the November election (?), or why the only things that ever seem to be on German television are amateur weightlifting, Sharon Stone's *Sliver,* Asian soccer, live rock concerts by the band Mastodon, and advertorial pornography that's marketed to the elderly. But I will not do any of that, as there is nothing less interesting than listening to someone explain why being somewhere foreign is not exactly the same as being wherever he was before. Those kinds of insights will be available on my blog.*

In fact, my original intention was not to write about Germany at all, unless something profoundly significant happened while I was here (such as an uprising at a Bavarian wind farm or the political assassination of Detlef Schrempf). However, I'm going to break my own imaginary policy. I've decided to write about which Americans are (evidently) fascinating to twenty-year-old Germans, mostly because these allegedly fascinating people serve as examples of how arbitrarily the mass media represents our society to the rest of the world.

* There is no blog.

Here's what happened: I'm teaching a class on twentieth-century popular culture at the University of Leipzig. I don't know why the school asked me to do this, but it did. And it turns out that *any* seminar on U.S. consumer culture is extremely attractive to every non-American kid majoring in American studies, because ninety-six students signed up for the class in the span of three days. Due to the size of the classroom, I was forced to immediately reduce this number to twenty. I was unsure how to do that fairly, so I decided to give them a competitive online essay test before the first day of class. The question was this: "Who do you consider the most interesting twentieth-century American — not necessarily the most historically important, but the individual you find most personally compelling?" The responses were well-written, habitually understated, and devoid of any pattern whatsoever. For example:

- Michael Jackson had more essays written about him than anyone else, which didn't shock me. What did surprise me was how sympathetically he is viewed: the general consensus seems to be that Jackson is an eccentric, philanthropic genius whose nation has turned against him, possibly due to racist motives. However, they do assume he's a child molester. Europeans are open-minded in unorthodox ways.
- George Gershwin did unusually well in this sampling, with two votes and a tangential mention in a third. In all three cases, Gershwin was closely associated with "the American dream," which may or may not exist.
- Kurt Cobain was not selected by anyone. Dave Grohl, however, was. Cobain was also referenced — somewhat negatively — in a paper focused on Taylor Hanson.
- Every significant Beat writer seemed to get one vote. Hunter S. Thompson got two.
- There was a female student who selected Jared Leto. I must admit — I did not see this one coming. He is perceived as a triple threat of acting, music, and environmental awareness (apparently, his tour bus runs on vegetable oil). Another girl selected Rob Thomas of Matchbox 20, although part of her argument may have been that Thomas was born on a German military base in 1972.
- One person wrote about the first black woman in outer space. This individual is named Mae Jemison, which was news to me.
- The only presidents referenced were Richard Nixon (three times) and Bill Clinton (once).
- Bob Dylan and James Dean both had five essays written about them

(and for the usual reasons one might expect). But a stranger collection of fellows all received two votes apiece: Andy Warhol, Dennis Rodman, F. Scott Fitzgerald, Jim Jarmusch, and Ian MacKaye.

• One person wrote about the Hummer all-terrain vehicle. This is not technically a human, but I could see her point.

• Sean Penn, Rosa Parks, Francis Ford Coppola, Johnny Depp, the mystery novelist Janet Evanovich, Jon Bon Jovi, Malcolm X, Elvis Presley, and New York Cosmos founder Steve Ross were all equally represented.

• Someone selected Ryan Adams. This made me happy for two reasons. The first is that I suspect Adams is something of an underrated semigenius, and I like the fact that he's more appreciated in places where nobody cares whether or not Paul Westerberg hates him. The other reason is that I think there's probably a 98 percent likelihood that Ryan Adams will read this sentence, put down the magazine, walk over to his four-track, and immediately write a psychedelic country song titled "Hey Little Leipzig Girl (I'm Glad You Dug Those Whiskeytown Bootlegs)," which I will be able to listen to on the Internet forty minutes from right now.

• Perhaps the most provocative essay argued for a tie between Ernest Hemingway and O. J. Simpson. The author's point seemed to be that Hemingway was "not the typical American," but that Simpson sort of was.

Now, I know these answers don't really *prove* anything, and I'm aware that ninety-six people in one city don't necessarily reflect the views of a nation of eighty-two million. I also realize that these icons were consciously selected by students who were trying to get into a class about populist mainstream culture, and some were clearly written by kids trying to predict what I might appreciate. (For example, one dude just cut and pasted James Hetfield's Wikipedia entry.) But I also think they illustrate a phenomenon that continues to make modernity more and more confusing: the proliferation of media has made it virtually impossible to tell the difference between a) what information is unilaterally interesting, and b) what information is merely available. I used to think Richard Nixon and Ryan Adams had nothing in common, but I now realize I was wrong — they both share an equal potential to be randomly fascinating to Germans.

Since my arrival in Leipzig, I have continually been reminded about the way many Germans view American culture. They essentially feel it does not exist. One grad student only half-jokingly told me that an entire semester of American cultural studies "should probably take about twenty-five minutes." But this, of course, is crazy. Now more than ever, I feel certain that the United States is as good at manufacturing culture as the rest of the world combined, probably because we often do so accidentally. A lack of culture is not our problem. The problem is we've become too effective at distributing that culture — at the same time, in the same way, and with the same velocity. It all ends up feeling interchangeable, which makes it all marginally irrelevant. As it turns out, my initial question was beyond impossible. There are no interesting twentieth-century Americans. There can't be, because they all are.

TONY PERROTTET

The Pervert's Grand Tour

FROM *Slate.com*

In Search of the Secretum

SEX HAS ALWAYS BEEN the unspoken inspiration for travel.

In Homer's *Odyssey,* the first travel book in history, Ulysses, the hero, spends more time in the arms of comely nymphs and enchantresses than actually under sail. Medieval pilgrims were notorious for spicing up their religious devotions with riotous fornication. By the nineteenth century, the erotic obsession had spilled from the bordellos and bars to suffuse the whole sightseeing agenda, creating a secret itinerary across Europe. For dirty-minded tourists, no visit to Paris was complete without a visit to the *Enfer,* or Hell, section of the National Library, where banned pornographic books from the Renaissance onward were conveniently hidden. The highlight of southern Italy was the ancient Roman brothels of Pompeii and their frescoes demonstrating sexual positions. Nobody had "done" Venice without visiting Casanova's prison cell or Provence without admiring the dungeon of the Marquis de Sade. In fact, the discerning traveler was spoiled for choice: Europe's major museums all had their off-limits rooms containing saucy relics, and every noble family boasted its private cabinet of naughty artifacts.

While researching my book on salacious history, *Napoleon's Privates: 2,500 Years of History Unzipped,* I realized that this deviant itinerary could still be traced through the underbelly of Europe — in short, a Pervert's Grand Tour. I'd always avoided the most popular attractions of Britain, France, and Italy, but this was an inspiring prospect: I would pick three "official" destinations and seek out some tasteful historical filth.

And I knew just the place to start.

Oh, Behave! The Wicked British Museum

Sexual imagery is so ubiquitous these days that only the most lurid display can raise an eyebrow, but there is still something deliciously furtive about tracking down a Victorian cache of "obscene objects" — the British Museum's once-forbidden Secretum.

The prospect had me as wide-eyed as a schoolboy as I made a beeline through the drizzling rain to that hallowed institution in the heart of old London. Once inside, wandering the stolid Georgian corridors of the King's Library, I fantasized that pulling a book from one of the mahogany shelves would open a secret passageway to a cave of sinful treats — the private collection, perhaps, of Sir Richard Burton, first translator of the Kamasutra; or Henry Spencer Ashbee, author of the Victorian porn classic *My Secret Life;* or even Sir William Hardman, "genial connoisseur of smut."

The reality was slightly less Merchant Ivory, but in my feverish state, nothing could disappoint. After muttering my name into an intercom, I was ushered into a waiting room by a little old lady, then pointed down some gloomy stairs into the storage areas. The public face of the British Museum immediately dissolved: marble splendor was replaced by institutional gray. The corridors were shabby, the paint chipped, and windows grimy in that *One Flew Over the Cuckoo's Nest* sort of way. Things were getting interesting.

Waiting for me was a young curator — Liz Gatti, a fashionable urbanite with an understated nose piercing, looking like a Marc Jacobs emissary now lost in *Bleak House.*

"We get a lot of inquiries about the Secretum," she began, as I signed the visitors' book. "But I'm afraid you'll be disappointed. There's hardly anything left!"

"Oh, that's not important," I said with what I hoped was sober aplomb.

We followed a corridor lined with antique wooden cabinets, each marked with a bronze number plaque, until we stopped in front of 55. This was it. The dreaded Cupboard 55 was the last known resting place of the Secretum.

"No whiff of brimstone," I joked. Ms. Gatti looked at me askance, then pulled out a fistful of keys.

The Museum Secretum was officially created in 1865, at the height of Victorian sexual hysteria, to protect the more impressionable public — women, children, and the working class — from the moral perils of erotica. At the time, boatloads full of archaeological finds were arriving from abroad, and these revealed the exuberant carnal habits of classical cultures. Excavations in the ancient Roman cities of Pompeii and Herculaneum, for example, included eye-popping images of uninhibited pagan copulation in every gender combination, the same images that had once graced every bedroom, street, tavern, and brothel of antiquity. Such guilt-free sex, it was decided in London, should be locked safely behind closed doors. (Naples, the city closest to the Pompeii dig, already had a Secretum in its Bourbon Museum; known as the *Gabineto Segreto,* or Secret Cabinet, it was created in 1819.) According to former curator Dr. David Gaimster, London's Secretum soon housed 1,100 objects. Only gentleman scholars deemed qualified to interpret such dangerous imagery could gain access.

As one would expect, the Secretum soon took on an underground cachet, luring a steady stream of randy tourists, dilettantes, and voyeurs, who would seek permission from the official "keeper of the Secretum" for a private session with the relics. The 434 phallic objects donated by an oddball collector named George Witt, a former medical doctor who had made a fortune in Australia as a banker, were a particular draw. Witt was convinced that all ancient religions had begun with phallus worship, and he amassed a huge array of examples to prove his thesis. Also in the dark and dingy storage room were a series of graphic Italian engravings from the 1500s called "The Positions," illustrating pornographic verse by Pietro Aretino; ancient Greek drinking cups adorned with explicit sex scenes; a replica chastity belt; antique condoms; a statue of the god Pan fornicating with a she-goat; and exotic erotica from the colonies, especially India and the Far East.

Wicked items were still being added as late as 1953, but finally, in the more permissive atmosphere of the 1960s, the Secretum collection was gradually redistributed to other parts of the museum. From the 1980s, its remaining relics were kept in Cupboard 55, which today is under the management of the Department of Pre-

history and Europe. I naturally assumed that anything still confined to the cupboard at such a late date must be pretty darned of-
fensive. And since the British Museum's entire storage collection is
open to the public by appointment on weekday afternoons, I applied to have a peek.

I actually held my breath as Ms. Gatti creaked open the doors
like a vampire's casket. Blinking in the half-light, I made out rows
of peculiar items that looked a bit like dreidels. I peered closer.
"Egad," I said, mystified. They *were* dreidels.

"Everything has been moved about," Liz explained. "Today we
use this cupboard to mostly house Judaica." This was deflating
and disturbing news: it turns out that most of the last items had
been redistributed in 2005. "There was no logic to the Secretum,"
she added. "Modern curators believe it's important to keep items
within their cultural context. Keeping 'immoral' objects together
in one place was a false premise."

But is there nothing here from the former collection? I pleaded.

"Well . . ." she said hesitantly, fingering the keys. "A few bits and
bobs."

That was when she cracked open the doors to Cupboard 54. And
there, embedded in neat rows of clinically white, acid-free foam,
was a selection of pastel-colored wax penises. These miniature or-
naments were used in the late 1700s as votive offerings in a village
in southern Italy, hung by the peasantry on the walls of Catholic
churches as fertility symbols. They had been collected by Sir William Hamilton, who had been posted as the British envoy extraordinary to the court of Naples during the Napoleonic wars (and
whose wife, Lady Hamilton, famously ran off with Lord Nelson).

Another foam sheet held ancient Roman rings and charms decorated with erect male members, laid out in neat rows like bright insects caught by a collector.

"Most of the supposedly 'obscene' items in the Secretum were
not originally created to be titillating," Liz explained. "These were
everyday objects for the ancient Romans. The phallic imagery was
actually used for good luck and safety. Even the Roman kids wore
little rings with phalluses engraved upon them."

My eye was drawn to the last display — four soft strips that
turned out to be condoms from the eighteenth century. These pioneer contraceptives were handcrafted from animal intestines, but

the result was very attractive. In a nice design touch, they were tied at the open end by little pink silk ribbons.

"They're like works of art," I marveled.

Finally, taking a deep breath, I stepped back onto the polished parquet of the real world. As a parting gift, Liz gave me a print-out of items that had once been in the Secretum and were now on permanent public display. I searched throughout the galleries and identified many of the items that were once too immoral to be seen — a classical roll call of satyrs, sodomites, hermaphrodites, and maenads, women driven to a sexual frenzy. In one cabinet, a woman was passionately copulating with a horse; in the next, a young girl was "tending *phalloi*," pouring seed over a series of erections like gnomes in a garden.

All very impressive — but somehow, under the bright lights of the regular museum, it wasn't quite the same.

The Devil's Playground

You should never visit the Marquis de Sade's castle on a pretty summer's day. No, to appreciate the site, you need an atmosphere of infernal darkness, with torrential rain and howling wind. At least, that's what I told myself as I tried to find the place while blinded by a brutal thunderstorm. I'd been soaked to the bone just walking to the car-rental agency. Now, with lightning darting about my cobalt-blue Picasso (yes, a Picasso — some sort of Citroën), I had to pull over for the twentieth time to make sense of the road map. Sade's castle is in a little village called Lacoste, only twenty-five miles east of Avignon in Provence, which is supposed to be southern France's most seductive idyll of lavender fields, vineyards, and quaint B & Bs. But paradise certainly wasn't behaving as advertised today. I might as well have wandered into the opening sequence of *The Rocky Horror Picture Show*, en route to the Annual Transylvanian Convention.

At last, a sign to Lacoste protruded from the murk. I parked by a medieval fortress wall; ahead lay a stone arch engraved with the words *Le Portail des Chèvres*, the Goats' Gate, the entrance to the upper part of the village. The marquis's old stomping ground was as welcoming as Salem on a witch-trial day. The houses were shuttered, so I walked cautiously up a steep alley, trying not to slip on the uneven cobblestones as the rain gushed in a channel between my feet, then I climbed a trail littered with weeds and loose chunks of masonry. And there, crouching like a wolf in the mist, was the Château Sade. It still appeared to be a half ruin, with a veil of crumbling outer walls, yet the core has been renovated to a habitable state — the ideal haunted refuge, you could imagine, for a deranged monk or bestial aristocrat from one of Sade's pornographic classics like *120 Days of Sodom*. At the very least, a Dungeons & Dragons computer game designer.

Au contraire. I climbed the wet stone steps and banged on the wooden door, but I was answered by grim silence. No lights shone in the windows.

I would have to come back to meet the new lord of the lair, Pierre Cardin.

France has always been a hot destination for literary tourists: the land is lousy with shrines like Victor Hugo's apartment in central Paris or Balzac's cottage in Passy, where even the author's old teapot is revered like a piece of the true cross. But only a certain type of traveler is lured to this corner of Provence, where the château of Donatien Alphonse François, Marquis de Sade, still looms in decaying grandeur. This forty-two-room redoubt was Sade's most beloved residence. He visited it often as a child, and after his father gave it to him as a wedding present in 1763, he lived here for long stretches of his twenties and thirties — his feral prime. The château soon became the core of his fertile imaginative life. As the biographer Francine du Plessix Gray points out in her classic *At Home with the Marquis de Sade,* its position hovering above the village fed Sade's outdated fantasies of feudal inviolability, where he could act out his rabid carnal desires with no fear of reprisal. Even while he was in prison, the château remained a font of inspiration for Sade's grisly literary works — a Walden Pond for the polymorphously perverse.

Essentially, the château was the mise en scène for some of his more outrageous real-life escapades. To take one example, it became the setting of a light-hearted romp dubbed by biographers "The Little-Girls Episode." At the end of 1774, the charismatic, thirty-four-year-old marquis came to winter at Lacoste with his family and a string of fresh-faced household servants he'd hired in Lyon, including five unsuspecting virgins. These were intended to

supplement his more knowing staff, such as the lovely housekeeper
Gothon, whom Sade had hired because she sported "the sweetest
ass ever to leave Switzerland," and the studly male valet Latour, by
whom Sade liked to be sodomized while prostitutes watched and
cavorted. For the next six weeks, Sade dedicated himself to cor-
rupting the captive minors. As far as historians can discern, he held
them hostage in the château's dungeon, forcing them to act out
scenes from pornographic literature as well as Sade's own intricately stage-managed sexual rituals. (A control freak, Sade like to
choreograph every detail: as a character complains in one of his
comic fictions, "Let's please put some order into these orgies!")
Modern French wives are legendarily indulgent of their husbands'
peccadilloes, but Sade's wife, Pélagie, took spousal freedom to new
levels by overseeing this marathon debauch, keeping the five girls
compliant, and then hushing up the ensuing scandal. When the
police came knocking, she helped bribe the outraged parents and
spirit the girls, decidedly damaged goods, away to convents.

Pondering this edifying tale, I puddle-jumped through the castle's former moat and climbed in the pelting rain up to the wild
plateau of Sade's old estate. This was once a splendid garden and
orchard, where the dashing young marquis and his three children
would frolic on summer days. (He was, by all accounts, a devoted
father, with a fondness for play-acting and games like hide-and-seek
and musical chairs.) Now, there were loopy artworks installed on
the grounds, including some fairly gross sexual cartoons painted
on panels by a Russian artist and a few surreal sculptures — a giant
fly, a human finger the size of a tree trunk, and an enormous skull,
its eye socket filled with pinkish rainwater.

But the most striking piece, perched on a strategic precipice,
was a shiny, new bronze sculpture of the Divine Marquis himself.
Erected in the summer of 2008, it displays Sade's bewigged eighteenth-century head surrounded by a cage — Sade the perpetual
prisoner. After being seized by police during a night raid in 1777,
he spent most of his life in prisons and nuthouses, including thirteen years in the Bastille and eleven in Charenton Asylum, the setting for the film *Quills*. Both proved futile efforts to censor his literary outpourings.

Some forty years after Sade's death, the poet Baudelaire wrote
that if a statue of Sade were ever erected, thousands would come to

lay flowers at its feet. Well, the crowds might have been thin on this rainy day in October, but there's no question that the marquis can bring in the fans. His presence in Lacoste 250 years ago has given the village a notoriety it might otherwise lack. And what began as a trickle of a few lecherous pilgrims has escalated exponentially since the Château Sade was snapped up by — of all people — Pierre Cardin, the elderly haute couturier based in Paris.

The billionaire fashion icon was evidently tickled by the Sade connection when he purchased the decrepit castle seven years ago for a nominal one million francs, including seventy acres of the estate and an oil painting of the marquis. In the village, rumors flew: some said Cardin was related to Sade; others whispered that Cardin is bisexual and thus wanted to vindicate the broad-minded writer's memory; still others alleged he was looking for some mythical Sade family treasure. Since then, Cardin has renovated the château as his holiday residence and has started an annual summer arts festival on the grounds, luring crowds from Paris and the Riviera. (Cardin's website presents it as an homage to Sade, who loved the theater and used to stage plays on the estate.) And Cardin has certainly caused more tumult in Lacoste than anyone since Sade himself: in recent years, the fashion designer has been buying many of the village's historic structures in a real-estate grab along the lines of Ted Turner in Montana. The reaction among some villagers has been violent. Lacoste is being torn apart by a miniature civil war with a viciousness that only the French can manage.

You could almost imagine the ghost of the marquis pirouetting in glee.

I wanted to stay in Lacoste for several days to see how Sade's mischievous legacy was playing out, so I'd booked a room above the Café de France, the only lodging available off-season. When I pushed open the door, four farmers were hunched over a wooden table, ripping into roast chickens like gourmandizing orcs, the one missing a leg pausing to shoot me a scowl. The barman also eyed me suspiciously, then led me up a dark, creaking stairway that smelled of last month's cooking oil.

As I sat sodden and hungry in my freezing garret, staring out at the ghoulish fog, I had to wonder if this was really Provence, and if so, what century.

It seemed to be less Brueghel and more Hieronymus Bosch.

The Marquis de Sade Is Dead! Long Live Pierre Cardin!

"Oh, he loved Lacoste, did the Marquis de Sade. He adored it! Every time he was on the run, he came back here. And Cardin, he loves the place, too."

Finn Mac Eoin, wild-haired gardener and local poet, was showing me around the renovation work under way in the Marquis de Sade's old village, which is being funded by the Parisian fashion king Pierre Cardin. Suddenly, carried away with the grand ambition of it all, he stopped and decided to orate a celebratory poem. "I call this one 'Resurrection,'" he said, striking a mock-heroic pose like a Shakespearean actor on the tiles. "It's dedicated to Cardin." Raising one hand, a knee up on a medieval wall, Mac Eoin swept back his curly hair and pronounced in a rolling Irish brogue:

> Up from ancient ruins in Phoenix flight,
> Domain de Sade Pierre'd before my very eyes —
> Stone by stone this titan feat rose and rose beyond a dream
> Where lark and passing cloud can meet . . .

Mac Eoin pointed with a flourish to another picturesque hilltop village, Bonnieux, in the distance, for centuries Lacoste's bitter Catholic enemy.

> Now, a beacon on this once Lacoste'd hill has
> Far-off Bonnieux put to shame. And soon the moon it will.

"Cardin's got that poem up on his wall in the château," Mac Eoin exulted. "Right next to the Marquis de Sade's portrait."

A villager stuck his head out of the window to see what all the noise was about, then, seeing it was Mac Eoin, pulled his head back with a snort of disgust.

"Ah, they hate me here," Mac Eoin chortled. "They fuckin' hate me! I don't care. Friends make you weak. Enemies make you strong! I'll make 'em hate me more."

That next morning in Lacoste, things had livened up in every sense. When I creaked open the shutters of my garret in the Café de France, the fog from the day before was rapidly burning off to reveal the sorts of views that would make an Impressionist drool. Lacoste, I now discovered, floats above the region called the Lubéron like a hot-air balloon, with sweeping vistas across verdant fields and succulent orchards. In the distance was Mount Ventoux, whose peak looks snowcapped but is actually bare white limestone.

So, this was the mythic Provence of Peter Mayle memoirs, beloved by British retirees and anyone with a passion for produce markets and renovating farmhouses.

Fine for some. But I prefer a bit of drama in my paradise, and Lacoste was delivering the goods. By 9 A.M., the village — which had been deserted the day before in the Gothic deluge — was ringing with activity. Construction workers were everywhere, scurrying like ants along the Rue Basse, Lower Street, where in the last year Cardin has purchased a dozen buildings, bringing his total to more than twenty-five. On all the work permits, I noticed Pierre Cardin's name had been crossed out by hand, and little slogans scribbled in — *"Sauvez Votre Village"* (Save Your Village).

Lacoste has always had a contrarian streak. It was a Protestant village in a sea of Catholics, and more recently, it was run by a Communist mayor for fifty years. Now many of the villagers are revolting again — against Cardin's renovations. In an inevitable conflation, the billionaire in the marquis's manor is being denounced as a haughty "neo-feudal" overlord trying to turn back the clock to prerevolutionary days. It's a theme that has delighted newspapers like *Le Figaro* and French TV. But not everyone in Lacoste is ready to light torches and storm the château. A minority view sees Cardin as saving the village from provincial stagnation. When the designer first arrived, several villagers actually donated houses for Cardin to renovate, saying they had been in the family for generations, but they could no longer maintain them. Others have approached him on the sly, aware that they could get up to three times market rate for ramshackle properties.

By chance, I was getting this positive view first, from Finn Mac Eoin, a one-man PR team for Cardin.

"I'm pro-Cardin, and I'm pro the Marquis de Sade," Mac Eoin declared, swearing that he had read every word Sade had ever written. (This is quite something; even some leading biographers admit they have never been able to slog through the deadening litany of carnal horrors.) "People don't know shit about the Marquis de Sade," he said. "They come here and they tell me, 'Oh, do you know he killed his wife and cut out her heart?' Such crap! So much misinformation. He loved his wife! She was like Florence fucking

Nightingale to him. Everyone wants to see blood. Everyone wants
to add to the rumors."

Certainly, there are subtleties to the marquis's life that get lost in
the sensation. As the biographer du Plessix Gray points out, he
should perhaps be termed "a nonviolent sadist." He never drew
blood in his rituals, preferring to use psychological torture. He denounced the death penalty, was never in a duel or even went hunting. The very word *sadism* was not coined until the 1880s, more
than sixty years after his death, and anyway, Sade was probably
more of a masochist: he liked to be whipped, often demanding
hundreds of lashes to provoke his erections. A lot of French aristo-
crats were at least as deranged.

"So what if de Sade was a rapist and a murderer?" Mac Eoin
railed. "You can't judge him by our modern standards."

Mac Eoin's wife was patiently making breakfast throughout this
tirade. I asked her if she shared his passion for the Marquis de
Sade. "I think it's good in a marriage to have different interests,"
she said sweetly.

Mac Eoin took me out into the warm autumn sunshine to visit
charming old houses that Cardin had renovated into gallery
spaces, and two mansions destined for hotels: one five-star, the
other budget. The marquis would surely have approved of Lacoste's artsy new life as host to Cardin's summer theater festival; he
was passionate about the stage, and his dearest wish was to be recognized not as a pornographer but as a playwright. Come to think
of it, he would have approved of Cardin's profession, too, since he
was obsessive about fashion. His prison letters are filled with demands for trendy new stockings, shoes, and suits. ("Send me a little
prune-colored riding coat," Sade ordered his wife in 1781, "with a
suede vest and trousers, something fresh and light but specifically
not made of linen." In the same letter, he requests a suit that is
"Paris Mud in hue — a fashionable color this year — with a few silver trimmings, but definitely not silver braid.")

Everything in the new Lacoste is cashing in on the Sadist theme.
We peered into the Cardin-owned Café de Sade, where a fortune
was being spent to raise the antique ceilings. And we looked in at
the new grocery, the Boulangerie du Marquis, which Cardin had
taken over from its former owner and expanded. "This used to be
such a shitty grocer," Mac Eoin scoffed. "The owner didn't even
bake her own bread!"

When I learned that Cardin had even opened a boutique gift store named after the Divine Marquis, my imagination ran riot. Would it be a high-end sex shop for the dominatrix and fetishist? Would it stock Sade's favorite accessories, like the hand-carved dildos he particularly liked for his autoerotic rites, or his beloved enema syringes, which bore tasteful engravings of men kneeling in worship before plump buttocks? At least it could offer some books from the marquis's secret library, I thought, classics like *The Fornications of Priests and Nuns,* or antique illustrated editions of his own phantasmagoric works, which were once passed secretly among the cognoscenti.

No such luck. Instead, when I entered the cool stone cavern that is the Boutique le Moulin de Sade, I was confronted with an array of gourmet food: foie gras, jams, pâtés, and honeys. When I quizzed the elderly shopkeeper about Sadist souvenirs, she gave me a bookmark bearing his profile.

The truth is, Sade would probably have been delighted. He was a fervent gourmand who loved Provençal delicacies like quail stuffed with grape leaves, cream of chard soups, and luscious jams. He once demanded that his wife send him a chocolate cake black "as the devil's ass is blackened by smoke." Fine food appears in all his writings about orgies, inspiring the participants to fits of lust. As one character notes, "Our cocks are never so stiff as when we've just completed a sumptuous feast."

Which, I guess, is a more direct way of saying that the way to a man's heart is through his stomach.

The Curse of the Château Sade

Every afternoon, I climbed up the castle steps and banged on the wooden door, hoping that Pierre Cardin might show me around the Marquis de Sade's dungeon, but the only answer was a dismal silence. The chatelain was still in Paris — he liked to visit only in summer, it seemed — so I tried to hang out with the rebellious villagers.

This was something of a challenge. After four days, I had become a familiar face in Lacoste, where the off-season population is only around sixty souls. Even the crustiest of the locals, *les Costains,* huddled outside the Café de France like illiterate goatherds, didn't shoot me quite as many scowls. And yet their world seemed remote and impenetrable. I was desperate to know what these former Communists thought of their two celebrity château owners, the Marquis de Sade and Cardin. But how would I get past their Gallic suspicion of outsiders — me, an interloper from that citadel of capitalism, Manhattan?

Then, in the Cardin-owned store, I noticed a flimsy little book on the history of Lacoste, filled with murky photographs and obscure old censuses. As I flicked through the pages, I froze in shock: there in the tax list of 1608 was my own name, *Antoyne Perrottet*. My family moniker had been, until now, fairly obscure, so this seemed quite a coincidence. From the Middle Ages, it turned out, a whole bunch of Perrottets were clustered together in this tiny village — about ten extended families. Wackiest of all, in 1806, one André Perrottet was the mayor of Lacoste at the height of Napoleon's glory.

Now, I've never been one for roots tours, but the idea that my forebears made up a good percentage of the local citizenry at the time of the Marquis de Sade put a whole new spin on things. All of a sudden, the village's history was personal. I had a blood connection. *Zut alors,* I was a *Costain* myself, give or take two centuries.

Now that I had my Gallic credentials — *one of the Perrottets,* mon ami, *used to be mayor under Napoleon!* — I considered I had an instant entrée to stop people in the street and ask their opinions. (Luckily, Finn Mac Eoin had already pointed out many of the more vocal anti-Cardin figures around town: "See that feller? He's an antichrist. Him? Fucking antichrist.") Suddenly, everyone was happy to talk. I ran into two weather-beaten farmers unloading firewood from a truck and quickly introduced myself. "Ugh, Cardin!" spat one, Jacques Trophemus. "He's a megalomaniac! What does he want with all these houses? One home, yes. But twenty-six? There's more to life than money!" He said the village life was being gutted by Cardin, who offers people far above market rate for their homes. Old people can't turn down the offer. Young people can't afford to live here. "These streets used to be filled with children playing! Where are they now?" He waved a hand theatrically. "The village is dead!" True *Costains,* he said, were even boycotting Cardin's new *boulangerie,* buying their bread from faraway villages.

This was obviously a feud in deadly earnest — but I soon found that interviewing the anti-Cardin forces was not entirely unpleasant. Usually, it involved sitting on a sunny terrace and quaffing wine while railing against the modern world. When I sought out Yves Ronchí, founder of an anti-Cardin group called the Association for the Harmonious Development of Lacoste, he turned out to be a vigneron in an old farmhouse. He came up from the cellar in wet rubber boots and purple hands, as if he'd just been stomping grapes. "This country is supposed to stand for liberty, equality, fraternity," he complained. "That is why we fought the revolution! But the rich today have taken on a new sense of privilege. They ignore laws and trample our democratic rights."

Ronchí took my business card and rubbed his straggly beard. He soon dug out a topographical map from his desk. "Did you know there is a village called Perrottet near here?" Instantly, we were old friends. He took me downstairs to see his great chrome vats of the latest harvest, and I tried the fresh red — an excellent drop, I thought. "Look, I don't mind Pierre Cardin personally," Ronchí confided. "It's what he represents, the sort of society. It's all about money, empty words, appearances. He is pouring a fortune into renovating these buildings, but the result is *bricolage* — a rushed job, makeshift, not serious. When you look inside, there is no character. Just empty space."

I had to admire the town's stubborn resistance to change, even though some feel they've become *fanatiques.* It reminded me of the Groucho Marx song "Whatever It Is, I'm Against It!" Perhaps the phrase should be on Lacoste's coat of arms. Still, sometimes it did seem a little extreme. Cécile Lendfors, a thirtyish artist who grew up in the village, told me that she was just waiting for the day the couturier keels over and croaks.

"I've bought a nice bottle of champagne to open when I get the news," she declared. "Cardin's eighty-six. He'll die before I do. I'm waiting for the day!"

When French TV journalists asked Pierre Cardin earlier in 2008 why he was buying up Lacoste, he adopted a provocative tone: "For my pleasure," he said coolly. Still, he has often seemed a little baffled by the villagers' reaction.

Things have clearly gone downhill for a feudal overlord.

Back in the eighteenth century, the Marquis de Sade could do no wrong in Lacoste. When he'd arrived in 1765, at the age of twenty-three, the pink-cheeked *Costain* yokels danced and sang for the lovely woman on his arm: "Oh, the happy news . . . Our marquis has married a young beauty. There she is! There she is!" The beauty turned out to be one of the most noted prostitutes in Paris, but the *Costains* took no offense. In fact, none of his regular scandals seemed to faze the villagers; it was really no less than was expected of a red-blooded French aristocrat. Sade took care to procure his victims from faraway cities, a considerate gesture to the locals. So, the villagers continued to warn him about police raids and assist his many white-knuckle escapes. On one occasion, he hid in the château roof; several times, he disappeared into the wild countryside of Provence.

Of course, the arrangement came to an end on the night of August 26, 1777, when ten policemen managed a 4 A.M. raid on the château and carried Sade away in shackles. He would never return: during the Revolution, a mob sacked the castle. It was not led by loyal *Costains,* of course, but radicals from the nearby town of Apt. Sade was devastated when he learned. "No more Lacoste for me!" he wrote. "What a loss! It is beyond words . . . I'm in despair!" Broke, he was soon forced to sell the castle.

He was less upset at never seeing his faithful villagers again. "I've come to the conclusion that all *Costains* are beggars fit for the wheel," he wrote in a 1776 letter, "and one day I'll surely prove my contempt for them . . . I assure you that if they were to be roasted one after another, I'd furnish the kindling without batting an eyelash." The outburst came after the father of one of his victims had burst into his château and tried to murder him by firing a pistol inches from his chest. The shot misfired, but the culprit had wandered the village for days, drunk on local wine, until the marquis had to bribe him to leave. Rather than form a lynch mob, the villagers had reacted with a Gallic shrug.

In fact, it's tempting to think that the ghost of the marquis has come back to plague the peasantry. After all, he has effectively skewed the village's fate through his notoriety alone. Without Sade, there'd be no Cardin dragging them into the modern world.

Now how would the Divine Marquis punish me, a direct descendent after all?

On my last night, I managed to get myself invited to a bacchanal in a remote farmhouse, where hundreds of Provençal hipsters converged to listen to live music around open fires, guzzle *vin rouge,* and gorge on fresh cheese. No hardship there. But the next morning, after only three hours' sleep, I had to drive back to Avignon. Under my windshield was an envelope: Finn Mac Eoin had left me a farewell poem.

It was called, appropriately, "Wine":

> Then what of morn, should all of night be chaste?
> The wine has gone and but the hourglass filled.

Sade was poised to take his revenge. I somehow managed to navigate my overpriced rental car back to a gas station and had just filled up the tank when I noticed a little sticker: DIESEL SEULEMENT. Oh, *merde*, I realized. Wrong fuel. The station attendant patiently advised me that if I now tried to drive the car on regular gasoline, the engine would implode. Three excruciating hours later, my car was on a trailer, and I was sitting beside a crusty mechanic who told me all about how he was going to come to New York and run the marathon, and maybe he could visit me and even stay?

When I checked my credit card statement back home, I'd been charged an extra four hundred dollars for that little Provençal screw-up. I guess Sade got me where it really hurts.

The Casanova Tour of Venice

With her bouffant red hair, thick-rimmed spectacles, and puffy overcoat, my guide, Luciana, hardly seemed Casanova's type as she clomped up the sumptuous Golden Staircase of the Doge's Palace in Venice. But then she paused, slipped open her coat, and dipped a hand coquettishly down her plunging neckline to produce a small key on a silver chain. This she inserted with a flourish into the wall, opening a hidden panel.

"*Signori* and *signore*," she whispered huskily. "Welcome to the Secret Tour of the Doge's Palace. There will be no bags permitted. No photographs. No video."

The half-dozen of us on the tour nodded obediently. Luciana, now coat-free, was instantly transformed into Sophia Loren in one of her later films — say, *The Priest's Wife* — and she beckoned us to enter. A crowd of milling tourists could only stare in slack-jawed envy as we, the chosen ones, stepped into the netherworld. As we passed, Luciana touched us each lightly on the hair, counting our numbers, then stepped inside to lock the door behind us, slipping the key with a smile back into her magnificent décolletage.

The Venetians certainly know how to stage a secret tour. At the Doge's Palace, the sumptuous nerve center of the old Republic of Venice, a special behind-the-scenes visit includes Casanova's prison cells. But it's difficult to learn about the trip, it's almost impossible to book, and then it's highly likely to be canceled on a whim. As a result, the mounting tension leaves travelers half-crazed and panting for more.

An illicit atmosphere goes with the territory in Venice, which flourished for over ten centuries as the erotic capital of Europe. Fabulously wealthy, sexually permissive, the whole city qualified as a beautiful red-light district by the late 1700s. Travelers flocked here from around Europe to cruise the canals with alluring local courtesans and beefy gondoliers. They flirted at masked balls, gamboled in the bordellos, and flocked to the nunneries where aristocratic convent girls would entertain foreign gents with musical concerts and sparkling conversation, then offer intimate favors for a modest fee.

Nobody sums up the lascivious pleasures of this era more than Giacomo Girolamo Casanova, the prototype playboy, who cut a virtual swath through the willing female population of Venice. He has been so mythologized in literature and film (most recently in a hokey 2005 Heath Ledger vehicle, *Casanova*) that many people now assume him to be a fictional character. In fact, he lived from 1725 to 1798, and most of his operatic love affairs — his passions for milkmaids and princesses, his *ménage à trois* with noble sisters under the nose of their father, his liaison with a female singer who was masquerading as a castrato, his seduction of his own illegitimate daughter — have been documented by historians. (Incidentally, Casanova was born fifteen years before the Marquis de Sade; the pair never met, although they had a mutual friend in Rome, a cardinal who seduced high-society ladies in the catacombs of the Vatican.) Casanova's many other achievements put Hugh Hefner to shame. He was the ultimate self-made man: the handsome son of two poor actors, he used his wit, charm, and *joie de vivre* to insinuate himself into the highest courts of Europe. Today, few realize that Casanova was also a translator of *The Iliad,* a successful theater director, a violin virtuoso, a spy, and creator of the French lottery. He debated with Voltaire and Benjamin Franklin and worked on one of Mozart's librettos. He penned a history of Poland as well as arcane mathematical treatises, a science-fiction novel, and a proto-feminist pamphlet.

Strangely, Venice prefers not to celebrate its most famous son, as if it is still rather ashamed of his reckless, wastrel ways. The only memorial is a plaque in the alley where he was born (nobody knows in which house). Which is why his prison cell in the Doge's Palace — where he was thrown in 1755, then escaped in spectacular fashion — has unusual status. It's the only place undeniably connected to the adventurer's fantastical life.

I felt like I was clambering about inside a galleon. Luciana led us up dark stairs and into corridors made of raw wooden planks, which began to shudder and sway as if we were at sea. The route to Casanova's cell ran through the original offices of the republic's most powerful bureaucrats. One door led to the chancellor's little no-frills cubicle; it was made with special hinges to create an airtight fit in order to prevent eavesdropping. Next came the State Inquisitor's Room. Then the Torture Room, where prisoners had their arms tied behind their backs and were dropped from ropes.

It was through these dismal corridors that the thirty-one-year-old Casanova was led after being arrested in his rooms on a hot July night in 1755. He had been denounced to the Inquisition for "irreligious behavior," but the real motive for the arrest was evidently to tame his overactive libido. Over the years, he had made many enemies by seducing the wives of powerful men; he had recently been courting a young lady fancied by a grand inquisitor. Now Casanova, who was never told of the trumped-up charges against him or the length of his sentence, was thrown into a cell in *I Piombi*, "the Leads" — so named because they were located beneath the prison's lead roof, which broiled in summer and froze in winter.

Climbing up into this attic, our little group became as hushed as if we were entering a cathedral. We stooped through a tiny doorway into a tight box; the floor, walls, and ceilings were dark planks encrusted with metal studs around an opaque window. Fixed near the door was a garroting machine, handy for quick executions.

"Alora," Luciana breathed sadly as we crouched inside. "This was Casanova's *first* cell. You can imagine what it was like for a man like him to be trapped here! He couldn't even stand up straight. He was

attacked by fleas constantly and tormented by boredom. In the heat, he could do nothing but sit stark naked, sweating. So he decided to escape, even though nobody had ever succeeded from the Doge's Palace before."

We all crouched as Luciana enthusiastically related the Great Venetian Breakout. Plan A, begun in this very cell, was an embarrassing flop. Casanova got hold of an iron bolt left by some workmen, and he began to dig through the floorboards. But after months of painful labor, the guards decided to do their amiable prisoner a favor and transfer him to a nicer cell. The tunnel was discovered. "But it was just as well," Luciana said. "Directly below us is the grand inquisitor's chamber. Casanova was about to break through the ceiling! He would have destroyed a Tintoretto fresco."

We filed into Casanova's second cell, which had slightly better ventilation and light, to hear about Plan B. Aware that he was being closely watched, Casanova slipped the iron pike, which he had somehow kept, to the prisoner in the next cell — a disgraced monk named Marin Balbi — and put him to work on the ceiling. At midnight on October 31, 1756 — Casanova had by now spent fifteen months and five days in prison — the odd couple were ready to make their break. The monk scrambled up through the ceiling, broke into Casanova's cell, and pulled him up. They then dislodged some lead tiles to get onto the palace roof itself, two hundred feet above the darkened San Marco Square. After nearly plunging to their deaths, the pair managed to get back inside another window using ropes made from torn sheets. But when they slunk down the Golden Staircase, they discovered, to their horror, that the main palace gate was locked from the outside.

This was when Casanova's fashion sense came to the rescue. In a bag around his neck, he was carrying the flamboyant party clothes he had worn on the night he was arrested — a lace-trimmed silk coat, ruffled shirt, tricorn hat with long feather — and now he put them back on. Glimpsing this chic man-about-town in the grille, a guard assumed it was a rich visitor accidentally caught inside after visiting hours, and he opened the door. Casanova elbowed past and scampered for the first gondola. "The escape made Casanova famous, but he would not return to our beloved city for eighteen years," Luciana sighed, as if mourning on behalf of Venetian womanhood. "When he returned, it was to a hero's welcome. Even the inquisitors wanted to know how he did it!"

"Signore and *signori,"* Luciana said in conclusion back at the Golden Staircase. "You, too, have escaped from the Doge's Palace! And perhaps you have learned that Giacomo Casanova was more than just a famous lover. He was a man of action, too."

When I emerged back out in San Marco Square, it took a while for my eyes to adjust to the sunshine and crowds. What now, to honor the memory of this Venetian demigod? I considered going to the Cantina do Spade, a restaurant housed in a former bordello, where the patriotic owner tells any diner who will listen that "Casanova was the greatest fucker in history," or to the convent of Murano Island, where he once lured the ravishing young nun "M.M." away for a tryst in a gondola. But my own short stay in prison gave me the answer. I decided to sit in the sun and read his autobiography, *The Story of My Life.* In his fifties, flat broke, Casanova took a position as a librarian in a castle near Prague, where he knocked out some 3,500 manuscript pages. His carnal adventures — 122 affairs — take up only about one-third of the final twelve-volume memoir, but they are the most energetically written pages and have always drawn the most eager attention. "I have devoted my life to the pursuit of pleasure," he declares without the slightest regret, and then he recounts why in hilarious, captivating detail. These tales would be published in uncensored form only in 1966, in time for the sexual revolution.

Well, I thought, maybe our view of Casanova as history's ultimate playboy is a little one-dimensional, since it ignores his other achievements. But it's hard to feel sorry for the guy.

LYNNE COX

A Dip in the Cold

FROM *The New Yorker*

IN JUNE 1972, I flew over the North Atlantic Ocean. I was fifteen
years old, and on my way to England to swim across the English
Channel. I gazed out the window of the plane and saw Greenland.
Glacial domes sparkled in the clear blue Arctic sky, fractured snow
and ice clung to the steep mountain walls, and rivers of ice and
snow extended in wide bands to the sea. I pressed my forehead
against the cool window and looked thirty-five thousand feet down.
Something small and white was floating on the dark-blue water —
an iceberg.

Greenland, the world's largest island, lies mostly within the Arctic Circle, and more than three-quarters of it is ice-capped. The
coastline is rocky and barren, but for centuries its harbors and in-
lets drew explorers who were searching for a northern sea route
from Europe to Asia. The frozen seas and inhospitable lands of the
Arctic thwarted one expedition after another. In 1820, the British
explorer William Edward Parry made it through Lancaster Sound
before being forced back by ice; in 1833, John Ross abandoned his
second attempt to traverse the passage after his ship was trapped in
ice for four years; and in 1845, John Franklin, commanding two
ships, disappeared. The first successful transit of the Northwest Passage was not completed until 1906, under the leadership of the
Norwegian explorer Roald Amundsen.

I have been a long-distance swimmer since I was fourteen. Initially, I was interested in breaking other people's records — the record for crossing the Channel, for example. When I was in my
twenties, I decided to tackle waterways that had never been swum,

and crossed the Strait of Magellan, went around the Cape of Good Hope, and swam between various Aleutian Islands. In 1987, I swam the Bering Strait, from the United States to the Soviet Union, and seven years later I swam through the Gulf of Aqaba, from Egypt to Israel and Jordan. Then I became interested in the limits of endurance. I wanted to know whether my body could tolerate extreme cold. In 2002, wearing only a swimsuit, I swam for more than a mile in Antarctic waters of thirty-two degrees Fahrenheit. In the Arctic, water can be two or three degrees colder; still, I wanted to swim portions of the Northwest Passage, traveling from Greenland to Alaska, using Amundsen's account of his journey as a guide.

Roald Amundsen was born on July 16, 1872, in Borge, near Fredrikstad, the fourth son in a family of ship owners and sea captains. His mother had wanted him to become a physician, but on May 30, 1889, when he was sixteen years old, he realized that his ambitions lay elsewhere. He was waiting on the shores of Christiania Fjord to greet Fridtjof Nansen, who had returned to Norway after successfully leading the first trip on skis across the Greenland ice cap. In his memoirs, Amundsen recalled the crowds that day. "I wandered with throbbing pulses amid the bunting and the cheers, and all my boyhood's dreams reawoke to tempestuous life," he wrote. "For the first time something in my secret thoughts whispered clearly and tremulously: 'If *you* could make the North West Passage!'" Four years later, Amundsen's mother died, and he abandoned his medical studies. He read accounts of polar explorations, studied the latest scientific papers from Germany about geomagnetism and the shifting location of the North Pole, and trained like an endurance athlete. He sailed with sealers in the Arctic and, from 1897 to 1899, served on the Belgian Antarctic Expedition, as a second mate.

On June 16, 1903, Amundsen and a crew of six men, along with six sled dogs, sailed out of Christiania, as Oslo was called then, on the *Gjöa*, a forty-seven-ton herring boat, which had been reinforced for the trip and equipped with a new engine. The Arctic seas were frozen for as much as ten months of the year, and they were barely passable when ice did break up, in the short summer.

Today, as a result of the changing climate, the sea ice starts to melt earlier and the seas remain open longer, but I still had a narrow window for my trip. I planned to begin in May 2007, off Green-

land, and then return to the United States in June to train while I
waited for the Canadian Arctic to thaw. I would swim in the Canadian Arctic in July and the Alaskan Arctic in August, before the sea
froze again. Even in the twenty-first century, it was hard to obtain
precise information on sea ice, water temperatures, and currents. I
wasn't sure where I would be able to swim in each location, and I
knew that I might have to wait for the right conditions. In January
2005, I began training in California, and organized a small team of
friends who would accompany me on different legs of the trip.

An obvious concern was the extreme cold. The frigid temperature of the water could cause an incredible shock to my body, over-
stimulating the vagus nerve and causing my heart to stop beating.
The cold could also cause my fingers and arms to become so numb
that I wouldn't be able to pull myself out of the water. I was also
worried about the Greenland shark, which can be as long as twenty-
one feet. An old friend, Adam Ravtech, who is a wildlife filmmaker,
showed me footage he had captured of a Greenland shark. It was
huge, but Adam told me that he had felt safe during the many
hours he spent filming it. What I really needed to worry about, he
said, was the walrus. One had tried to grab a diver by the leg while
Adam was filming a documentary in the Arctic. Adam had had to
pluck the diver out of the water.

Amundsen's trip across the North Atlantic was smoother than he
and the crew had expected, with relatively little sea ice and mostly
favorable seas and plentiful seals for food. On July 24, they reached
Disko Bay, halfway up the west coast of Greenland. The *Gjöa*'s first
stop was Godhavn, where the governor of Greenland, which was
administered by the Danish, was waiting to greet Amundsen. "A
barrier of grounded icebergs seemed to block the entrance to
Godhavn," he wrote. "But soon Nielsen, the governor of the colony, came out to us in a boat to bid us welcome and pilot us in. We
met a violent squall and had to tack, as the motor could not manage it alone."

Greenland was sparsely populated in the early twentieth century,
and most of its Inuit inhabitants lived in small communities along
the coast. Even today, fewer than sixty thousand people live there. I
had intended for my first swim to start in Godhavn, a town of 108
people in 1903 that now has a population of a thousand, but it was

too remote. Instead, I decided to stay about sixty miles away, in Ilulissat, a bigger town, on the eastern side of Disko Bay, close to the Ilulissat Icefjord, where icebergs that have broken off from the ice cap begin their slow journey toward the shipping lanes of the Atlantic. I arrived with my crew — Bob Griffith, Gretchen Goodall, and Bill Lee — in late May. Two locals, Karen Filskov and Konrad Seblon, who worked for Destination Disko, promoting tourism in northern Greenland, had agreed to help organize the first swim. We met in the lobby of the Hotel Icefiord, and sat around a wooden table, with a map of Disko Bay spread out in front of us, discussing our options.

We considered one large bay as a starting point, but it was near a shrimp-processing plant, and inedible parts of the shrimp were discarded in the water. I pointed at another bay, and Konrad shook his head. That was where a raw-sewage pipe drained directly into the sea. Konrad and Karen talked to each other softly, in Greenlandic and in Danish, then one of them would translate into English for us. They suggested that I cross Church Bay, where I could swim in clean water and finish near the town center. It was a distance of just under a quarter of a mile. Then Karen asked, "When you swim, will you be wearing a wetsuit or a dry suit?"

"I'll be wearing a swimsuit — a TYR Lycra swimsuit," I replied.

It took a moment for my answer to register. Karen drew in a quick breath and said, "Are you crazy? Do you know how cold that water is?"

I thought she'd understood what we were doing.

"From the research I've done, the water temperature could be between twenty-eight point eight and thirty-four degrees," I said.

Konrad looked concerned. He asked Karen something in Greenlandic, and they spoke for a few minutes. Eventually, he said that he knew someone who had a Zodiac — a hard-shelled inflatable motorboat — that we could use as an escort vehicle, in case anything went wrong and I needed to be pulled out of the water. The swim was on.

When we arrived in Ilulissat, I had noticed that the land was covered with granite boulders, and that most of the quaint homes that we passed, painted red, yellow, turquoise, orange, purple, magenta, and blue, were perched on rocks. There weren't any beaches at the water's edge.

We walked out of the hotel into a light snow shower and followed the main dirt road that climbed into town. Dogs with long coats were staked in tiers along the steep hillsides. When, at one point, a puppy bounded down to greet us, the adult dogs broke into loud, anxious barks and high-pitched howls. Karen warned us not to play with the puppy. These were working dogs, Konrad explained, not pets or companions. They were conditioned to withstand the harshness of the environment, and they were strictly trained. There was no room on a sled team for a dog that didn't listen. The result could mean death for the dog, the team, or the driver.

We went along a narrow boardwalk that ran between houses and over marshland. The boards had snapped here and there, and the footing was unsteady. When we reached the southern end of Church Bay, we followed the cliff edge, and decided on an entrance point — some low rocks that tapered gradually into the water. But the grass-green algae that covered the rocks concerned me.

We passed below Zion Church, a small eighteenth-century wooden building, where the father of the polar explorer and anthropologist Knud Rasmussen had been a minister. The rocks near the church were covered by a foot of melting ice and snow. Below, a rocky ledge encircled the bay, but most of it was two or three feet above the water. If I were swimming, it would be too high for me to reach up and pull myself out.

The next morning, we scouted the northern part of Church Bay for an exit point. We watched a powerfully built man of medium height, who was wearing rubber boots and carrying two large plastic buckets, slip, slide, and swing his arms to catch himself as he walked to the water's edge. If a local man was this challenged, what was I going to do? I thought. The man lifted a log-size piece of clear blue ice from the water. He used a pick to split off chunks, which he dropped into the buckets. This ice had once been rainwater. It had entered the cracks of an iceberg and frozen there, and, when the iceberg broke up, the clear ice had floated away on the seawater. It was pure and sweet and would be used as drinking water.

Two days later, on May 28, I put on my swimsuit and sweatsuit, and gazed out the window of the Hotel Icefiord, studying the movement of the icebergs. Some seemed as big as battleships. In 2002, just before I jumped into the waters off Antarctica, I had been overwhelmed by the thought of swimming among icebergs. Now, five years later, I was using the icebergs like buoys; they made the water currents visible.

Karen walked with me while the rest of the crew motored to the starting area in the Zodiac. They had taken the water temperature. It ranged from 28.8 to 29 degrees, three degrees colder than the water had been in Antarctica. The bay was calm. There was no wind, and there weren't enough icebergs to make navigation difficult, but the tide was lower than we had expected, and the exposed algae-covered rocks would be too slippery to walk across. We searched for another spot and found a bare rock. It wasn't ideal — I would have to drop five feet off the rock and hope that the water would slow my impact enough so that I could land safely on a ledge two feet below the surface and give my body a few moments to adjust to the temperature.

I handed my sweatsuit to Karen and felt the forty-degree air on my skin. I put on my cap and wrapped the elastic band of my goggles around my wrist so that I wouldn't lose them when I hit the water. I took a deep breath and stepped off the rock. My feet touched the ledge, and in twenty seconds my arms and legs and torso were numb, but I had expected this. I pushed off the ledge and started swimming with my head up. I couldn't really feel my arms or legs, but I could sense them rapidly moving against the water. I was breathing fast and deep, but even so I wasn't getting enough air. I was struggling from the moment I hit the water. I might have to get out, I thought. I tried placing my cheek and then my nose in the water, and held my breath.

I lifted my foot — my swimmer's high five — to indicate that I was all right, but my breathing was faster and more labored, my lips were pursed, and I was not able to catch up on the oxygen my body was demanding. The cold was seeping into my body, invading me. I saw the church, heard the bells tolling, saw the doors opening and the congregation stepping outside, climbing onto the snowbanks. I was just two hundred yards from shore. I was sprinting, but suddenly I couldn't go any farther. "Backstroke. Swim backstroke," I said to myself. "Roll over on your back and catch your breath." I did, then I rolled back onto my stomach. "Fifty yards. You've got it. Go. Go. Go."

I saw the ledge we'd decided on as an exit point, but I couldn't find a handhold. I swam to one side and grabbed a rock. My face slipped across the cold green slime as I pulled myself onto my hands and knees. I felt as though I had cut my knee, but I couldn't tell, because I was so numb. Then I noticed blood on my leg. I looked up and saw the man who had been collecting ice earlier in the week. The local people looked as if they were trying to make sense of what they were seeing. They had always been told that you would die in a matter of minutes if you fell into the water with your clothes on, and now they were watching someone in a swimsuit climbing out of the water.

As Amundsen sailed farther north along the Greenland coast, the *Gjöa* encountered dangerous drift ice and dense ice fog in Melville Bay (near Thule Air Base, the northernmost U.S. military installation), before finally reaching Dalrymple Rock, where the crew loaded provisions that they had arranged to have waiting for them.

On August 17, they turned west, leaving Greenland behind them, and crossed Baffin Bay. Five days later, at 9 P.M., the *Gjöa* anchored in Erebus Bay, off Beechey Island, the last known stop of John Franklin, the British Royal Navy officer whose two ships had been lost in 1845. Amundsen wrote:

> It was about 10 o'clock when twilight came on. I was sitting on one of the chain lockers looking towards the land with a deep, solemn feeling that I was on holy ground, Franklin's last safe winter harbour. My thought wandered back — far back. I pictured to myself the splendidly equipped Franklin Expedition heading into the harbour, and anchoring there. The "Erebus" and "Terror" in all their splendour; the English colours flying at the masthead and the two fine vessels full of bustle . . . Certainly these brave men had succeeded in discovering much new land, but only to see their expectations of the accomplishment of the North West Passage that way brought to nought by impenetrable masses of ice. The winter of 1845–46 was passed here on this spot. The dark outlines of crosses marking graves inland are silent witnesses before my eyes as I sit here . . . it is the farewell of the Franklin Expedition. From this point it passed into darkness — and death.

Franklin and his entire crew of a hundred and twenty-nine were lost to the ice and to starvation.

In Ilulissat, I had swum for a quarter of a mile and been in the water for less than ten minutes, but the swim had felt much farther and much longer. I knew that I had never worked so hard in my life, but I wanted to do better on the next leg. I planned to swim from a point on Baffin Island about three hundred miles south of Beechey Island, in the Canadian Arctic. Baffin Island, part of the territory of Nunavut, is shaped like a lobster, and I was heading for Pond Inlet, just below the claw, an Inuit hamlet of about thirteen hundred people and some twenty-five visiting civil servants, construction workers, and scientists, perched on the edge of Eclipse Sound.

During Amundsen's time, the Inuit were nomadic, following the food sources — the herds of caribou, the Arctic char, the seals, narwhals, and polar bears — but in the 1960s, as a way to secure Canadian sovereignty, they were moved into government-built communities. In Pond Inlet, there was a small airport, government buildings, a hamlet office, some police holding cells, a library, a community health center, two stores, and a number of modest houses. For the most part, the Inuit on Baffin Island were still hunters and fishermen, and many of the families also received government assistance. Jobs were scarce, but the Baffinland mining company had recently submitted an application to open an iron-ore mine a hundred miles south of Pond Inlet, a project that would involve the construction of a railway and a deep-water port.

Bob Griffith was coming with me on this leg of the trip, and we flew from Los Angeles to Montreal and on to Iqaluit, the largest city on Baffin Island; then we flew north to Pond Inlet. On July 3, 2007, the sound was frozen solid. The ice looked like a sheet of blown glass, with whirling patterns of opaque white on a clear blue background.

As we circled and began our descent, I searched the sandy shores for open water but didn't see any. We landed on a dirt runway and made our way to a one-room terminal. Jared Arnakallak, the manager of the Sauniq, the hotel where we'd be staying, met us in a beat-up white van. The hotel was a single-story building, painted chocolate brown, and looked like a large extended trailer.

Adam Ravtech had suggested that I get in touch with David Reid, who ran a company called Polar Sea Adventures. We met David in the hotel cafeteria. He was a six-foot-tall Scotsman, with a buzzcut and sunburned cheeks. He had just returned with a tourist group from the floe edge, which was about fifty miles from Pond Inlet, where the frozen waters of Eclipse Sound met the open waters of

Baffin Bay. Narwhals were waiting at the floe edge for the ice to break so that they could migrate into the sound and the nearby fjords, where they would spend the summer. Local hunters were catching narwhals and seals, and polar bears were there, too, feeding.

We planned the swim for July 9, Nunavut Day — a celebration of the signing of the Nunavut Land Claims Agreement in 1993, which led, in 1999, to the region's recognition as an official Canadian territory, allowing it to have some degree of self-rule and control over its own institutions. For the next six days, we watched the ice slowly crack. There were small leads, then a larger one, where the Salmon River flowed into the sound, but the open water was too far from shore, and we wouldn't be able to get a boat out there safely. Bob and I walked along the beach. We had been told that the locals played a game of sorts to see who could keep a snowmobile on the ice the longest without it falling through, and as we watched some snowmobiles start to sink we realized that it was melting.

We met most of the construction workers, scientists, and engineers who were staying at the hotel, and became friends with nurses who worked at the health center, but Pond Inlet always looked deserted. To the Inuit, the normal state of water was ice, David explained. When the ice thawed, it was dangerous, particularly because the majority of the hunters couldn't swim. It was already too thin for hunting, so many of the local people had gone "on the land." They would camp for most of the summer and hunt caribou and other game.

By Nunavut Day, the ice had broken up. Near the center of Pond Inlet was the small area of water, about two hundred yards wide, that had been created by the flow of the Salmon River. A mile and a half west, more water had opened up at the mouth of a stream. Beyond that, there were five- to six-foot-high blocks of sea ice. Even there, the ice had not broken up enough to allow us to use a Zodiac; instead, David would paddle a kayak and I would swim behind him. David carried a yellow kayak over his head down a steep grass hill, past two wary sled dogs, and set it in the water. He looped a rescue rope once around his waist, and then pushed off from the shore and paddled out to the sea ice.

My first goal here was to swim out to one of the chunks of sea ice. If I managed that, I would follow David through the narrow passages between the ice. I dragged my feet as I walked slowly into the water, so I wouldn't step on any stingrays. A chill ran from my feet, through my body, and out along my shoulders and arms.

"This is great," I said, when I reached David. "Let's go to the right." The water felt as cold as it had in Greenland, but I could breathe much more easily.

Swimming with my head up, I followed David around a small block of sea ice and entered an area where there were larger blocks of ice on either side of me. It was like entering a snowy sculpture garden, one that might have inspired Henry Moore — the ice had been rounded and smoothed by the wind and the waves and the tide. To my right was a block of ice that looked like a reclining polar bear. On my left, another resembled a snowy egret taking flight. As I continued through the maze, though, I became a little afraid. There were ledges that extended under the water; David pointed to them with his paddle, but I still misjudged my position moving through the water and hit them. It hurt dully.

I caught up with David, and I gradually put my face in the water. It was easier to swim that way — my hips were not dragging, and I could see well below the water's surface. It was glacial blue and as clear as spring water. The bottom was a soft, silty brown, and a pure white starfish was resting on a sandbar. I felt more confident as we moved into deeper water, and at the same time I was gauging the distance we had traveled, making sure that I had enough left in me to get back. Although my outer body was numb, my core felt warm.

I continued sprinting through the passages, but I wasn't paying attention to my forward motion. I turned too soon at one point, and got hung up on an underwater ice shelf. David glanced back, and I shouted that I was fine and asked how long I'd been swimming.

"Twenty minutes," he said. "One more crossing of the bay?"

Once I'd finished my final loop, I had been in the water for twenty-three minutes and had covered about a mile. It was my coldest swim — four degrees colder than in Antarctica.

Back in town, we joined the Nunavut Day celebrations. Two community leaders were grilling hot dogs and hamburgers, and a pair of caribou carcasses were being butchered by two others. Some large pieces of raw meat had already been given out, and some of the adults were holding big chunks between their teeth and using an ulu knife — with a very sharp, half-moon-shaped blade — to cut the meat into smaller pieces. An elderly woman made a fire of a small pile of dried heather, to heat water for tea. The burning heather created a swirling stream of smoke that filled the air with a fresh and clean fragrance.

I noticed that one woman's fingers were green. She was eating the stomach of the caribou, and her fingers had been stained by its contents. A nurse from the health center accepted a slice of raw caribou. She told us that it tasted like rare roast beef and that we didn't have to worry about parasites with caribou, although one could get trichinosis from raw walrus or polar bear. She added that we might want to avoid the aged meat, too — anything that had been hunted or fished would often be put in a hole for two to three months. It was an acquired taste, she said.

When Amundsen left Beechey Island, on August 24, 1903, he sailed southwest, through Peel Sound and into unknown waters. He wrote, "Our voyage now assumed a new character. Hitherto we had been sailing in safe and known waters, where many others had preceded us. Now we were making our way through waters never sailed in, save possibly by a couple of vessels, and were hoping to reach still farther where no keel had ever ploughed." But Amundsen almost lost his ship. In James Ross Strait — named for the British naval officer who reached the magnetic North Pole, in 1831, and later led the first search for Franklin — the *Gjöa* ran aground. The crew managed to free her, but that evening a fire broke out in the engine room. Three days later, the ship ran aground on a reef. A storm hit, and under full sail the crew succeeded in prying the ship off the reef, leaving splinters of the *Gjöa*'s false keel behind. By the time Amundsen sailed through the Rae Strait, more than five hundred miles from Beechey Island, he and his crew were exhausted, and hoped to find a place where they could spend the winter. On September 9, on the shores of King William Island, a crewman noticed, Amundsen wrote, "a small harbour quite sheltered from the wind, a veritable haven of rest for us weary travelers."

Amundsen named the harbor Gjöahavn. "The harbour itself was all that could be desired," he wrote, and went on:

The narrow entrance would prevent the intrusion of large masses of ice, and the inner basin was so small that no wind could trouble us there from whatever quarter it blew . . . A number of cairns and tent circles showed that Eskimo had been there, but that, of course, may have been a long time ago. Fresh reindeer tracks gave hope of sport . . . The spot seemed eminently suitable for a magnetic station.

The crew built a storehouse and, because Amundsen's second goal on his voyage was to determine the current location of the magnetic North Pole, a small observation hut. He and his men ended up spending almost two years in Gjöahavn.

Inuit — or Eskimos, as they were widely known — were living on the island. Amundsen and his men became friendly with the Ogluli Eskimos who camped near Kaa-aak-ka Lake, not far from Gjöahavn, and with the Nechilli Eskimos who lived in the area. The Europeans studied the Eskimos' dogsledding techniques, observing how they would let the runners on the sled get a fine covering of ice so that, Amundsen wrote, "they slide like butter." To prevent frostbite, Amundsen's men closely watched other crew members' faces, "detecting a white nose on one or a frozen cheek on another. We did as the Eskimo do; we drew our warm hands out of the gloves and applied them to the frozen spot till the blood came again into circulation." The Inuit also taught them how to build igloos. The Europeans traded with the Inuit for fish and reindeer, giving them knives and sewing needles, and introduced them to Christmas and New Year celebrations. Amundsen became close friends with an Inuit named Atikleura, whose wife, Nalungia, made fine clothes of reindeer skin. Knowing that these would keep him warm in the Arctic, Amundsen hinted that he would greatly appreciate some undergarments:

> Evidently very pleased at my request he now brought out some old, worn underclothing, put them on in place of those he was wearing, and handed me the latter with every indication that I was to change there and then. Somewhat surprised, I hesitated; I must say, I was not in the habit of exchanging underwear with other people, especially in the presence of a lady. But as Atikleura insisted, and his wife, Nalungia, showed the most complete indifference as to what I did, I quickly made my decision, seated myself on the form, veiled my charms as well as I could with the bed clothes, and was soon clad in Atikleura's still warm underclothing.

Today, Gjoa Haven (the name has been Anglicized) is a hamlet of about twelve hundred Inuit and a few visiting government and medical workers from the Canadian mainland. I had decided not to swim there, but I wanted to see the town. Bob Griffith returned to California from Baffin Island, and I flew across the frozen sea to King William Island.

Jackie Flynn, the manager of the Amundsen Hotel, where I was staying, and her husband, Leo, who ran the town's co-op, were from Newfoundland but were working in the north until December. Jackie offered to take me on a tour of Gjoa Haven, and we walked along dirt roads, past rundown homes surrounded by rusting snowmobiles and old ATVs. There were four markers in and around the town, Jackie told me, noting where Amundsen and his men had camped, but we discovered that one of the markers had been stolen. The plaques in two old cemeteries in the town center indicating who had been buried there had also been vandalized, and the crosses destroyed.

In Gjoa Haven, I saw several twelve- and thirteen-year-old girls with babies, and I found out that this was the norm. By the time girls were in their twenties, they often had five or more children. With the twenty-four hours of summer sun, children and teenagers stayed up all night long, playing in the streets and hanging out in vacant houses.

For all the difficulties of their lives, though, the Inuit I met were hospitable people. They invited me into their homes, showed me how they played traditional games with dice, and served me hot tea. Through Rita Hummiktuq, a student-support assistant and the coach of the girls' soccer team at the local school, I met Jimmy Qirqqut, one of the town's elders, who recounted a story he had been told by his mother about the day his great-grandfather met Amundsen. Jimmy's story was similar to one that Amundsen told in his book, except Jimmy was more dramatic when he described the initial tension between the Europeans and the Eskimos. One of Amundsen's men had been carrying a gun, and once he put it aside, Jimmy said, the two groups realized that they could be friends.

While a hundred years had passed between Amundsen's visit and mine, the Inuit showed the same warmth — and were still on the edge of survival.

On August 13, 1905, Amundsen left Gjöahavn, sailing 250 miles west through dangerously shallow waters. On August 16, he entered Victoria Strait, and the following day anchored in Cambridge

Bay, on Victoria Island, the farthest point that ships traveling eastward from the Pacific had reached, thus completing, Amundsen wrote, the last "unsolved link in the North West Passage."

Ten days later, the *Gjöa* met the Charles Hanson, a whaling ship that was sailing east from San Francisco. The sight was "magical," Amundsen wrote. "I could feel tears coming to my eyes." He thought that he was on the home stretch, but sea ice stopped his progress at King Point, on the Yukon coast. He had to anchor the *Gjöa* onshore and spend a third winter in the Arctic.

The following summer, the *Gjöa* sailed more than eight hundred miles from King Point, until sea ice forced a brief stop on Herschel Island, which lies just off the Yukon. Once the ice cleared, Amundsen set off again, and made slow progress through more ice and fog and between sandbars, until he entered the quiet, open waters of Prudhoe Bay.

Prudhoe Bay, an inlet of the Beaufort Sea and the Arctic Ocean, covers more than 140 square miles. In 1968, one of the largest oil reserves in North America was discovered there. Oil production didn't begin until 1977, when the Trans Alaska Pipeline was completed and oil could be transported from Alaska's North Slope eight hundred miles south, to Valdez. Today, roughly five thousand transient workers who are involved in oil production, transport, and support services work in Prudhoe Bay and the neighboring town of Deadhorse. The oil field, which is owned jointly by BP, ExxonMobil, ConocoPhillips, and Chevron, and is operated by BP, produces roughly 150 million barrels a year, although the amount has begun to decline.

Prudhoe Bay would be the next leg of my swim. I asked the head of security of Prudhoe Bay for permission to explore the waters, but my request was denied. It was only after approaching the offices of Alaska's U.S. senators; enlisting the help of Charles Prince, at that time the chairman and CEO of Citigroup, in getting in touch with BP; and gaining an endorsement from Alaska Clean Seas, the organization hired by the oil companies to handle oil spills, that I was able to get the necessary clearance.

Bob Griffith joined me from California, and Royce O'Brien and Tom Flynn, who worked for Alaska Clean Seas, offered to pilot their company's Zodiac to accompany me on my swim. On July 29, at around 8 P.M., with the sun shining as brightly as if it were noon, we stood on a causeway on the west side of Prudhoe Bay that extended about two miles out from the shore. The air temperature was fifty degrees, the bay was calm and clear, and there was no trace of oil seepage or other pollution in the sparkling water. Then I noticed something in the tiny waves. It was small, shaped like a ball, the color and texture of clear Jell-O tinged with plum, with inch-long tentacles extending from its base. "Tom, what's that?" I asked. "Is it some kind of jellyfish?" Tom said, "I've never seen anything like that in these waters in my life." Neither had Royce. For a moment, I wondered what other creatures might be in the bay, but I put the thought out of my head as I entered the water. I swam parallel to the causeway, about fifty yards offshore. Every time I turned my head to breathe, I saw an elevated pipeline. At the end of the causeway was a seawater-treatment plant, which processed seawater and pumped it back into the oil field. And as I swam I moved through shoals of the small, plum-colored jellyfish. They didn't sting, but when I touched them, they trembled.

Bob called out when I'd reached the thirty-minute mark, and I swam for another minute before giving the crew the signal that I was ready to stop.

As I dressed on the causeway, Royce said, "I've just seen you swim in thirty-degree water for thirty minutes, and from everything I know this isn't supposed to be possible."

In August 1906, Amundsen was nearing the end of the Northwest Passage, but three miles off Cape Simpson, roughly fifty miles from Point Barrow, now the northernmost point in the United States, bad weather was approaching. Amundsen wrote, "As the weather was still very hazy and the gale was stiffening to a hurricane, we sought shelter in the lee of some ground ice close by, and made fast to it."

According to Amundsen, the Arctic current ran strongest near Point Barrow, and flowed northeast at a sometimes torrential pace. Although the *Gjöa* needed shelter, Amundsen knew that it was dangerous to let a vessel lie near ice whose boundaries cannot be seen; it is easy to get caught inside a mass of ice without any outlet, and so risk an involuntary trip as the ice drifts to the North Pole. But then one of the propeller shafts warped, and the gaff — part of the ship's fore-and-aft rig — broke. "We were in a very awkward predicament, no engine and no sail," Amundsen wrote, but the crew raised the trysail, and the *Gjöa* continued on.

There was heavy drift ice at Point Barrow, and Amundsen knew that he would have to force the *Gjöa* through it. In open water, under full sail, the ship gained speed. Then the *Gjöa* violently struck the ice with her bow and slowly parted it.

> It seemed as if the old "Gjöa" knew she had reached a critical moment. She had to tackle two large masses of ice that barred her way to the North West Passage; and now she charged again into them to force them asunder and slip through . . . A wild shout of triumph broke forth when the vessel slipped through.

Amundsen had reached the Chukchi Sea.

Today, about 4,500 people live in Barrow, which is 330 miles north of the Arctic Circle; more than 60 percent are Iñupiat, and the surrounding villages are almost entirely Iñupiat. Traditionally, many of the Iñupiat hunted bowhead whale and fished in the Chukchi and Beaufort seas, but most of the money coming into Barrow today is from oil. Although it is a tourist destination, increasingly the visitors are scientists working on projects that directly address global warming — studying changes in the tundra and the permafrost, and in carbon levels. They are observing the increasing rate at which the sea ice is melting, and the erosion caused by the reduction of sea ice at Point Barrow. Many of the scientists are based at the Barrow Arctic Science Consortium, a not-for-profit research organization established in 1995. Three of its employees — Lester Suvlu, Vernon Kaleak, and Henry Elegak — had volunteered to help with the swim.

Bob and I thought that we had nearly reached our goal. I hadn't seen any sharks, I had grown more comfortable swimming in the frigid seas, and in Barrow we were really concerned only about polar bears. Lester told me that he had seen more bears swimming ashore in recent years than he had in his whole life. The ice was receding, and there was no place for the polar bears to hunt seal during the spring and summer. In 2005, the ice was more than a hundred miles out, he said, and the wildlife people found four polar bears that had drowned. Recently, a mother and her cub had swum ashore and stopped, exhausted, to lie down on the runway at the old airport. While I was in the water, one of the crew would follow on the shore, riding an ATV and carrying a rifle, in case we had a bad bear encounter.

When I stepped into the Chukchi Sea on August 2, the water was warmer than I had expected — forty degrees. The wind and the current would be at my back, and I was certain that my final swim would be the easiest. Vernon was with Bob in a Zodiac, waiting for me to start. I didn't see a polar bear, but there were jellyfish, large ones, with purple-and-white striped domes about three feet in circumference. They were stranded on the sand, inverted, ten to fifteen feet below me, their ten-foot-long tentacles splayed out around them.

I paused in midstroke when I noticed a scarlet jellyfish the size of an apple moving toward me. The tentacles, fire red and as thick as spaghetti strands, trailed behind; they were six or seven feet long, and I knew that they would hurt if I touched them. As I swerved right, my left hand grazed the dome and I recoiled. Staring down into the sea, I saw hundreds of these red jellyfish. They were beautiful — like flowers blossoming in an underwater garden — and terrifying. I pulled my hands in tight under my body, trying to get higher in the water so that I wouldn't get stung.

A tentacle grazed the soft underside of my arm, and it felt like a very bad bee sting. Reacting, I swung wide and hit something else. It appeared to be a small, clear jellyfish, but it had four creased sides that were edged with purple and glowed. It looked magical. I stopped to examine it more closely, treading water as I tried to understand how it was propelling itself. I couldn't see any kind of cilia or jet, but I saw another clear jellyfish, this one edged with glowing pink, and another that was edged with neon green. I was concentrating so intently that Bob later told me that he thought that I might be in an advanced stage of hypothermia, and was on the verge of pulling me out. He had never seen me swim so erratically.

The red jellyfish were moving up to the surface, and their tentacles were fanning out. Then I noticed that the big purple striped ones were being flipped over by the Zodiac's wake. In a few minutes, they would be on the surface.

"How long have I been swimming?" I asked Bob.

"Twenty minutes, but with the current you've swum more than a mile. Do you want to go farther?"

"Let's go ashore," I said.

At this point, Amundsen turned the *Gjöa* south, and sailed through the Chukchi Sea. He had traveled seven thousand miles, from Oslo to the Bering Sea. On August 30, 1906, he passed through the Bering Strait. The *Gjöa* and its crew had made it through the Northwest Passage. Amundsen caught sight of the Diomede Islands, and, just when it seemed that the *Gjöa* had entered calmer water, the ship was hit by a squall and its gaff broke again. Then a dead calm set in, and the *Gjöa* sailed slowly into Nome, Alaska. Amundsen wrote:

> Suddenly a steam launch appeared in front of us, and we heard whistling, shouting, and cheering, the Americans' mode of expressing enthusiasm. Dark as it was, we could still discern the Norwegian flag floating side by side with the Stars and Stripes on the launch. So we had been recognised . . . The heartiness with which we were welcomed, the unbounded enthusiasm of which the "Gjöa" was the object, will always remain one of my brightest memories of our return . . . The boat touched land. I really cannot say how I got ashore, but a jubilant roar of welcome issued from a thousand throats, and through the darkness of the night a sound burst forth that thrilled me through and through, bringing tears to my eyes; it was the strains of our national air.

As I climbed out of the Chukchi Sea, I felt a sense of elation. These weeks in Greenland, Canada, and Alaska had taken me into waters that few had entered or ever swum. I had traveled through the same Arctic world as Amundsen had, a place where one misstep could mean disaster. And at the same time I felt as though I was exploring a different place. I thought of the frozen waterways that were now opening up to exploration. They were so tempting, but first I needed to turn south, as Amundsen had.

MATTHEW POWER

Mississippi Drift

FROM Harper's Magazine

FOR SEVERAL YEARS, beginning when I was six or seven, I played a hobo for Halloween. It was easy enough to put together. Oversize boots, a moth-eaten tweed jacket, and my dad's busted felt hunting hat, which smelled of deer lure; finish it up with a beard scuffed on with a charcoal briquette, a handkerchief bindle tied to a hockey stick, an old empty bottle. I imagined a hobo's life would be a fine thing. I would sleep in haystacks and do exactly what I wanted all the time.

Since then, I've had occasional fantasies of dropping out, and have even made some brief furtive bids at secession: a stint as a squatter in a crumbling South Bronx building, a stolen ride through Canada on a freight train. A handful of times I got myself arrested, the charges ranging from trespassing to disorderly conduct to minor drug possession. But I wasn't a very good criminal, or nomad, and invariably I would return to the comforting banalities of ordinary life. I never disliked civilization intensely enough to endure the hardships of abandoning it, but periodically I would tire of routine, of feeling "cramped up and sivilized," as Huck Finn put it, and I would light out for another diversion in the Territory.

It was on one such outing, a hitchhike up the West Coast in the summer of 1999, that I met Matt Bullard in a palm-fringed city park in Arcata, California. A dumpster-diving, train-hopping, animal-rights-crusading anarchist and tramp, with little money and less of a home, Matt was almost exactly my age, and from that first time we talked I admired his raconteurial zest and scammer's panache. He considered shoplifting a political act and dumpstering a civil right. As we sat on a park bench in the sunshine, Matt reached into his backpack and pulled out what he called a "magic dollar," an ordinary bill save for its twelve-inch tail of cellophane packing tape. He would dip it into a vending machine, select the cheapest item available, collect his purchase and change, and pull his dollar back out by the tail. An unguarded machine could be relieved of all its coins and every last one of its snacks in the space of an hour. It was a very impressive trick.

Matt was convinced that there was something deeply wrong with most Americans: they were bored and unfulfilled, their freedom relinquished for the security of a steady paycheck and a ninety-minute commute, their imagination anesthetized by TV addiction and celebrity worship. He had decided to organize his life against this fate. He utterly refused to serve; he lived exactly as he desired. Matt's was the kind of amoral genius that I had always longed to possess. He not only had quit society altogether but was gaming it for all it was worth, like some dirtbag P. T. Barnum. I, meanwhile, would soon be returning to a temp job in a Manhattan cubicle. Matt couldn't understand why I needed to go back, and I couldn't really myself, but I went back anyway, tugged by the gravity of expectations. In the ensuing years, I got occasional e-mails documenting Matt's drift, describing days on grain cars passing through Minnesota blizzards, nights in palm-thatched squats on Hawaiian islands: dispatches from a realm of total freedom beyond the frontiers of ordinary life.

Two summers ago, Matt sent an invitation that I could not ignore. He was in Minneapolis, building a homemade raft, and had put out a call for a crew of "boat punks" to help him pilot the vessel the entire length of the Mississippi River, all the way to New Orleans. They would dig through the trash for sustenance. They would commune with the national mythos. They would be twenty-first-century incarnations of the river rats, hoboes, and drifters of the Mississippi's history, the sort who in Mark Twain's time would have met their ends tarred, feathered, and run out of town on a rail. Catfish rose in my mind; ripples expanded outward and scattered any doubts. I wrote back straightaway and asked to join up.

I met Matt on a scorching July afternoon and followed him through leafy, upper-middle-class residential streets toward Minneapolis's West River Park. The industrious hum of weed-whackers

and leaf-blowers filled the air, and helmeted children tricycled
along a path, their watchful parents casting a suspicious eye at us.
But through a small hole in the foliage by the edge of the bike
path, we instantly stepped out of the middle-American idyll, scrambling down a narrow path through the tangled undergrowth,
through cleared patches in the woods littered with malt-liquor cans
and fast-food wrappers, hobo camps with the musty wild smell of an
animal's den. I clutched at the roots of saplings to keep from tumbling down the slope. The sounds of civilization receded to white
noise. We stumbled out of the trees onto a sandy spit, and I suddenly saw the river before me, narrow and amber-colored, flowing
silently south, lined on both banks with forested bluffs.

Matt's raft was moored to the bank next to a storm sewer outflow
pipe. My first impression was of the Unabomber's cabin set afloat.
A brief description of the vessel: ten feet in the beam, twenty-
four feet stem to stern, its decks had been laid down over three
rows of fifty-five-gallon drums, twenty-three in all. "I got them from
a dumpster behind a chemical plant," Matt told me. "Some of
them still had stuff sloshing around inside." The barrels had been
framed out with lumber, mostly two-by-fours swiped from construction sites, and a deck of marine plywood set on top. On this platform Matt had built a cabin, about ten by fourteen feet, leaving a
small motor deck aft and a front porch fore. The porch connected
to the cabin through a pair of French doors, and a screen door ex-
ited the rear. The cleats, railroad spikes welded to diamond plate,
were "punk as fuck," said Matt, admiring his amateur blacksmith-
ing. On the roof was bolted a large solar panel of larcenous provenance, as well as a small sleeping quarters and a worn-out armchair
from which the boat could be steered. A wheel salvaged from a
sunken houseboat was connected by an ingenious series of pulleys
and wires to the outboard motor on the back deck, a thirty-three-
horsepower, two-stroke Johnson, which was showroom-new during the Johnson administration. It was one of the few purchased
items on the boat, bought by me as a gesture of my commitment to
the mission. Several workbenches lined the cabin, and there was a
galley with a propane stove, a chest of drawers, and a rusty high
school gym locker for storage. Matt had brought everything he had
scrounged that could possibly be of use: old fishing anchors, tied-

up lengths of rope, lawn furniture, a folding card table. Three bicycles. Several five-gallon gas tanks. A stereo speaker system with subwoofers made of paint cans, hooked up to a motorcycle battery. A collection of practice heads from the dumpster of a beauty college. In keeping with the rustic theme, the boat's front had a porch swing made of shipping pallets and a pair of plastic pink flamingos, "liberated from some lawn," screwed to its posts.

Matt's six-foot-two frame had bulked up since I'd last seen him, and his hair had grown into a waist-length mullet of dreadlocks hanging behind a battered black baseball cap. He wore a goatee, and his round face squeezed his eyes to mischievous slits when he smiled. He had added to his tattoo collection to form a sort of identity-politics résumé: NOT REALLY VEGAN ANYMORE advertised an amended dietary philosophy on his wrist; a piece on the back of his hand showed crossed railroad spikes and the free-associative motto WANDERLUST ADVENTURE TRAMP; on his left biceps was a black-masked figure standing behind a dog, above the phrase ANIMAL LIBERATION.

Matt hadn't held a steady job since a brief stint at Kinko's in the late '90s. One time in court, he said, a judge had admonished him: "You can't be homeless the rest of your life. You have to work." He laughed as he recalled this. "I fucking hate work," he said. "If I could see some result from it, besides money, maybe I'd do it. I went into the welfare office to apply for food stamps, and they took one look at me and said, 'Clearly, you're unemployable.'" He saw no shame in this, and he looked at food stamps as a way of getting back the taxes he paid when he was at Kinko's. From the hundreds of hours he had put into the boat, it was evident that what he hated was not doing work per se but rather trading his time for money. Matt had been working on the boat for over a year and had spent almost nothing on it. What wasn't donated or dumpstered was procured by extralegal means. "Half this boat is stolen," he chuckled, with unmistakable pride in his handiwork and resourcefulness.

The neo-hobo lifestyle, such as it was, often blurred the boundary between ingenuity and criminality. On the legal side, there were the old standbys: "spanging" (bumming spare change), "flying signs" (asking for money with a cardboard sign), and the governmental largesse of food stamps. Matt was also a big proponent of pharmaceutical studies, which gave out nice lump-sum payments as well as free food. In one study, he said, he had taken the largest dose of ibuprofen ever administered to a human being. In that instance, the result of being a human lab rat was only diarrhea, though he hadn't landed a new study in a while. "I had plans to buy a house with drug studies," he said wistfully. The only semilegitimate work Matt was willing to pursue was seasonal farm labor, particularly the sugar-beet harvest in North Dakota, which has become something of an annual pilgrimage for the punk traveler community. From three weeks of driving forklifts or sorting beets on a conveyor belt, enough money could be earned to fund months of travel.

On the illegal side of gainful unemployment, there were many techniques of varying complexity. The digital revolution in retailing had led to gift-card cloning (copying the magnetic strip on an unused gift card, returning it to the store display, and then waiting until it is activated) and bar-code swapping (either printing up low-price bar codes on stickers or switching them from one item to another). Various lower-tech shoplifting methods could be employed anywhere, from the primitive "wahoo" (wherein the shoplifter walks into a convenience store, takes a case of beer, screams *Wahoo!*, and runs out the door) to "left-handing" (paying for an item with your right hand while walking through the checkout with another item in your left) and "kangarooing" (the more theatrical use of a dummy arm and a pair of overalls with a large hidden pouch). One of the most lucrative scams was called "taking a flight" and involved having an accomplice steal one's luggage from an airport baggage carousel, which, with enough persistent calls to customer service, could result in a three-thousand-dollar payday from the airline. Matt and his friends saw stealing as a form of revolt, a means of surviving while they chipped away at the monstrous walls of the capitalist fortress.

For Matt, the river trip was to be a sort of last great adventure before he left the United States for good. As long as he stayed, he felt the ultimate unfreedom of jail lurking around every corner. For years he was heavily involved with the animal-liberation movement and logged weeks of jail time in three different states for protests at animal-testing facilities. He claims to be on a domestic-terrorist watch list. "When I get my ID run by the cops, it comes up 'Suspected member of Animal Liberation Front. Do not arrest.'" A recent homecoming for Matt in LAX resulted in a five-hour interview with Homeland Security. He related all these stories with thinly veiled pride, the way a parent might describe a child's performance in a Little League game.

After the river journey, he was moving to Berlin, a squatter's paradise he had visited once and found far more livable than anywhere in the United States. "I hate America," he said, without the menace of a McVeigh or a Zarqawi but nevertheless with feeling. I asked what he would do with the raft once we reached New Orleans and he left for Germany. "Only one thing to do," he said. "Torch it. I'm gonna give this motherfucker a Viking burial."

To inaugurate the voyage, Matt had planned a launch party a mile downstream, at a beach on the river's edge. With a few more arrivals, our little crew swelled to five: me and Matt, plus Cody Dornbusch, a compact, bearded twenty-four-year-old from South Dakota; Chris Broderdorp, a twenty-one-year-old bicyclist and master dumpster-diver from Minneapolis, rail-thin with a half-shaved mop of curls and a high-pitched laugh; and Kristina Brown, a fetching, levelheaded twenty-five-year-old from Seattle, who among them had the most schooling and seemed most to be play-acting at the pirate life. I was the only crew member without a pierced septum. The general mood among my boatmates was upbeat: the overflowing dumpsters of Middle America would be more than enough to sustain our bodies, and adventure would nourish our spirits. Matt fired up the ancient engine, and in a haze of blue exhaust smoke we chugged slowly out into the current, which had the color and foaminess of Coca-Cola, and headed downstream, hidden from the city by the limestone bluffs. The abandoned mills around the Falls of Saint Anthony — the falls that had brought the city here — had been converted into million-dollar condominiums. The Minneapolis–St. Paul metroplex, tidy and forward-looking, seemed to have turned its back on the river that birthed it.

The party, advertised among the local punk scene through word of mouth and printed flyers, commenced at sundown. The raft was hung with Christmas lights, and a driftwood bonfire blazed on the sand. Kids drank 40s of malt liquor and climbed over and over again onto the roof of the raft, jumping, diving, and cannonballing in various states of undress into the muddy brown river water. The night was humid and sultry, tinged with menace, and a thick darkness pressed down upon the river. Amid all the wild shouting and splashing, the dirt-smudged faces lit up by flames and colored Christmas lights, it seemed as though the raft had run aground on some cargo cult's island, the natives working themselves into a frenzy as they decided whether to worship us or eat us or escort us to the edge of the volcano at spearpoint. Someone stumbled into me in the dark, dripping, and grabbed me by the shirt, smelling of sweat and booze and the river, his voice slurred. "Hey! You're the writer. From New York." I reluctantly confirmed this. "Well, your fuckin' story better be about *solutions*." (He dragged out the word for emphasis.) "Otherwise it's bullshit. Solutions!" His grip tightened. He attempted to fix his gaze to mine and failed. He shouted "Solutions!" once more for good measure before shambling away and jumping into the river again.

In the morning, with the ashes of the bonfire still smoldering and a half-dozen half-dressed casualties of the bacchanal sprawled on the beach, we pulled the lines in and pushed the raft's barrels off the sandbar, drifting out and spinning like a compass needle until the boat nosed at long last into the flow of the river. With the Lyndon Johnson (the nickname I had given the forty-year-old engine) at half-throttle, the raft meandered with the current, the green wall of trees slipping by at walking pace. The five-gallon gas tank was draining disturbingly fast. I sat on the front-porch swing, rereading a dog-eared newspaper. Chris idly strummed a guitar as Cody and Kristina sat up top with Matt, who was steering from the captain's chair. "You know, you're going to be reading that fucking July 16th *New York Times* for the next month," Cody told me, sticking his head over the edge. I put the paper down. A Hmong family fished from a railroad embankment, waving excitedly as we passed, perhaps remembering the long-tail boats of their far-off Mekong. Eagles wheeled and dove into the river, which unscrolled before us as we rounded each bend. It was high summer, blue skies and sunny, about as auspicious as one could hope for the start of a two-thousand-mile journey. We had hung up ragged pirate flags, and now they fluttered behind us in the breeze, the grinning skulls wearing a look of bemused delight.

Our first obstacle was Lock and Dam #1. To maintain a navigable channel on the upper Mississippi, which would otherwise be too

low in the summer for commercial traffic, the U.S. Army Corps of
Engineers built a system of twenty-nine locks and dams between
Minneapolis and St. Louis. These serve as a stairway for ships to
survive the Mississippi's 420-foot drop during its 673-mile journey
to St. Louis; below that, the river (joined by the Missouri and then
the Ohio) is sufficiently deep not to require locks, and there the
Corps built levees instead. This engineering work has altered the
natural flow of the Mississippi, allowing millions of acres of former
flood plains and wetlands to be converted into intensively culti-
vated industrial farmland, which in turn sends fertilizer- and pol-
lutant-rich runoff from thirty-one states coursing back into the
channel and downstream. Floods are held back by levees, and the
resulting pressure, like that of a thumb pressed over the nozzle of a
hose, erodes fifteen thousand acres of wetlands a year from the
Delta, creating an oxygen-starved "dead zone" the size of New Jersey each summer in the Gulf of Mexico. The Mississippi is one of
the most managed, and mismanaged, river systems in the world.

The upper river may be restrained by dams, but it is not without
its hazards, both natural and man-made. I flipped through our
photocopied set of charts of the upper river, on the cover of which
there was a hand-drawn picture of a squarish boat, seen from above
as it travels in a circle, about to plow over a stick figure flailing in
the water. Underneath was written: CIRCLE OF DEATH.* Each
page of the charts covered ten miles of river, and each enumerated
a frightening array of obstacles. "Wing dams," long jetties of rocks
that jut out into the river to direct flow toward the channel, lurked
just inches below the surface, waiting to tear our barrels from under us. "Stump fields," the remnants of clear-cut forest lands that
had been drowned by the river, appeared as crosshatched forbidden zones that would strand us in an enormous watery graveyard.
But of the many things we had been warned about, barges were by
far the most dangerous. Seventy-five million tons of wheat, soy-
beans, fertilizer, coal — the bulk produce of mining and industrial

---

* Matt explained this rather gruesome nautical term: when a speedboat operator
stands up and catches the throttle, he can be tossed overboard, yanking the tiller to
one side. The unmanned boat, at full throttle, will then trace a wide circle and return to the same spot where its pilot was sent overboard, running him down and
causing death by hideous propeller wounds. Although the two-mile-an-hour cruis-
ing speed of our vessel made such a scenario unlikely, the crew decided to christen
our raft the SS *Circle of Death.*

agriculture — are shipped by barge along the upper river every year. A standard fifteen-barge tow, three hundred yards in length, can carry the freight equivalent of 870 semi trucks. They are as large as a high-rise building laid on its side, and about as easy to steer. A tow plying the river under full steam can take as long as a mile and a half to slide to a stop, plowing over anything in its path. The Lyndon Johnson sputtering out in the navigation channel while a tow bore down on us was not something I wished to contemplate.

As if reading my thoughts, just yards from the mouth of the lock chamber, the motor coughed a few times and then quit. We spun in place, and Matt flew down the ladder from the top deck to try to get the engine started. "Shit, shit, shit!" he yelled. "I forgot to mix the oil in with the gas!" The old two-stroke lubricated itself with an oil-gas mix, and we had very nearly blown the engine by running straight gas through it. Matt popped open a bottle of oil and sloshed it into the gas, measuring by eye. The rest of the crew scrambled for our canoe paddles, hacking at the water futilely to try to guide the raft into the lock. Matt barked orders that no one heeded, and the general response of the crew (myself included) to our first emergency was unrestrained panic. Finally, after loud cursing and many wheezing turns of the starter, the engine roared to life, leaving an oily rainbow on the water and a cloud of blue smoke in its wake.

"That's fucking great," said Matt. "Dead fish and dead Iraqis."

The lock loomed ahead of us, and we slid into its chamber, cutting the engine and bumping up against the concrete retaining wall. A lock worker walked along the wall to us and threw down ropes to keep the raft in place. I had hoped he'd be excited at our arrival, or at least amused, but he had the world-weary countenance of a man who had seen all things that float, and our jerry-built vessel of scrap lumber and barrels was insufficient to impress him. I asked him what other strange things had passed through his lock. A guy came through rowing a raft of lashed-together logs just last year, he said. I realized that we were just the latest in a long line of fools, and not even the most hard-core.

Behind us, the door to the chamber swung silently shut, and like a rubber duck in a draining bathtub we began sliding down along the algae-slick wall as millions of gallons of water drained into the next stage of the river. Within a few minutes we had dropped thirty feet, and the top of the chamber glowed distantly as if we were at the bottom of a well. With the majesty of great cathedral doors swinging open, a crack appeared between the gates of the lock, and the murky green waters of the chamber joined the still waters of the lower river, glinting in the sunlight. Matt whooped, to no one in particular. New Orleans, here we come.

The first night, still in St. Paul, we pulled up to a hobo jungle, a firepit-pocked stand of trees below a rusting railroad bridge where in the past both Matt and Cody had waited to catch freight trains. The jungle sits on land that floods out yearly. Wrack and trash were scattered about; it looked like the desolate set of a horror movie. Chris rode his bike off to search dumpsters, and the rest of us carried the gas cans ashore to fill them up. Having covered barely ten miles in about the time it would take to walk that distance, we had already used up an enormous amount of gas. While the Lyndon Johnson got slightly better mileage than, say, an Abrams tank, it was nowhere near as fuel-efficient as a Hummer. This appalling carbon footprint aside, at three dollars a gallon our meager gas budget would be eaten up before we got out of the Twin Cities. My back-of-the-envelope calculation suggested that it would take somewhere near five thousand dollars' worth of gas to make it the whole length of the river. Matt, however, felt no guilt about this use of fossil fuels. "I figure since I never use gas the rest of the year, it all balances out. We'll make it. We're gonna bust our asses, get some work somewhere, do some scams, look for a Wal-Mart."

Wal-Mart was frequently invoked by Matt as a source of almost limitless material bounty, a natural resource as rich as the midwestern prairies its parking lots had buried. Enormous and ubiquitous, the megastores offered almost everything we needed to survive. Aside from outright theft (the most straightforward procurement strategy), there were the wonders of Wal-Mart dumpsters, overflowing with inventory that was slightly damaged or barely past its expiration date. There were also a wide variety of "return scams" as elaborate as anything the Duke and the Dauphin could have pulled over on the rubes. "Receipt diving" involved plucking a crumpled receipt from an ashtray by the exit, entering the store, selecting the same object off the shelves, and promptly returning it, receipt in hand, for store credit. Another ruse involved finding goods in the trash (a bag of chips, perhaps), to which a PAID sticker had been affixed. This sticker was removed and placed on a small, expensive object, which was then returned for store credit; and since many of the larger Wal-Marts in the Midwest had their own gas stations, a half-eaten bag of chips could thereby be converted into a large supply of free gasoline. Or so my crewmates told me. We paid retail for our new load of gas, hauling the heavy jerricans a mile through the woods to where the raft was moored. I was beginning to realize that there was a considerable amount of heavy lifting involved in dropping out.

Chris returned with a garbage bag full of cold pepperoni pizza slices, a new staple of our shipboard diet, removed from under the heat lamps of a convenience store and discarded only hours before. We all dug in to the congealing bounty. Chris's dumpstering was a good supplement to our ship's stores, which were stacked against a wall in stolen milk crates, a depressing harvest from community food banks: government-commodity-labeled cans of cheese soup, string beans, creamed corn; bags of generic Froot Loops, some Kool-Aid powder to fend off scurvy. The crew's dietary ethos was what is commonly referred to as "freeganism," wherein foodstuffs that are about to be thrown away are rescued from the waste stream and thereby ethically cleansed. An estimated seventy-five billion dollars' worth of food is thrown out yearly in America, and it doesn't take a great leap of logic to connect the desire to live sustainably with the almost limitless supply of free food that overflows the nation's dumpsters. Thus the opportunivore can forage either overtly or covertly, by asking up front or diving out back.

"We're going to dumpster everything we can," Matt told me. "Plus food shelves, donations, and you should apply for food stamps the first chance you get downriver." I'll eat out of the trash as happily as the next guy, I told him, but I didn't feel right applying for food stamps; this set Matt off on a series of gibes about my "so-called journalistic ethics." Matt was happy enough to sustain himself on the detritus of a world he saw as careening toward self-destruction, and equally happy to scam a government he despised. "I'm glad everyone's so wasteful," he told me. "It supports my lifestyle."

In the middle of a watery expanse of grain elevators and moored barges to the south of St. Paul, our engine emitted a tubercular hack and died again. There was a stiff headwind, and the ungainly raft acted as a sail, dragging us against the current and back up-river. We paddled and poled ourselves to shore and tied up just before the skies opened up with a thunderstorm, and we huddled inside the cabin, soaked, as the robot voice on the weather radio warned of dime-size hail carpet bombing the Twin Cities. Matt stomped around the boat, dripping and furious, yelling at the disorder in the galley and the general uselessness of the crew. Most orders were monosyllabic, the commonest being "Move!" Rain hissed on the plywood roof of the cabin, thunder rattled the windows, lightning tore the air. The flashes burned photonegatives of the landscape onto my vision. The river had removed its bucolic mask to show a darker, wilder aspect.

The mood was grim. Cody stared off into the distance every time he heard a train whistle in the nearby yard, freights being his preferred mode of transport. We spent two nights tied up along the rocky, wave-swept shoreline, the roof leaking in half a dozen places, with every pot in the galley set out to catch the water. The cabin became increasingly claustrophobic, smelling of sweat and mildew and cigarette smoke and rotting produce. I waded ashore and walked through a shuttered suburb in the pouring rain to buy spark plugs. In the hardware store, I overheard the two tellers discussing a care package to be sent to their coworker, now a roof gunner in Iraq. Would the pudding separate in the heat? Would applesauce be better? Our drifting life felt mean and meaningless in comparison. I walked back down to the river in the rain. We changed the fouled plugs and limped on again under bleak gray skies.

Matt had arrived at a magic solution to the fuel dilemma, a way to absolve ourselves of complicity in the Iraq War and reduce the *Circle of Death*'s carbon footprint. We were going to drift to New Orleans, taking advantage of the gravitational pull of a quarter-mile drop over the two thousand miles of river. I pointed out the folly of this. There were twenty-eight dams still in front of us, slowing the river down. A breath of headwind would hold the raft in place as if we had dropped anchor. He dismissed my doubts with a sneer. Matt was even harder on Chris, upbraiding the young biker for his lackadaisical work ethic and enormous appetite. As a dumpster-diver, Chris had proven to be overeager, and our galley was perpetually full of overripe fruit and moldering doughnuts. And he was always eating, even during crises: he would have been grazing the buffet on the sinking *Titanic.* Matt barked orders at him constantly and generally considered him to be an oogle.*

Twain, writing in *Life on the Mississippi* of his days as a cub pilot, describes a certain Pilot Brown: a "horse-faced, ignorant, stingy, malicious, snarling, fault-hunting, mote-magnifying tyrant." In a section unsubtly headed "I Want to Kill Brown," Twain deals with his hatred of his superior by lying in his bunk and imagining dispatching the tyrant "not in old, stale, commonplace ways, but in new and picturesque ones, — ways that were sometimes surprising for freshness of design and ghastliness of situation and environment." At night, swarmed by mosquitoes on the beached raft, I entertained some of the same fantasies that sustained a young Sam Clemens, feeling the fellowship of oppression through all the years that had passed down the river. There is a long record of psychotic sea captains in literature, and Matt, by historic standards, was somewhat less formidable than Bligh, or Queeg, or Ahab. He was a bit hard to take seriously, even when he launched into a tirade. But he was still profoundly unpleasant to live with and sail under on a ten-by twenty-four-foot floating platform. I became increasingly of the opinion that Matt resembled a romantic anarcho-buccaneer less than a narcissistic sociopath. Perhaps he had traveled alone too often, depending on no one but himself, to be a leader of others. And this, I had come to realize, was what a functioning crew — even of anarchists — demanded.

We passed at long last beyond the Twin Cities, below the flaring stacks of an oil refinery that looked like a postapocalyptic fortress, a column of orange flame swaying in the night sky. Matt cut the engine and drifted whenever the wind allowed, and our pace slowed to a crawl. We averaged a handful of miles a day. A drop of water from the Mississippi's source at Lake Itasca will flow down along the river's length to the Gulf of Mexico in ninety days. In 2002, an overweight and lanolin-slathered Slovenian named Martin Strel swam the entire length in just over two months. It would have taken us at least nine months at the rate we were drifting. I made a game of watching dog walkers on the shore outpace us. Bloated catfish floated past belly-up, bound to reach New Orleans long before we

* A poser; a street rat without street smarts; the lowest caste in the nominally nonhierarchical gutterpunk social hierarchy.

would. Hundreds of spider webs garlanded the raft; they draped across the curved necks of the lawn flamingos and between the spokes of the ship's wheel. I spent hours on the front-porch swing, chain-smoking like a mental patient at the dayroom window. I learned quickly not to bring up the glacial pace of our progress toward the Gulf.

"This is my boat, and my trip, and nobody is going to tell me what to do," Matt snapped. "If it takes two years, it takes two years. I won't be rushed." The paradox of Matt's position had become clear to all but him: by building a raft to escape the strictures of society, he had made himself a property owner, and subject to the same impulses of possessiveness and control as any suburban homeowner with a mortgage and a hedge trimmer. He was as much a slave to civilization as the locked and dammed river on which we drifted, and far less likely to break loose.

Meanwhile, a shipboard romance had blossomed between Matt and Kristina. None of us talked about it, though it was hard not to notice, as every movement of their accouplements in the captain's quarters was telegraphed through the entire raft in minute detail. Although Matt showed her more deference than he extended to anyone else, he still condescended to her, barked orders at her, got jealous over phantoms. She told me she was having fun and wanted to stay on the river as long as she could stand to be with him. I pointed out that it wasn't a particularly healthy way to have a relationship, and she laughed. "It's kind of ironic that he's so big on animal liberation and can't stand people," she said. "It's because animals can't contradict him."

As if to augur my own psychological dissolution, the raft itself was falling apart. The heavy oak transom to which the two-hundred-pound engine had been bolted was pulling out from the raft's wooden frame. A little more torque from the engine and it would rip itself right off, sinking to the bottom of the channel like an anvil. Thrown up against the shore by wakes, we tied up to a tree outside the town of Hastings, Minnesota, where Matt told us we would need to stay for several days to fix the broken frame. He ordered me to find a Wal-Mart and return with a little electric trolling motor, which could help steer the drifting raft or pull it out of the way of a tow. I walked up through Hastings, down the main street of curio shops and antiques stores, past the end of the town sidewalks, and out along the highway.

One can bemoan the death of the American downtown at the hands of exurban big-box stores, but to truly understand the phenomenon, try reaching one without a car. It was a triple-digit day, the heat shimmering up from the softened blacktop, the breeze hot as a hair dryer. I tried to hitchhike, sticking my thumb out as I stumbled backward down the road. Cars flew by, their drivers craning to look or studiously avoiding eye contact. I wasn't a very appealing passenger: I hadn't showered or shaved in the week since we'd left Minneapolis, and had worn the same clothes throughout. I had a permanent "dirt tan," a thick layer of grime that no amount of swimming in the river could fully remove. My black T-shirt had been torn by brambles and faded by the sun, and a camouflage trucker's hat covered my matted hair as I trudged for miles along the grassy shoulder. Shame eroded; I didn't mind if I was seen peering into dumpsters behind convenience stores, looking for cardboard to make a hitchhiking sign. But still no one stopped.

After walking for almost an hour, I reached the edge of a wide sea of blacktop, and walked across to the vast shed of a building that wavered on its edge like a mirage. Enormous doors slid open, and arctic air engulfed me, pulling me into the glorious air-conditioned acreage of the largest Wal-Mart I had ever seen. I pushed a cart through the aisles, picking out a trolling motor and a deep-cycle marine battery to run it. No one paid me much mind, not the too-young couples arguing in Housewares, not the carbuncular stock boys tallying inventory on the vast shelves. As I rolled up to the counter, the checkout girl offered some scripted pleasantries, asked if I had a club card. She rang up the trolling motor, a large oblong box sticking out of the cart, but didn't notice the seventy-dollar battery lying under it.

All I had to do was keep smiling and push the cart straight out the door, across the parking lot, back to the river, and the battery would be mine. Who would miss it — my seventy dollars, from Wal-Mart's billions? Matt would have walked out proudly, or bluffed his way out if confronted by security. He would certainly have called me a coward for passing up the chance. I told the girl about the battery, and she rang it up, and I struggled back across the sea of asphalt in the blazing sun.

When I returned to the raft, which was tied up amid bleached driftwood and plastic flotsam on the shoreline, I found Matt waist-deep in the water, rebuilding the transom, and Cody, drunk on malt liquor, busying himself by stuffing his gear into his backpack. I asked him where he was going.

"I don't really feel like going half a mile an hour along the river with people I don't really get along with. I'd rather go fast as hell on the train. Go work the beet harvest, make four grand, and go to India with my girlfriend." On the far side of the raft, Matt said nothing, only scowled and hammered on the boat. "Matt's a fascist," he whispered to me. "If I stay on the boat, I won't be able to be his friend anymore." The raft, which for Huck and Jim supplied the only space where they could be friends, had wrought quite the opposite effect on our crew.

With no goodbyes, Cody threw his skateboard and pack to the shore and jumped after them, walking off in the direction of the railroad trestle that spanned the river downstream. Half an hour later, a pair of Burlington Northern engines pulling a mixed string of grainers and boxcars rattled over the bridge, bound for Minneapolis, and I wondered, with envy, whether Cody had clambered aboard.

Day after day I studied the charts and traced our snail's progress. Each marked buoy passed like a minute hand making its way across the face of a schoolroom clock. The time, the date, all the measures of normal life were stripped of meaning. But just when boredom threatened to overwhelm the senses, the river would offer up some bit of unimpeachable beauty. Bald eagles circled overhead and landed in snags to watch us with wide yellow eyes. Deer startled from the shore, crashed into the understory, white tails flashing. Opalescent sunsets silhouetted herons at dusk. The great birds paced their own glassy reflections before pulling up like brush strokes to stand in the shallows of the far shore.

Late one night we motored along a stretch of the dark river and pulled up at Latsch Island, a houseboat community in Winona, Minnesota. Several hundred young anarchists from around the country had train-hopped and hitchhiked there to attend the annual event known as the CrimethInc Convergence. CrimethInc is more a mindset than an actual organization, but its stated credo is essentially anticapitalist and antiauthoritarian, serving as a catchall for a host of other social and political viewpoints, from postleft anarchism to situationism to violent insurrection against the state. A large group gathered on the darkened beach when we arrived and cheered the raft, strung with Christmas lights, as we beached it at full throttle.

I wandered around the encampment the next day. Grimy and feral-looking, the CrimethInc kids squatted in small groups around a clearing. The campsite was overgrown with poison ivy, and many legs were covered with weeping red blisters. It was the first time in weeks I hadn't felt self-conscious about being filthy, but now I felt self-conscious about not being punk enough, and I worried I was being eyed with suspicion. Almost none of the kids were older than twenty-five, as if there were a sell-by date on radical social philosophy, a legal age limit after which one must surrender lofty ideals and shave off all dreadlocks. CrimethInc's core function is the creation of propaganda, mainly in the form of books and zines, and they held a swap of such anarcho-classics as *Days of War, Nights of Love; Evasion;* and *Fighting for Our Lives.* One of my favorite free pamphlets was "Wasted Indeed: Anarchy & Alcohol," a searing indictment of the revolution-sapping properties of the demon drink, which offered potent slogans: "Sedition not Sedation!" "No cocktail but the Molotov cocktail!" "Let us brew nothing but trouble!"

The CrimethInc kids were in the middle of several days of self-organized workshops, seminars, and discussions ranging from the mutualist banking theories of the nineteenth-century anarchist philosopher Pierre-Joseph Proudhon, to an introductory practicum on lock-picking, to a class on making one's own menstrual pads. One well-attended discussion was on consent ("Not the absence of no, but the presence of yes!"), and it seemed to underscore the CrimethInc goal of reevaluating the rules and customs of society and creating new ones. Consent was central to the idea of functioning anarchism, which they believed to be the purest and most direct form of democracy. Everyone ate as a group, and a huge cauldron of dumpster-dived gruel bubbled over a campfire, tended by a grubby-handed group of chefs dicing potatoes and onions on a piece of cardboard on the ground. Huck may have been right that a "barrel of odds and ends" where the "juice kind of swaps around" makes for better victuals, but it occurred to me that the revolution may well get dysentery.

Anarchism has not made much of a mark on American politics since 1901, when Leon Czolgosz assassinated President McKinley; but neither has it entirely vanished, and running through the

American ideal of the rugged individualist is a deep vein of sympathy for the dream of unmediated liberty. What would happen, I had often wondered, if their anarchist revolution ever got its chance? If everyone just up and quit, and did exactly as he or she pleased in an orgy of liberated desire? Who would keep the lights on? Who would make the ciprofloxacin or, for that matter, the calamine lotion? What kind of world would the sun rise on after that victory?

But the revolution hadn't happened, and it probably never would. The kids were naive fantasists, but I could see their basic point: there was a huge amount wrong with America and the world, from impending environmental collapse to widespread sectarian warfare to a real lack of social justice and equality. CrimethInc's adherents had come together there because they wanted to live their lives as some sort of solution. They saw "the revolution" not as a final product but as an ongoing process; they wanted not just to destroy the capitalist system but to create something livable in its place. I didn't want to smash the state, but I realized that in my adulthood I had faced those same dispiriting questions: How should we live in a world so full of waste and destruction and suffering? What *were* the "solutions" that the inebriated oracle insisted I find, that first dark night on the riverbank? I didn't know if I had ever been one of these kids or if I had just been playacting, wishing I were an idealist and acting as if it were so. There were solutions, I felt sure. But they were not to be found there, adrift, disconnected from the world.

We floated ever southward, through rolling farmland and beneath chalky bluffs, past tiny towns clinging to the riverbank, the raft bobbing like a cork in the wakes of tow barges and jet skis. We were averaging about seven miles of drifting a day, and there were still more than sixteen hundred miles of river between us and the Gulf. Sometimes I'd look up from a book after twenty minutes to see we hadn't moved. Matt became more aggressive and bossy as the days passed, exploding over tiny things: an open dish-soap cap, a pot of leftovers uncovered, an empty matchbook not thrown out. A week after Cody left, Chris had unloaded his bicycle from the top deck and in a single afternoon pedaled back the mere fifty miles we had come from Minneapolis; and with both of them gone, the brunt of the abuse fell on me. We got into an argument about money one night, as I had financed pretty much every purchase of un-dumpsterable or otherwise freely procurable necessity for the past several weeks. Matt had seventeen dollars to his name and wanted money to tide him over until he took a break from the river and went to the beet harvest. I told him I didn't want to be his banker, and that he was clearly resourceful enough to figure things out just fine.

After that, Matt refused to talk to me at all. He and Kristina spent their days playing cards and dominoes, and I either took shifts at the steering wheel or sat on the porch, trying to read. We drifted in a heavy silence for two days, passing Victory, Wisconsin, and at last making it out of Minnesota and into Iowa, the river unraveling before us into a swampy waste of braided channels and black backwaters, widening out at times into half-submerged fields of rotting stumps.

We tied up for a night at a dock above the Black Hawk Bridge, and the tires of tractor-trailers moaned on its steel grating, ghost-like as they flew over the river. I walked up the hill above the river to use a pay phone at a smoky bar, the regulars hunched over their stools like heartbroken gargoyles. When I came outside, I saw Matt and Kristina surrounded by local police next to a convenience-store dumpster, framed in a circle of streetlight. They had been fishing out some food, and the manager had called the cops on them. But after checking their IDs, the police let them go. Matt walked back to the boat, and Kristina and I went for a drink at the bar before returning to the same dumpster, filling a bag with cold cheeseburgers and pizza slices. The petty authoritarianism of the police had been confounded, but it didn't feel like much of a victory. Staring out at the neat lamplit lawns of Lansing, Iowa, I felt weary of being a stranger. I told Kristina I had to leave.

As much as I had wanted to see the raft down the entire river, as much as I had wanted the strength to quit everything and live on river time, to see Hannibal and Cairo and Memphis and New Madrid, I couldn't do it. I woke up at sunrise, packed my bag, and sat on the dock in the dawn glow. Matt and Kristina were asleep inside his quarters. Mist rose off the river, which wound south past dark banks hung with wisps of fog. I heard Matt stir; he squinted and grimaced as he stepped out onto the porch and saw me sitting on my pack on the dock. We seemed to understand each other.

Kristina undid the lines from the cleats, and Matt pushed away from the dock. With a wave they motored out into the middle of the channel and then cut the engine, catching the current and drifting along to wherever the river would bear them. I sat watching for what seemed like hours before the *Circle of Death* rounded a far bend and vanished. I shouldered my pack, walked up to the bridge, and began hitchhiking east toward home, borne along by kindly strangers. Waiting for a lift at sunset, I found myself on a stretch of blacktop rolling to the horizon through a landscape of wheat fields and grain silos. Swarms of grasshoppers flitted around me, flashing golden in the fading light, leaping out of the fields at the highway's edge. Alone in the middle of the country, far from home but heading there, I felt more free than I had since leaving Minneapolis, since I'd first set eyes on the Mississippi. But the ground still seemed to rock below my feet, as though a ghost of the river rolled beneath me.

Kristina sent me occasional updates, but soon she left the raft herself and went off traveling on her own. Two months later I got an e-mail from Matt. With astonishing persistence, he had made it all the way to St. Louis, through the entire lock-and-dam system, nearly seven hundred miles down to the wild reaches of the lower river, where the current, freed at last from its restraints, flowed unhindered to the Gulf. Drifting through St. Louis, the raft had been hemmed in between a moored barge and a pair of tugboats. A third tug had pulled through, creating a huge bow wash that sent water rushing sidelong into the cabin. Inundated, the *Circle of Death* had keeled over and sunk, almost immediately, to the bottom of the Mississippi. Matt, barefoot in only shorts and a T-shirt, had narrowly escaped drowning by swimming to the barge and climbing out. All his clothing, his journals, photographs, identification — everything but his life had been lost, and he found himself in a place he had often been: broke and homeless, coming ashore in a strange city. The river, of course, continued on without him.

SETH STEVENSON

The Mecca of the Mouse

FROM *Slate.com*

The Wide World of Disney World

SOON AFTER CHECKING IN to my hotel room, I discover a mouse in the bathroom. Three mice, in fact. One is imprinted on the bar of soap. One peers out from the shampoo label. And a third, on closer inspection, is a washcloth — ingeniously folded by hotel staff to create two protruding, terrycloth ears.

I'm growing used to these rodentophilic touches. Earlier today, as I drove into the enormous Walt Disney nation-state here in Florida, I noticed a tall electrical stanchion topped with a pair of Mickey ears. Soon after, I spotted a water tower with the ears painted in black. When it comes to branding, Disney's aim is total immersion.

Which is good, because that's my aim, too. I'm here to envelop myself in the Disney World experience. I've obtained lodging deep within the compound, at a Disney-owned resort. I've bought a $280 multiday pass, granting access to more Disney attractions than any person could reasonably endure. For the next five days, I plan not to stray beyond the borders of the Disney empire. (Don't worry, that still leaves me forty-seven square miles, an area roughly twice the size of Manhattan, in which to roam.)

Why on earth would I, a childless adult, visit Disney World by myself? Basically, to figure out what the hell's going on in this place. Because America has clearly decided it's hallowed ground.

More than one hundred thousand people visit Disney World every day. I went when I was a kid. Nearly all my friends went. A few went more than once. Heck, I know Jews who weren't bar mitz-vahed but did go to Epcot.

Somehow, this cluster of amusement parks has grown into a rite of American childhood. Kids are born with homing beacons set for Orlando. Meanwhile, parents — despite the hefty costs — often seem just as eager or more so to make the pilgrimage.

My question is: what exactly are we worshipping at this mecca?

Day 1: Epcot

I drive the three minutes from my hotel and ditch my rental car in the lot. After swiping my pass-card and getting my fingerprint scanned (a new security measure), I enter through Epcot's gates. Once inside, I'm immediately jaw-dropped by the looming mass of Spaceship Earth.

It's tough to ignore — being a sixteen-million-pound, 180-foot-high disco ball. One of Walt Disney's personal rules for theme-park design involved a concept he curiously termed the "wienie." A wienie is a showstopping structure that anchors the park. It is meant to be iconic and captivating, so that it lodges in your visual memory forever.

Spaceship Earth is perhaps the wieniest of all wienies. And it announces right off the bat that Epcot will not be your standard kiddie fun park. Over at the Magic Kingdom, the wienie is the fairy-tale Cinderella Castle. Here, it's a geodesic sphere inspired by the theories of R. Buckminster Fuller.

When I enter Spaceship Earth, I board a ride tracing the history of communication — from the first written symbols to the advent of the personal computer. It's low season now, so there's a mercifully short wait for the ride. That's the good news. The bad news is that once the ride is under way, I discover that it's a vague, aimless snooze. Toward the end of it, we pass what I believe to be an animatronic Steve Jobs. He's pneumatically gesturing inside a replica of a 1970s California garage.

When the ride is over, we spill into an area called "Innoventions." It's sponsored by a company called Underwriters Laboratories, which specializes in product-safety compliance. Among the fun activities here for kids: try to make a vacuum overheat! Also: see if you can fray the cord of an iron! (I'm not kidding about this.

There are nine-year-old boys with furrowed brows attempting to cause product failures.)

Several other exhibit halls surround Spaceship Earth. According to my guidebook, they feature "subjects such as agriculture, automotive safety, and geography." Well, gosh, that's what being a kid is all about!

Inside a pavilion labeled "The Land," I find myself being lectured on sustainable development. The lecture is delivered by the animated warthog from *The Lion King*. I can overhear the nice mom behind me trying to distract her whimpering toddler. "Look, honey," she says, reading from her Epcot brochure, "the next ride is a 'voyage through amazing greenhouses and a fish farm!'" The kid cries louder.

Though I was only eight, I still remember the day Epcot opened in 1982. The TV networks treated the event as news, airing live coverage. Every kid in my third-grade class was desperate to see this wondrous new place.

Once the fanfare faded, though, we began to sense that Epcot was a slightly odd duck. Disney had purposefully designed it to appeal more to young adults than to their offspring. It was bound to disappoint all but the nerdiest of children. It had been the largest private construction project in all of American history — requiring three years and one billion dollars to complete — and in the end, it was essentially a tarted-up trade expo.

A perusal of Disney history suggests that Epcot was in some ways the brainchild of the man himself. What Walt envisioned was an Experimental Prototype Community of Tomorrow — a real town, serving as a laboratory for cutting-edge ideas about urban planning. But after Walt died in 1966, his dream was gradually perverted into the theme park we see today.

Sponsors were called in to defray the huge costs, and in return, Epcot's "Future World" exhibits became an ode to giant corporations. The automotive safety ride is brought to you by General Motors. The agricultural science ride is compliments of Nestlé. In his tome *Vinyl Leaves: Walt Disney World and America* (the title refers to the fake leaves on a Disney "tree"), the mildly paranoid anthropologist Stephen M. Fjellman writes that Epcot's attractions are meant to "convince us to put our lives — and our descendants' lives — into the hands of transnational corporate planners and the technological systems they wish to control."

When I leave the Future World area, I walk around the Epcot lagoon to the other half of the park. Here I enter the "World Showcase." It consists of eleven separate pavilions, each dedicated to a different nation.

I like the idea of the World Showcase. And some of the architecture — the faux Paris street scene, for example — displays an astounding talent for mimicry. But if you've ever actually been outside America, this nod to the rest of the world is mostly just insulting.

Half the pavilions have no cultural content at all. The Morocco complex is just souvenir stores selling carpets and fezzes. The ride meant to encapsulate Mexico is a collection of slapstick Donald Duck skits. (Donald loses his bathing suit while parasailing in Acapulco, Donald flirts with some *caliente señoritas,* etc.) I guess none of this should surprise me. Lots of tourists view travel abroad as basically a chance to shop for regionally themed trinkets.

By the early evening, it's getting dark, and both kids and adults are getting crankier. A lot of strollers get wheeled into corners as moms whisper-shout, "Settle down, Hunter" and "You stop that right now, Madison." I'm also noticing a lot more people buying the $8.50 margaritas available next to the Mexico pavilion.

I take this as my cue and head back to the parking lot. Tomorrow's another day — and another theme park.

Disney's Hollywood Studios

The keynote attraction of Disney's Hollywood Studios, listed first on the park brochure, is something they call the Great Movie Ride. This ride purports to trace the history of American cinema. "Travel through classic film scenes and Hollywood moments," the pamphlet promises.

Eager to see what sort of curatorial stamp the Disney imagineers might put on this topic, I line up, wait my turn, and hop aboard a conveyor pod. Soon, I'm rolling along past various iconic movie stuff. There's Jimmy Cagney cracking wise. There's Humphrey Bogart wooing Ingrid Bergman. And oh, look, it's Sigourney Weaver battling an alien. (To my great disappointment, we at no point pass Debbie doing Dallas.)

There are two big problems with this ride (besides there being no Debbie). First, as best I can tell, the kids sitting all around me have no idea who any of these actors are. Never seen any of these movies. They perk up solely at references to films that were released after 2005.

Second, these aren't video clips we're watching: those famous scenes are being performed by animatronic robots. They have waxy faces and whirring pneumatic limbs. Frankly, they're weird. And they, too, leave the kids completely cold.

I'm sure "audio-animatronic" creatures were nifty when Disney pioneered them in the 1960s. They became possible after Wernher von Braun lent his pal Walt Disney some magnetic computer tape — the same kind that was used by NASA to synchronize its launches. (Pause to contemplate: Wernher von freaking Braun! He gave the world not only the V-2 rocket and the Saturn V superbooster, but also the means to create an android Sigourney Weaver. Perhaps the greatest innovation of all!)

In 1964, an animatronic Abe Lincoln wowed the crowds at the New York World's Fair. People were convinced he was a live actor. Impressive achievement. Four decades later, though, who's impressed when a mannequin blinks and raises its eyebrows?

Sadly for Disney, many well-known rides throughout all the parks — even the famed Pirates of the Caribbean — still rely on animatronics as a central selling point. I'm guessing that within a decade all these robot performers will get phased out. Robot Humphrey and Robot Sigourney will get powered down one final time, then tossed on a pile in some dark, archival closet. A few classics — maybe android Abe — will be left out on display to appease the nostalgists.

However dated, it's still very Disney — this notion that the ultimate entertainment is to watch a machine impersonate a human. It hints at Disney's core philosophy. If I had to choose a single word to describe the Disney theme parks, that word would be *inorganic*. Or, as a cultural studies post-doc might put it: "Blah blah simulacra blah blah Baudrillard." As has been noted in many a dissertation, we visit Disney World to savor the meticulous construction — physical, mythical, and emotional — of a universe that's completely fake and soulless.

But oh, how beautifully soulless it is. Upon leaving the Great Movie Ride, I walk down a facsimile of Sunset Boulevard. Here, I notice the asphalt under my feet has rubbed away in spots, revealing the old streetcar tracks beneath. Of course, there never was a streetcar. And its tracks were never paved over to make way for the automobile age. And that pavement was never subsequently eaten away by the ravages of time. In fact, this entire fake history came into being all at once, fully formed, plopped on top of some Florida scrub land. As the famed Baudrillard scholar Michael Eisner announced at the opening of the park in 1989: "Welcome to the Hollywood that never was and always will be."

I think it's these interstitial moments — the seamlessness and the attention to detail — that really stun Disney visitors and stay with them long after they've left. The rides are great, sure, but every amusement park has rides. Disney creates fully realized narratives.

Consider the Tower of Terror, located at the end of Sunset Boulevard. It's just a classic drop tower, where the goal is to send your stomach up into your sinuses. A regular amusement park would put you in a windowed gondola, crank it up high, and drop it. But here the complicated backstory is that we're visiting a haunted, 1930s-era Hollywood hotel. The hotel lobby contains accurate period furnishings — battered velvet chairs, musty lampshades.

As I wait in line, shuffling forward, I eavesdrop on the couple behind me. The woman (I've gathered she's from a show-business background) is marveling at Disney's set design. "Look at the distressing on all the surfaces," she says with real admiration. "That's not easy to do. You can't just let the set hang around and age for fifty years." She's right: the place is yellowed, stained, and cobwebbed to a perfect patina. You'd never guess the whole thing was built in 1994.

After passing through the lobby, we're shown an expensively produced film about the hotel's haunted past. Then "bellhops" in *Barton Fink*-ish costumes lead us to our seats. And then, at last, the actual ride happens. It's about forty-five seconds of screaming our tonsils out as we plummet down an elevator shaft. All that effort and ingenuity wrapped around such a simple thrill. But this is precisely what draws folks all the way to Disney World instead of to their local Six Flags.

When the ride's done, I go back outside and watch people strolling down Hollywood Boulevard. It turns out that the most farfetched fantasy in Disney World isn't the magic spells, the haunted buildings, or the talking animals. It's the fact that there aren't any cars.

For the mostly suburban Americans visiting here, this whole pe-
destrianism concept is at once liberating and bewildering. People
don't seem ready for it. On the one hand, they adore walking with
their children in a totally safe environment (one that's outside and
is not explicitly a shopping mall). On the other hand, they're getting extremely winded.

It's pretty far to walk the whole park. "Slow down! Stop walking
so fast," I hear over and over — sometimes from fat adults, other
times from their chubby children. They sweat through oversize T-
shirts. They breathe heavily with every step. Their plump calves go
pink in the sunshine, contrasting with their bright white sneakers
and socks. Self-propulsion appears to be a wholly unfamiliar challenge.

Still, the rewards for their efforts are many. Around any given
corner there might lurk Power Rangers, mugging for photographs.
Sometimes a troupe of fresh-faced teens will suddenly materialize
and perform dance numbers from *High School Musical*. Later, you
can buy a multipack of *High School Musical* socks at one of the sidewalk souvenir stores. (Okay, I actually bought some of these socks.
They were for my twenty-six-year-old sister. We share a refined sense
of humor.)

As the afternoon wanes, and I grow tired of the masses, I duck
into the least-attended attraction I can find. It's called "Walt Disney: One Man's Dream." Inside, there's a small museum dedicated
to Walt's life and a theater screening a short biographical film.
There are about twelve people in the auditorium when the film begins. One family leaves halfway through because their toddler is
cranky.

Poor Walt, I think to myself. One day you're chilling with Wernher von Braun, inventing lifelike robots. The next day you're just
some dude who drew a mouse.

(Hey, let this be a lesson to you, *High School Musical* brats. There
will come a time when no one will be buying your licensed hosiery
anymore. Who will sing and dance with you then? Allow me to answer: you will sing and dance alone.)

Disney's Animal Kingdom

The Imagineering Field Guide to Disney's Animal Kingdom reveals that
the imagineers deliberately left the parking lots out in front of this

Disney-style zoo as bleak and barren as they could. A wasteland, with no strips of grass to interrupt the endless asphalt slab. They wanted to heighten the contrast we feel when entering into the lush, wooded Animal Kingdom park. The scheme "ensures that the immersion into nature . . . will be very impactful."

My first thought upon reading this was: Screw you, imagineers! Parking lots suck enough as it is. You're saying you made yours even more depressing than necessary, just so you could showcase some cutesy landscaping idea? Go imaginuck yourselves!

Once I'd gotten this indignation out of my system, my second thought was: Gosh, they sure do put a lot of thought into this stuff. Leafing through these behind-the-scenes books (I also have *The Imagineering Field Guide to Epcot*) brings to light, yet again, the insane attention to detail you find at every Disney property.

For instance, once you've made that transition from the parking lot through the gates into the Animal Kingdom entrance area, the imagineers' next goal is to carefully orchestrate your first glimpse of the massive Tree of Life. (It's one of this park's two wienies — the other being a replica Mount Everest.) Various inclines, berms, and hollows have been arranged so that you're forced to ascend a small rise before suddenly stumbling onto a gorgeous, unimpeded view of the tree. (The tree itself is an impressive feat of engineering. And is, of course, totally fake.)

I've been curious to see how this obsessive nano-focus would be reconciled with the challenges of a zoo. Live animals seem decidedly un-Disney, as they can't be compelled to perform a repeated, synchronized sequence. (Unlike an animatronic robot. Or a low-wage employee.) With the animals' free will involved, it's impossible to ensure that every guest will receive the same, focus-group-approved experience. This sort of thing makes the imagineers extremely uncomfortable.

Their response was to make the animals into a sideshow. In many cases, you don't even get to watch the animals from a static viewing point, as you would at a regular zoo. Instead, there's a "ride" with a silly narrative structure (about, for instance, chasing poachers), during which you get quick, oblique glimpses of the animals as you speed by. The true stars of Animal Kingdom aren't the lions, apes, and elephants. The stars are the precision-crafted environments you walk through.

Here, come with me as we visit the delightful little village of

Harambe. Harambe is the perfect East African port town of your mind's eye. When you first come upon it, it's hard not to feel you've been teleported to Kenya.

All the signs are in the right typeface. The buildings are lovingly dilapidated. The paint-color choices are perfect. (The imagineers say they took paint chip samples on research trips and did surface rubbings to get the building textures right.)

Having traveled to Africa myself, I can tell you that Harambe gets only two minor details wrong. The first is that Africa has many more flies than this. And the second is that Africa has black people.

Given the otherwise remarkable accuracy of Harambe's set design, I'm sort of surprised that Disney didn't manufacture fifteen thousand animatronic Africans. Okay, so they did import a few actual, nonrobot Africans to work the snack stands. *Jambo!* But perhaps the bigger issue is: where are the black tourists visiting the park? I've seen maybe two black families all day. As in the rest of Disney World, there are literally more French people here than African Americans.

Another population dynamic I've noticed: the dearth of children at this supposed family destination. I've seen lots of adult couples with no kids in tow. Even when there's a token toddler present, there are often six or seven grownups attached to it. I'm beginning to suspect it's the adults who really want to be here, while the kids are just serving as fig leaves.

This theory is bolstered by a scene I witness while waiting in line for food. An elderly, gray-bearded gent is in front of me, trying to buy a soda, when all of a sudden he's interrupted by his twentysomething daughter, who is scurrying toward us. "Daaaaaad! She's not tall enough to go on the ride!" whines the woman, gesturing with a pout at the tiny girl clinging to her thigh. "So now *I* can't go! And you wandered off!" The man says nothing. "Take her hand," the woman demands. The poor old fellow is mortified by this behavior (and is in the middle of his beverage transaction, to boot). But he silently takes his granddaughter's hand so his horrid daughter can go enjoy her fricking roller coaster.

Admittedly, Disney has some pretty great roller coasters. Toward the end of the day, I walk over to Anandapur (a fake Himalayan village, complete with Tibetan-style prayer flags) and board the Expedition Everest ride. I'm seated in a rickety rail car, which creaks up to the top of the two-hundred-foot mountain before swooping, banking, and dropping at insane speeds. Everyone screams together. It's a group outpouring of white-knuckle terror. When the ride's over and I disembark, I find I've broken out in a light sweat. My dazed fellow riders look at each other in total awe: Can you believe what we just went through?

The same thing happens on the nearby Kali River Rapids ride. There are seven other people on my raft, and as we float down the rushing river, I can feel us starting to gel into a team. We shout warnings to each other when the white water rages ahead. ("Look out, here it comes!") We catch each others' eyes and can't help but smile. The little girl sitting next to me cackles every time we get hit with a splash. She's shouting, "I'm soaked!" with a big, adorable grin.

If I've found one redeeming feature of the Disney World experience, it's the community spirit that's fostered when strangers all join together for a primal shriek of fear — or joy.

Celebration and Downtown Disney

I've spent three straight days inside the Disney World fortress. The incessant magicalness is starting to wear on me. I'm feeling a need to escape Big Rodent's clutchy claws. At the same time, I don't want to risk too much corruption from outside influences. I'd rather not stray too far — geographically or spiritually. The perfect compromise: a visit to Celebration.

This insta-town was conceived by Disney, built on Disney-owned land, and initially managed by Disney executives (though the company has shed much of its involvement over time). And it's only a few miles from my hotel. I make the short drive, park my car downtown, and hop out for a look.

I've long been a fan of planned communities. I once lobbied my editor at *Newsweek* to let me write a story about Co-op City — those ugly brick apartment towers in the Bronx, New York, next to I-95. My resulting (very short) article included a quote terming Co-op City's architecture "a disgrace to humanity." The piece also noted that Co-op City had been constructed on the rubble of an abandoned theme park. The park was called Freedomland, and it was the creation of a former Walt Disney associate.

Celebration, though it wasn't built until the 1990s, was in some ways the creation of Walt himself. Walt's original plan for his Florida swampland was to create a brand-new living town — the true Experimental Prototype Community of Tomorrow. Celebration is the belated (and mangled) realization of that dream.

Walt had envisioned a high-tech, sci-fi city, in appearance not unlike Epcot's Future World area (monorails whizzing by and whatnot). That's not how things turned out. Celebration is instead *backward* looking, with neotraditional, faux-prewar houses. Its oldtimey, Norman Rockwell vibe is less Future World and more Main Street U.S.A.

Celebration's planners were proponents of New Urbanism (in itself a somewhat nostalgic credo, what with its emphasis on marginalizing the automobile). The town's layout is pedestrian-friendly, the retail and restaurant district is a short stroll from many houses, and all the car garages are hidden in rear alleys not visible from the street. Sure enough, within moments of my arrival, I find myself smack in the middle of a New Urbanist/Rockwellian moment: children walking home from school together as a friendly crossing guard holds up his stop sign.

The thing is, I can't help but wonder if these kids might be animatronic. Everything looks waaaaay too perfect. The town famously has a strict rulebook legislating things such as yard upkeep, what color your curtains can be, and what kind of furniture (if any) you can put on your porch. This results in a place so scrubbed of individuality that the houses seem to resent their human residents.

All the streets here have the same power-washed gleam as the streets in the Disney theme parks. The neighborhoods have the same built-all-at-once aesthetic. I actually like some of the downtown buildings designed by shnazzy architects. (Favorites include the toylike post office by Michael Graves and the retro cinema by Cesar Pelli — though I feel Philip Johnson's town hall with its forest of pillars is a facile, unfunny joke.) But having spent the last few days surrounded by maddeningly perfect Disney habitats, I'm now getting the sinking sense that I haven't escaped the Mouse at all.

Celebration forces upon you the same seamless, manufactured experience you get when you walk through the "villages" of Harambe and Anandapur. The inhabitants of Celebration are essentially *living* inside a theme park. (We might call it Suburb Land.) Each night when the park shuts down, they're still inside the gates.

In the evening, I decide to check out Downtown Disney, back inside the fortress. It's basically a very high-end strip mall — with a Planet Hollywood instead of an Applebee's, and a Virgin Megastore instead of a Hot Topic. I grab dinner at Bongos Cuban Café (celebrity owner: Gloria Estefan) and then stroll over to Pleasure Island as it gets dark.

Pleasure Island is where adults on vacation at Disney go at night to escape their children. Also here: businesspeople stuck in Orlando for conferences and locals who treat this as their regular hangout. (Pleasure Island doesn't require a Disney Pass.) There's a club for every taste, from the disco lounge (8-Trax) to the hip-hop spot (BET Soundstage) to the mainstream, top-forty dancehall (Motion).

A single cover charge gets you in to all the clubs, all night. So people bounce back and forth among the venues. This creates the sort of nightlife melting pot that you rarely, if ever, find in the real world. Because it's Disney, and we all feel safe and emboldened, no one's afraid to venture into what might be perceived as alien territory.

Nerdy white people stride confidently into the "black" club. Older couples wade onto dance floors packed with whippersnappers. Gay dudes sashay through the redneck-y rock club. (When I say that, I'm not trying to play on a stereotype. I literally watched three gay men prance about and do ballet jumps while the house band played Lynyrd Skynyrd. These guys were egging each other on, trying to get a rise out of the crowd, but none of the lumpy heteros seemed to pay any mind.)

I find the whole scene oddly hopeful — at first. If people can all get along together here, maybe we can bring that tolerance back home with us. As the night wears on, though, different groups begin to self-segregate.

Early in the evening, for instance, I had a drink at a club called Mannequins. It had a mixed crowd: moms and dads in dorky khakis, some college-age kids getting blitzed, and one pair of gay guys dancing up a storm under the disco ball. I was heartened by the diversity. But it didn't last.

When I popped back a few hours later, I ordered a drink and scanned the room again. It appeared the demographics had undergone a radical shift. Now there were 150 men positively swarming the rotating dance floor. They were accompanied by about three women. And I couldn't help but notice that these men, as a group, seemed extraordinarily handsome, trim, and well dressed.

Ohhhhhhhhhh. I suppose that name should have been a clue, now that I think about it.

Anyway, it's all good in the Disney 'hood. When we envision a "magic kingdom," we, each of us, have our own ideas.

The Magic Kingdom

Inside every Disney theme park, you'll find at least one booth — often more than one — stocked with information about Disney Vacation Club Resorts. A nice man or woman will hand you a brochure, offer to take you on a tour of model rooms, and talk you through a few different time-share options. Apparently, it's a terrific deal if you want to bring your family back to Disney World every year.

Query: why would *anyone* want to go to Disney World every year? You can pretty much see the whole thing in a week. Okay, fine, kids might like it enough to go back again — once, or maybe twice. But this time-share makes financial sense only if you return about seven times.

Holy frack! I'd go mental if I had to spend seven precious vacations trapped inside the Disney universe. But let's put my personal feelings aside. Let's say you're a parent. Mightn't it be better to broaden your children's horizons just a tad? Like, maybe visit Canada — instead of just the Canada pavilion in Epcot?

According to Disney, there are more than one hundred thousand member families in the Vacation Club. These people have handed over all their foreseeable leisure time to the Walt Disney Company. It's an astonishing decision, no? And it's surely less about a destination than an ideology. We'll call it Disneyism. These families aren't choosing a vacation so much as a religion.

Walt Disney, the man, is a singular character in American history. He gets his start as an animator, then becomes a movie mogul, an amusement park baron, and eventually a mythmaker — a sort of unprecedented high priest of American childhood. By the mid-1960s, with his techno-utopian plans for the living city of Epcot, Walt had even turned into (in the words of the anthropologist Stephen M. Fjellman) "a social planner and futurist philosopher."

It's these later incarnations of Walt that really fascinate me. The guy is sculpting the toddler id while also designing a domed metropolis with a monorail. How did this happen? A man who got famous drawing a cartoon mouse was now going to solve all America's urban problems?

It's hard to think of a comparable career arc. But as a parallel, evil-twin figure, consider Scientology founder L. Ron Hubbard. He was born ten years after Walt, also in heartland America. His career likewise took off on the strength of mass-market entertainments (in Hubbard's case, sci-fi). And then midcentury — during that Atomic Age moment when everything somehow seemed possible — he turned his attention to a grand, ego-gratifying social project of dubious utility.

Who knows what ambitions might have bubbled up in Walt if he'd lived past 1966. But I think one way to look at his life is as L. Ron Hubbard gone good. This is a long way of saying: Disney isn't just a media outfit with some theme parks. It's a worldview — sprung from the head of a lone, imaginative man. And ultimately, for the people who come back to Orlando year after year, it's a church.

On my last day here, I visit the Magic Kingdom — the original and still best-attended of the Disney World parks. After walking down Main Street U.S.A. (a fake, turn-of-the-century boulevard lined with yet more Disney souvenir stores), I come upon the famous Cinderella castle. Fairy-tale spires everywhere. It's so gleaming, it looks like they repaint it every night. (Over the last several years, furthering my Disney-as-religion theory, the castle has become a prime location for wedding ceremonies. Up to five weddings per day are held on Disney World's grounds. Mickey and other characters will even attend your wedding reception. For a fee.)

As I get closer to the castle, I see the familiar Disney apostles (Mickey, Minnie, Donald, Goofy) performing musical numbers on a stage, enthralling a large crowd. The lyrics to their songs shuffle around a few key words — *dreams, magic, imagination, wonder* — and weave them into some upbeat string arrangements. Hymns for the Disneyist congregation.

Many of the little girls watching this are wearing princess dresses (bought at those souvenir stores). For years, Disney must have sought a boys' version of the princess obsession, and it seems they've finally found it — thanks to the blockbuster *Pirates of the Caribbean* films. Lots of little dudes are running around in pirate costumes, waving plastic swords.

Disney has increasingly managed to find characters to leverage for each different demographic group. Tinkerbell, from *Peter Pan*, has been rebranded as the slightly saucier "Tink" and now graces T-shirts targeted at your tween daughter. Meanwhile, your death-metal son will be drawn to the skull-and-bones imagery of *The Nightmare Before Christmas* franchise.

Even adults wear Disney gear here. There are moms in Mickey ears and dads with giant sorcerer hats. This is a safe place for everyone to act like a kid, and I'll admit there's a certain sweetness about that.

I'm not a fan of the gender dynamic implicit in the princess/pirate split. (Visiting Mickey and Minnie's side-by-side houses does little to reassure me on this score. Mickey's house has a nonfunctioning kitchen and is full of sports equipment, while Minnie has a to-do list on her wall with the entries "Bake a cake for Mickey" *and* "Make a box lunch for Mickey.") Still, my heart melts when I see a little girl wearing a princess dress while sitting in her wheelchair, beaming ear to ear as her even beamier parents take pictures.

I can understand why families love Disney World. And there's nothing wrong with making kids happy. I just think we'd all be better off if we didn't indoctrinate our kids in the Disneyist dogma.

After spending the past five days here, I've come to the conclusion that Disney World teaches kids three things: 1) a meaningless, bubbleheaded utopianism, 2) a grasping, whining consumerism, and 3) a preference for soulless facsimiles of culture and architecture instead of for the real thing. I suppose it also teaches them that monorails are cool. So there's that.

I end my day with the "It's a Small World" ride. Yes, it's a prime example of bubbleheaded utopianism. Yes, it features animatronics, which are dated and lame. And yes, that song just never ends. No matter: the ride somehow manages to charm me anyway.

Designed for the UNICEF pavilion at the 1964 World's Fair, it shows us children of many cultures all living in harmony. (A color-saturated, Pop Art harmony.) It's an unassailable message, and there's also something comforting in the ride's retro simplicity.

Our open-top boat floats along, and I love the gentle bump and re-direct when it hits an underwater guide rail. I even have a soft spot for the music. (Though I prefer to reimagine it as a slow, melancholy ballad.)

As I leave the park, I decide that after all my cranky complaining, I'm glad my week came to an end this way. "It's a Small World" makes for a nice, pleasant memory to finish on. I'm feeling positive about Disney again. And then there's an incident on the parking tram.

I'm seated on the tram, ready to ride back out to the parking lot where my rental car's waiting. The driver has already blown the horn and announced that no more boarding will be allowed. Suddenly, I notice a woman twenty yards away, running toward us.

The driver spots her, too. The tram is in motion now, and he screams over the loudspeaker: "Ma'am! Stand back! There is no more boarding!" But the woman can see that there's no real danger here — the vehicle is moving at, like, three miles an hour — and fer crissakes she doesn't want to wait fifteen minutes for another tram if she doesn't have to.

The driver keeps shouting. The other passengers are tut-tutting at this rule-breaker. The tram keeps rolling. The woman is getting nearer.

As I watch all this, I start to think about the totalitarian seamlessness of Disney. The berms that hide the loading docks and the dumpsters. The fireworks that go off every night at precisely 9 P.M. The impeccably G-rated entertainment. The synchronized rides. The power-washed streets.

"Ma'am!" the driver yells again, with real exasperation. She's just a few strides away, with her eyes on that slow-moving prize. "Ma'am, there is no more boarding at this time!"

I can't help but break into a satisfied grin as the woman hops up on the running board and takes a seat.

TOM SLEIGH

The Deeds

FROM *The Virginia Quarterly Review*

1

"When we drove into Qana last year," Joseph told me, scanning the
gray concrete houses on either side of the road, "we heard flames
roaring, the sound of the jets, people screaming, and the ringing
of cell phones." He looked at me and shrugged. "The relatives of
people were calling to see if they were okay." Joseph worked for
the Red Cross during the 2006 war with Israel and was one of the
first to enter the village after an Israeli bombardment massacred
twenty-eight Lebanese civilians. Soft-spoken, slight, he was solici-
tous on the surface but, like many Lebanese, reserved, even wary.
When I hired him as my driver and interpreter to take me south
from Beirut, I knew only that he drove a taxi with his father and
worked as a draftsman in an engineering firm to pay his way at Lebanese University. But then he offered to take me to Qana. He could
show it to me, he said; he could tell me what he'd seen.

To get to Qana, we needed military clearance, and so we'd
stopped at the central army compound in Sidon, one of the major
cities in southern Lebanon. The Lebanese intelligence officer who
handled foreign press was dressed in blue jeans and a checked oxford, his shirttail hanging out. His wire-rimmed glasses gave him a
bemused air, and his thoroughly unmilitary bearing unsettled me.
I knew that he knew that I knew he had all the power, and while he
seemed to enjoy this, he also seemed to appreciate the absurdity of
his own position. Why should he be the one to control who went to
the south of Lebanon?

"This is not my decision," he said. "You need to get permission from the military authority in Beirut."

"But," I explained, "when we came yesterday to the base, I was told that we were to talk to you and that you could grant us permission."

"Who are you writing your story for?"

I tried to explain that *VQR* was a general-interest magazine and that I wanted to tell the Lebanese side of the story of the 2006 war against the Israelis. He could barely keep from rolling his eyes: how many times had someone like me come in and said the same thing? And which side of the war would that be — the Druze, the Shia, the Sunni, the Christians?

I wasn't exactly a seasoned reporter — as a matter of fact, I'd spent most of my writing life as a poet. This was my first so-called assignment, and the role of foreign correspondent felt a little outsized. As the officer stared me down, I realized his checked oxford was, in fact, a cowboy shirt, complete with snaps and pocket flaps. And when I noticed his cowboy boots shining under the rickety metal table, on which a comic book and various official-looking papers were spread in casual disarray, I began to feel a little desperate, realizing that whatever I'd expected to find in Lebanon would be of an order of complexity beyond any of the books I'd read, or the people I'd talked to, in preparation for the trip. I started to babble about how close to Washington, D.C., my magazine was, that it was read by important D.C. politicians. I could picture my editor grinning, exhorting: *Shovel faster, boy-o, shovel faster.* At last the officer smiled — quite genially, actually — and lifted his hand the way a casting director might to spare himself one moment more of a bad actor. He asked Joseph where we wanted to go.

Joseph, his face tense during the entire exchange, wanting to help but knowing how capricious the military authorities could be, said simply, "Qana." The officer wrote a few words in Arabic on a scrap of paper and said, "This will get you where you're going. Show it at all the checkpoints." He then shrugged good-naturedly: "Beirut has many good nightclubs and shops. I hope you will visit them." I assured him I would. Then he looked at me and said: "Everyone says that we Lebanese are good at two things. Fighting. And shopping." I nodded and smiled, he nodded and smiled, and Joseph and I went back to the car.

On our way south we inched along in the dust cloud kicked up
by dump trucks, by convoys of United Nations Interim Force in
Lebanon (UNIFIL), and Lebanese Army transport vehicles. All the
coastal bridges had been bombed to rebar and rubble and were
now being jackhammered apart by work crews. As the sun beat on
the sea in the distance and the rocks riled the waves into scuffed-up
patches of foam, I remembered that Qana was the place where Jesus worked his first miracle. At a wedding feast, Jesus turns water
into wine and inadvertently humiliates the bridegroom for serving
up a wine far inferior to Jesus' miraculous vintage. That I was on my
way to this scene of biblical faux pas and realpolitik slaughter in a
cab I'd rented for the day — the logo TRUST TAXI emblazoned
across the rear windscreen — was just the sort of irony that made
Lebanon Lebanon.

Checkpoint after checkpoint, we flashed our flimsy scrap of paper and my passport at the soldiers lounging in their flimsy wooden
booths, or just as often leaning on stacks of tires painted red and
white. Between checkpoints, I studied the map, locating Qana,
then searching out each of the twelve official Palestinian refugee
camps in Lebanon — though by now there was nothing camplike
about them. These were established neighborhoods built alongside Lebanese neighborhoods, in the capital city of Beirut and
throughout the country, and they were home to somewhere between 250,000 and 400,000 refugees, depending on whose statistics you believe. Three generations had grown up in these makeshift cinder-block-and-rebar quarters since the Arab-Israeli War of
1948 and 1949, when over seven hundred thousand Palestinians
had fled or been driven from their homes by the Israeli forces. In
the subsequent armed conflicts between Israel and Lebanon, Israel
had labeled these camps "terrorist strongholds," while Palestinians
saw them as centers of resistance against Israeli aggression.

I hadn't expected violence when I came to Lebanon. I'd originally been scheduled to leave the United States in December 2006.
But when a prominent Christian politician, Pierre Gemayel, was
shot dead by three gunmen, and the country seemed on the verge
of civil war, the trip was postponed to May 2007. By that time, everything was supposed to have calmed down. But the violence that
had been building for months erupted the moment I stepped off
the plane — and only got worse, in a series of car bombings, shoot-
ings, and a full-fledged siege by the Lebanese Army on a Palestin-

ian refugee camp where Islamic fighters, led by Fatah al-Islam, had holed up.

To Joseph, now twenty-two, none of this seemed unusual. He was a child of war. During the first five years of his life, Beirut was a chaos of sectarian zones, a dizzying swap meet of shifting alliances, arms deals, and gangland struggles. He lived through the Israeli and the Syrian occupations, which ended, respectively, only in 2000 and 2005. And that's not counting the everyday threat of political assassinations carried out by car bombings, an occurrence so frequent that you'll see television ads for car-bomb detectors. "ProSec: For a World of Security." A man dressed in an expensive-looking leather jacket holds a device emitting an electronic beam that senses plastic explosive under his Mercedes's fender. A useful gadget, really, in a country where five anti-Syrian ministers of parliament have been assassinated in the last two years. What one thousand kilograms of plastic explosive will do to a motorcade — enveloping in the blast not only the target vehicle but also anything moving within fifty meters — obsesses Lebanese news channels.

I confess that as we drove I was feeling a little paranoid, eyeing cars and their drivers. On TV, two nights running, I'd watched cars exploding into flames — just as they do in movies — and later I visited the scorched remains. There were no "security zones," just a casual-looking ribbon of yellow caution tape declaiming, in Arabic and English, STAY BACK. I could stand close enough to see how the blast heat had annealed the body paint to a glassy blue-black sheen. Doors and windows blown away, upholstery fire-gutted. One skeletal chassis resembled the fossil remains of some docile, plant-eating dinosaur. The locals who walked by barely gave it a second glance. When Joseph spoke of this kind of destruction, he was deadpan, unimpressed by its drama for an outsider like me. "Welcome to Lebanon," he said. *Welcome to Lebanon:* how often I heard it repeated, followed by a half-humorous, half-stoical shrug, when I asked about the car bombings. Cab drivers, hotel clerks, soldiers, politicians, professors, Palestinian refugees: *Welcome to Lebanon.*

2

"This is the first time for me to be in Qana since last year," said Joseph. "It's strange to see it so quiet." Where bombs had fallen now resembled construction sites, rubble piled high on the side of the road, though clearly much of it had been removed. "There was another massacre here," he told me, "during the 1996 war with Israel. They bombed a UN compound where the farmers came to keep safe. There is a memorial. People from all over Lebanon come here to see it." One hundred six people died when Israeli howitzer shells collapsed the roof. The 2006 massacre was the result of two bombs — one almost certainly precision-guided and made in the United States — that exploded into a three-story building with a subterranean garage where members of the extended Hashim and Shalhub families had gone for cover. Twenty-eight of them were killed.

The Israeli Defense Force insisted it had proof that the building was housing Hezbollah fighters and weapons, including missile launchers. These claims were disputed by a top Israeli military correspondent, who said, "It now appears that the military had no information on rockets launched from the site of the building, or the presence of Hezbollah men at the time."

"Our [Red Cross] team," Joseph told me, "was called by the military on July 30, at 1:50 A.M., and we left Beirut as soon as they called. We got to Qana at 4 A.M., but the Hezbollah soldiers ordered us not to enter the village. They were waiting for the Israelis to tell them that it was safe to go in, that the bombing was finished. The Hezbollah soldiers said that they would shoot us if we tried to enter without their permission. We could see nothing but smoke and rubble. We wanted to enter the town, but they held us back for two and a half hours."

Joseph told me it was common practice for the Israelis to issue general warnings about impending bombardments. But at Qana, he said, the villagers had been too afraid to leave while all the roads out were being so heavily bombed. When I asked him how he felt about Israel, he began to talk about the United States — something that happened again and again, from Lebanon's former prime minister Selim al-Hoss to taxi drivers and hotel workers. "Before 9/11, all of us wanted to go to America to work or study, but that has changed. America is seen as not friendly to us. And also because of Bush and his support of Israel." He glanced sidelong, as if worried he might offend me. "In our eyes, there is no difference between what Israel wants and what Washington wants. They are the same voice speaking."

As we drove past makeshift scaffolding around half-rebuilt cinder-block houses, Joseph was careful to distinguish between the actions of the Israeli and U.S. governments and ordinary citizens. And he had equally complex feelings about Hezbollah, which most Lebanese of whatever sect regard not as terrorists but as both a resistance movement against Israel and a mainstream political party. But nothing is ever simple in Lebanon. Joseph was ambivalent about their religious and social agenda — feelings only deepened by his Christianity, which in Beirut is almost a form of tribal identification. Since the Lebanese Civil War (1975–1990) pitted every sect against every other sect, with the major division falling between Christian and Muslim, survival depended on religious solidarity and the willingness to band together with other sects in sometimes surprisingly short-term alliances. Even the current legal system is divided. Lebanon recognizes eighteen different religious sects, called confessions, and each confession has its legally binding religious courts that handle social issues such as marriage, divorce, intermarriage among faiths, and inheritance. So eighteen different law codes operate simultaneously. For example, according to Muslim codes, a Muslim woman can't marry a Christian, but a Christian woman can marry a Muslim — though according to Muslim law, she cannot inherit.

Joseph, despite navigating these divisions, was a fairly secular Christian who loved the Rolling Stones and didn't seem much interested in politics as they broke down along sectarian lines. "During the Civil War, things were not good between Muslims and Christians," he explained. "My father is a fireman — after a battle, the firemen picked up the bodies and put out the fires — and so he saw the worst part of the war. People stayed with their own people. But for my generation, it is different. As a boy, I played with Muslim children. To me, religion is much less important." Still, he said, "If you are a Christian, you tend to live among Christians, marry a Christian. I have many Muslim friends, but your main connections are to other Christians." Each sect is similarly divided over its view of America. "Because America is seen to be anti-Muslim, Muslims hate Americans. But we Christians tend to love Americans, because America supports us. Both points of view are wrong. All the leaders are wrong," Joseph said, as we drove under a banner of Hezbollah's leader, Hassan Nasrallah, a chubby, bespectacled cleric

with a bushy black beard. Beneath his smiling face ran an Arabic
caption: THEY RESISTED. THEY FOUGHT. THEY WON. "We
Lebanese are good at blaming the other side. There is enough
blame for all sides. We must look at ourselves, but we are bad mir-
rors. All we see are the things done to us by the other side."

Joseph let down his reserve for the first time. "I live war. I've lived
only eight years my whole life in peace. But I lose my nerve when I
hear this thing from this mother." He spoke softly, but fiercely: "I
saved children out of one home, two were suffocating under rubble and bricks, two had broken bones, they were two and seven
years old, and their parents, their faces, they were stone — I cried
as I worked, their mother did not cry, she said, 'This is for Hassan
Nasrallah.' If I wasn't in uniform, I would have killed her. I would
die for my children. She said it was a sacrifice for Hassan Nasrallah.
I would not sacrifice my children for anything. Yes, to see the reac-
tions of the parents killed us. We all have martyrs, but I do not call a
boy or a girl of seven or eight years a martyr. How many sins did he
make?"

He parked near a mosque pocked by shrapnel. "We saw bodies of
children. There was rubble and dust. We were four ambulances in
all. Our first job was to look for the living. Then we took care of the
most serious cases. I could hear lots of screaming, but it was sometimes hard to see where it was coming from. We found five children. I did CPR on one until we could get him to the ambulance.
One had broken bones, and the other was wounded in the thigh.
We put them in the ambulance, and then the driver took them to
a hospital thirty kilometers from Qana. Three of the people we
pulled out of the wreckage died on the way to the hospital."

We walked by a house that had collapsed into itself, just the
doorframe standing and a fragment of the back wall of what had
once been someone's living room. Joseph and I stepped through
the doorway, and he pointed to a pile of mangled rebar and concrete. "This door was blocked by rubble, but the door was still on
its hinges. We could hear two women screaming inside, but they
wouldn't open the door. They didn't believe us when we said we
were Red Cross. So we had to break down the door. We were all
completely covered in dust and it was hard for them to see our uniforms. We could still hear the jets circling overhead, and they were
scared that we were Israelis. They had a flashlight and lit our faces

so that at first we were blinded. But they hugged us when they saw we were Red Cross."

We walked past a bombed vacant lot where an old man in a Mercedes was assessing his property. A tall, dapper fellow, he offered us a cigarette, and told us how the Israeli bombs demolished his five stores and the villa that he'd built here for his retirement. "The Israeli drones must have spotted weapons here. Hezbollah was hiding rifles and grenades between my houses. So that's why they bombed me. I am lucky to have family in Detroit. They all sent me money to rebuild. But since I have a green card to work in the U.S., Hezbollah would not give me any money, even though it is their fault this happened." He then insisted that UNIFIL — the UN peacekeeping force — had told the Israelis about the weapons cache in the corner of his lot, and I could sense him trying to control the anger and frustration in his voice. "They are supposed to help us but they help the Israelis."

Joseph gave me a skeptical glance, but many Muslims in southern Lebanon make this same charge against the UN forces. Whatever the merits of such accusations, the UN has been powerless to stop the fighting. During the five years prior to the war, the Hezbollah militia and the Israeli Defense Force shrugged off UNIFIL and played cat and mouse with each other's fighters. According to the rules of the game, each side was supposed to restrict raids and combat operations to military combatants. Civilians were more or less off-limits. But it turns out that between the time of the 1982 Israeli invasion and the 2000 pullout, the five hundred Lebanese and Palestinian civilians killed "by accident" totaled more than the combined dead from the Hezbollah militia, the Israeli Defense Force, and the South Lebanon Army, Israel's proxy army. And this number was thirty times the number of Israeli civilian deaths. This kind of grim accounting breeds an internecine calculus of how many people you have to kill to get the other side to stop killing, and continually weighs blood shed against how much blood remains to be shed in order for scales to balance.

3

In a little village just beyond Qana, we met an old man scornful of both Hezbollah and the Lebanese government. "Six died at that

house up the way and ten were wounded," he told me as Joseph
translated. "And none of the buildings that were bombed belonged
to Hezbollah. But we, we have nothing left. In our fields we found
two Israeli missiles ninety centimeters long. And as you can see, our
house is destroyed."

The old man's disdain for Israel began long before last year's
war. From 1978 to 2000, the Israeli Defense Force had occupied a
so-called security zone in southern Lebanon to protect their northern border population. The zone expanded by 1985 to comprise
about 10 percent of Lebanon's territory. This sparked Palestinian
and Hezbollah militia resistance. When things quieted down, the
Israelis told themselves that their policy was working, and had to
continue. And when things heated up again — car and suicide
bombings, Katyusha rockets, guerrilla-style ambushes — the Israelis insisted on the absolute necessity of the zone. On the opposing side, the notion that Israel would withdraw once resistance
stopped seemed ludicrous to Hezbollah and to neighboring Syria,
which was embroiled in its own conflict with Israel over the Golan
Heights, a casualty of the 1967 Arab-Israeli War. Such is the nature
of wartime logic: all signs of goodwill are interpreted as weakness,
and any sign of weakness is to be exploited. And, of course, the
weakest of the weak, those most easily exploited, were the un-
affiliated civilians.

The old farmer and his wife now lived in two rooms — the only
ones still standing — of what had been a seven-room house spacious enough for sons and daughters, children and grandchildren.
Down the middle of his yard he'd cleared a path through the rubble that led to the remains of the bathroom, where only the mirror and a hanging light bulb remained. "My wife and I stay here,
but everyone else is gone to Tyre or to Beirut. We have sixty-three
children and grandchildren, and when the bombs dropped we
thought it was our last day on earth — the sea, the air, the ground,
from every place there were explosions. One minute, and everything was destroyed."

From the wreckage of his garden, the old man plucked three
pink roses and a white flower that Lebanese Christians associate
with the Virgin Mary. He gave them to me. Across the street was a
dump truck painted with the Islamic symbol of the eyes of Fatima,
the daughter of the Prophet. Fatima and Mary seemed weirdly at

odds at that moment. As we left, he told us that his orange groves would go unharvested this year; his fields were seeded with Israeli cluster bombs, making it far too deadly a business to try to pick oranges.

While we walked toward the car, Joseph took me to where the most recent massacre in Qana had occurred. "When we arrived, we began to collect the dying people. I'm used to it, it's ordinary to me, I grew up with dead people, people eighty or ninety years old who died not from old age but from war. They had no names, nothing to remember them by, they were just bodies to be picked up. Nobody could tell what body part belonged to what body. And all the time you were deciding what piece of flesh to put in which body bag."

On most days, we would have seen buses of people who'd come to pay homage at the site, but there were none that day, probably because of the heightened security. And so the village was extraordinarily quiet for the middle of the afternoon. You could smell the oranges rotting, off in the distance, and see the hills' outcrops. I thought of Armani clothes strewn across a showroom by the bomb blast in a Beirut shopping district (it was just as the intelligence officer in Sidon had said — fighting and shopping); I recalled the seismic pattern of the blast wave that knocked out windows on one side of a building but left the other side's windows intact when the wave caromed among concrete walls. Such sights were beginning to seem commonplace. But I wasn't prepared for what Joseph told me next.

"I couldn't see anything, there was so much smoke and dust. But right here, yes, it was right here" — and Joseph pointed to a scraped-bare, chalk-white patch of ground near the edge of where the three-story building must have been — "I saw what I thought was a child's hand. We had no tools, really, to move the rubble, and so I began to move rocks with my hands to dig the child out. And as I dug, I uncovered her head and had dug her out to just under her armpits. People were screaming, and I could hear a cell phone ringing. And I thought that if I could just lift her up under her armpits, then I could pull her free. And so I reached under her armpits and pulled, but she was not there. I mean the bottom half of her was not there. She had been blown in half."

We stared at the spot he was describing and suddenly, at the same

moment, saw the gleaming, flesh-colored plastic thigh and leg of a
baby doll. I nudged it with my shoe, wanting to pick it up as a kind
of gruesome souvenir, but restrained myself. It seemed a coincidence so bludgeoning that it made you disgusted with reality and
the atrocious nature of a war that could unleash such banalities of
heartbreak and despair. Joseph shook his head — as if there were
something absurd and unsubtle and ludicrously contrived about
that leg lying there in the heat of afternoon — then holding out
his arms before the bomb site, he said, "All this . . . how embarrassing."

Beginning our drive back to Beirut, we passed under a poster of
Hassan Nasrallah that declared, in Arabic, DEFEAT HAS GONE
WITH YOUR PATIENCE. Of course, the poster meant to praise the
patience of the Lebanese people in their victory against the Israelis, but the real meaning lay in the ambiguities of the syntax. "What
have they won?" Joseph asked softly. He stared into the dust cloud
billowing from the military convoy ahead of us. "Here, they declare
a holiday for the liberation of the south. But why not a day about
Qana's dead? We do not care for the dead."

He looked at me, then looked away, and I told him that we could
talk about something else — but he cut me off midsentence. "I
hope that this is the story you are after. I hope you are satisfied, Mr.
Tom, with what you have seen. But what did they win? They lost
children, houses, they lost the trust of the people. I left the Red
Cross because of the war. Do you remember *Top Gun*? Tom Cruise?
He says the first rule of engagement is that you do not kill civilians."

4

In September 1982, between eight hundred and two thousand Palestinians (depending on whose estimates you credit, Israeli intelligence's or the Palestinian Red Crescent's) were slaughtered in
Shatila and in the southern Beirut neighborhood of Sabra. The
Christian Maronite militia, outraged by the assassination of their
leader, Bashir Gemayel — his head was blown off his body by a two-
hundred-pound bomb — bayoneted men, women, and children,
trampled babies to death, slaughtering whole families in retaliation
against the PLO, which had been driven out of Beirut by Israel a

short time before the massacre. Gemayel's militia carried out the killings, but Ariel Sharon's invading army looked on and refused to intervene, occasionally launching flares over the area so that the two nights of hard work could be carried out more efficiently. And once the killing was over, they loaned Gemayel's men bulldozers to facilitate the digging of mass graves. Hundreds of thousands of Israelis protested, but the Israeli government never condemned the incident.

But as Hicham Kayed, a Palestinian filmmaker, led me through Shatila's poorly lit, narrow, winding streets, raw sewage spilling out from pipes here and there, I was more focused on keeping up with him and trying not to collide with anyone than on thinking about the massacre. As I stumbled and slipped on the hard-beaten dirt-and-gravel street, I kept glancing into the small, rudimentary storefronts: an open doorway leading to shelves piled with canned goods or clothes or used automobile parts and tires, and a surprising number of electronics shops selling all kinds of ancient gadgets and computer components. We were going to meet Hicham's fixer, a man who knew Shatila intimately and secured permission for Hicham's shoots.

At the fixer's apartment block, we climbed narrow, unlit stairs to the rooftop, from which we could see the entire neighborhood, rooftop courtyards like the one we looked out from looming over the expanse of cinder-block buildings. The sun was just starting to set, the moon had risen, and there was a heavy fog creeping in from the Mediterranean. Down below, you could make out thick vines of electric cable dangling just above the heads of passersby. The swooping lengths of bundled wires were fastened to the sides of the buildings in the most casual manner by what looked like U bolts, and though there must have been some form of urban planning, the jungle of branching wires indicated the haphazard, improvised aspect of Shatila. This gave the whole neighborhood a provisional feel, as if there was an unspoken understanding among the Palestinians that their exile in Lebanon would end, and everyone would exercise "the right of return" — go back to their homes in Palestine and resume their lives before the *Nakba* (Arabic for "catastrophe"), what Palestinians call the flight from their homes during the 1948 to 1949 war between the Arab states and the newly founded state of Israel. A war that the Israelis, by contrast, call the

War of Independence. Between *catastrophe* and *independence,* there is a vast and fiercely contentious literature about the founding of Israel, war atrocities committed on both sides, whether the Palestinians fled or were driven out by the Israelis. But up on the roof, the Sabra and Shatila massacre and the *Nakba* seemed historical events only.

We sat on an assortment of old wooden and plastic chairs while chickens roamed free from their coop, pecking for grain, their little eyes focused monomaniacally on that next kernel of feed corn, their heads jerking up and down as they wandered among our chairs, taking no notice of us. Hicham pointed to the chickens and joked, "Look at them, they all look like they are running for office."

He had talked earlier that day about the way every political party in Lebanon was mired in its own corruption. They were all hypocrites spouting democratic slogans, he thought, and all they cared about was maintaining power. "At least Hassan Nasrallah and Hezbollah say what they stand for. Maybe I don't like what they stand for, but at least you know who they are." When I asked him if there were any younger politicians who gave him hope, he looked at me incredulously, smiled, and shrugged. "No. Absolutely not." Amused by the gormlessness of my question, he asked, "Why would there be? The Lebanese president must be a Maronite Christian, the prime minister a Sunni Muslim, and the speaker of parliament a Shiite. Each of them wants to be the boss, and not just for their term of office — but forever. So whoever is in power tries to change the law to keep himself in power. This is why they are afraid to give Palestinians citizenship — a civil right that Palestinians should not have to ask for. The Christians want to give Christian Palestinians citizenship because they think that will give Christians more power. But not Muslim Palestinians — the Christians are afraid they will support Hezbollah. So to us to be a citizen means almost nothing. And many Lebanese still resent the way the PLO carried on a war against Israel from our soil. But what we are asking for is this — our civil rights. So no group or party in Lebanon wants to give you your right as a right but as a business move."

Some Muslims are more sympathetic than the Christians to the Palestinian's situation, but religious solidarity doesn't go as far as you would expect. The PLO, with its often arrogant, gun-toting, thuggish behavior toward the local Shia population, alienated many southern Lebanese. Many blamed the PLO and the Palestinians in general for Israel's continued military presence. Plus, the various sects, especially the Christians, worry how the Palestinians might change the way power is divvied up in Lebanon. And so the Palestinians are denied Lebanese citizenship and are subjected to legalized discrimination.

"Because I am not a Lebanese citizen and have not asked to be one," Hicham said, "the law makes it difficult, if not impossible, for me to inherit my father's house. I might be able to live in it, but I cannot sell it or rent it. There is even a chance that it might go to a Muslim religious organization," a possibility that gave him great amusement. "And for years there were seventy professions that Palestinians were barred from entering. Those restrictions have been loosened, but you still have to be a member of a professional syndicate, and only citizens can join them. And since we are denied our civil rights, and are not citizens, we cannot join, and so we cannot work." Professions such as architect, engineer, doctor, pharmacist, lawyer, and journalist were proscribed. Hicham waved his hand as if gesturing to the whole camp: "And you see how everything is old and in need of repair and how crowded everything is. We cannot build beyond the borders of the camp so we have to build up. And for years we were forbidden from bringing in building materials, and the army makes sure of that by the checkpoints they man outside the camps. The government claims that if we are allowed to bring in materials and repair our homes, then Israel will think we no longer wish to return to Palestine. So the government is really taking care of us by not letting us live in decent housing." He gave me an arch look. "The government is looking out for us by supporting our right of return by forcing us to live in overcrowded, substandard conditions." He grinned and shook his head.

All the while the fixer's wife, a young, pregnant, black-haired woman in a headscarf, brought coffee and fruit that she peeled and cut into quarters and handed to each of us on plastic plates, encouraging us to eat, eat. Her little boy ran in circles, pretending to be one of the airplanes that you could see in the distance. A minaret's loudspeaker announced a funeral service for the next day, the crackling voice high-pitched and resonating in the calm evening air. The moon had risen and Hicham's fixer passed out water pipes to us, what they call a "hubble bubble" for the bubbling sound the water makes when you inhale. We took a toke, drawing the cool smoke into our lungs. When Hicham finished exhaling, he said, "We are like your American Indians. This is our reservation. We have control over our internal affairs in the camp, but what is there to control when you cannot own property, you cannot work outside the camp except illegally in the worst jobs no Lebanese wants, you cannot go to school unless there is a place left over by the Lebanese, and you cannot have any say in Lebanese politics?" And then he shrugged at the absurdity of his own situation. "Yes, of all possible governments, this one is the worst."

5

We smoked in silence for a while. Staring out over Shatila, I couldn't help but think of what it must have been like to live through such a massacre, and of the Palestinian's determination to endure by rebuilding the camp after its destruction. Only a few days before, I'd visited Quneitra, a Syrian town in the Golan Heights — a town that had been "razed to the ground." The very term — razed — had always seemed like literary artifice from histories of the war between Carthage and Rome. But in Quneitra, the word was inescapable.

Before pulling out of Quneitra at the end of the 1973 Yom Kippur War, the Israeli army evicted the thirty-seven thousand Syrian Arabs living there, then stripped buildings of fixtures, windows, doors, anything that could be carted off, right down to the hinges and knobs. Once the town was completely picked clean, bulldozers and tractors moved in and knocked down most of the buildings. It was odd, disturbingly odd, to hear bird song in the clear, quiet air, and to see a herd of cows, heads bowed to graze among the ruins overgrown with flowers and weeds, roses run wild in what used to be somebody's garden. Now, Quneitra served the dual purpose of a Syrian memorial and propaganda site.

When, later that day, I had ducked into a carpenter's shop in a Palestinian camp near Quneitra, I met an old man who invited me to his home. His house was modest but comfortable: cushions and an industrial-style brown carpet covered the concrete floor, a ceiling fan whirled close to a modest chandelier, family pictures and crockery were stacked in a wooden hutch, and plastic roses sat snug in a wall sconce. This was luxury compared to the bare, unadorned

Palestinian homes I'd seen in Lebanon. The signs of domestic order — including an old computer and a TV — were hard won. "All
you see in our camp we have built by ourselves," he told me. "We
do not have paved streets, no sewer system, no drinking water. People build their own sewage system, and it flows to an open outfall
pipe at the end of the village. The international community keeps
promising to improve things, but it's just a lot of noise. Nothing
changes. Still, our lives here are much better than in Lebanon. At
least in Syria a Palestinian can work in any job, and we have most of
the same rights as Syrian citizens. We are issued identity cards that
are temporary, but they are valid until our return to Palestine."

As he spoke the room filled with his neighbors, who listened intently. Most of them were too young to have experienced the *Nakba*
or even remember a time when the right of return still seemed a
real possibility. He paused to sip his tea, then continued in a low,
strong voice, staring straight ahead. "In 1948, the Israeli army invaded my village. Right before my eyes they killed my mother, and
four of my brothers. My father was hit by a bullet and died. We left
the house while shots were still being fired. I was three years old,
and I remember it with complete clarity. The house was blown up,
and we were forced to go to Lebanon, then Syria. When we got
here, we had nothing but tents, we had no shoes, no clothes against
the cold. My first school was a tent, and my teacher wept for us. To
live in such conditions, in a tent, was like living in a spider web in
the heart of a well. I was raised here until preparatory school, then
I went to Damascus to high school, and then to Saudi Arabia."

He paused again to sip his tea, then said in a quiet voice, "It was
like a lake of blood, and the deeds are stained with blood." I assumed he was speaking in metaphors, until he asked, "Would you
like to see the deeds?" He called his nephew on a cell phone. A few
minutes later a heavyset young man of about twenty arrived on a
motorbike to show me the deeds to the family's property in what is
now Israel. I could see that the paper was discolored with blood,
the legalese obscured by three long, brown, faded stains. "The
deeds were found by accident when my uncle and cousin came
over to our house — after the soldiers dynamited it — to see if
there was anything they could do to help us. I saw my home blown
up. But the worst thing I saw, the worst thing I ever saw, was my
brother, still a baby, suckling at my dead mother's breast."

This was no rehearsed performance trotted out for my benefit.

The effort to say this, to remember it, had cost him, and it had also cost us to listen. The old man's words seemed to have nothing in common with the doublespeak of Lebanon's ruling elite or Syria's police state under Bashar al-Assad. Everywhere in Damascus propaganda photos of the president stared down at you, declaiming in Arabic and English: I BELIEVE IN SYRIA AND I BELIEVE IN JUS-TICE. Bashar's father, the previous dictator, had once, after putting down a rebellion by the Sunni Muslim Brotherhood, bulldozed whole neighborhoods in the Syrian city of Hama and killed an estimated twenty thousand Sunnis. Over Quneitra there was a banner that declared, apparently without irony, PEACE IS OUR TARGET: THE PEACE WHICH RETRIEVES OUR OCCUPIED SYRIAN GOLAN.

But I found that the old man had accusations and agendas as well. I kept thinking of a quote from Robert Frost. "Politics is an extravagance," he wrote, "an extravagance about *grievances*. And poetry is an extravagance about *grief.*" I confess that it was easier to accept the old man's grief than his grievance. His voice hardened and grew louder, almost fierce: "The Israelis," he said, "should return to the place where they came from. The Arab Jews, we love them, they are our brothers. But we wish that the colonial European Jews would go home to Europe." He paused for a moment and said, "The blood of my brother is on these deeds. This proves that this land is for us, and not for them. Our only hope is that America will wake up. The Jewish lobby manipulates American opinion, even though they know nothing about Palestinians. Daily, the Israelis commit crimes that Europe and America do nothing about. The Nazis' crimes are documented, and their crimes are as bad as the Nazis. The war criminals should be prosecuted, but the Americans help them. And as Arabs and Palestinians, we do not know how to talk with America and Europe. We must learn to do that better so that people in America will see the truth. I saw on Al Jazeera a film that told the story of Israeli crimes. But the Israelis know how to get their story told. My last word is this: we will resist the Jews by word, by sword, until the last drop of blood."

6

Later that same evening, having left Quneitra, I spoke with a high-ranking member of the Syrian government. He wore a dark blue

suit, a black-and-silver silk tie, and displayed the smooth manner of
a professional diplomat — the courtly, subtle smile that indulges
an opponent in his errors, the calm, reflective voice that seems
somehow edged with steel. He had received his doctorate from a
European university, and as we talked, he confessed a penchant for
Graham Greene — for Greene's obsession with betrayal, his weighing of treacheries and brutalities committed for good causes and
enlightened reasons, his portrayal of characters who are inevitably
corrupted by their own goodness. We sat in the minister's office, a
well-appointed, utterly nondescript room in one of the ministries
in Damascus, and I was immediately drawn to his intelligence, his
nuanced explanation of Syria's support for the Palestinian people
in their struggle with the Israeli Defense Force. That, and his deep
appreciation for the opportunity to meet a writer described to him
as "an important American poet." In other words, it was farcical; it
was like fog talking to fog, his words designed to get his message
across and appeal to my vanity, my words to appeal to his civility.

Meanwhile, I kept wondering how much personal responsibility,
if any, he bore for the imprisonment of Syrian activists who recently
received brutally hard sentences, twelve years in the case of prominent human-rights activist Dr. Kamal al-Labwani. Who was this
functionary, really? Who was I, talking to him? It was clear to me,
however, when I left his office, that I had made a good impression,
and he, in fact, had made a good impression on me. I liked him.
He offered to do anything he could to make my trip more enjoy-
able, and I have no doubt that he would have. Like him, I was shov-
ing feeling out of sight, avoiding either grief or grievance in order
to maintain a cordial decorum. I was as guilty as anyone of speaking the language of policy.

On my way out of the ministry building, I remembered a kitschy
painting at the Quneitra propaganda center: Bashar al-Assad and
his father, dressed in white robes and mounted on white Arabian
steeds, their hands brandishing sabers at an enemy in flight, no
doubt the Israelis being driven from the field by heroic *père et fils*.
Somebody had painted the thing, and somebody had placed it
right next to the door with the obvious intention of glorifying the
Assads (though to my mind it emphasized the Assads' wounded
pride at having lost the Golan). I got a weird sense of multiple
exposure, the old man's straight talk overlaid by my minister's
spokesmanese overlaid by the painting's anti-Israeli mythmaking.

But Assad wasn't the only one putting out propaganda. As I traveled back and forth between Lebanon and Syria, every government source I spoke with — and without exception these ordinary men and women were courteous, hospitable, even likable — directed me to websites showing powder-burned children and heroic rescue workers pulling them from rubble. Another click of the mouse would link me to almost hysterical charges and countercharges about the authenticity of such photos. It's as if each side's partisans — and certainly our own media is no exception — fear that the emotional immediacy of grief will verify the righteousness of one side's grievance, or one's sense of grievance will be weakened by having to feel the other's grief.

But given the hard conditions in the Lebanese Palestinian camps that I visited, the real extravagance would be decoupling politics and grievance from poetry and grief — hence the old man's desire that the Palestinians find a way to get their side of the story told in the West, not as propaganda but as a collective truth. Mahmoud Darwish, who, if there were such a thing as a Palestinian homeland, would be the unofficial Palestinian national poet, a man who endured *al Nakba,* as well as the personal *Nakba* that every refugee undergoes, has a poem called "Murdered and Unknown":

> Murdered, and unknown. No forgetfulness gathers them
> and no remembrance scatters them . . . they're forgotten in
> winter's grass gone brown along the highway between
> two long stories about heroism and suffering.
> "I am the victim." "No. I alone am
> the victim . . ."

The voices seem to compete for the honor of victimhood, as if Darwish were satirizing as much as memorializing the collective wound. Or as a Hezbollah official said to me about the Israelis, quoting an Arabic proverb, "He hit me and then he cried." Of course, it didn't seem to occur to this official that this same logic might also apply to Hezbollah.

Once you refuse to see someone else's grief and focus strictly on your own grievance, it becomes far easier to reduce your rival victim to a villain — someone you need to protect yourself against and, if necessary, harm before he can harm you. But in Qana, where Joseph wanted to kill the woman who said that her child was a sacrifice to Hassan Nasrallah, he resisted the impulse. True, his grievance sprang from his own grief at what he saw, and certainly his urge to kill her was tied up with his sense of grievance, possibly with his Christian upbringing, his lifelong experiences of war, and his understandable anger at what he thought was her unfeeling response. But some powerful inkling of the woman's grief, her need to see her child's suffering and death as a sacrifice for the community rather than just another random event of war, must have kept him from harming her, must have let him get on with what he'd come to do: save lives, not take them.

But Darwish's poem hints at something darker. Most of the people I met — the old Palestinian man, Joseph, the people I talked to in Qana — were just trying to lead their lives. Some of their relatives indeed had been murdered, and were, for all the world cared, virtually unknown. No one would much notice if the survivors thought of themselves as victims or not.

7

It was pitch-black as Hicham drove us back to downtown Beirut, the night strangely edgy, the streets almost deserted except for soldiers in camouflage who manned tanks and armored vehicles at checkpoints throughout the city. The UN had just approved the formation of a special tribunal to look into — what else? — the assassination in 2005 of Rafik Hariri, a Sunni and the former prime minister of Lebanon — and one of the richest men in the world — who was killed by a car bomb of three hundred kilograms of C-4, the explosive equivalent to one thousand kilograms of TNT. Seventeen other people, "murdered and unknown," died with him in the blast. Because Hariri had had a conflict with Bashar al-Assad, it was widely assumed that the Syrians were behind the assassination. But then a story was also circulating that he'd been killed by a Palestinian suicide bomber, a follower of Osama bin Laden. And there were other stories, all equally plausible, all equally unsupported by hard evidence.

I saw Hicham tense up when we drove through a neighborhood in which hundreds of flickering candles, celebrating the approval of the Hariri tribunal, lined the streets. While making a left turn, we were stopped by a group of Sunni men. They wanted to know if we lived in the neighborhood, and if we didn't, what were we doing here? Hicham explained that he lived on the next block, and so they let us pass. I had never seen Beirut so deserted, and it seemed that the bombs, and the anticipation of violence at the announcement of the tribunal, had worked a kind of fatal magic on the populace. Everyone was hunkered indoors, eyes glued to TV screens for news of the next bomb, the next killing, the next atrocity in a never-ending series of atrocities.

After Hicham parked the car and we said a hasty good night, I took a cab back to my hotel. I paced nervously in my room, waiting for some sign of violence to break out, for the pro-Syrians to attack the Hariri supporters, and vice versa. And then I heard it: the rattle and crack of gunfire down in the street just below my window. I ran to the light switch and turned off my lights, but my curiosity got the best of me, and like a fool I opened my balcony doors, stepped out, and looked down into the street. Two small boys were running away from a string of lit firecrackers.

The moon was high now, and I could see on the horizon a silver light that must have been reflected back into the sky by the invisible sea. Below, in the dark, a little farther down the street, a Lebanese soldier, palm leaves woven in his helmet mesh for camouflage, lolled behind his tank's gun turret, talking amiably with another soldier. His friend was making an obscene gesture known the world over, and the one up on the tank burst out laughing. I gripped the balcony with both hands and tried to catch my breath, all the while half expecting to be shot and knowing that I wouldn't be. I caught a heavy whiff of jacaranda mingling with the sulfurous odor of gunpowder drifting up to my window. I was shaking with fear, and felt utterly ridiculous, a real drama queen. *Welcome to Lebanon,* I said to myself, *welcome to Lebanon.*

JAY KIRK

Hotels Rwanda

FROM *GQ*

ON OUR SEVENTH DAY in Rwanda, somewhere between Kibuye and Ruhengeri, on yet another devastated dirt road winding through yet another breathtaking landscape, Darren informed us that the hair on his arms appeared to be growing much more quickly than usual. Not at an alarming rate, but still, more growth than he'd ever noticed back in Los Angeles.

He put an arm between the front seats of the Land Rover so we could see for ourselves. Ernest and I agreed: his arms looked ape-y. One expected to be changed by travel; one looked for little symptoms in oneself, signs of alteration, but did this count as a valid transformation?

Ernest had never heard of such a thing. Once, he'd had a client who'd come all the way from Australia just to punch a mountain gorilla in the face, but nothing quite like this.

Jenn and Michael were in the Nissan Patrol somewhere behind us. We'd passed them not long ago, pulled over to the side of the road, handing out crayons to a group of children dressed in rags. Maridadi, their driver, was standing off to the side, laughing at the mayhem. All their friends back in New Hampshire thought they were crazy to come here on vacation. Darren had come to make a documentary, and I was here writing a piece about the alleged rebirth of the country's tourism trade, but Michael and Jenn had just come along for the experience.

Of course, by now we had each privately grown suspect of our own motives for taking a vacation to a country forever defined by bloodshed. At the worst moments, I wondered if we were soul-sick vampires, in search of souvenirs among the ashes. Or were my friends and I just benumbed Westerners looking for something to startle us awake? Very likely we were not so different from the man willing to travel halfway round the world just to punch a mountain gorilla in the face. Sometimes you'll do anything to remember you're alive.

And who's to say? Perhaps the Australian who traveled to Rwanda just to punch a mountain gorilla is not so very different from the Hutu who, when asked why he had participated in the genocide, reported that "killing was less wearisome than farming."

But the killing is long over. The country of Rwanda has woken from its dreadful nightmare and is open for business. If you believe most reports, relative stability has been achieved, the country is truly safe, and the borders are more or less secure from incursions by the ousted Hutu militias that still haunt the contiguous forests of the Democratic Republic of Congo. The whole country has a feel of rejuvenation. The capital city of Kigali is thriving. Everywhere you look, there are cranes poised like red metal giraffes, slabs of concrete bristling with rebar, and cairns of clean bricks piled up along Boulevard de la Révolution. There's a new American embassy going up, and they're rebuilding the parliamentary Conseil National de Développement, damaged during the war. The Supreme Court building is getting a fresh coat of paint, and on every other corner is a shiny new bank. And while tourists aren't exactly flocking to Rwanda yet, the annual numbers are not unimpressive: sixteen thousand visited in 2003; thirty-one thousand in 2006 — this in contrast to the sixty-one tourists who came in 1994, the year of the genocide.

To its credit, the tourism board, or Office Rwandais du Tourisme et des Parcs Nationaux — whom we will come to know affectionately as the ORTPN — has not tried to sweep its nation's violent history under the rug in order to lure tourists, but has actually integrated it into the package, offering visits to very graphic and disturbing genocide memorials right alongside its ample eco-menu of awe-inspiring biodiversions. Though Rwanda is one of the poorer nations in Africa, so of course it needs the dollars, I do not believe it means to capitalize on the tragedy at all. On the other hand, there is this other thing the tourism board *might* capitalize upon, wittingly or not. And that is that there is no other place on earth where you can visit mountain gorillas one day, discover the true cosmic dimensions of the banana the next, feel haunted and overwhelmed and harrowed to your very brink, and for the same price of admission, feel more awake than you have ever felt.

Maybe it's the cold bucket of history over the head. Maybe it's the collective effort of everyone around you to stay conscious, the shocked look of so many people who are still just waking up from the worst nightmare of their lives to realize that, yes, it was all for real. And while it's true that you may question whether or not you were fully awake before you got here, you will also probably spend an inordinate amount of time trying to lull yourself back to sleep, wherever you can find alcohol, because part of you will realize that being awake, really awake — well, it's just not in your nature. That is, if you're like me and you hail from the land of the Xbox, and you've become accustomed to — even begun to desire — the substitution of the virtual for the real, you probably prefer the dream to the directly experienced. But no matter how stuck you are in your digital simulator, however "experientially avoidant" you may be (as I was recently diagnosed by a cognitive-behavioral therapist), you will not remain immune to this odd sensation of waking up in Rwanda to discover, however disconcertingly at first, that not only do you have hair growing out of your arms, but your body also appears to possess these extra dimensions you had not taken into account of late. That you have been going around for some time a mere half-awake version of yourself. Just as you now realize that all along you've been eating these things that bear only a half-awake resemblance to a banana. And this is because, in Rwanda, a banana possesses at least seven dimensions, whereas in America, like most everything else, you get two at best.

On our third day, we drove toward Akagera National Park, where we hoped to see the sort of big game that roams in abundance in bordering Tanzania. As we travel east, the landscape broadens, the banana groves thicken, and my eyes cease to sting from the haze of smog that clings to Kigali. Along the way, we see crews of men in tart pink uniforms doing roadwork with pickaxes, clearing rubble or digging ditches. These are the many convicted *génocidaires*. As young men, most of them were recruited into the civilian Hutu militia, or Interahamwe, and trained to kill with an efficiency that

would make the Rwandan genocide the most rapid in human history.

As we get farther into the countryside, we see these same men
working the fields with machetes, always dressed in the same easily
spotted outfits. The sight of men in pink is commonplace, if not
quite mundane. They are everywhere, chopping at the weeds. The
sight of the killers becomes ordinary in the worst imaginable sense
of the word.

There are virtually no cars on the roads, only countless pedestri-
ans moving along both shoulders and overladen bicycles wobbling
out of the way as quickly as possible as we fly through villages.
Women wear *kitenge,* plain floral wraps, maybe matched with a
D.A.R.E. T-shirt or one emblazoned with Ren and Stimpy or Hulk
Hogan, babies tied to their backs, baskets filled with bananas or
cassava balanced on their heads — not only these but also large,
unwieldy bundles of firewood, men and women alike performing
the feat, head-balancing large mud bricks, foam twin mattresses
stacked four high, cases of orange Fanta, small engines, battered
plaid suitcases, sacks of onions and carrots. I see people carrying
backpacks — backpacks! — on their heads. Only the truly onerous
hauls are saved for the national pack animal — the bicycle — upon
which they somehow miraculously transport even more mind-bog-
gling quantities of freight: eight cases of Primus beer balanced on
the crossbar, a hut's worth of sorghum, and always, always bikes
struggling under great clumsy pyramids of the plastic yellow jerricans, salvaged ten-gallon oil containers, a dozen or more at a time,
which are used to transport water for its every conceivable use.

On the hillsides, here and there, are shiny corrugated metal–
roofed shanties, little Levittowns along the edges of the coffee
plantations. These are new villages, Ernest says, built for Tutsi exiles back after the war. Before joining the Rwandan Patriotic Front
and returning home, Ernest himself had lived in exile as a boy. He
had fled with his parents in the early '6os, shortly after Rwanda
gained independence and the first wave of massacres followed the
handover from the Belgian colonizers to the Hutu majority. By
1963, as many as fourteen thousand Tutsi are estimated to have
been killed. Prior to this, the Tutsi had enjoyed a position of privilege, having been left with a modicum of the status they'd held for
hundreds of years as feudal lords, before the arrival of the Europeans. By 1990 there were between two hundred thousand and five

hundred thousand Tutsi living in exile. It would later be out of this great displaced populace that the RPF would build its army and fight its way to victory under Major General Paul Kagame. In Kenya, where the Ntagozera family had fled, Ernest eventually got a job as a professional guide for Abercrombie & Kent, one of the big safari operators there. For eighteen years, he took clients out on tours of his adopted land, including a few big stars like Kim Basinger, James Earl Jones, and Robert Wagner. In 1985 he took out the Holy Father himself, Pope John Paul II.

"He loved the animals a lot," Ernest says. "He blessed every single animal that we met," including one baby rhino who'd been specially flown in to the pope's camp from an animal orphanage in Nairobi on a DC-3 — no doubt in hopes of getting his kind taken off the endangered-species list. On the other hand, during the genocide, the Vatican's effectiveness would be limited to a synod of African bishops called together in Rome, where discussions were quickly bogged down by lengthy and irrelevant debate over liturgical vestments, polygamy, and drumming in church.

After the war, Ernest's mother, who died in 2006 at the age of eighty-four, finally returned from exile. "She always said, 'I don't care if I step in Rwanda and I die the next day. I just want to go home.' It was the most important thing to her in the world," he says.

We are stopped in the road, waiting for a herd of goats being led across by a small boy with a switch, and Ernest watches the boy as if watching a part of his own memory.

"She was a little bit sad because my father never got to see home again," he says. He gives the horn a toot to hurry along the memory. His father, who had worked as a professional hunter, had died in exile. Most of Ernest's family, of course, who did not go into exile, who stayed behind, were killed. His uncle Xavier was killed in Kibungo prefecture with his wife and seven children. In all he lost 122 relatives.

As we get farther into the country, mud huts with corrugated-metal roofs give way to mud huts with thatched roofs, and little cheering kids leap out of the red dust left in Maridadi's wake to howl at us. *"Agachupa! Agachupa!"*

"What are they saying?"

"Agachupa," Ernest says. "They want your plastic water bottles." Our empties. To carry water on their long walk to school. They are

the children's version of the ubiquitous yellow jerricans. We can't drink enough water to keep up with the demand, but we try our best.

Inside the park, we are now eating Maridadi's dust — blood-red particles of laterite soil, to be geologically specific. It coats the inside of the Land Rover and within a few hours will turn my white shirt pink. We are in bush country — a dry and sparsely treed woodland of low acacias and termite mounds that look like Khmer temples — grinding along a road that is entirely without mercy or forgiveness or hope of redemption.

Ernest identifies a few trees: *Grevillea robusta, Euphorbia candelabrum*. He points out a blob of crumpled blue tinfoil in a tree. *Lamprotornis superbus*. Superb starling. Before starting his own private company, Ernest was director of tourism for the national parks and worked steadily to help resurrect those parks, most of which had been free-for-all zones for poachers and illegal timber interests until the government began to focus its energies on preservation, tourism, and subsidizing community projects to keep locals from poaching wildlife. Ernest himself trained an army of professional guides, trackers, and park rangers and personally oversaw the building of countless lodges, trails, roads, etc., while the ORTPN secured international funding to save the parks' native flora and fauna and began educating villagers that it really was in their best interest not to deplete the objects of wonder that brought in tourists, since with those tourists came money that, through revenue sharing, is now funneled back into the villages for schools, medicine, irrigation projects, and the like. Boundaries were demarcated. The presence of armed soldiers put a stop to logging and curtailed illegal hunting. There are now plans under way to restock rhinoceros in Akagera, and eventually the same will be done with elephants.

"Oh, look there," Ernest says. "Impala." It is our first African wildlife sighting. The impala look like your garden-variety suburban white-tailed deer but with lyre-shaped horns. They graze, get nervous, then bound off. After an hour we have seen more impala, butterflies, a few more starling *superbus*, and a sun-bleached cow skull, but not much else.

"It is too hot," Ernest says. "The animals are in there, in the shade." He points at the endless tawny grass. Ordinarily, he says, this area would be chock-full of zebra. But it hasn't rained for some time, everything is brown, and the animals have gone higher in search of water and greener grass. Of course, a lot of the animals were poached for food during the war. The entire time we will pass only one other group of tourists, an older couple with their college-age son, to whom, as we skirted their vehicle at a tricky spot in the road, Darren grinned out the window and delivered a cheerful if unreciprocated "Howdy."

"They are French," Ernest said. "I do not think they say 'Howdy.'" He has a sour look on his face when he says how the Rwandan government blames the French for having helped facilitate the genocide. Their involvement was plain to all Rwandans, he practically shouts. It was the French who sold machetes to the Hutu, French soldiers who trained the militia, the French who provided refuge for deposed Hutu extremist leaders.

After another hour or more of gameless viewing, we climb up to a stunning view over the rounded rolling hills and a slate blue lake. We get out at the top to stretch and pee. The acacia trees are splatted on the hillside below like meaningless Rorschachs.

"Did you dudes see the lion?" Michael says.

Frustrated that he hasn't been able to show us more game — any game, really — Ernest suggests that, it being close to lunch, we head to the lodge, and then we can go visit one of the tea plantations in the afternoon. We'll have better luck looking for big game early tomorrow morning.

Apparently, Maridadi knows a shortcut to the lodge. But no sooner have we accepted defeat and started back than Maridadi's truck lurches to a stop ahead of us.

"Look!" Ernest says. "Baboons!"

They are under a fig tree. A group of maybe twenty olive baboons. A few are in the branches, but most are on the ground below. The dominant male sits in the shade while the others take turns presenting their asses to him to inspect at close range, lick, and then dismiss with an approbatory smack.

"Have you ever seen one attack a human?" Darren asks.

"No, but I've seen them fight amongst themselves. They are very vicious. They have teeth like a dog's."

Next we see a group of gazelle, wagging their tails like puppies. A few topi spring by, mixed in with a few oribi, just to confuse us. Then a herd of eland — the largest of the antelope species — makes a grand, quivering-dewlapped appearance. As if choreographed

for maximum effect, below them a giant herd of black Cape buffalo thunders by in the opposite direction over the hill. As I follow
with my binoculars, watching as they make their way over the crest,
my view is suddenly obstructed by a yellow webbed blur. I focus,
glass upward. Refocus, glass a little higher. What exactly do I have
here?

"Holy mother of God!" Darren shouts.

Gasps all around. A giraffe! It is no more than twenty yards away,
nipping the leaves off the upper reaches of a nearby tree. Where
did it come from? While it chews, it stares at us unafraid. When we
drive closer, it does not run away. Then, as if from nowhere, two
more giraffes materialize out of the trees. Then six.

"Holy shit!" Perched in the back seat window, Darren pans his
camera over the gathering of extraterrestrials. "This is fucking obscene!"

With their black-and-yellow fur, their stubby horns like eye stalks,
and the way they move, lurching almost aquatically, they look like
gigantic yet infinitely graceful banana slugs. They are hyperclose.
One giraffe, even more gigantic than the rest, steps out in front of
us and blocks the road to get at the sweet tips of an acacia. They are
so strange-looking. Despite their apparent benevolence, it is not a
stretch to imagine laser rays shooting from their eyes, scorching
everything in sight. In the other truck, Jenn's awestruck face is
pressed to the window, gaping at the giraffe, silently mouthing the
words, it seems to me, *I love you.*

"All roads must go somewhere, right?" Ernest sounds as if he's trying to convince himself. Though, technically, we are really only interested in the road that will take us to the lodge. I guess we should
have been tipped off that we were lost hours earlier when Ernest
started saying things under his breath like "This road is bothering
me" and "This road keeps appearing and disappearing." And then,
long after we had driven clear of anything resembling an actual
road, "See? There are tire tracks in the grass. Somebody has come
through here."

So much, we thought, for Maridadi's shortcut.

After an hour or so, when we ask if we can get out to take a leak,
Ernest won't let us. "I do not trust this grass," he says. "There may
be lions."

I duck from the window as the encroaching bush scrapes against the car. Thorny branches screech like bats across the windshield. We are now just following a faint path in the grass, going deeper and deeper into the bush. Despite an occasional sigh, which is more of a trailed-out baritone *zzzzzzz,* Ernest never loses his cool. A man must learn a great deal of patience when he has had to live in exile for thirty years.

Finally we stop, and he and Maridadi have a tense tailgate conference. When he comes back, he says he thinks we've basically gotten off the road and onto some kind of cow path, but that it would make more sense to continue down the cow path than to return down the four or five hours of rutted and directionless path we came in on. If we went back the way we came, it'd be dark before we got off whatever path we're on — assuming, that is, we were even going in the right direction.

"We might be sleeping in the bush tonight," Ernest says.

The notion that we are on a cow path is soon confirmed by cows blocking our way — giant Ankole cattle with eight-foot-long horns — and then we eventually come to a small cluster of huts at the base of a hill. We had actually passed this squalid habitation a while back. There is a small, greasy fire outside the main hut, and a handful of children creep toward us and stand around the Rover staring, shyly responding to Ernest's questions. *"Amakuru?" "Meza." "Nibyiza."* After a little while, a wizened skinny old herdsman comes out wearing a purple sweatshirt that looks like he must have found it buried in his backyard. Ernest and the man exchange words for a few moments before the man gets in the back seat with Darren and the warm reek of livestock and banana beer fills the cab. He chats with Ernest in Kinyarwanda ("He's telling me, 'What do you expect, it's a bush road!'"), and then, about twenty minutes later, we come to a visible fork in the cow path. Ernest gives him a few francs and the man hops out and begins his long walk back to his hut. We quickly come to the road, and in no time we're passing a sign to the entrance of the Akagera Game Lodge that says PLEASE BEWARE OF BABOONS.

After my shower, and the expulsion of a few pints of bloody grit from my nostrils — enough laterite soil to build my own miniature imitation Khmer termite mound — I go down to meet my companions. Coming out of my room, I nearly trip over a couple of wolfy-looking baboons in the corridor, so I take the long way down to the poolside bar.

Evidently, after the war, they had a hard time getting this lodge back in running order. This is one of the great victories, so far, for Rwandan tourism, however chilling the story is in its own way. During the genocide, when the place had shut down, baboons had taken over the abandoned resort and turned it into their own fortress on the hill. Then, when the ORTPN reopened the lodge, in 2003, the squatters refused to go peacefully. They'd been living here almost ten years, hundreds of them, holed up like bandit kings. They had the best view in the park, a safe haven from their natural predators, the leopards. The government couldn't just pass out eviction notices. Rangers had to come in with Kalashnikovs and clear the place, fighting it out with the baboons all the way down to the front gate, all just to reclaim it for the *turistas*. After they patched the bullet holes, swept up the glass, and hosed off the tennis courts, they were open for business again. Ever since, the baboons have been exiled to the forest, presumably regrouping, making the occasional sortie into the dining room, waiting for their chance to take it all back.

I find Michael and Jenn down by the pool, lounging on the brink of an unbelievable panorama of the park's valleys below. Across the lawn is a conical, mansion-sized thatched hut going up on the edge of the property, which I am later told will be the presidential suite. Michael made inquiries about getting it for us, but it is not yet ready for guests. Just below the pool, at the edge of the grounds, near the woods, is an old stone cistern. Pink blossoms float on the muddy water.

There are few tourists in this grand resort. There is the French family with the college boy we passed earlier in the park before getting lost. The son is drinking a Coke and looks suicidally bored. A little bit later, a Belgian couple in matching Indiana Jones safari-style garb appear, but they keep to themselves. Why, I wonder, would they come here as tourists if not to torment their own consciences? To needlessly prod the colonial ghosts? Can a vacation be billed as historical catharsis?

Jenn, in a bikini bottom and a Sleater-Kinney T-shirt, is sitting on the edge of the pool, splashing her feet, and Michael is sprawled out on a chaise longue. Darren is in the water, elbows propped on the ledge. We are sharing our awe over how long Ernest and Maridadi managed to conceal from us the fact that we were lost. Personally, I was grateful not to have known sooner than necessary.

Jenn, being unafraid in general, did not seem to mind that we were lost going on five hours. In fact, after a few beers, she says she wants to take a walk back down into the park come midnight.

"That's insane," Michael says.

"Definitely insane," Darren says. "You'll get eaten by a lion."

"I'll cast a spell to protect myself," she says.

Darren looks into the darkening woods with an air of gloom. "It's amazing how many animals out there could snuff us out."

Elephant, lion, buffalo, hyena. We compare and contrast and attempt to impose some sort of hierarchy onto the nearly infinite variety of horrible deaths by which nature holds it over us. It would be worse to be stomped to death by an elephant than exsanguinated by a lion, but not as bad as being mauled by a buffalo and not nearly so bad as being hamstrung and slowly eaten alive from the ass up by a pack of ravenous hyenas. Much of this fodder is generated by Darren, who before our trip had been conscientious enough to consult a website specializing in beast-on-human fatalities in Africa.

"Hyenas, snakes, a lot of lions, but a lot of them were chimps. Completely unprovoked, too. One minute they look perfectly normal. The next minute —" He shakes his head. "Guess what they go for, Jay."

"I'm gonna say testicles."

"Exactly. They're seriously fucking violent. First they disembowel you, and then they tear off your testicles."

I ponder this for a moment, since we are, in fact, half-planning to go chimpanzee tracking in a few days.

"We'll be fine," I say.

"The guy I read about got his balls ripped off right in front of his wife."

"If one attacks you, rip its balls off first," Michael says.

"No, that's the thing," Darren says. "They attack like eight at a time. You wouldn't stand a chance." He is quite in earnest. "As a pack, they all go for the male and they rip them right off. It's the first thing they do."

"So what are the chances this is gonna happen to us on our chimp tracking?"

"I've thought about it a lot, believe me."

"You've been thinking about this all along?"

"Honestly, I don't fear the gorillas at all. But I fear the chimps. And I think they're gonna smell that on me, and that's what scares me."

"Should we carry clubs?"

"My girlfriend suggested pepper spray."

"Or a stun gun or something."

"Dude," Darren says. "Once it happens, there's nothing you can do. It's like a riot, you know what I mean? And nobody can stop it. They're half your size, and they're as strong as you, and there's like eight of them."

"And they're right at your testicle level, obviously."

"Can't you just kick them in the face?"

"No, no, they kick *you* in the face."

"Jesus. So let's play golf instead," I say. "Screw the chimps."

He nods. "We can bag the chimps. I've seen chimps, man."

"You have?" I say. "No, you haven't."

"I've seen them in zoos."

Jenn is floating on her back, half listening to us with a euphoric smile, when she abruptly kicks out into the deep end of the pool, exclaiming, admonishing us, "Nothing is dangerous! Nothing is dangerous."

"Jesus," Darren says, "what if the baboons decide to take back the hotel and kill us all in our sleep?"

Michael cackles blackly. "That would be bad."

When Jenn and Michael retire to bed, Darren and I go to the upstairs lounge, where we run into a couple of nice-looking American NGO workers. They're at a table, playing a game with black marble-sized tree pods in a pocked board of wood. They live in Kigali and, if memory serves, work for an organization dedicated to curbing AIDS in Africa, which also has something to do with the fact that there's a package of Prudence Plus condoms in the nightstand of every room I stay in — as standard as the portrait of His Excellency President Paul Kagame over each hotel's check-in desk, more reliable than Gideon's Bible. Allison and Allison — the girls' respective names — are in Akagera for a little weekend R and R. When we ask if we can get them anything from the bar, they tell us to get another bottle of *waragi.* Having already taken a few slugs of this stuff out of a flask from a stranger at a nightclub in Kigali a few nights earlier, the same night I had found myself onstage between dance acts doing my best Frank Sinatra impression, I make a face, to which the dark-haired Allison says that we just haven't had it mixed properly and orders us to procure a pint, a bottle of tonic water, and a bucket of ice. Properly mixed, it turns out, *waragi* tastes like a very good gin and tonic.

Once we've exhausted the subjects of AIDS and recent genocide tribunals, and then ordered up yet another bottle of *waragi,* our expat friends ask what's latest in the States, which leads to the topic of who won the Oscars, which naturally leads to the topic of movies in general, which leads me to declare that my favorite movie of the past few years is still *Grizzly Man,* which leads Darren to say, as I knew he would, "I fucking hate Werner Herzog."

"Why?" (blond) Allison asks.

"Because he had no right to just sit there like an asshole with the headphones on and deny the audience, that's why," he says, referring to the famous scene where Herzog listens to the final entry in Timothy Treadwell's video diary as he is eaten alive by a bear. The lens cap of the camcorder had been left on, so only the audio portion is available to Herzog, who refuses to let the audience hear Treadwell's footage as he listens to it, leaving us to ponder only the expression on his face.

"We already know what happened," I say. "He doesn't need to exploit it to get the terror across."

"C'mon. It's the only reason anybody wants to see the movie," Darren says. "So why the fuck doesn't he have the balls to play it?"

"It's not the only reason people went to see it."

"Fuck yes, it is, Jay! Of course it is!"

"He's being eaten alive! Why do we need to hear it? We know he's screaming and begging to God. The violence is implicit. Besides, it's his choice to show restraint." I grin. "Artistically." The girls seem to be in agreement with me, which pisses Darren off more, even though one of the Allisons hasn't even seen the movie.

"Oh, Christ. That is such bullshit." Darren waves away my cigarette smoke. "The only reason anybody, and I mean *anybody,* went to see it was because he gets killed."

"You're ridiculous."

"Everyone going into the movie knows he gets killed by the bear!"

"Exactly!" I say. "We already know going in that he gets eaten by a bear, so why belabor the fucking point? The shock comes from watching the guy goofing around, or whatever, showing off in front of the camera, being 'normal,' and then you remember what happens next — or what already happened. The tension underlies every moment of the film. You never completely forget about what the fucking bear did, so you're always a little off-guard."

Actually, come to think of it, watching Herzog is sort of like being in Rwanda. You become complacent. You're going along, and for a moment or two you forget where you are. You actually start to have a pretty good time, you begin to enjoy the beautiful scenery, until the next awful reminder comes along and kicks your legs out from under you, and you think you might vomit at the mere thought of it, at the unspeakable truth beneath every scenic vista and preternaturally tasty banana. It has almost become a game of sorts, in my mind, seeing how long I can go between each moment of remembering. Perhaps it also explains why we are drinking like such fiends.

At some point we have shifted, moved ourselves, taken our drinks, and gone down to the pool, where we continue the argument. One of the Allisons asks if Darren thinks Herzog robbed him of the pleasure of hearing the death throes of a man being eaten alive. "Do you feel you were denied the experience?"

"Hell yes, that bastard denied me! He denied the audience something he had absolutely no right to withhold. He had absolutely no right!" The girls are wrapped up in blankets on the chaise longues watching Darren fulminate. There is a certain charm to his indignation. Each word is suffused with such conviction, we can't help but feel partially swayed. Perhaps we have been denied a valuable life experience. And what could be worse than that?

But even more than that, it is starting to worry me just a bit that this mutual obsession we share — this incessant question of what it would be like to be eaten alive by: a) a bear, b) a chimpanzee, c) a rabid dik-dik, whatever — may have less to do with the animals themselves and more to do with the relative acceptability of being eaten alive by a mindless animal, whereas we do not sit around reflexively asking each other to imagine what it would really be

like, what it would really *really* be like, to watch a neighbor of many
years hack apart your wife and child before your very eyes. Somehow the fear of animals is more bearable. They make a tidy stand-in
for our darker, less rational, if altogether more probable fears.

At some point, we realize that Allison and Allison have departed,
maybe after the second time a member of the hotel staff came
down to courteously request that we stop shouting so the other
guests might sleep, and momentarily, left alone, we sit glumly beside one another on the diving board, but then a sudden thump in
the woods snaps us out of our drunken reverie.

"What was that?"

"I bet it was a baboon."

"Dirty savages."

We creep over to the edge of the wall, and then, peering into the
dark, we see motion down by the edge of the woods. A glimpse of
jagged white stripes. After a moment we realize what we're looking
at. They are drinking out of the muddy cistern, their stripes faintly
glowing in the dark. Seven zebras. I shudder when I think of the
leopards out there, waiting for them, maybe lurking just beyond
the invisible trees. At the same time, I have an overwhelming desire
to wake Jenn, to go for a walk in the woods, to descend into the jungle. Foolishly, even though it's three in the morning, I wake her
anyway. Despite the hour, half asleep, she doesn't want to miss the
zebras and comes down to see them, but by then the zebras have already slipped back into the woods, as stealthily as they emerged.

In the western part of the country, bright green crops of tea and
coffee grow on beautiful, Tuscan-like hills so artfully terraced they
look like lumps of scrimshawed jade. At a higher altitude, the air is
sweet and cool, and the landscape has an enchanted and hobbity
vibe to it. Silver-blue eucalyptus and orange-blossomed jacaranda
dot the hillsides. The beauty here is sublime: one could never stage
the horrors of history in such a setting. Far below the winding road
— about forty-seven barrel rolls down the steep drop to our immediate left that it would take, by my best estimate, before our truck
burst into a ball of flames — are tiny figures carrying tiny hoes.

The little kids who run toward us as we speed up the winding
roads are much more raggedy than in the east. Dressed in tatters
that, to be honest, I would probably not use to clean my bike chain,

they stand by the side of the road selling overripe avocados. Clearly, however, they have had much more exposure to tourists than the children of Akagera; instead of shouting *"Agachupa!"* they hold out their hands, or make the finger-rubbing gesture for money, and shout *"Muzungu!"*

"Muzungu means white man," Ernest says. "Actually, it has nothing to do with being white, per se. The word *muzungu* means literally 'the person who goes in circles.'" The original term apparently referred to the first missionaries — the shock troops of the colonists — who would set up a mission, convert the natives, and then move on, set up another mission not far away, convert the natives there, then another, etc., before their eventual return to ground zero. Ergo, the person who goes in circles.

Given the original missionaries' success, the country of Rwanda, like many other African nations during colonial times, was washed clean of its pagan culture and replaced with the frayed belief system of the Europeans. They were so successful that until recently, the country was 90 percent Christian, with more than 60 percent Roman Catholic. Since the genocide, however, many have been leaving the church, and behind their departure is a truth that is difficult to fathom: in the most Christian of African nations, many of the worst massacres actually took place *inside* the churches. And what's even more sickening, the massacres often took place with the complicity of the clergy.

During earlier rehearsals for the genocide, such as the massacres that took place in the early '60s and in the '70s, people had naturally turned to the church for sanctuary. But in 1994, the Hutu anticipated that people would flock to their places of worship seeking refuge. By this point, severe restrictions had been imposed on the Tutsis. A Tutsi could not become an army officer, and soldiers could not marry Tutsi. Only certain quotas of Tutsi — 9 percent — could get jobs or go to school. Compulsory identity cards revealed the ethnicity of each citizen, and vigilante groups enforced the quotas imposed by the government. At the university in Butare, there were tribunals set up to determine the bloodlines of each student. The Tutsi had become utterly marginalized in society. The Catholic Church, by this point, was blatantly pro-Hutu. Instrumental in helping to organize racist political groups like Parmehutu, a central Hutu Power operation, Catholic missionaries and clergy spread genocidal ideology in their parishes and schools.

At the Roman Catholic Church in Cyangugu, 1,500 parishioners were killed. Seven thousand Seventh Day Adventists were killed at their church in Mugonero. One pastor, according to Philip Gourevitch's book *We Wish to Inform You That Tomorrow We Will Be Killed with Our Families*, told a congregant, "You must be eliminated. God no longer wants you." Both priests and nuns alike were found guilty not only of turning a blind eye but also of assisting in the actual killing. In Nyange, Father Athanase Seromba first helped usher his Tutsi parishioners into the church, then worked side by side with militiamen who threw grenades through the open windows. Prior to coming, I had read that four thousand people had been killed at the church in Kibuye alone, but when we went to see for ourselves, the plaque put the figure at 11,400.

"There are quite a number of people who don't want to go back to the churches because of the genocide," Ernest says. "Because they believe that the Catholic Church participated in it — which is true."

It makes me think of the images I had seen at the genocide memorial in Kigali: fallen bodies crammed between the pews, bullet-riddled tabernacles, bloodstained altar cloths, statues of Mary in her blue robes looking over the carnage, as indifferent and inscrutable as the rafters. When we left, at first we were all silent. We had expected to be fucked-up, and for a while we were just that. I had found Michael and Jenn outside, by the mass graves — half a dozen austere slabs of concrete, each the size of a city skating rink — trying without luck to collect themselves. Darren looked cachectic. Walking around the perimeter of the mass graves, I felt ashamed for even attempting to penetrate a grief that was not properly mine. But I could not shake the gallery of family photographs I had seen inside — more harrowing than the room of skulls, or the room of leg bones and arm bones stacked like split firewood, worse than the rooms of bloodied clothes, the torn skirts, the spattered Superman bed sheets, for me at least, was this dimly lit gallery, where the walls were pasted with thousands of snapshots of the once living. Three little boys in matching white suits and black bow ties. A girl home on college break. A ladies' man on a red couch, wearing a warm, come-hither smile. A priest baptizing a cow. A church potluck. A couple calming their swaddled newborn. A college professor in a black turtleneck. A teenager in tight blue jeans and denim jacket. Here is a grandfather. A grandmother in pearls. A stern-looking man drinking from an orange gourd. A nun. A man in a purple running suit. A dumbstruck bride. A man reading a book in a public garden. A faded Polaroid of a holiday dinner. A secretary at her desk, touching flowers in a vase. More babies. More grandmothers. More granddaughters. Newlyweds cutting a pink cake. Friends drinking Primus. Friends playing chess. Friends laughing. Friends mugging for the camera. Unsuspecting friends. Friends not anticipating death.

But then, on the way back to the hotel, the strangest thing happened. A sense of euphoria came over us. Now, on the streets, everybody seemed so intensely alive. More alive than anyone had ever seemed. The electric, frenetic pace of humans on the move, rush hour in Kigali, motorcycle taxis zipping around us, boys riding bicycles two at a time, people just getting off work and walking along the roads in small and large groups, women with woven baskets on their heads, people on cell phones, laughing schoolgirls in bright blue dress uniforms, boys in clean khakis, everyone looking so defiantly alive!

We suddenly very much wanted to be part of it, to get as close to the living as possible. The appropriate thing to do — with no thought of disrespect to the dead — was to go out. Check out the reopened nightclubs we'd heard about. We wanted music and alcohol. So we went hopping, to Cadillac and Club Planet and then to KBC, but each place was tamer than the last: the night had not yet caught fire. And so we went in search of something livelier. Maridadi, amused by our ebullient demands to get us to the next place, drove us around the city, with 50 Cent blasting on the radio — *Y'all niggas better lay down / Yeah, I mean stay down* — until finally, finally we landed at a dingy hall called the Sky Hotel. It was here where, at a sort of open talent show, between two equally gyratory and barely clad dance acts, I'd found myself onstage with a mike, in front of three hundred drunken, hooting Rwandans, doing my worst Frank Sinatra . . .

One day, after returning from seeing an enormous clan of colobus monkeys, creatures who look like robed judges swinging through the forest canopy in their black-and-white fur — who line up on branches, maybe ten in a row, to take turns diving out into the abyss, making great daring leaps, thrilling leaps, leaps of faith and leaps of madness, jumping twenty, thirty feet, the long white locks that grow out of their cheeks streaming like magnificent side-

burns — Darren confesses that the entire day, to his great annoy-
ance, he has had the song "Lady in Red" going through his head.
He says it's driving him nuts.

Ernest glances at him in the rearview mirror. "It's because you
drank *waragi* last night." He shrugs as if this fact could not be more
plain.

In a village outside the Nyungwe Forest, we pass a large crowd on
a hillside, dressed in their Sunday best, many holding colorful
parasols. They are quietly gathered, sitting in the grass, a hundred
or so, an entire village, by the looks of it. What are they doing, we
wonder, waiting for a priest? I look for the bride. It's a beautiful
day. Blue skies. The air is sweet and blowsy. A perfect day for a wedding. But then Ernest points out the men with official-looking
sashes, and the now conspicuous man in a chair beneath a tree,
dressed in pink.

"It is a *Gacaca*," he says. One of the local tribunals set up for villagers to try members of their community who participated in
the genocide. So many people are guilty, so many people participated, killed their neighbors, raped their neighbors, chopped
their neighbors to pieces, that if they relied on the conventional
court system alone, it is estimated it would take more than one
hundred years to try everyone involved. Something like seventy
thousand suspects remain in jail awaiting trial. By using the Gacaca
tribunals, they hope to speed trials and sentencing.

Ernest says he has personally known individuals who have been
tried but whom he had no idea were guilty. Once when he attended
a local *Gacaca,* he was surprised when the name of a neighbor of
his, a friend he drank beer with in the evenings, was suddenly
called out by the chairman. "He stepped forward, and when his
turn came, he was asked very many questions. About allegations
of what he did during the genocide. He answered some questions; others, he claimed they were lies." At the next *Gacaca*, Ernest
said, more people testified against his neighbor, and several prisoners were brought in to testify that he had been a driver for the
Interahamwe and that he had personally killed Tutsis in the sub-
urbs. Ernest was stunned. He had never suspected a thing. But that
is precisely the distinctive, paranoid feature of this particular genocide: how so many ordinary citizens were enjoined to participate in
the killing. They will never sort out all the guilty.

*

On the way into Ruhengeri, we pass a bored teenager absentmindedly scraping his machete across a guardrail. On the shoulder of the road, beside a spilled sack of carrots, a man attempts to repair his bicycle by hammering the derailleur with a rock. All safari trucks eventually converge on Ruhengeri, being, such as it is, the nearest village to Parc National des Volcans. It is here where the majority of tourists flock to see the mountain gorillas. And it is because of them that the highest denomination of Rwanda's Kool-Aid-colored currency features, instead of a general or politician, an image of *Gorilla berengei berengei* (so named after Captain Robert von Beringe, the first lucky white man to shoot one). But when one of the linchpins of your economy is an endangered species — there are only 720 mountain gorillas alive today — one wants to proceed with caution, as the ORTPN and the government of Rwanda have so conscientiously done. They have not treated their lucrative spectacle as a sideshow, selling tickets at the bottom of the mountain to all comers, but in fact allot only a limited number per day, and for only one hour per visit (admission is five hundred dollars). If you show so much as a sniffle that they deem possibly infectious to the gorillas, you are bumped from the hike.

When we meet early the next morning at the base station, we are broken up into groups, are given a guide, and receive our briefing, which I had assumed would include strict instruction on how to behave in an adequately humble way conducive to not being pummeled to death — like, for instance, how to make that weird pig-grunty noise Sigourney Weaver used in *Gorillas in the Mist* to pacify the apes — but we find ourselves hitting the trail with nothing more than walking sticks and Ernest's advice (he does not come with us) to just relax in the event one of them decides to sit on you.

"What can you do to avoid getting sat on?"

"Nothing," he said. "They are so big, they can do anything they want to do to you."

"Anything?"

"*Any*-thing."

The first leg of the hike is easy going, up a mild grade across an open heath of low grass and mossy rocks. The weather is sweet and the ground is soft on the feet. Given the altitude, our breathing is a little labored, but the hike is not half as difficult as we'd been led to believe by the guidebooks. We walk in single file, with our guide and one of the two armed guards who accompany us in the lead and the other guard bringing up the tail. The machine guns they carry are as much to protect us from the Cape buffalo who share the mountain with the gorillas as they are to protect us from any hostiles lingering on the DRC side of the forest. But we are told we have little to fear; it has been nine years now without a single tourist dragged off into the woods and hacked to death with machetes.

When we come to a broad stone wall, we rest. The wall separates the bosky meadow from the bamboo forest above. One side of the wall is light and open; the other, dark and treacherous. Rare golden monkeys frolic along the wall and chatter at us from the eucalyptus trees. We're lucky to see them.

While our guide waits to hear from the trackers, checking in periodically on his walkie-talkie, Jenn kneels, her staff pressed to her forehead, praying before the wall like a knight errant.

"Is she praying to God?" our guide asks me.

"No," I say. "She's praying to the gorillas." Which I think is true. It's the sort of thing I might do myself if I were alone. Get down on my knees and rejoice inwardly at the immensity of it all. The magic of the day. Looming above us, the volcano Mikeno presses vertiginously against the cloudless blue sky. Once the ranger gets the call on the radio, we clamber over a breach in the stone wall and enter the forest one at a time.

Now the climb is more difficult, steeper, the trail a mess of churned mud. It is also claustrophobic: a narrow tunnel through the tangled forest, with the occasional detour where buffalo have blazed their own trails, the bamboo squashed under their hooves like reeds. As we climb higher, there are so many of these extra game trails bisecting our own that it becomes a labyrinth, and it seems ever more urgent to keep up with our guide lest we end up on the wrong trail. If you have ever read Ernest Hemingway's story "The Short Happy Life of Francis Macomber," then you will know that the Cape buffalo is widely considered, even by the most stoic of hunters, to be the most dangerous animal in Africa, and will understand when I say how unsettling it was when our guide stopped midway to call our attention to the pungent anxiety-inducing musk from the buffalo that were now "surrounding us."

Darren asks, in a whisper, why the buffalo will charge us but leave the gorillas alone.

"All the animals give each other a good natural vibe," Jenn says. "We give them a weird vibe."

What, I ask Jenn, is her current level of fear on a scale of one to ten?

She turns and smiles at me as if I'm crazy. "Zero!"

I confess mine is a solid seven. Not that the fear is paralyzing, but I am able to think of little else as we continue upward — especially as the ominous ramshackle openings in the brush left by the buffalo seem to multiply as we gain altitude. I linger toward the back, sticking as close as possible to the guy with the AK-47.

We talk in whispers now. The gorillas, our trackers say, are just yonder. So we leave our backpacks and walking sticks behind in a pile and then creep through the underbrush, into an overgrown glade. It looks like we're in the middle of a Rousseau painting. Giant ferns, bamboo, a mess of exotic oversize designs in green. All the trees are upholstered with shaggy moss. And there, in the center of this greenery, is a quarter-ton male mountain gorilla just sitting in the open, stuffing leaves into his mouth.

Darren struggles to stabilize his tripod in a scrub of nettles — they have warned us not to scream if the nettles sting our arms or legs, for fear our cries of pain will upset the gorillas. Hours earlier Darren had confessed to me that he didn't expect to be in complete awe. Not really. He's done enough nature documentaries now not to expect to experience a subluxation in space. He's seen polar bears. He's seen emperor penguins. Like me, he was a little skeptical about the lasting impact the whole thing would have on him, that it would ultimately feel as mundane as anything else, more or less, so long as nobody got any arms ripped out, but for now we are as giddy as schoolchildren. We would do anything to prolong the magic of this encounter. The expression on Jenn's face betrays a visible strain: the sincere efforts of a mind at work to make the moment count.

The gorilla moves over to a spinney of trees and begins yanking down the vines and stripping them with his teeth. Every time he yanks down a vine, it makes sound like a meth addict ripping copper wiring out of a plaster wall. His arms are absurdly long. His head is the size of a vault. This is the biggest primate on the face of the planet: the hominid equivalent of a grizzly.

Not too far away, in a shaded grotto of leaves and vines, is a mama gorilla holding her infant. The apeling looks like one of Spielberg's animatronic trolls: the perfect synthesis of ugly-cute. Their ripe musk fills the air as in a sauna; the scent is peppery sweet, like jalapeños frying in molasses. The guides, eager to let us take pictures, say the gorillas are "habituated" to us *muzungus* with cameras, which clearly they are, but at the same time it somehow seems like the wrong word when it's so obvious that what they are is profoundly indifferent to our presence. Or even worse: as if we don't even exist. And not as if they're only pretending we don't exist . . .

On the way back down the mountain, even though I slip in just as much buffalo shit as I did on the way up, on a scale of one to ten, I feel zero fear. The mountain gorillas have liberated me for the time being. On the other hand, I'll admit, strangely enough, that I am also left a little sad. This experience has been checked off the list. It isn't just that it's over, but also because it no longer belongs to the exclusive realm of imagination, and to be quite honest, I think my imagination will miss it. Memory will distort it for its own doubtful purposes. Which makes me wonder if there's really any value to this experience thing at all. Why is having done something better than having imagined doing something? I mean, what if the so-called value of experience is overinflated? Why do we expect to be changed by experience at all?

Since traveling to Rwanda, I am more _____.

I have become increasingly plagued by thoughts of _____.

I am no longer _____.

I am more inclined to believe in _____.

But less inclined to believe _____ about humanity.

How have your thoughts about the world in general changed since you left your hotel one morning and saw a woman missing her legs sitting in the grass on the shoulder of the road? Please explain: _____.

Midafternoon on our last full day, Darren and I are down on the beach, under the shade of an umbrella, reading, with a bottle of South African sauvignon blanc chilling in a silver ice bucket. Michael and Jenn have been secluded in their room for the past few days, recovering from some intestinal flu they picked up in Ruhengeri. Nearby is a little girl digging in the sand and a group of middle-aged British women getting pleasantly snockered, their own ice buckets askew in the khaki sand, their many accumulated glasses sparkling in the merry beach air.

The lake is choppy and shimmers enticingly, though Darren and I have already decided that we are strictly abiding advice given by our respective Stateside travel doctors to avoid swimming in the water at all costs. Something about microbes piloting up your urethra and laying poisonous eggs in your bladder. This plus the underwater pockets of volcanic gas — they're extracting the methane as an energy source — leaves us happily on the beach. Just across the lake, looming above the Congolese city of Goma, is the diabolical volcano known as Nyiragongo. When it erupted six years ago, it killed one hundred people and left tens of thousands homeless. They say it will blow again, and when it does there's no telling how many will die. Vesuvius killed 3,300; Nyiragongo could kill two million. But the next time, death won't be limited to those across the lake (morose volcanologists predict). The sulfur dioxide will sneak across the water and kill anyone here as well. They won't smell it; they'll die in their sleep. When I share this piece of information with Darren, which I gleaned from a PBS special, he asks when it's due to erupt.

"Pretty soon, I think."

"God, I hope it's not today or tomorrow," he says. "I really do."

"I wouldn't worry about it," I say.

"Ole ORTPN doesn't advertise that, does it? Exploding volcanoes and methane gas. Jesus." He lifts the bottle from the ice bucket, sees that it's empty, and starts scanning the beach for our waiter.

The grounds of the hotel really are paradise: radiant palm trees, ornamental cacti, euphorbia trees, purple-blossomed jacaranda, taut white volleyball nets. The cheerful sound of kids playing in the water comes from the other side of the fence, where a guard is posted between the hotel property and the have-nots of Gisenyi. The guard looks bored, twiddling his nightstick in the sand. A short while later, I glance up and watch two dugout canoes slowly plying their way across the water; when they get closer, we can hear the passengers chanting as they paddle. For a minute, unthinkingly, I take it to be some kind of tourist gimmick before recalling where I am. Again I have forgotten, only to have memory stab back under the door like an envelope bearing unwanted news, when I look farther down the beach.

Not twenty yards beyond the fence, out on a rocky outcrop, is a crowd of loitering men. Each holds an Easter-yellow jerrican, a detail made all the more vivid and disheartening by the fact that the mob is attired entirely in pink. There are at least a hundred of them. I didn't think of it till now, but not a five-minute walk from here is a prison. On our way into town yesterday morning, we saw families waiting outside to visit. Near them, a group of naked boys are in the water tossing a ball. The convicts take turns, one at a time, wading out a little bit, to submerge their jugs. They hold them down for what seems like a long time, until the air bubbles dwindle, while the others wait patiently for their turn. Their pink shirts billow gently in the placid breeze.

When Michael and Jenn finally rejoin us, close to dinnertime, they seem a little wracked out, but their intestines are evidently strong enough for them to order beers from the waiter when he makes his way back around. Jenn is dressed ready to swim. This despite my best efforts to remind her of the lurking schistosomiasis: the infected fluke larvae waiting to burrow into her skin, the fevers and coughing, the seizures and lesions of the brain she has to look forward to for her recklessness. Does she really want bladder cancer? Is a dip in the lake really worth it?

"There's no way I'm not going swimming in Africa," she says. "That's ridiculous. Look, plenty of people are swimming. They're fine."

She takes off her towel and strolls down to the water's edge. After a moment, Michael says, "Fuck it," ties his hair in a ponytail, drops his shirt, and follows.

She waits for him, and then, holding hands, they start out into the beautiful poisonous lake. Just watching them brings my fear level to 3.5. The water turns out to be shallower than you'd think, so they have to wade out farther before it rises to their shoulders. They are floating now, holding on to each other, and Jenn lifts her glistening arms as if to embrace the sky. They look like people who truly know they are blessed. For a long time, they stay like that, bobbing and grinning, looking up in awe as the heavy military planes rumble low overhead into Goma. The war goes on there, despite recent elections. Nyiragongo smolders in the distance. And slowly,

one jug at a time, the men in pink haul water out of the lake as if
exhuming the incomprehensible mystery of their crimes. Who of
us would have known that in five short months, back up in the
Virungas, their militia friends would slaughter seven of our friends
the mountain gorillas, and would even set one pregnant female on
fire? There will be speculation that the massacres are meant to in-
timidate park rangers who've become critical of the charcoal-smug-
gling interests and the risks posed to the gorilla sanctuary. Then
again, perhaps they killed the gorillas just as a reminder, to let their
enemies know that they are still there, unvanquished, that they are
still capable of unspeakable acts. When I get the news, I will wish
that Jenn could have been there to protect them; I will wish her
prayers had worked. But she is getting farther away from me now,
out in the water, and it takes some effort to control my fear as the
shrieks of the children playing in the water near the men drowning
their plastic jugs reach a frenzied pitch. But then, as I see the waiter
coming back toward us, walking calmly across the sand, a bottle of
wine balanced on his tray, I remember, and repeat under my breath
the reassuring mantra until I can almost stand to believe it: *Nothing
is dangerous . . . Nothing is dangerous . . . Nothing is dangerous . . . Nothing is dangerous . . .*

KIRAN DESAI

Dragon Season

FROM *Travel + Leisure*

THE MURAL IN THE TASHIDING MONASTERY is of a graceful woman mounted on a yak in a lotus blossom garden. "That is Tara," explains a monk: a virtuous form of Buddha.

"And that?" A fierce figure resembling something out of a Japanese cartoon sits astride a snow lion, scattering thunderbolts. "He disperses ghosts, chases evil spirits."

Another mural shows creatures in a mountain pond, a beast with an elephant trunk emerging from a conch shell, a winged lion with a bird's beak and horns.

"These you will not find here. If you go farther north into the jungle, you will find them."

"And these?" The monk smiles, wraps, and rewraps his scarlet shawl. "You know, in the rainy season they come out of the ground and fly about."

"I'm sorry?"

"Dragons, you know how they fly about?"

It is dragon season in Sikkim. Monsoon storms hurtle against mountains with a savagery matched only by the ferocity with which the earth responds to this onslaught. Overnight, things sprout and grow. Little clusters of huts are lost in a wild exuberance of cardamom, banana, and deadly nightshade. The Tista and the Rangit rivers leap through jungle of teak and incandescent fields of paddy. Ginger is being harvested, and the freshly dug roots spice the air.

Sikkim is possessed of an almost mythical bounty. The mountainside is so steep, the vegetation seems confounded: everything grows. Cactus, orchids, orange trees, rhododendron, oak. Higher,

in the alpine reaches where rumors of the yeti and Loch Ness mon-
ster–like beasts live on, the gullibility of travelers is tested by yak
herders attempting to sell shriveled ginseng root as a bit of a yeti
arm, or the pelt of a Himalayan bear as yeti fur. Higher still, prof-
fering an aching beauty that alters constantly with the light, is
Kanchenjunga, the third-highest mountain in the world, a plume
of snow blown by dervish winds at its summit.

The Monastery of Tashiding was built in 1717 when a rainbow
was seen connecting the site with Kanchenjunga. The interior is
aglow with the fluttering flames of copper lamps. Before images of
the Buddha and various high lamas, there are offerings of rice and
oil, water, incense, bananas. The monks sit in two rows on either
side. Old spectacled monks, tiny novices in toddler-size robes, looking like so many marigolds. Earlier, these little monks had helped
me pull off the leeches — five, ten, fifteen — that I'd collected on
my walk through the jungle from Kalimpong to Tashiding. They
carried them out, placed them gently, respectfully on leaves, giggled madly when I suggested delivering them the death sentence
with a big stone. Surely I was making a very funny joke? True to the
teachings of the Buddha, the monks will kill no living creature. Not
even malevolent bloodsuckers.

The sound of chanting rises; it catches the rhythm of the rain
outside. Conch shells trimmed in silver and long horns encrusted
with turquoise are blown, cymbals are clashed together, bells rung.
The murals, in addition to the Tara and the ghost chaser, present
a demon with the wheel of life clasped in its fangs and talons to indicate the knot that binds us: rooster-snake-pig as lust-anger-fool-
ishness, each chasing, each feeding on, each consumed by the
other. Also displayed is the tantric symbol of the Kalachakra, demonic forms of male and female power in grotesque sexual union,
Dracula teeth and pink tongues fiercely intertwined, multiple
heads crowned by skulls, a snatch of leopard-skin skirt for modesty's sake, tiny naked humans being crushed under their careless
feet. Nearby, a Buddha sits, serene despite this arresting sight. Lust
upon these walls, and fear, peace, grace, and fantasy. Images that simultaneously inspire and terrify.

Guru Padmasambhava (Lotus Born), the tantric master who is
depicted with a wrathful smile ensconced in a curling mustache, introduced this particular brand of Buddhism, "the ancient Nyingma
(Red Hat) order," into Tibet in the third century. When the re-

formist Gelugpas (Yellow Hats), the order of the Dalai Lama, rose in power in the fourteenth century, three Nyingmapa monks convened at Yuksom in Sikkim to reestablish power. They crowned the first *chogyal* ("Righteous Monarch") of Sikkim, then called Denzong, or Valley of Rice.

In all, there are about two hundred monasteries in Sikkim. Some are being renovated with poster paints and fluorescent lighting, bathroom-tile floors, jail cell–like steel crisscross doors, metal grilles in the windows. Some are as yet unspoiled; the pigments are jade, bronze, and garnet. They are faded, but the demonic energy still seems potent. The floors are of teak and the prayer wheels are made of buffalo hide. Photographs of head lamas are displayed at the altars, and should you ask, "Is he still alive?" you sometimes get the answer "Yes, his reincarnation is here already."

In the years after the Chinese invaded Tibet in 1950, Sikkim became a haven for fleeing monks. Residents describe the hillside burning scarlet as if with fire while lines of monks came streaming down the old salt and wool trade routes from Lhasa. They're still leaving. The monasteries of Tibet are being emptied at these borders. Visit antiques shops in Darjeeling, and if they deem you a serious buyer, bundles of dirty cloth and newspaper are taken from beneath the counter, unwrapped to reveal treasures being offered for a pittance. It is so dreadfully sad to see the heritage of a nation being sold in this soiled, ignominious way, sold by the desperate, bought by the unscrupulous. Silver and gold prayer books and scroll containers; prayer wheels made of bone, silver, copper, leather, wood, coral, and turquoise; and jade bowls so transparent the day shines through to illuminate patterns of deep thunderclouds approaching.

Delicate border politics with China, Bhutan, and Nepal account for a heavy military presence here. The north is largely off-limits to even Indian visitors, and in the rest of the state, passes are checked and rechecked, policemen making a little extra finagling bribes for permission to drive through sensitive areas. Foreign nationals must request permits to visit Sikkim. Their stays are limited to fifteen days.

Terrible landslides. The roads falter across a vast morass of boulders. Sometimes they are transformed into riverbeds. I travel from Gangtok in the east to Pemayangtse in the west, stopping at all the monasteries along the way in a hired diesel Jeep Commander, a skeletal frame attached to a rough, kicking machine, so every organ is given a tremendous shake. Monsoon clouds billow into the vehicle, hiding everyone from each other, oneself from oneself. Now and then, a brief moment of sun, and dozens of butterflies sail forth, yellow, iridescent blue.

On these broken roads, squatting in circles, sitting on the rocks, having a leisurely chat as if in a living room, for it is the single place at this time of year that is not squelchy and overgrown with foliage, are bands of resting villagers. A group of women in ruffled, flowered nighties, which have become a daytime fashion here, admire a baby held by one of them. The baby has big kohl-lined eyes and a large black painted spot to ward off the evil eye. They get up to let our Jeep pass, resettle, and entertain the laughing baby by pelting him with lantana flowers.

Large signs — BARRACKS, CANTEEN, OFFICERS' MESS — mark sad concrete buildings. Little groups of soldiers go jogging by in comically big shorts, skinny legs sticking out, looking not nearly sturdy enough for combat. But when I ask the driver if he thinks India is properly defended against the Chinese, so close across the mountains at Nathu La, the old trade pass into Tibet, he says, "Oh, we are well defended. No need for worry. With roads like these how many Chinese will make it over? Ha ha ha!"

Perhaps the bad state of the roads has also kept many monasteries remote. They feel so far from the world and its dirty problems, it is jarring then to descend to military checkpoints and see these two aspects of Sikkim side by side, to witness how this place with a fairy-tale reputation has faced the problems of the modern world, with particularly tragic consequences.

The British began their forays into this region in the early 1800s, starting tea plantations in the drenched and misty landscape after they lost their monopoly on the tea trade with China. Darjeeling was forcibly annexed from Sikkim by the Raj in 1861. The British took Kalimpong from Bhutan after the Anglo-Bhutanese war of 1864. They brought in Nepalis to work the tea plantations, for the area was too sparsely populated to provide sufficient labor. Soon the Lepchas, who practice Bon, a form of animism, and who believe that they are descended from sacred Kanchenjunga snow, became a minority in their own hills. The population is now 75 percent Nepali, less than 20 percent Lepcha. Later India adopted much the same attitude toward Sikkim as the British had earlier. Despite a desperate attempt to keep his kingdom's sovereignty, the last *chogyal* of the only Himalayan Buddhist kingdom other than Bhutan was forced, after a plebiscite, to succumb to the vote of the Nepali majority. Sikkim was annexed by India in 1975. Wary of a similar fate, Bhutan adopted an aggressive policy against its Nepali population, attempting to keep out new immigrants. Nepalis were also hounded from the Indian states of Assam and Meghalaya in bouts of terrible violence. And in yet another twist of history, shaken Indian Nepalis demanded a separate Nepali state, Gorkhaland. For years, through the 1980s, the mountains were engulfed by a separatist movement called GNLF, Gorkha National Liberation Front. Perhaps it was an inevitable occurrence in a nation cobbled together in this fashion, with shifting populations and borders, with so many competing loyalties. Ownership will always be contested — it is just perspective, after all.

When I was a child, my family had a house in Kalimpong, across the Tista River from Darjeeling. The hills of Sikkim were blue in the distance. Some twenty years ago now, and I still remember how the air was thick with the threat of what was to come. People here refer to what occurred as "the Agitation." What exactly happened will always be debated. Bridges and police stations were bombed, roads destroyed, government buildings went up in flames, police brutality was sanctioned by politicians. Business came to a standstill. Tea plantations were shut down, the tourism industry vanished, schools and colleges closed. No water, no phones, no electricity, no food. In the end, the GNLF was granted a political platform and greater autonomy, which stopped, however, short of statehood. In the air today is the stink of something not quite over.

The ghost of the Raj lingers on not merely in the politics, but in moldy buildings that once were grand. I have an aunt who still lives in Kalimpong, in an old English stone house that she discovered as a ruin, roof loaded with ferns, seemingly deserted, but with a blind Englishwoman being eaten alive by maggots in her big brass bed, abandoned by her servants. Eventually the woman died, and the house was sold by relatives in England. My aunt bought it, she says, because this place offers something that life elsewhere never could.

She loves it for its beauty, fierce beyond the reach of civilization. Above her home, the mountains soar in twisted, hornlike peaks and convolutions that seem to mirror the region's history and politics.

We spend a rainy-season dusk on her veranda. Below, the army is eating dinner in the mess. Above, in forests of bamboo, the monks are chanting their last prayer of the day. It is so peaceful now, but it is impossible not to reflect on the fact that life here is a complicated endeavor. As a doctor working in a clinic in the bazaar, my aunt has seen the darker side of life here, the worst effects of poverty and political upheaval.

I ponder, then, the particular form of tantric Buddhism that is nurtured in the Himalayan monasteries, their reflection of the complex human soul that seems related to this landscape, this history. I think of the monks housed in dark, swampy rooms, living so remotely, so simply, so as to pour all they have into keeping this faith fervently burning, this form of Buddhism even more ancient than the one practiced in Tibet, close to Bon and the spirit worship of the Lepchas. I think of those phantasmagoric murals, the dragons that we have scoffed at, condemning ourselves to savor them only in meager ways, illustrations in a children's book or a cartoon film. Here they are free and freeing, and something precious to the human spirit, lost elsewhere, is yet vibrant.

We sit as people do most evenings, in the wavering light of uneven voltage, grand moths with the wingspans of birds flying by. We eat mutton, stuffed *momo* dumplings with red-chili chutney on the side, and drink *chang* through bamboo straws in mugs, topping and retopping the fermented grains of millet with warm water from a big copper kettle. We wait for the evening's usual episode of rain. When it arrives, the storm blocks everything out but itself, drowns out all observations and meditations, ruins all conversations. The dragons the monk at Tashiding assured me were alive are writhing and gnashing. They are far too compelling to balance against any human consideration. In these hours, there is immense relief.

We sit and watch, lighting the lanterns when the electricity fails entirely.

CAROLINE ALEXANDER

Tigerland

FROM *The New Yorker*

THE OLD MAN stepped onto our boat out of the utter blackness
that falls between the abrupt fall of twilight, at five o'clock, and the
rising of the full moon. His name was Phani Gayen, and he was employed at the Saznekhali Wildlife Sanctuary, in the mangrove forest on the northern border of India's Sundarbans Tiger Reserve,
where we were moored. Formerly, he was a crab fisherman, taking
his small, pole-punted boat down along the forest's brackish tidal
creeks and narrow channels. On June 23, 1984, at half past noon,
he had gone into the forest with companions to collect wood. He
turned and found a tiger springing for him, roaring. "I was then
forty-five years old and very, very strong," he said. "I did not allow
the tiger's face to touch my face." He stroked his Adam's apple.
"The tiger's throat is very hard, *here.*" As the tiger gripped him with
its paws, its head hung over his shoulder, drenching his shirt with
saliva. "I knew I was going to die. So I embraced the tiger. He was
soft. The tiger was soft. Like a sponge." Somehow, this surrender
freed him — the tiger released him and turned on one of his companions. Taking the companion by the throat, the tiger headed
back into the forest.

The claw wounds on Gayen's head and face kept him in the hospital for three months. The wounds healed, but his ear was damaged permanently. Over the years, he had told his story many
times. "I no longer fear the tiger," he declared, his scarred face lit
by the yellow bulb that our boat's generator powered. "It is the tiger's nature." But he avoids entering the forest.

The bulb's light did not extend to the shore, and Gayen vanished into darkness on the long, narrow gangplank. The camp where he worked was one of only a few small stations in the 4,263 square kilometers of protected forest. At the mouth of the Ganges Delta, the Sundarbans encompasses the largest single mangrove ecosystem in the world, of which roughly 40 percent lies in India and 60 percent in Bangladesh. The 9,630 square kilometers of the Indian Sundarbans, designated a UNESCO Biosphere Reserve, are in turn divided into two more or less equal regions. Of the hundred and eight islands lying in the web of tidal rivers, creeks, and channels, fifty-four are inhabited — or "reclaimed" — supporting a rural, poor population of more than four million people. To the southeast lies the tiger reserve, whose swamp forest and intricate waterways are the improbable domain of the uniquely aquatic Royal Bengal tiger.

Washed by powerful, twice-daily tides flowing from the Bay of Bengal, and regularly buffeted by cyclones, the Sundarbans has always been unstable, its low landmasses constantly being eroded, silted, and reconfigured. Upstream pollution, from Calcutta; increasing salinity, caused by naturally occurring displacement of freshwater sources; and depredation of the forest by villagers cutting wood are long-standing threats. Still, the Sundarbans remains "intact," thanks partly to stringent conservation measures and to its inaccessibility, and partly to the Sundarbans tiger, whose presence ensures that the forest is too dangerous to enter casually. "Without the tiger, we would have no forest," I was told by villagers, fishermen, wood collectors, honey gatherers — by all who cautiously skirt the forest.

I had come to the Sundarbans in late November, after the rainy season, with members of a not-for-profit agency, the Anudip Foundation, which offers livelihood training, and whose members were interested in producing a film about the region. Kushal Mookherjee, a Calcutta-based naturalist and wildlife consultant, who had been coming to the Sundarbans regularly for field study for more than a decade, was also on board. Another companion, Dr. Pranabes Sanyal, an authority on mangrove ecosystems, was the former field director, from 1980 to 1986, of the Sundarbans Tiger Reserve. The forest reserve can be reached only by boat, and our plan was to travel the rivers and back ways haunted by one of the most viable tiger populations remaining in the wild.

We had joined our launch, the sixty-two-foot *M. V. Tanaya*, at a

small port on a channel off the Matla River, one of the main arter-
ies through the reserve. Little other traffic was going our way as we
wended through the waters of the reclaimed Sundarbans. On either side, broad embankments of baked clay fortified the land
against the tide, giving each village the appearance of a walled city.
Fishing vessels listed in the mud below them; hours later, the same
boats would be floating as much as fifteen feet higher, level with
the walls. In recent years, the tides have become more menacing, as
the sea levels have climbed inexorably. Toward the end of 2006,
two islands from the western edge of the Sundarbans archipelago
were reported to have vanished beneath the water.

"If the Sundarbans goes under, the tiger episode on earth is
over," Kushal said, a belief shared by many authorities. The plight
of tigers worldwide is critical, with the most optimistic estimates
positing a population of between 3,300 and 4,300. Some four hundred tigers are cautiously estimated to inhabit the combined Sundarbans of India and Bangladesh.

From time to time, we passed solitary women trudging through
the water near the shoreline, pulling nets behind them as they
trawled for prawn seed. This practice, introduced in the past twenty
years or so, has disastrously reduced prawn and other fish populations, and the constant pacing along the fragile shore by the
women and children who drag the nets has contributed to erosion.
In their flowing saris, the women presented picturesque silhouettes
that belied the danger of their work, up to ten hours a day waist-
high in the murky water. As many as ten fatal crocodile attacks are
documented each year, and, I was told, too many shark attacks to
report. The most common are by dog sharks, which take a bite of
soft tissue — a leg or buttock — but do not kill. "They are considered minor hazards," Dr. Sanyal said, with a sympathetic grimace.
The Sundarbans's occupational hazards — crocodiles, sharks, co-
bras, kraits, swimming tigers, and cyclones — make it one of the
most dangerous places in the world.

As we passed from the reclaimed area into the waters of the
protected tiger reserve, the villages petered out, the occasional
wooden ghat or jetty the only evidence of human presence. On the
right bank, there were, suddenly and starkly, no structures at all,
but only a barely discernible web of netting draping the forested
waterline — a fanciful strategy intended to deter straying tigers.

The boat arrived at the long jetty of the Saznekhali Wildlife Sanctuary, in a buffer zone established around the tiger reserve's most stringently protected core, which is off-limits to everyone except personnel and vetted researchers. The river was at very low tide, and a compound loomed above the river and fifteen feet of exposed mud banks like a fort bristling with defenses. Stoutly staked at the high-tide mark, a quadruple row of bamboo pylons formed a palisade, patrolled by a troop of rhesus monkeys. Inside the compound stood a shrine to Banbibi, the divine protectress of the forest, and to Dakshin Roi, the tiger god.

"In most of the forest stations, there is a deity statue," Dr. Sanyal said as we stood before gaudily painted representations of the gods. The inhabitants of the Sundarbans are both Hindu and Muslim, but the wilderness has forged its own idiosyncratic beliefs, honored by people of both faiths. Banbibi is depicted as an attractive, sari-clad woman; she does not accept sacrifices of animals or blood but is propitiated with sweets. She is serene and kind, and is often shown riding unconcernedly on a roaring tiger, like Dionysus on his leopard.

"Mother, we are going to your kingdom," runs a characteristic *puja*, or prayer, offered to Banbibi by devotees who must enter the forest. *"Kindly protect us, please see that we get a safe return, we do not fall prey under your tiger's paw."* Sometimes Banbibi's brother, Shajangali, is depicted with her. In "dress and countenance," as one authority has written, he seems to belong to "Muslim gentry." The dashing Dakshin Roi, depicted as a mustachioed, gun-carrying, horse-riding, sporting gentleman, is Tiger incarnate. He is deep yellow, with large, compelling eyes. Within this nexus of sometimes contradictory associations, he is, like Vishnu, the Preserver, principally worshipped for his curative powers: "A god can create life and can take it," as a village woman told me with some energy. An actual tiger might be Dakshin Roi, or the animal on which Banbibi rides, or Vishnu.

"Tiger is the king of the Sundarvans," writes Tushar Niyogi in his "Tiger Cult of the Sundarvans" (from which the quotations above are also taken). "Any account of the Sundarvans remains incomplete if it does not include elaborate notes on Tiger."

The boat pulled away from the Saznekhali jetty at dark. Some miles upstream, we dropped anchor at another village. By eight o'clock, the full moon had risen, and sky and river alike became milk white. The sound of the generator *chug-chugged* pleasantly across the water, and when it was shut off there was nothing to be heard at all. The few dhows also at anchor appeared as half-moon silhouettes. When dawn broke the next day, they had already departed.

We continued generally east, going against the tide in a narrowing of the river, which smoked with dawn mist. A small fishing boat appeared ahead, and as we drew abreast our captain hailed it. A man dressed in a ragged blue-and-white-striped shirt and a checked *longi* waved uncertainly. He was joined by his wife, who wore a heavy sweater over her sari against the morning cold. His name was Parimal Biswas, and he was a crab fisherman. A swath of tattered awning sheltered their bedding and tiny kitchen, and the bow was filled with a huge basket teeming with crabs, which Biswas uncovered with obvious pride; there were, he estimated, some fifty to sixty kilos. At a hundred rupees, or two dollars and fifty cents, a kilo, he expected to get more than a hundred dollars from this trip — a lot of money. His line was already rebaited, and he was punting along the shoreline, looking for a likely place to make a final drop.

Yes, he said, in answer to Dr. Sanyal's query, he had often seen tigers. "When we see one, we cross to the opposite bank and lie down low," his wife explained. "We pretend no one is around." Biswas knew his work was dangerous. "But I have to eat," he said with feeling. Digging into a pocket, he drew out a document, reaching across the water to hand it to Dr. Sanyal. "It is a permit to fish here," Dr. Sanyal said. "He was born a cripple, and is allowed to fish here," in the reserve. The permit, issued by the Government of West Bengal, Forest Department, was important: among other things, it ensured that his family would be recompensed in the event that he was taken by a tiger.

We were still heading east, toward the most remote part of the reserve. Fronds of the great nipa palm and of the phoenix palm burst out of the leafy mangrove greenery. According to folk etymology, "Sundarbans" is Bangla for "the forest of beautiful trees," and the mangroves shimmered in the low morning light — literally shimmered, as the leaves of some species are covered with a glossy protective wax, which is secreted, along with excess salt, as one of their strategic adaptations to the saline water. The vast majority of the Bengal coast's marine life begins in the nursery of the Sundarbans;

fifty-three species of reptiles are harbored here, more than two hundred species of birds, and at least fifty species of mammals, including the endangered Irrawaddy and Gangetic dolphins, the Smooth Indian otter, and the cheetah-spotted fishing cat. A hundred years ago, there were Java rhino, wild buffalo, and swamp deer.

Sitting under the bow breezeway, Dr. Sanyal was watching the forest drift past, noting with pride its many accomplishments: the pneumatophores, or respiratory roots that rise in perpendicular spikes above the mud, like snorkels, carrying oxygen to the mangrove plant; the "derricks," or elaborate root scaffolding that secures the mangrove in the tugging tides and the region's many cyclones. "There are twenty-eight true mangrove species in Sundarbans," Dr. Sanyal said, and he seemed about to embark on a loving recitation of them all. Reed-slender, inherently elegant even in bush attire, Dr. Sanyal exuded an aura of gentleness and humility. To meet him in civilian life, in his home city of Calcutta, say, one might have surmised that he belonged to some contemplative priestly order; in reality, of course, he was a renowned authority on the hero-beast *Panthera tigris tigris*, the Royal Bengal tiger.

The adaptation of the Sundarbans tiger to the mangrove ecosystem is every bit as remarkable as that of the mangrove system to tidal ecology. Tigers, the largest of the world's big cats, migrated to India twelve thousand years ago from south China and southeast Asia; the time of their arrival in the Sundarbans is not known. In the marshy land and brackish channels caused by encroaching tides, the huge terrestrial animals took to the water. "The Sundarbans tiger is amphibious," Dr. Sanyal said. The tiger's diet is not only meat-based; it also includes aquatic prey, such as monitor lizards and other reptiles, frogs, and fish. The variety of the tiger's prey — ranging, as one field manual cheerfully notes, "from fish to human beings" — is another advantage that the Sundarbans tiger has over other tiger populations.

It was only nine o'clock when the boat arrived at a neat compound of concrete-block buildings and gardens, where reserve officials and staff, some with their families, lived, surrounded by high, stout wire fencing. The day before, a tiger had sauntered along a creek outside the compound and left its pugmarks. "This was a female," Dr. Sanyal said, pointing out that the four pads were slightly rectangular, each measuring about two and three-quarters inches. The pad marks of a male would be squarer and broader.

The prints had been made not far from a "mangrove cage walk" — a two-hundred-meter-long path through the forest under a protective wire tunnel, such as one might find in a maximum-security prison. The path ended at a thirty-foot-high watchtower, level with the tops of the tallest trees and overlooking a broad river that marks both the eastern limit of the Indian Sundarbans and the international border with Bangladesh. Historically, bandits have operated on both sides of the border, but the Bangladesh Sundarbans, which is also under protection, is considered the more lawless. The possibility of closer collaboration between the two Sundarbans is being explored, but for now the little-patrolled seventy-kilometer-long river border remains vulnerable to traffic and to poachers.

"A male tiger on this side who hears a female over there will swim over to her," Dr. Sanyal said. Tigers can swim five miles, so the two-mile dash to Bangladesh would be a mere jaunt. "Once, I was following a tiger in a motorboat," Dr. Sanyal said, as we continued looking across the river. "And the tiger was swimming faster." A tiger is said to have clocked more than eighteen hundred feet at seven minutes and eighteen seconds — against the tide. Put another way, a tiger's time for a hundred-meter freestyle would be a respectable one minute and twenty seconds. "Tiger is a very silent, very swift swimmer," Dr. Sanyal said.

The Royal Bengal tiger is solitary and "secretive" — the last attribute regularly appears in the language of even the most sober field manuals. A group of tigers — should one be so fortunate to see one — is called a streak. A male tiger can be as large as ten and a half feet in length and weigh more than five hundred pounds. The tiger's coat is deep amber, the lines of its characteristic black shadow-stripes abstract and sophisticated. Its claws retract, like those of a domestic cat; it "prusts," or chuffs, rather than purrs, as well as roars. The iris of the tiger's eye is amber yellow. The tiger is one of the few anointed animals commonly referred to as "charismatic"; "Nature's masterpiece of the creation," to cite a recent book; or, as Kushal put it, "something to look up to," both beautiful and powerful. The tiger is also a very clever animal, and a very effective predator. Stories abound of its strategic, chess-player ma-

neuvering of prey and of its extraordinary stealth. Every story told
to me by a witness or survivor of a tiger attack included words to the
effect of "it came from nowhere."

Project Tiger was inaugurated by the government of India in 1973,
following the first tiger census, which disclosed that, of the estimated forty thousand tigers living in India at the turn of the previous century, fewer than two thousand remained. For decades, the
conservation program had the reputation of being one of the most
effective in the world, but in recent years tiger populations in India, as elsewhere, have plummeted, with drops in many reserves of
as much as 50 to 60 percent. In 2005, it was learned that every tiger
in the Sariska Tiger Reserve — some hundred miles from India's
capital, New Delhi — had been killed by poachers.

A booming Chinese market for traditional medicines, responsible for other wildlife losses, remains the primary incentive for tiger
poaching. In the Sundarbans, developments such as building projects and new roads within the reclaimed land are also cause for
concern: roads, jetties, even cell-phone towers make remote Tigerland more accessible.

"Sundarbans is a very, very difficult place — it's one of the most
difficult places. That is why tigers are surviving in Sundarbans,"
Kushal said. "The poachers don't know exactly how the tiger
moves, where it's living. That is why they could possibly not do what
they have done to other places. That is the only reason — the terrain itself is protecting the tiger in Sundarbans."

The results for the 2006 census of the Sundarbans population
have not been announced. Estimates by scientists who know the
area intimately suggest somewhere in the region of two hundred tigers. The Wildlife Institute of India, which was responsible for con-
ducting the nationwide survey of all reserves under the auspices of
Project Tiger, has cited the logistical difficulties presented by new
methodology. Previously, a plaster cast was made of the rear left
paw of each individual set of pugmarks — a task that, from the
deck of the Tanaya, at least, seemed of almost Sisyphean impossibil-
ity. For the 2006 census, pug counting was combined with camera trapping and prey and habitat assessment, and in 2007 the
census undertook the new strategy of radio-collaring representative Sundarbans tigers — a momentous development. Hitherto,

Tigerland has existed as a world unto itself, protected, as Kushal had pointed out, by its inscrutability — impenetrable, secretive, inviolate.

Veering southwest, we entered a new network of creeks, cutting diagonally into the interior of Pirkkhalli, a block of islands measuring roughly a hundred and fifty square kilometers and marked on maps as being "dense mixed jungle." "There are resident tigers at Pirkkhalli," Dr. Sanyal said. "As well as those that visit." We entered an arm of the Gosaba River, which broadened to open, long views down its straight course.

Ahead, lazing on the mud, was a small crocodile. As the boat ambled on, Dr. Sanyal told of an eyewitness account reported many years ago: Crossing a broad river, like this one, a tiger had been followed by a crocodile. Maneuvering alongside the tiger, the crocodile thrashed its great tail, striking the tiger across his nose. Here Dr. Sanyal straightened his back and raised his head imperiously; unconsciously, he assumed the mien and manner of the hero-beast. "Tiger had blood coming out of his nose," Dr. Sanyal said, majestically. "But he did not say a thing. He kept on swimming. As soon as he got to the other side, he put one paw on the ground, and he turned with the second paw and came up under the crocodile's belly, and flipped him" — eighteen hundred pounds of estuarine crocodile, which the tiger then ripped open. There was a pause while we savored this tale of strategy and courage. Dr. Sanyal had regained his own gentle manner. "And this is why we love Tiger," he said.

Netidhopani Camp stood at the southern limit of the buffer zone and on the edge of the reserve's most protected core area. Unusually, the site had historic remains: the ruins of a three-hundred-year-old brick temple, built to commemorate a young widow whose prayers to Shiva were said to have brought her dead husband back to life. The interior was rumored to house a lingam of Shiva; two weeks earlier, it had also housed a tiger, which had borrowed its convenient shade.

The quarters of the camp's officials were domestic and attractive, with paths lined with pots of hibiscus, marigolds, and roses — the whole surrounded by a palisade of wire. The fence bore a large inward dent, which had been made by a tiger charging at chatting forest officials. The warden told us that he had lived here for a year and a half, and had seen a lot of tigers. Just five days earlier, two had strolled in together and rolled around on the ground near the sweet-water pond outside the compound, and only two days ago a man in a small fishing party had been killed by a tiger very nearby. One of his companions, who had witnessed the death, had "lost his senses" from fear. It was the third person killed in the area this year — all victims, it was believed, of a single tiger. As the warden put it, "There was a true man-eater around."

The warden was about to go on patrol, and agreed to let us follow his boat. It is not known why Sundarbans tigers have a propensity for man-eating, although theories abound: because the saltwater makes them irritable, because human bodies floating down from the Ganges have whetted their appetite, and so forth; more plausibly, Sundarbans tigers, in their remote domain, have never learned to fear man. Their taste for humans is not, however, as happens elsewhere, because the tigers are old or infirm and humans make easy prey. A distinction must be made, as Dr. Sanyal pointed out, between the "circumstantial man-eater," such as a tigress protecting her cub, and man-eaters like the one across the river, the site of whose last kill the boat had now reached.

It was a pretty bay at the entrance to a narrow channel, and it was easy to see why someone might use it as a mooring. Ahead of us, suddenly, the warden's boat began churning backward; the officials in their khaki park uniforms crowded the starboard rail, pointing into the forest; remembering us, some turned and urgently beckoned. Less than two minutes later, when we pulled up, there was nothing to see but low-growing mangrove trees. The tiger had been resting on the shaded beach afforded by the low tide. Peering deeply into the forest recesses through high-powered binoculars, I could see the natural paths that wound among the mangrove clusters, shelters made of a matting of branches, lairs, and dark shadowy areas — a thousand places to hide a tiger.

"After Project Tiger was launched, it was our duty to minimize the man-animal conflict," Dr. Sanyal said afterward, recalling his years as a forest officer. "Whenever a tiger strays inside a village, one has to go immediately . . . It's an emergency." As field director of the Sundarbans, he had been equipped with two jet speedboats and a marksman with a tranquilizer gun. "I used to take a hand mike with me so that I could guide the people — 'Don't come very near Tiger, keep a distance.'"

In his monthly rounds to the islands and villages, Dr. Sanyal sought to persuade the local people that officialdom was committed to the region, not just to the tigers. Initially, there had been resentment; villagers pointed out, "The tiger is killing *us* — why is *it* protected?" "When they saw that we were attending to them, their enmity to Tiger was gradually reduced," Dr. Sanyal said. "Quite a few tigers were killed before by the villagers." He continued, "Fortunately for me, all the six years I stayed there as field director, not a single tiger was killed by the local people — not a single one. It was only due to the cooperation I got."

Sundarbans tiger attacks were documented as early as the 1600s, and legend has it that during the British colonial era tigers every year claimed hundreds of lives. Today, the number of reported deaths has averaged around ten a year for the past decade. This reduction involved an aggressive campaign to modify the conduct of both man and tiger, which inspired an arsenal of hopeful and imaginative tiger deterrents: masks with a painted human face worn on the back of the head to trick the tiger, who prefers attacking from behind; Tiger Guard Head Gear, a fiberglass casing for the head, neck, and chest, issued to forest staff, who, like villagers, are highly vulnerable. Hot and awkward in the summer, the outfit was, according to Dr. Sanyal, "very comfortable" in the winter, which is the working season. "I went inside the forest many, many times without attack — you look something like an astronaut," he said, which alone may have deterred the baffled tigers. Another measure was the creation of life-size electrified clay dummies, dressed in the clothes of honey gatherers and fishermen and left to stand in the forest, administering a 230-volt jolt to any attacking tiger.

But the primary strategy to "minimize man-eating" was to keep as many people as possible out of the forest. "During my entire stay, I did not find a single case where a tiger came inside a village and killed a man," Dr. Sanyal said. Livestock, not people, were the victims; in 2004, a tiger famously killed sixteen cattle in a single night. "The problem is when the people are going inside the forest," he went on. "That's what I tried to convince them. 'This is what is happening: when Tiger is coming to your territory, he is not killing you; but when you are entering Tiger's places, then the killing takes place.' They realized that, but they said, 'Our living is fishing, honey collecting, and woodcutting, so what to do? We have to venture to Tigerland.'"

We had arranged to meet with a group of honey gatherers, who, of all who venture into Tigerland, undertake the most dangerous forest work. Joining us on a small launch that we had acquired for the outing, they gave instructions to the captain, who took us to a place where the gatherers commonly entered the forest.

A spokesman emerged from the honey collectors, a thin man, with gray hair and beard stubble, named Haldar. He had been going into the forest for honey since he was about twenty, some thirty years ago. There was a protocol for his profession, which he outlined with much authority: around the first of April of every year, when the forest was in full bloom, you went to the Forest Department to obtain a honey-collecting permit, and were issued a tiger-tricking mask, for the back of the head. "We leave them in the boat," he said matter-of-factly, to Dr. Sanyal's consternation. "The mask gets in the way when you are climbing trees." A team of men works together; this year, he had gone out with five companions. Before you went, you made a *puja* and prayed to Banbibi.

To find honey, you followed the bees, climbing a tree and looking up to sight them. The bees must be *full* bees; an empty bee wags his tail and flies erratically, a full bee flies in a true beeline. You spent all day in the forest, smoking out hives.

Traditionally, honey collectors and wood gatherers entered the forest only with a *gunin,* a man credited with knowledge of charms to keep tigers at bay; but, as "Tiger Cult of the Sundarvans" notes, in recent times "more than once their tricks have been proved ineffective . . . to check the howling beast," particularly when *gunins* themselves have fallen to the tiger's paw. The book continues, "And it is interesting that, usually, when a tiger attacks a jungle entrant it breaks the neck of the victim and carries away. But while a tiger attacks a spirited *gunin* . . . it generally puts its paw on the face of the person so that he cannot utter his charm." In thirty years of honey gathering, Haldar said, he had seen twenty-five tigers, and, like the other collectors on the launch, he had been attacked. His friend Sardar, who was sitting beside him, said that years ago he had been jumped from behind and held down under a tiger's paw while one of his companions hit the animal with a wood axe until it released him. Here, Sardar turned his back and lifted his shirt to show a large, dark, unmistakably pug-shaped scar.

Following animated directions, the launch turned and nosed into a shallow inlet. A frisson of expectation passed over the boat, as palpable as a cold shadow, while the mangrove foliage closed around the bow. "Well, here we are," Haldar said with glee every bit as palpable. "Let's all get out!" Dr. Sanyal frowned and gently shook his head, and, after a face-saving pause, the launch reversed and slunk back downriver. Hugging the mud banks, now at low tide, we passed very close to a large snake, which, even with its head buried in a muddy hole, was at least six feet long. Yelping in unison, Dr. Sanyal and Kushal leaned over the boat's rail for a better look. "King cobra!" Kushal exclaimed, as the snake withdrew its head with cold dignity. "You have been asking us about the tiger, but there are other dangerous creatures," Haldar said indignantly. "There are a lot of snakes inside, and in particular the cobra."

Some minutes later, the launch drew abreast of a small, shaky hut set back from the forest fringe and looped with colorful garlands — one of the numerous small shrines to Banbibi that stand along the rivers. "Our families pray to God when we go into the forest," Haldar said. "The wives, the parents — everyone cries. Our wives treat us as dead when we are gone. They eat only at night; imagining us in the forest in the day, they don't eat then. They imagine us in the boat, safe, at night — then they eat." Throughout the Sundarbans, it is common for wives to live like widows while their husbands are in the forest, forgoing the prerogatives of married women, such as colorful saris and the splash of vermillion in their hair. There are also villages of real "tiger widows," women whose husbands entered the forest and simply never came out. At the threat posed by tigers, Haldar waved a hand. "There would be no Sundarbans if there were no tiger," he said, echoing a familiar sentiment. "People will remove the wood." He added, philosophically, "I would be risking my life anyway, whatever I did."

In the settlement of Jharkhali, on Namkhana Island, we sought out the companion of the man who had been killed two days earlier by the tiger we had almost seen. His name was Monoranjan Mondol, and we met in an attractive bungalow of vaguely colonial-era style, with tightly closed green shutters. A few years earlier, two tigers had ambled into the building, and it was now little used. Mondol was a tall, athletic-looking man, with handsome, distinguished features; he walked carefully, very erect, and with the reserve of a man who was still visibly stunned.

The sun through the green shutters formed bands of light across Mondol's face as he described how his party of three men had moored their small boat in the pleasant creek we had seen. At some point, the men noticed pugmarks on the right bank. Someone said, "There's a tiger here; let's hurry and finish." They were looking to the right but the tiger came from the left, and roared. Together, the three men rushed forward, making a noise. "But the tiger was not to be frightened," Mondol recalled. Leaping toward the victim, it caught him by the throat and simply carried him into the forest. Mondol ran after them for some thirty or forty feet and then stopped. "Such a big animal, but there was not a branch broken," he said, and even before his words were translated it was possible to catch the wonderment in his voice: not a branch, not a twig out of place.

Our last hours in the Sundarbans were passed in a narrow creek just beyond the Sundarkati Eco-Conservation Camp, in the western buffer zone. Although not under the jurisdiction of Project Tiger, Sundarkati was known to have a lot of tigers; according to Pradeep Vyas, a joint director of the Biosphere Reserve, over the past several years some twenty-five had strayed across the river into villages in the vicinity, two of which had been trapped or tranquilized recently — one, an old tiger with one hind leg, was transported to the Calcutta zoo.

We had been told of a strategic creek, at the intersection of two channels, and arrived at dawn to find a small boat moored off one of the banks, with a solitary fisherman on board. Fresh pugmarks, made in the night, circled the boat — from right bank to left, from left bank to right. Yes, said the fisherman, looking worried, he had known a tiger was around, but — asking the familiar question — what was he to do?

As the fisherman punted to the river, our boat anchored in the channel. The right bank bore thick stands of phoenix palms, a favorite of the tiger. The sun beat down on the channel. The phoenix palms, striped with dried orangish fronds and dark shadows, were surely tiger territory. As time passed, our talk became idle, and in a low moment I encouraged Kushal to give his tiger roar, as the fishermen and honey gatherers had done in the course of their narratives. Laughing and leaning back against the port rail, Kushal roared — *"AAA-uuugh,"* a sound that swallowed space rather than projected into it.

There was a brief pause, and then, from the starboard side, an answering roar.

"Something big is moving in there," someone called from the roof, but by the time I scrambled up there I saw only the briefest tremble of movement in the fronds.

"If it had been a mating call, he would have responded immediately," Dr. Sanyal said afterward. "Tiger was curious, just testing us."

On four occasions, Dr. Sanyal had alluded to an incident that had taken place years earlier and obviously still haunted him, and on the last day of our voyage he told the story. In 1989, he had been summoned to a village on Basanti Island into which a tiger had strayed. Arriving at dusk with a marksman and a tranquilizing gun, he found the animal lying low in a bamboo grove. The tiger was darted, and Dr. Sanyal and his colleague loaded it onto the flatbed of a rickshaw van. In the dark, with the tiger lying between them, they began the hour-and-a-half journey across the island to the motor launch that would deliver the tiger safely across the river.

"After about an hour, I found that Tiger was coming to," Dr. Sanyal said. As the tiger tried to sit up, Dr. Sanyal asked his assistant to administer Valium. "Then he brought out his box and found there is no Valium," Dr. Sangal recounted. "So I was in a fix." A second, two-milligram dose of tranquilizer was reluctantly administered to the tiger, and they continued on. At the motor launch, the sleeping tiger began salivating heavily, and then blood came from its mouth. It had been over-tranquilized.

"Ultimately, it died," Dr. Sanyal said. He paused before continuing, "The great experience was the next day. I found hundreds of people were coming to see this tiger. I was not feeling well, because it had died. I was sitting there in a chair. Everyone who was coming and seeing the tiger was telling me, 'What is this? Could you not save this animal? It is a beautiful animal! You could have saved it.'

"This thing we say — 'If Tiger is not there, our forest will not be there, we will not get our honey' — that is a secondary thing. But this was the direct impact: they were looking at me — 'You could have saved this beautiful animal.'"

PAUL SALOPEK

Lost in the Sahel

FROM *National Geographic*

Darfur — The Road to Furawiya

THE ROAD WAS NOT REALLY A ROAD. Its two ruts led into
Darfur, to the war in western Sudan, from the unmarked border of
Chad. So much of the Sahel was like this — unmapped, invisible,
yet a boundary nonetheless. The land stretched away in a monot-
ony of gravel pans and dried grasses so translucent — so brittle —
they seemed made of blown glass. The iron horizons never budged.
Yet we were crossing boundaries with every passing hour, mostly
without seeing them.

After I was arrested and imprisoned in Darfur, an American soldier told me, shaking his head in disgust, "You fly over this place
and all you see is miles and miles of nothing." But that was an outsider's delusion. Every outcrop and plain was parsed by unseen tan-
gents, lines, ghostly demarcations. They portioned off the claims of
tribes, individuals, clans. They bulged and recoiled according to
war and season. No-go zones encircled water holes. Certain unseen
lines, *masars,* dictated the migration routes of nomads. There was
nothing haphazard about any of this. To cross one line or to venture too far from another might invite retribution, even death. And
that was the ultimate line of them all in the Sahel: the one between
knowing and ignorance.

The Sahel itself is a line.

The word means "shore" in Arabic, which implies a continental margin, a grand beginning and a final end. Stretching across
northern Africa roughly along the thirteenth parallel, the Sahel di-

vides — or unites, depending on your philosophical bent — the sands of the Sahara and Africa's tropical forests. It is a belt of semiarid grassland that separates (or joins) Arabs and blacks, Muslims and Christians, nomads and farmers, a landscape of greens and a world of tans. Some fifty million of the world's poorest, most disempowered, most forgotten people hang fiercely on to life there. And for thirty-four days in Darfur we joined their ranks.

There were three of us.

Idriss Anu drove the Toyota truck that would be stolen by militants. Daoud Hari was the translator, and for this he would eventually pay with severe beatings. We were en route to the village of Furawiya when the progovernment guerrillas rose silently from the grass.

"Stay in the car," Daoud said.

But it was already too late. Even as the gunmen sauntered up, their hair matted in dreadlocks and their chests slung with small blackened things that looked like dried ears but which were Koranic amulets, we still hadn't grasped that we had crossed a threshold where it no longer mattered what passport you carried, that you were young and loved, that your skin was supposedly not of a torturable color, or that you were a noncombatant. Words had lost all currency as words, and by the time the grinning teenager with the Kalashnikov reached for my door handle, we were condemned to live and die according to choices made by others. We had become truly Sahelian.

The Sahel is a line.

But it is also a crack in the heart — a tightrope, a brink, a ledge. See how its people walk: straight-backed on paths of red dust, placing one foot carefully before the other, as if balanced upon a knife-edge. The Sahel is a bullet's trajectory. It is the track of rains that fall but never touch the sand. It is a call to prayer and a call for your blood, and for me a desert road without end.

Gaga Refugee Camp, Chad

My journey began among refugees in eastern Chad. This is where I met George Bush's father.

Bush tyrannized his family's small plot of sand. He threw his mother's battered dishes to the ground, pulled on visitors' noses,

and scampered away giggling. He got away with this because he was
an only son. His elder sister, age four, despised him. Bush was fat-
cheeked and two. "Boosh!" the refugees cooed. "Boosh-ka!" He was
clearly a great camp favorite. This was in the Gaga settlement,
where more than seven thousand Darfuris lived and died under
UN canvas.

"Only George Bush can stop the Arabs in our land," said Bush's
papa, Ahmed Juma Abakar. He corralled the boy in his lap. "When
he grows up, he will help kill them."

Multiple lines of identity were braided through Abakar. He was a
coffee-colored African with a puff of white hair on his chin. He was
a Masalit, a member of one of the African farming tribes driven out
of Darfur at gunpoint by the janjaweed, the Arab nomads armed by
the Arab-dominated government of Sudan. He detested Arabs. Yet
he himself spoke Arabic. He also served sugary tea in shot glasses
like an Arab, wore a white Arabic robe, and prayed five times a day
toward Mecca. I, too, find this puzzling.

The war in Darfur has killed at least two hundred thousand people and displaced more than two million. It may be the first genocide of the new century. But it also happens to be one of several
similar, if smaller, conflicts boiling across the Sahel. Chad, Niger,
Mali, Nigeria, and Senegal — low-intensity battles smoldered in
each nation I visited. Niger was expelling its Mahamid nomads.
Tuaregs were ambushing African soldiers in Mali. These clashes
were parochial, obscure, yet part of an overarching quarrel: the
eternal struggle over grass, water, and soil between pastoralists and
settled peoples. Viewed this way, the Sahel represents the oldest
killing field in human history. In the Sahel, Cain is still trading
blows with Abel.

In Darfur the violence is infamous because Sudan's government
had cynically armed one side — the Beni Husseins, Ereigats, and
other Arab herders — against rebellious African farmers such as
the Masalits and Furs. These two rivals, both Muslim, had earlier
evolved a complex entente. When a farmer speared a nomad's
camel, elders docked part of his harvest. The plaintiff usually
claimed the grain in a hungry year. It was an antique food bank system. Murder between tribes was settled with a sliding scale of blood
money — a hundred camels for a man, fifty for a woman.

A ten-pound machine with eleven moving parts has erased this
legacy.

The flood of cheap Kalashnikov rifles into Darfur has devalued individual responsibility in warfare. It has undercut the tribal authorities. Young men who once sang songs to their favorite cows now serenaded their guns: "The Kalash brings cash / Without a Kalash you're trash."

"We used to get along," Abakar said. "The Arabs would graze their camels on our fallow fields. They were my father's friends."

I asked when Arabs and Africans would be brothers again. Abakar looked at me with genuine incredulity. He then tuned his transistor radio to the BBC. The Israelis were bombing Lebanon. *"Allah-u akbar!"* the old Muslim tribesman said, cheering on the Israel Defense Forces. He raised George Bush's chubby little arms in triumph.

Darfur — Towé Village

On our first night in Darfur, the gunmen forced Idriss and Daoud into a pickup truck and drove them off into the moonlight. They tortured them out there, tied to a thorn tree for three days. Me they pummeled without enthusiasm inside an abandoned hut in the burned-out village of Towé. Between sessions, I lay trussed on my belly, breathing hard against a dirt floor that smelled of rancid butter. I squinted out a brilliant doorway at two women.

They were planting sorghum in a dry wadi.

The women's work appeared rudderless. They planted their seeds in lines that wriggled across the field, nudged here and there by whims of conversation. The older woman swerved whenever she told jokes, and her seed rows lurched like cardiograms. She giggled into her hands often, and I decided she must be mad. The younger one was more solemn. She toiled briskly, with a sense of purpose, as if engaged in a race, and her planting was much straighter. A tiny child crawled at her side, trying to eat the seed grain. The women labored like this all day. Then, late in the afternoon, they quarreled, and their plantings veered apart in rancor.

It occurred to me that the women were doing more than growing food. They were sowing their autobiographies.

Sex jokes, village gossip, little wisps of song, rebukes to children — all of it lay scribbled in the eccentric lines of their crops.

Women have been singled out for maximum violence in Darfur. Mass rapes by the janjaweed are systematic and well-documented.

As part of a Sudanese campaign of ethnic cleansing, women have been burned alive, shot, bayoneted, and dumped down wells. These stories, too, would be recorded in their fields. Lying in the hut, I imagined flying low over the savannas of Darfur and reading the women's lives inscribed in plots of millet, peanuts, and sorghum. (See that row of melons ending abruptly at midfield? A Fur grandmother dropped her seed bucket and ran at the sound of approaching hoofbeats.)

In Towé the women were Zaghawa seminomads. The laughing one was named Fatim Yousif Zaite. She wasn't crazy. She was forty, with the burning, clairvoyant gaze of the starving, and a smile that transmitted the innocence of her heart. She brought me gourds of *asida*, a yellow lentil paste she could hardly afford to share. Once, while untied to eat, I grabbed both her dusty hands in mine. She sprang back in fear.

But I only wanted to thank you, Fatim. You will always be with me. The janjaweed may toss your kids into vats of boiling water as they had done to children in another village, and the Sudanese Air Force may bomb your wretched fields as they had before, killing five of your family members. But for three days in Darfur you were my mother.

Kirou Bugaje, Niger

A few months later I was in Niger. I took a bus east. The plains turned lush.

Oxcarts jerked along red roads, hauling mountains of peanuts. Children's laughter dribbled from the high grasses. The *thok-thok-thok* of women pounding millet telegraphed the news of full granaries.

This was a surprise. The Sahel of the imagination is a geographic hunger pang. Cataclysmic droughts scorched northern Africa in the 1970s and 1980s. The most recent famine lashed Niger as recently as 2005. In places, the Sahel continues to starve, to lose ground to the Sahara. On the banks of the Niger River houses lie buried in coffins of sand.

Yet in Niger, a country twice the size of France, researchers have been fascinated to discover that nineteen thousand square miles of savanna are more vegetated today than twenty or thirty years ago.

Similar regeneration of trees, grasses, and bushes appears to be under way in parts of Mali and Burkina Faso. The most precious line in the Sahel has always been green. And lately it has been growing thicker, brighter, more lustrous.

Why?

Ecologists disagree. Some credit global warming, which may be boosting rainfall in sections of northern Africa. Others say years of warfare and chaos in the Sahel have depopulated the African countryside, allowing millions of acres to lie fallow and recover.

At the Hausa village of Kirou Bugaje, the plump chief, Abdurahaman Ademu, had his own explanation: the miraculous leaf of a tree.

"The gao improves our yields of millet and sorghum," Ademu said, padding in a white robe and sandals across his tree-shaded fields. "That's why we don't cut the trees down anymore. We plant around them."

The gao, an indigenous acacia known to biologists as *Faidherbia albida,* is a nitrogen-fixer like the alfalfa plant. Its leaf litter is rich in nutrients. Twenty-five years ago Ademu and his people had wiped out virtually every tree within a day's walk to feed themselves in a famine. When their crops failed, they ate the leaves. When the leaves were gone, they razed entire groves to sell for firewood and buy food. But eventually, somewhere, someone remembered that the yields of grain were richer when sown in the fertile shade of surviving gaos. Husbanding wild trees is an ancient practice in the Sahel. Its importance was rediscovered. And from there, the dusty boughs of the gao spread in widening circles of green. Today, without fanfare or mercy concerts, some of the world's poorest farmers are busy stitching huge tracts of the Sahel back together again.

Ademu had three wives. Their names were Zeinahu, Hajara, and Hadjia. He had twenty children whom he called Hey You and This One. He was amused that I found his village beautiful.

At dusk the sky turned orange, and we ate spaghetti drowned in palm oil. The village chirped and squealed like a playground. A white moon rose, and out on the savanna the Fulani nomads were driving their lyre-horned cattle south into Nigeria. They were armed with bows, and some carried broadswords strapped to their backs. There hadn't been a war for years. Drifting to sleep on a prayer rug outside Ademu's family mosque, it was possible to imag-

PAUL SALOPEK

ine that there was nothing in the world that could not be reclaimed.

Darfur — Ghost House Prison

On the third day of our captivity in Darfur, the gunmen traded
Idriss, Daoud, and me to the Sudanese Army for a box of uniforms.

A military helicopter ferried us to El Fasher, the capital of North
Darfur, but over Kutum, a loud banging made my muscles grab. We
were taking rebel ground fire. Holes blinked open in the fuselage,
and a bespectacled officer sitting across from me toppled out of his
seat. He rolled around on the deck clawing at his back. It was just a
spent round, so he survived. His comrades congratulated him as if
he'd won the lottery. But the pilot knew better. After a hard landing at the airport, he jumped out of the machine and strode away
without looking back.

We were taken to a "ghost house" — one of Sudan's many secret
prisons. It was night. A gang of armed toughs screamed into our
faces and shoved us against a mud wall. They called us spies and
waved their cell phones in front of my eyes. The tiny screens displayed burning towers and Lilliputian images of Osama bin Laden.
I thought: This is the end. But of course it was only the beginning.

What can be said about those days?

An agent of the *istikhbarat* pawed through my cell's pit toilet each
morning, looking for what I can't say. His work was unrewarded because I was on a hunger strike. I was protesting my being held sepa-
rately, in solitary confinement. I resumed eating on the eighth day
when the guards informed me they would force-feed me through a
rubber tube. "Like Guantanamo," they said.

My dreams reached malarial intensity. I dreamed of my wife and
of running through the wheat north of Mosul where the falling
Iraqi shells made the sound of bed sheets ripping and of Don
Benito soaking his oak plow in the ranch well in the Sierra Madre. I
dreamed of men I had worked with at sea, and where did you go,
Edie Brickell, and of *la vida loca*.

During one of the midnight interrogations, I spotted a small,
spiky animal sniffing its way across the interrogation room floor. It
looked like a hedgehog. I was lightheaded with hunger. I had long
since run out of things to say. I reached down from my chair.

"Don't touch the hedgehog," the colonel said.

"Okay."

I reached down again.

"Don't — touch — the — hedgehog!" It was his pet.

I remember this distinctly: my face felt odd. It was my first smile in ten days.

Kano, Nigeria

I bumped south in a bush taxi shared with five Fulani nomads and 140 pounds of goat cheese bound for the markets of Nigeria. There were flies.

But for a fly, all of Africa might be Muslim.

Islam galloped across northern Africa by horse and camel while Christian Europe dozed under rulers like Henry the Quarrelsome or Ethelred the Unready. By A.D. 1000 Muslim emissaries — warriors, gold merchants, slavers, scholars, holy men — had planted the green flag of Muhammad and Allah on West African shorelines that wouldn't see the bleached sails of a Portuguese caravel for four centuries. But the bite of the tsetse fly, *Glossina,* barred the way south. A vector for the blood parasite that causes sleeping sickness, the insect killed off numberless waves of invaders and their horses in its lethal domain, the open woodlands below the Sahara.

Today the tsetses still reign, and the religious border still holds. North of the fly zone, Africa remains austerely Muslim; to the south lies a steamy patchwork of Christianity. I encountered this frontier in Kano.

Nigeria's second largest city lay smeared inside its smog. It received few tourists. It had a reputation for pious mayhem.

Hundreds had died in riots between hotheads among Kano's majority Muslims and thousands of minority Christian migrants from Nigeria's south. Conservative imams encouraged the governor to impose Islamic law, or sharia, on the state — a provocation in secular Nigeria — further inflaming tensions. Street signs in the city were written in Arabic, and the shops were stocked by Lebanese, Yemeni, and Egyptian traveling salesmen. Motorcycle taxis didn't pick up women: contact with male drivers was deemed unseemly. A few years ago, local officials boycotted a UN antipolio campaign, claiming the vaccines were sterilizing Muslim girls.

Polio, which had been almost wiped out in Africa, has since rebounded in Nigeria and is reinfecting surrounding countries.

There is now a black Taliban movement in Kano. One local mullah dubs himself "Kandahar," after the capital of Afghanistan's fanatics.

"I would pay with my blood if I preached inside the Old City," said Foster Ekeleme, the Methodist bishop in Kano's Christian outskirts.

Ekeleme was an Igbo from the southeast who moved with the stiff gait of a retired boxer. He had survived good and bad times between Kano's two great faiths. When I visited, he complained bitterly that his flock was targeted every time the United States bombed another Muslim country, but he ended with a plea. "I am hopeful! We Christians and Muslims must learn to coexist. Look — even my night watchman is Muslim!"

It was true. A bored Hausa youth in a white skullcap leaned against Ekeleme's church. The church itself was a fortress of raw concrete circled by a high iron fence. The fence was spiked. All that was missing was a moat. Suspecting that the Christians were speaking from a position of weakness, I consulted a Muslim thinker.

Salisu Shehu was a mellow scholar with droopy eyelids. He taught Islamic studies at Bayero University, where hand-painted billboards exhorted students to Dress Fashionable and Decently.

This is what the professor said: while it was lamentable that people had been burned, hacked, and shot to death for their choice of gods in Kano, the real enemy was poverty. Christian Igbos and Muslim Hausas required jobs. The youths were unemployed, restless. As for Islam in the Sahel, it was neither extremist nor intolerant — it was a very old type of Sufism expounded by the moderate Imam Malik; a nomad's faith rooted in the traders' live-and-let-live ethic.

"The Sahel isn't a wall between Africans," Shehu said. "It's a crossroads — a bridge."

Today that bridge is groaning. Both the Muslim and Christian populations of Africa have boomed over the past ten years. In the Sahel, where birthrates are among the highest in the world, mosques financed by conservative Middle Eastern states have sprouted in cities and villages. For their part, many of Africa's Christians aren't of the turn-the-cheek Presbyterian sort. Church loudspeakers boom out sermons, preachers bless militias, and several of the riots in Kano were ignited by Christian massacres of Muslims elsewhere in Nigeria. But I never got to meet the extremists.

At five in the morning, my hotel phone rang. It was a secret policeman.

"Whatisyourpurposehere?" he demanded.

"Beg your pardon?"

"Youmustcometothelobbynow!"

The tone was clear if the English wasn't. My paperwork was in order. But I panicked. I raced through the list of sources who might have betrayed my presence in Kano, settling on a dour pharmacist who must have Googled my name and pounced on the recent headlines: SUDAN CHARGES U.S. JOURNALIST WITH ESPIONAGE.

With the echoes of cell doors clanging inside my head, I made excuses to the agent in the lobby. I frantically began hiding my notes but only managed to throw out my back lifting the room's refrigerator. I tossed my bag out the second-floor window, eased myself down the exterior sill, and dropped the last nine or ten feet to the ground. My back exploded. So I quit. I gave up. Hobbling into the lobby jackknifed at the waist, with my T-shirt on backward and my surviving notes tucked into my socks, I found the place empty. The policeman had got tired of waiting. This was Nigeria.

By sunrise I had bought all the open seats in an old Peugeot bush cab and left for Mali.

Darfur — Police Station Jail

The Russians were very drunk. There were three of them — small, medium, and large — and the Sudanese police had shot out their truck windows. The guards pitched them into our cell at midnight. The Russians had broken curfew.

They were helicopter pilots contracted to AMIS, the beleaguered African Union peacekeeping force in Darfur. One began singing patriotic songs that would last all night, and the other two asked why I was there. I told them. I had crossed into Darfur illegally, through the side door of Chad, like scores of other Western journalists. But I had been caught. I faced a twenty-year sentence. I had to repeat "spying" three times until they understood.

"Sudan" — spat the small one — "is fakit." He wore a mullet

hairdo and yellow Beatle boots that curled at the tips like elf shoes. Eventually they would all be deported.

Another prisoner had meanwhile escaped in the night — a Darfuri gunrunner — leaving a cupful of his blood splashed on the jail yard wall. He'd maimed himself on the concertina wire. As a result, Idriss, Daoud, and I spent the next two days locked down with sixteen other prisoners inside a fifteen-by-fifteen-foot cell. We hunkered against each other in fetal positions like eggs incubating in a carton. Pickpockets, con men, goat rustlers, two street kids, and a lunatic took turns pissing out the barred door.

This was at the civilian police station, our second place of internment in El Fasher.

The cell's interior walls were polished black with human grease from the backs of sitting men. Above this wainscoting of grime rose thousands of scrawled names. And some of them were ours.

Timbuktu, Mali

In Mali I took a ferry up the Niger River to see the Sahel's most fabled backwater.

Timbuktu started as a nomads' watering hole, grew by the sixteenth century into the Oxford of the Islamic world (twenty-five thousand scholars once resided there), and has faded back into a geographic coma. Its sand alleys were like solar ovens. Goats jaywalked on the main street, and dehydrated tourists sent letters postmarked from a town synonymous with the uttermost end of the Earth. I ducked into the shade of the Imam Ben Essayouti library for a glimpse of a golden age.

Banzoumana Traore was a Malian albino with hazel eyes and a loose cotton suit ablaze with blue and yellow polka dots. I looked again and saw that the dots were antimalaria capsules. Traore was the archivist at the library, which housed a remnant of Timbuktu's priceless trove of medieval manuscripts. With money from South Africa, the United States, Arab countries, and Europe, small private libraries like this one were popping up all over Timbuktu. They held the Sahel's most astonishing intellectual legacy: tens of thousands of hand-lettered manuscripts, some stored in caves and household cupboards since the city's fall to the Moroccans in 1591. There was love poetry composed in Moorish Spain. There were tracts on Islamic jurisprudence and centuries-old essays on, among other subjects, astronomy, optics, medicine, ethics, and botany. Gazing on these fragile treasures, it was hard not to lament the dearth of book learning in the Arabic-speaking world. A recent UN study found that only ten thousand books have been translated into Arabic over the past 1,200 years — barely equivalent to the number of books Spain translates every year.

Traore's bright pink index finger slid across inks concocted from lampblack. He read aloud of a slave girl in ninth-century Baghdad who shamed the caliph's advisers in a contest of wits (a lesson on women's worth), of a discourse on the Islamic propriety of smoking tobacco (the 223-year-old conclusion was positive), and of an antique memory aid for learning algebra (by matching certain tones to numbers, students could sing out equations).

Timbuktu had been ruled by the kings of Mali and Songhai, by the Moroccans and the colonial French. "Local families guarded the manuscripts through it all," a proud Traore said.

When I arrived, yet another empire was eyeing desolate Timbuktu.

U.S. Special Forces bucked through town in dusty Humvees. Having learned a lesson from Afghanistan — ignorance isn't bliss, and ruinscapes of poverty, violence, and neglect incubate a murderous rage — Washington was taking a renewed interest in Muslim black Africa. The Pentagon was spending a hundred million dollars a year to train impoverished Sahelian armies in antiterror tactics. A brand-new Africa command center, AFRICOM, would come on line in October 2008, though few African countries wished to host it.

This murky front in the global war on terrorism was yet another invisible line in the Sahel.

It zigzagged across the dunes north of Timbuktu where Green Berets taught Malian soldiers how to ambush Algeria-based jihadists. The Malians were underfed, hypercourteous, and lacked even the most basic equipment. Some were deaf. Others needed eyeglasses. "They shoot into the sand," drawled a U.S. master sergeant. The world's elite soldiers swooped down on outlying villages like well-toned aid workers, vaccinating babies, filling cavities, and deworming bony nomad cattle. But the most effective hearts-and-minds operation I saw was illicit.

His name was David. His shaved head was burned puce by the sun, his eyes glittered with resolve, and he was a sixteen-year U.S.

Army veteran. He had been deployed to Africa before and wished to convert to Islam, which shows that there is no occupation without counteroccupation. He slipped out of the Special Forces compound at 9 P.M. and drove to the mud-brick palace of Timbuktu's imam. "My gun — I forgot about my gun," he said, realizing he couldn't very well take his pistol to a conversion ceremony. He stashed the weapon under the SUV seat.

The imam was round and jolly and sat cross-legged under a whirring ceiling fan. A television muttered the latest soccer score between Lyon and Real Madrid. The imam instructed David to repeat the *shahadah* three times and lectured him at length on the five pillars of faith, in both Songhai and French.

"I missed some of that," David said.

A half dozen Malian youths took pictures with their cell phones. They were trembling with excitement. A modern centurion embracing Allah in exotic Timbuktu was a once-in-a-lifetime sight. It made almost anything seem possible. David would later be reprimanded for violating security procedures. But for a few electric minutes amid the tan dunes of Africa, the shadows of Abu Ghraib receded.

"Fin du cérémonie!" declared the imam, clapping his hands. He added for David's sake, "Mission accomplished!" I liked the imam immensely. He was dying to catch the end of the soccer match.

Darfur — Judiciary Prison

Thursdays were judgment day in El Fasher.

At our third jail, a concrete cellblock outside the local courthouse, Sudanese magistrates in pale blue leisure suits rendered their verdicts according to *hudud,* the Islamic punitive code, and police meted out sentences on the spot with an ox-hide whip. I had never seen anyone flogged before. They forced us to watch.

The whip landed with a muffled pop on the backs, buttocks, and legs of prisoners. It was astonishing: how could human beings sweat so much — so fast? After ten blows, the prisoners were wet as swimmers. At twenty, the courtyard wall behind the whipping post was spattered with their sweat. The men's muscles spasmed. Their torsos writhed like trees in a gale. But their grit beggared belief. One middle-aged convict, a Darfuri with the respectable, middle-class look of a schoolteacher, took a hundred lashes without crying out.

When it was done, he walked with great purpose across the yard, as if on some errand, and toppled facedown in the dust. He was an adulterer.

The chief whip man was Corporal Salah.

He was built square as a butcher's block, and at age thirty, his hair was leached of color. Near the end of our imprisonment, on the days when I was feeling bright, I accepted his challenges to play chess. He almost always won. He was a student of the aggressive moves of Bobby Fischer. When he spoke, it was usually in the immature certainties of jihad — "once the world converts to Islam" — but his frequent sighs told a story of repressed ambition. At night he pored over textbooks on microbiology. He dreamed of laying his big, blunt-fingered hands on the brows of patients in hospital wards. He saw himself clad in the snowy whites of a doctor, not the coarse fatigues of a cop.

Will you believe me when I tell you that there was gentleness in Corporal Salah's heart? That he spoke to his victims tenderly, urging them not to be afraid, even as he scourged the hide on their backs?

By this time our whereabouts had become known. An American Air Force lieutenant colonel and a Marine major brought us Cheez Whiz and every other thing, and an American diplomat brought me Faulkner. Eventually Bill Richardson, governor of my home state of New Mexico, intervened. Daoud and Idriss returned to Chad, to the high wire of the Sahel. I tumbled twenty hours across the Earth in the governor's borrowed jet.

I was doing laundry two months later when the telephone rang. It took me a moment to connect the wiry voice of the caller to certain muscular hands — the fingers clamped on men's shoulders, guiding them firmly to a wall flecked with sweat.

"Hello, my friend," Corporal Salah bellowed.

He was shouting over a poor connection. He was in Khartoum, he said, where he'd been transferred, unhappily, to a bigger prison. He asked after my health. But what he really wanted to talk about was the U.S. visa lottery.

Saint-Louis, Senegal

The last line in the Sahel was the Atlantic.

The Senegalese capital of Dakar had the fevered feel of an embarkation point — a maritime city of pushy touts, whores for every pocketbook, and scraps of cardboard flattened on sidewalks where visa hunters camped in lines outside European embassies. A reverse trickle of European youngsters, tattooed, puffing cigarettes, self-conscious in their skins, strolled the waterfront. They rode ferries to Île de Gorée, to see the famous "doorway of no return" for slaves bound for the Americas and Europe. (In truth, few of the estimated ten to twenty-eight million Africans sold into bondage in the New World ever passed that way.) Senegalese papers told lurid tales of a new exodus: African migrants dying en masse while trying to reach the Canary Islands, an outpost of Europe, in motorized canoes.

For me the Sahel ended at the door of Didier, the captain of one of these boats. I met him in Saint-Louis.

He lived on the beach in a shack above the high-tide mark. He agreed reluctantly to talk. What he was doing was illegal. He had already steered two shiploads of Senegalese, Malians, Guineans, Nigerians, and Burkinabes to the Canaries. All had hocked their bicycles, their wives' treadle sewing machines, their parents' barren farms, their slum shacks — everything they owned to make the $900 passage to a Sahelian's version of El Dorado: washing dishes in Valencia or hustling leatherware in the piazzas of Rome. Twelve paying customers had died on him. They had gone out of their heads, Didier explained. They guzzled seawater on the five-day, eight-hundred-nautical-mile journey through the Atlantic's swells.

"We read the Koran over them and threw them over," he said. "Otherwise they start to stink."

Didier was leaving that evening with another canoe. He would earn a small fortune, a thousand dollars (a good year's wages) in a week. He was beautifully muscled. Yet despite his virile swagger in brand-new jeans and red T-shirt, his glances collapsed inward with fear. He was a man poised on a gangplank. Ambulances were wailing that entire afternoon in Saint-Louis. An emigrant canoe had foundered offshore. Bodies washed up with all the skin abraded from their arms where they had clung to the doomed boat's gunwales. More than a hundred people were missing.

Tens of thousands attempt this passage every year. Hundreds die. The Europeans were sending naval vessels to try to stop them.

What was going on here could just as well be called the mass evacuation of Africa as much as "illegal migration." It was a desperate flight from a way we'll never be. An underpaid schoolteacher in North America or Europe earns not ten times, not twenty times, but a hundred times more than millions of Sahelians. To think such ravening disparity will somehow never touch you is foolish. In the teeming fishermen's quarter of Saint-Louis, among the shanties where battered TVs disgorged idiotic French reality shows, and in the sand alleyways speckled with goat droppings, there was talk of bigger canoes, of more barrels of diesel fuel crammed into holds — reenacting the old slave crossing to the Caribbean, to America.

I watched Didier leave at sunset.

I last saw him standing stiffly at the tiller of his boat, wearing a red slicker, nosing out of the harbor amid a screen of other fishing smacks. He did not acknowledge my wave. A little girl did cartwheels on the beach among piles of human waste. Impossibly clean white birds pecked at things. Didier's canoe diminished into a darkening sea that seem sketched in charcoal. I was secretly with them. I saw myself huddled in that plank boat. But even if we all survived, I wasn't sure we would ever truly escape the Sahel.

ERIC WEINER

My Servant

FROM *New York Times Magazine*

SOME YEARS AGO, I was looking for an apartment in Delhi. I had just moved to India, and everything about it was frenzied and raw. Every place I saw was either too pricey or noisy or prone to attack by flying cockroaches the size of small birds.

Finally I found a flat with heavy wooden doors and a terrace that overlooked a pleasant street. The landlord, an imperious man with tufts of wiry black hair sprouting from his left ear, proudly pointed out the apartment's features, including Western-style toilets, air-conditioning (a real luxury) and, he added matter-of-factly, a "servant." I wasn't entirely comfortable with the way that sounded, but I can't say I was shocked either. I had been told that a great many people in India had servants (or what Americans would call household help), and I figured this was the sort of cultural difference I had better get used to.

A few days later, the servant loped upstairs and reported for duty. He was skinny, alarmingly so, with mahogany skin and sharp features. His name was Kailash, and he was eleven years old. This was a cultural difference that I was not prepared to accept. I started downstairs to confront the landlord, but then hesitated. I rationalized that if this boy, an orphan from a neighboring state, didn't work for me, he would work for someone else, and who knows how that person would treat him? Washing my hands of Kailash seemed like a cop-out, or so I told myself.

And so every afternoon Kailash climbed the stairs and knocked meekly on my door. He was, truth be told, not much of a cleaner: he didn't remove the dirt; he just rearranged it. But he was naturally kind, honest beyond reproach and, it turned out, a wizard with temperamental fax machines and printers.

Kailash picked up English by eavesdropping. Before long he was saying "I'm history" and "Get outta here." Over time he began to tell me things, like how his parents died years ago, or how much he loved cricket, or how the landlord beat him if he didn't cook the *chapatis* right. I'm not sure when I decided to help, but it didn't cost much to hire a tutor, and soon he was in school for the first time in years. Later, when I moved to another apartment, Kailash moved with me. He was, technically, still my employee, but at some point he began referring to me as his parent. This made me uneasy, yet there was no denying my new role. I said horrible, parental things to him like "If you're going to live in my house you're going to live by my rules."

One spring, puberty arrived, and suddenly I was the "father" of a hormonal Indian teenager. Once, while I was out of town, Kailash and a few friends rented porn movies and a VCR. I was appalled but also secretly pleased by his initiative. Whenever I asked Kailash about his aspirations, he demurred. "Whatever you want me to do, sir," he would say. "As you wish."

I always imagined that our relationship would follow a linear, screenplay trajectory. Orphaned Indian boy has fateful meeting with bighearted American; boy struggles to overcome disadvantaged youth; boy finally perseveres and is eternally grateful for bighearted American's help. But more than a decade after I left India, Kailash and I were stuck in the second act.

Thanks to my quarterly wire transfers, Kailash lives in a tiny apartment in Delhi that is too cold in the winter and too hot in the summer. His main companion is a Pomeranian named Envy. A while ago, he turned down a job I arranged for him serving tea at a packaging company — a job he would have accepted before he met me. I have raised his expectations, a dangerous thing in a country of more than a billion restive souls.

My Indian friends have watched from the sidelines, skeptical of my efforts to "save" Kailash. "You're thinking like an American," they say, as if it were a mental illness. "Kailash is from a lower class, a lower *caste*. He can only go so far. Face the facts."

They're right, I've said to myself, trying to come to terms with the notion that this Indian orphan and I will be tethered for life.

Yet I haven't been able to shake the naive idea that one day Kailash will float free into a life of his own making. I was pleased when, a few months ago, he began attending computer school, learning code, hoping to grab his sliver of India's shiny, high-tech future.

On a recent visit to Delhi, I sat down with Kailash at one of the coffee joints that are sprouting there. I needed to do some work first, I told him. It wouldn't take long. My laptop, as usual, was slow to boot. Kailash glanced over my shoulder and was appalled to discover that I was still using Windows 2000. "It's too slow," he said. "You really should get Windows XP."

"Okay, Kailash," I said, looking at the handsome twenty-three-year-old who has replaced the scrawny boy of years ago. "As you wish."

ALMA GUILLERMOPRIETO

Bolivia's Wrestlers

FROM *National Geographic*

AT THE LARGEST PUBLIC GYMNASIUM in El Alto, Bolivia, daylight is fading from the windows, and hundreds of people along the bleachers are growing impatient. They have been sitting for more than two hours now, jeering and whistling and yelling encouragement at the succession of *artistas* who have faced off in the center of the gym to match wits and perform dazzling feats of strength and skill. But it is growing late, and over the blaring disco music, foot-stomping and impatient whistles can be heard in crescendo: "Bring them on!" The music grows louder, the whistling, too; there is a sense that rebellion may be about to erupt, but at last the houselights flash and dim, and the music shifts to the *chunka-chunka* beat of a modern Bolivian *huayño*. An announcer emotes into the microphone, the curtains leading to the locker rooms part, and "Amorous Yolanda" and "Evil Claudina," this evening's stars, make their longed-for appearance to ecstatic applause.

Like many of the women of Aymara descent in the audience, Yolanda and Claudina are dressed to the nines in the traditional fashion of the Andean highlands: shiny skirts over layers of petticoats, embroidered shawls pinned with filigreed jewelry, bowler hats. Their costumes glisten in the spotlights while they make a regal progress around the bleachers, greeting their public with the genteel smiles of princesses, twirling and waving gracefully until the music stops. That's the sign for the two women to swing themselves deftly onto the wrestling ring that has been the focus of this afternoon's activity. Swiftly they remove their hats, unpin their shawls, and . . . *whap, whap, whap!* Claudina belts Yolanda one, Yolanda slaps Claudina, Claudina tries to escape, but Yolanda grabs Claudina by her pigtails and spins her around, and *WHAM!* Claudina whirls through the air, petticoats and braids flying, and lands flat on her back on the mat, gasping like a fish. The audience goes nuts.

Welcome to the delirious world of Bolivian wrestling. In the cold, treeless, comfortless city of El Alto ("high point"), thirteen thousand feet above sea level, there are one million people, most of whom fled here over the past three decades to escape the countryside's pervasive misery. The lucky ones find steady jobs down in the capital city of La Paz, which El Alto overlooks. Many sell clothes, onions, pirated DVDs, Barbie dolls, car parts, small desiccated mammals for magic rituals. The poorest *alteños* employ themselves as beasts of burden. All of them battle hopeless traffic, a constant scarcity of fuel and water, the dull fatigue of numbing labor, the odds that are stacked against them. When they're done working, they need to play, and when they want to play, one never knows what they will come up with. Lately, they've come up with the extraordinary spectacle of the *cholitas luchadoras* — fighting cholitas — which has given new life to Bolivians' own version of Mexican *lucha libre,* a freeform spectacle somewhere between a passion play, a wrestling match, and bedlam.

"Watch out!" the entire audience shrieks. Yolanda has been celebrating her victory, but Claudina, as proof of her evil nature, is about to lunge at her from behind. Yolanda spins too late; Claudina knocks her flat and clambers like a crazy person onto the ropes. "I'm the prettiest!" she yells at the audience. "You're all ugly! I'm your daddy! I'm the one the gringos have come to see!" Indeed three rows of ringside seats are filled with foreigners, all popeyed, but they're actually irrelevant. It's their fellow Bolivians the cholitas are performing for.

Claudina, who is officially a *ruda,* or baddie, has taken a swig of soda pop and is spraying the public with it at the precise moment that Yolanda, a *técnica,* or goodie, pounces on her and drags her up to the bleachers, sending the spectators there scattering in blissful, screaming alarm. Yolanda wins! No, Claudina wins! No, Yolanda! But wait! The audience screams in warning again because a new menace has silently made his entrance: "Black Abyss" — or maybe it's "Satanic Death" or the "White Skeleton"; it's hard to keep track

— has leaped into the fray and has Yolanda in a ferocious leg lock. The situation looks hopeless, but no, here comes the "Last Dragon," out of nowhere, and he's carrying a chair! And he's whomping Black Abyss, or maybe the Skeleton, or maybe Yolanda, on the head with it! Even Claudina seems to have lost track of who's who: she's taking a flying leap at her own ally, the loathsome "Picudo." "He is destroyed forever!" the announcer yells frenetically.

Or almost forever: in *lucha libre,* no defeat is ever final.

"What I want to make absolutely clear," says Juan Mamani, who fights as a *rudo* under the *lucha* name of "El Gitano" and who runs the show, "is that it was me who came up with the idea of the cholitas." Mamani is a tall, angular man whom it would be kind to call unfriendly. He cuts phone conversations short by hanging up, does not show up for appointments he has been cornered into making, and tries to charge for interviews. His cholitas are terrified of him. "Don't tell him you called me; don't tell him you have my phone number!" one of them begged.

I hunted him down near the El Alto gym, and after an unpromising start — he kept trying to duck past me — I said the magic words "Mexico" and "Blue Demon." The face of Juan Mamani, the ogre, was suddenly wreathed in smiles. "My greatest passion is *lucha libre,*" he said. "And for us, Mexico is the example. Blue Demon is for me *lo mas grandioso.*"

Mamani's wrestlers all hold daytime jobs, and he makes a living from a small electrical-repair shop. But he has invested a good part of his life's earnings in a huge wrestling ring at home, where his group trains. He pays his wrestlers between twenty and thirty dollars a match and probably doesn't clear vastly greater amounts himself. "Here in Bolivia, it's impossible to make a living from this great passion of mine," Mamani said. His dream was to create a Bolivian school of wrestling heroes to equal the feats of the great Mexican *lucha* legends; their daring leaps and backflips, their unique costumes and regal bearing. Had I seen Blue Demon fight? Really? He shook my hand as I left.

About seven years ago, when he was fretting about the diminishing audience for the weekly *lucha libre* spectacle at the El Alto gym, Mamani had the inspired idea to teach women to wrestle and put them in the ring in cholita clothes. "Martha la Alteña," an outgoing *luchadora*, not remarkably muscular but very strong, was among the sixty or so young women who answered Mamani's open audition call. Like several of the eight or so who ended up staying, she comes from a wrestling background. "My father was one of the original Mummies," she said proudly, referring to one of the best loved, or most dreaded, of Bolivian *lucha*'s creatures.

Amorous Yolanda was also inspired by her *luchador* father, and even though her parents separated on unfriendly terms when she was an infant, she used to sneak into El Coliseo in downtown La Paz — long since gone — to watch him perform. "But a lot of times men don't believe in women," she told me. "Once I heard my father say that he wished he'd had a son instead of me, so he could follow in his footsteps as a *luchador*." When she heard about Mamani's casting call, Yolanda, then still called Veraluz Cortés, raced to audition, leading to a temporary rift with her father. Whether her *lucha* stardom also contributed to the breakup of her marriage is not clear.

Outside the ring, Martha la Alteña generally wears what is called the señorita style of dress — blue jeans and sweaters — and part of the glamour of her cholita costume is provided by turquoise-blue contact lenses. Yolanda, on the other hand, who is thin and very intense, wears a bowler hat and petticoats and skirts, even when she is knitting sweaters at her day job, and considers herself an authentic cholita.

"Sometimes my daughters ask why I insist on doing this," she said. "It's dangerous; we have many injuries, and my daughters complain that wrestling does not bring any money into the household. But I need to improve every day. Not for myself, for Veraluz, but for the triumph of Yolanda, an artist who owes herself to her public."

Esperanza Cancina, forty-eight, who sells used clothing for a living, has installed her large family and her ample self, in all her petticoats and skirts, in the choice ringside spot behind the announcer's chair, at a safe angle from the popcorn and chicken bones and empty plastic bottles the audience likes to pelt the *rudos* with. Ringside seats cost about $1.50 each, which is hardly cheap, but Señora Cancina comes faithfully to the show every other Sunday. "It's a distraction," she explains. "The cholitas fight here, and we laugh and forget our troubles for three or four hours. At home, we're sad."

Around us, the youngest members of the audience, including her grandchildren, are skittering around the edges of the ring in an adrenaline frenzy, trying out *lucha* leaps and swarming after a wrestler who has just been defeated, trying to hug him, touch his costume. The music is booming, and it's hard to conduct a conversation, but Señora Cancina is amiable and cooperative. She had twelve children, she says, but after a pause adds that six died. How? Her face takes on a distressing blankness. "Scarlet fever, diarrhea, those things . . ." she murmurs, and has to repeat the answer over the noise. Would she have wanted to be a *luchadora*, too? Definitely, she says. "Our husbands make fools of us, but if we were wrestlers we could express our fury."

Over on the long side of the bleachers, in the prime chicken-bone-throwing area, Rubén Copa, a shoemaker from La Paz with an easy, friendly smile, is waiting impatiently for the afternoon's final match — one in which the "Mummy Ramses II" will take on cholitas yet to be announced. "Bolivian wrestlers aren't half bad, you know," he says with a touch of pride. Not even the women? He huffs and waves his hands in protest. "There's none of that anymore! Every kind of work is for everyone now." I want to know if it's true that men come to the *lucha libre* just to see the cholitas' (very modest) underpants. For a moment he looks offended, but then he smiles again. "Not at all!" he says. "I come to see them wrestle! You'll see for yourself how good they are."

And indeed, a few minutes later the Mummy Ramses II is staggering around invincibly in a red-stained jumpsuit and a fright wig, dragging one cholita behind him while another one looks for something to set him on fire with, and the kids are screaming in delicious terror, and Señora Cancina is yelling things at the Mummy that cannot be printed in this magazine, grinning broadly as she does so. The Mummy is slamming his victim against the wall, and it looks tough for the cholitas, as the announcer warns us, in this *definitivo y final combate* — it looks very, very tough. But something tells me that you can't keep a cholita down.

Here comes Martha, flying through the air!

ROGER COHEN

The End of the End of the Revolution

FROM *New York Times Magazine*

ON MY FIRST DAY in Havana, I wandered down to the Malecón, the world's most haunting urban seafront promenade. A norte was blustering, sending breakers crashing over the stone dike built in 1901 under short-lived American rule. Bright explosions of spray unfurled onto the sidewalk.

I was almost alone on a Sunday morning in Cuba's capital city of 2.2 million people. A couple of cars a minute passed, often finned '50s beauties, Studebakers and Chevrolets, extravagant and battered. Here and there, a stray mutt scrounged. Washing flapped on the ornate ironwork balconies of crumbling mansions. Looking out on the ocean, I searched in vain for a single boat.

It was not always so, ninety miles off the coast of Florida. In 1859, Richard Henry Dana Jr., an American lawyer whose *To Cuba and Back* became a classic, sailed into Havana. He later wrote: "What a world of shipping! The masts make a belt of dense forest along the edge of the city, all the ships lying head into the street, like horses at their mangers." Over the ensuing century, Cuba became the winter playground of Americans, a place to gamble, rumba, smoke *puros*, and sip *mojitos*, the land of every vice and any trade. Havana bars advertised "Hangover Breakfasts." They were much in demand. The mafia loved the island, the largest in the Caribbean; so did the American businessmen who controlled swathes of the sugar industry and much else.

Then, a half-century ago, on January 1, 1959, Fidel Castro brought down the curtain on Fulgencio Batista's dictatorship. America's cavorting-cum-commerce ceased. Miami became Cuba's second city as, over the years, hundreds of thousands fled communist rule.

The confining shadow of Fidel's tropical curtain, on the fiftieth anniversary of the revolution, was captured in the emptiness before me — of the Malecón, but even more so of the sea. I noticed over subsequent days that Cubans perched on the seafront wall rarely looked outward. When I asked Yoani Sánchez, a dissident blogger (www.desdecuba.com/generaciony), about this, she told me: "We live turned away from the sea because it does not connect us, it encloses us. There is no movement on it. People are not allowed to buy boats because if they had boats, they would go to Florida. We are left, as one of our poets put it, with the unhappy circumstance of water at every turn."

It is unnatural to perceive the sea and a distant horizon as limiting. But in Cuba a lot of things are inverted, or not as they first appear. A repressive society long under a single ruler — the ailing eighty-two-year-old Fidel still holds Cubans in his thrall even if he formally handed the presidency to his younger brother, Raúl, in 2006 — develops a secret lexicon of survival.

Through a labyrinth of rations, regulations, two currencies, and four markets (peso, hard currency, agro, and black), people make their way. Stress is rare but depression rampant in an inertia-stricken economy. Truth is layered. Look up and you see the Habana Libre, the towering hotel where Fidel briefly had his headquarters after the revolution: it began life as the Hilton. The seafront Riviera hotel, now so communist-drab it seems to reek of cabbage, once housed the rakish casino of the mobster Meyer Lansky.

Turning west along the seafront that first gusty day, I encountered a strange sight that summoned the United States from its tenebrous presence: a phalanx of poles, topped with snapping flags displaying a five-pointed Cuban star against a black backdrop, bearing down on the eastern facade of a boxy concrete-and-glass structure that houses the U.S. Interests Section in Havana. The flag barricade was put up to block an electronic billboard on the side of the building. In 2006, U.S. officials put political slogans on the billboard; it now transmits news not otherwise accessible to Cubans.

This seafront tableau is laughable: the United States unreeling red-lettered strips of unread news into a sea of black flags and defiance. It captures all the fruitless paralysis of the Cuban-American

confrontation, a tense stasis Barack Obama has vowed to overcome. Diplomatic relations have been severed since 1961; a U.S.
trade embargo has been in place almost as long; the Cold War has
been over for almost two decades. To say the U.S.-Cuban relationship is anachronistic would be an understatement.

But changing it won't be easy. As with Iran — the only country
with which noncommunication is more pronounced — bad history, predatory past U.S. practices, and the expediency for auto-
cratic regimes of casting the United States as diabolical enemy all
work against bridge-building. When, a little farther west down the
Malecón, I met with Josefina Vidal, the director of the Foreign Ministry's North American department, I found her anger as vivid as
her elegant purple dress.

"I once saw a slogan on that U.S. billboard saying Cuban women
have to prostitute themselves because they do not have the re-
sources to survive," she told me. "This is totally unacceptable, a vio-
lation of the Vienna Convention!" (The Vienna Convention of
1963 regulates consular relations.)

Vidal continued: "The U.S. wants to punish Cuba with its blockade. It cannot accept us the way we are. It cannot forgive us our independence. It cannot permit us to choose our own model. And
now along comes Obama and says he will lift a few restrictions, but
that in order to advance further Cuba must show it is making democratic changes. Well, we do not accept that Cuba has to change in
order to deserve normal relations with the United States."

But on Havana's streets the name Obama is often uttered as if it
were a shibboleth. Many people want to believe he offers a way out
of the Cuban web that Fidel's infinite adroitness and intermittent
ruthlessness have woven over a half-century.

Wayne Smith, who ran the U.S. Interests Section under the Carter
administration, has observed that "Cuba seems to have the same effect on American administrations that the full moon used to have
on werewolves." There is something about this proximate island, so
beautiful yet so remote, so failed yet so stubborn, that militates
against the exercise of U.S. reason.

It's not just the humiliation of the botched 1961 Bay of Pigs invasion, when 1,500 CIA-backed Cuban exiles tried to overthrow the
nascent Castro regime. It's not just the memory of the Soviet intro-

duction in 1962 of missiles to the island that almost brought nuclear Armageddon. It's not just the traded accusations of terrorism, the surrogate conflicts of the Cold War from Angola to the Americas, the downed planes, the waves of immigrants, the human rights confrontations, the espionage imbroglios, or the custody battles. It's something deeper, and that something has its epicenter in Miami.

Just before the Obama victory, I lunched in the city's Little Havana district with Alfredo Durán, a former president of the Bay of Pigs Veterans Association. Inevitably, we ate at the kitschy Versailles Restaurant, long a social hub of the Cuban-American community. Durán, who was imprisoned in Cuba for eighteen months after the Bay of Pigs fiasco, is a man mellowed by age. Furious with Kennedy and the Democrats in the invasion's aftermath — "there was a feeling we were sacrificed, left to eat possum in the swamps around the bay" — he decided after the Cold War that anti-Fidel vitriol was a blind alley and the trade embargo counterproductive. Fellow veterans were furious; they stripped his photo from the premises of the veterans' association.

"I say, 'Lift the embargo unilaterally, put the onus on Cuba,'" Durán told me. "If we negotiate, what do we want from them? They have very little to give."

As he spoke, a little ruckus erupted outside between Republicans and Democrats. Durán smiled: "You know, the only place Cuba still arouses passions is right outside this restaurant. Yet U.S. policy toward Cuba is stuck with old issues in Florida rather than logical strategy."

The old Florida issues boil down to this: it's a critical swing state with a significant Cuban-American vote, and a hard line toward Fidel has been a sure-fire political proposition. Once again this year, Miami's three Cuban-American congressional Republicans won reelection. And yet: their victory margins narrowed. Some 35 percent of the Cuban-American vote in Miami-Dade County went to Obama, a big bounce, ten points better than John Kerry's showing in 2004. Fifty-five percent of those under twenty-nine voted for Obama.

Obama's victory is particularly significant because he bucked conventional wisdom on Cuba during the campaign. He lambasted Bush's "tough talk that never yields results." He called for "a new

strategy" centered on two immediate changes: the lifting of all
travel restrictions for family visits (limited by Bush to one every
three years) and the freeing up of family remittances (now no
more than three hundred dollars a quarter for the receiving household). Obama also called for "direct diplomacy," saying he would
be prepared to lead it himself "at a time and place of my choosing,"
provided U.S. interests and the "cause of freedom for the Cuban
people" were advanced. He said his message to Fidel and Raúl
would be: "If you take significant steps toward democracy, beginning with the freeing of all political prisoners, we will take steps to
begin normalizing relations."

Three generations on from the revolution, being a Democrat is
no longer equated by Cuban-Americans with being a Communist.
The fixation on removing Fidel, the dreams of return, and the raw
anger of loss have faded. "We have gone from the politics of passion to the politics of reality," Andy Gómez, an assistant provost at
the University of Miami who left Cuba in 1961 at the age of six, told
me. "We are here for the long haul. We worry about the economy,
health care. Next Christmas in Havana — that's over."

So could the convergence of a president who is as mestizo as
countless Cubans, a new pragmatism in Miami's Little Havana, and
the looming passing of Cuba's revolutionary gerontocracy provide
a framework for that elusive U.S.-Cuban reconciliation? Durán is
hopeful. "I'm seventy-one, and I know I'll see the day," he told me.
"The day you can get in your speedboat in Coconut Grove after
work and be in Havana at nine P.M. for dinner."

Nonsense, Jaime Suchlicki, a conservative Cuban historian who
teaches in Miami, told me. Raúl is a Soviet admirer "and no Deng
Xiaoping." The Cuban situation — buoyed by Chinese, Venezuelan, Russian, and Iranian support — is not desperate enough to
force concessions. Every past rapprochement has turned to rancor.
"Cuba is an absolute disaster, but it will not fall apart," Suchlicki
said.

Yet Cuba does stand at a fulcrum of generational shift, from
those formed by Fidel to those who will hardly know him. Seizing
this opportunity will require a measure of American humility.
Obama has a strong sense of history and the historical moment. He
would understand the deep roots of the conflict, going back to the
U.S. military intervention in 1898 that left Cubans with the linger-

ing sense that their own hard-won independence from Spain had been snatched from them. What followed were four years of direct U.S. rule and Cuba's emergence as a nearly independent republic in 1902 — "nearly" because, under the Platt Amendment, the United States kept the right to intervene in the island's affairs. It also got Cuba to cede in perpetuity a little thing called Guantánamo Bay, a forty-five-square-mile area in the southeast of the island.

"All this left a deep frustration in the popular imagination," Fernando Rojas, the vice minister of culture, told me in Havana.

It is this history that has allowed Fidel to claim that his revolution was, in effect, a second war of independence. It is this history that has made the United States the enemy of choice for Cuba long after the exigencies of Cold War confrontation vanished.

This is the history that turns otherwise rational heads in both Washington and Havana, as if the full moon had got to them. My impression is that Obama has the cool temperament that can factor the charge of this past — similar to the heavy legacy of the CIA-organized 1953 coup in Iran — into his diplomacy. Cuba is certainly ready for a change it can believe in.

Lealtad (loyalty) Street runs from the Malecón down through the densely populated district called Centro Habana. I first went there at night. The city is dimly lighted, but one of Fidel's achievements, along with an impressive education system and universal health care, is security. It might be said that's because there is very little to steal, but that would be uncharitable. The revolution, anything but puritanical, has nonetheless instilled a certain ethical rigor.

A residential street, Lealtad beckoned me with its silhouettes lurking in doorways, its clatter of dominoes being banged on tables, its glimpses through grated windows of lush interior courtyards, its old men playing cards in high-ceilinged living rooms of brocaded furniture and sagging upholstery, its melancholy. As I wandered, I stumbled on a bar called Las Alegrías — Joys. What I saw struck me with the force of a vision. Under harsh fluorescent lights, drinking shots of rum, were a white man with a bulbous red nose pickled by drink, a black man with unfocused eyes, and a black woman with head bowed, all of them at a distance from one another and seemingly inhabiting an Edward Hopper painting where each lonely element etched another detail of despair. The feeling of being transported is very Cuban: Hopper's "Nighthawks" was painted in 1942.

I resolved to return to Lealtad in an attempt to understand the despair at Joys, but also in the conviction that the secret lexicon of fifty-year dictatorships can be read only in the details of daily life. Secrecy and obfuscation are the lifeblood of such regimes. They alone preserve the mysticism that absolute leadership requires, allowing an aging man with severe intestinal problems to remain Zeus on Olympus. It's not for nothing that the whereabouts of Fidel, who has not been seen in public since he fell ill in July 2006, are an official secret.

The next day I came back and, dodging boys playing baseball with a ball made from tightly rolled paper, stopped at a chicken-egg-fish store with nothing in it. Antonio Rodríguez, fifty, the affable, bald Afro-Cuban running it, explained to me the mechanics of rationing, in which he is an often-immobile cog. Every month, each Cuban is allocated ten eggs (the first five at 0.15 pesos each, the second five at 0.90 pesos); a pound of chicken at 0.70 pesos; a pound of fish with its head at 0.35 pesos (or eleven ounces without the head); and half a pound of an ersatz mince at 0.35 pesos a pound. It's hardly worth converting these sums; they're trifling. Suffice to say that, at twenty-five pesos to the dollar, you get the whole lot for no more than twenty-five cents.

That may sound like a steal, but there are catches. Rodríguez, after seventeen years at the store, where the broken cash register is of prerevolutionary vintage and the antique refrigerator of Soviet provenance, earns $15.40 a month. The average monthly salary is about twenty dollars. I asked him when some chicken or eggs might arrive. Beats me, he said. As many as fifteen days a month, he's idle, waiting for something to be delivered so he can announce it on the blackboard behind him and get to work crossing off "sales" in his clients' frayed ration books. Rodríguez pointed to a man outside. "That guy standing on the corner, and me working, there's no real difference," he said. "We get paid almost nothing to spend the day talking."

Luiz Jorrin, the man in question, approached. "This is all due to the U.S. blockade," he said, pointing a finger at me and using the exaggerated term that Cubans favor for the embargo. "Look at your financial crisis! Maybe you'll get over it with time. Well, we'll get over this with time. I don't believe in capitalism. Look what it did in Africa and Latin America. It's destructive."

This was too much for Javier Aguirre, a slim fellow who helps Rodríguez. "We're wrecked, and after three hurricanes, we're even more wrecked," he said. "I just don't believe in the system. Give me Switzerland! Of all the Cubans who have gone to the United States, how many want to come back?"

The question prompted a silence. Aguirre, it transpired, tried twice to escape, only to be caught, once by the Cubans and once by the U.S. Coast Guard. Under the current "wet foot, dry foot" policy, most Cubans who reach U.S. soil are allowed to stay, while most intercepted at sea are repatriated. Go figure.

Now twenty-nine, Aguirre, an aspiring artist, is waiting. Cubans are used to waiting. Along with baseball and quiet desperation, it's the national sport. They talk; they joke at the Beckett play that is their lives; they tap their fingers to the beat of drums and maracas. They lament the billions of dollars of damage caused in recent months by Hurricanes Gustav, Ike, and Paloma; an offer of U.S. assistance was rebuffed. At least, they laugh, there's no traffic problem.

The little storefront exchange was typical, I found, in its surprising openness, in its mention of the U.S. embargo as the source of misery, and in its vindicating reference to the global economy's collapse. Cuba, it has to be said, is one of the very few places the Dow's meltdown has scarcely touched. But tumbling oil prices may affect Venezuelan and Russian largess over time, and slumping European economies may hit tourism. Meanwhile, Cubans go on trying to make sense of the senseless.

"Obama should ask Congress to lift the blockade for ninety days after the hurricanes," Rodríguez suggested.

"We're always asking for the kindness of strangers," Aguirre retorted. "This is not communism or capitalism, it's a Cuban mess."

The more I learned of the centralized Cuban economy, the more that seemed a fair summary. Cuba has two currencies, one for communism and one for a limited, state-dominated capitalism. The pesos that people get their salaries in are essentially good for nothing but rationed or undesirable items. By contrast, the convertible dollar-pegged pesos known as "CUCs" (pronounced "kooks") are

good for international products. Pass a dimly lighted peso store
and you might see a bicycle tire, a yellowing brassiere, and a set of
plastic spoons. Pass a convertible-peso store and you will see cell
phones, Jameson whiskey, and Heineken in a bright, air-conditioned environment.

As a result, many Cubans spend their lives scrambling to get in
on the convertible-peso economy, which largely depends on getting access to foreign visitors. A highly qualified electrical engineer
opts to work in a cigar factory so he can hawk Havana cigars to
tourists. Others offer to be their guides. Whatever goods can be
sneaked out of state-run businesses are good for black-market sale.
Cell phones — recently permitted in what was portrayed as a liber-
alizing measure by Raúl — cost about $110. That is half a year's sal-
ary for most Cubans. A gallon of gas goes for about six dollars, or
nearly a third of an average monthly salary. No wonder Cubans see
access to the CUC universe of tourists as salvation.

A kind of economic apartheid exists. People are stuck in a reg-
ulation-ridden halfway house. They want to escape the socialist
world of Rodríguez's store for the capitalist world of the mini-
Cancún on the Varadero peninsula east of Havana, a hotel-littered
ghetto of white sand and whiter Scandinavians snapping up Che
Guevara T-shirts without worrying too much about what Che
wrought on Lealtad Street.

The Cuban government gave me a courteous welcome. I was escorted to a few official meetings, but otherwise left without a
minder (as far as I could see) to do what I wished. One official stop
was with Elena Álvarez, who was fifteen when Fidel's revolution
came and now, at sixty-five, works as a top official at the Ministry of
Economics. She tried to make sense for me of the voodoo economics I'd seen.

Here's what she wanted me to grasp. Cuba, at the time of the revolution, was "one of the most unjust, unequal, and exploited societies on earth." Illiteracy was running up to 40 percent, a quarter of
the best land was in U.S. hands, a corrupt bourgeoisie lorded it
over everyone else. Fidel's initial objective was a more-just society,
but U.S. pressure radicalized his revolution and pushed it toward
all-out socialism within the Soviet camp.

Álvarez reeled off some numbers. There were six thousand doctors in Cuba at the time of the revolution; there are now close to

eighty thousand for a population of 11.3 million, one of the highest per-capita rates in the world. The U.S. embargo has cost Cuba about two hundred billion dollars in real terms. When the Berlin Wall crumbled, 80 percent of Cuba's international trade was with Soviet-bloc countries. About 98 percent of oil came from them. Back to the Communist bloc states, at inflated prices, went Cuba's sugar and rum.

"We've had to reinsert ourselves in the global economy twice in thirty years, once in 1960 and again in 1990," Álvarez said.

Okay, I said, that shows some resilience, but when the Soviet Union collapsed, why didn't Cuba do what Moscow's other satellites did: take down totalitarianism, become a market economy, and set people free? The real totalitarianism, she countered, was Batista's. Cuba now has different values. Despite scarcities, attributable in large part to the embargo, it's a society that wants to protect everyone. The rationing system guarantees that all citizens have a minimum. Everyone gets low-cost food at work. Free health care and education mean a twenty dollar monthly salary is the wrong way to view the quality of Cuban life. Going to a market economy in 1990 would have meant wholesale factory closures, as in East Germany, and 35 percent unemployment. "We decided we had to protect our workers," Álvarez said. "We have another philosophy."

That "philosophy" has produced results. According to the World Health Organization, life expectancy for men and women in Cuba is seventy-six and eighty years, respectively, on par with the United States. The comparative figures in Haiti are fifty-nine and sixty-three, and in the Dominican Republic they are sixty-six and seventy-four. The probability of dying before the age of five is seven per thousand live births in Cuba — nearly as good as the U.S. figure — compared with eighty per thousand live births in Haiti and twenty-nine in the Dominican Republic. Illiteracy has been eliminated. United Nations statistics show 93.7 percent of Cuban children complete high school, far more than in the United States or elsewhere in the Caribbean.

That raises the question: Why educate people so well and then deny them access to the Internet, travel, and the opportunity to apply their skills? Why give them a great education and no life? Why not at least offer a Chinese or Vietnamese model, with a market economy under one-party rule?

Álvarez said there was some "space for the market." She insisted,

"We are not fundamentalist." But the bottom line, of course, is that the authorities are scared: opening the door to capitalism on an island ninety miles from Florida is very different from doing that in Asia.

In the so-called Special Period, initiated in the 1990s, Cuba did open to foreign investment in sectors like nickel and tourism, allowed tourists in, introduced the convertible peso, and began putting more farmland in private hands. But it stopped there. Just how much land is now private is disputed, although one thing is clear: not enough to prevent Cuba from having to import more than $1.6 billion worth of food a year. Those imports, in a development remarkable even by upside-down Cuban standards, have included sugar. Domestic production has collapsed.

So I put it to Álvarez: at the half-century mark, with Fidel fading, was it worth persevering with a revolution that has left Cuba with dilapidated buildings, deserted highways, and a need to import sugar?

"The revolution has been a success," Álvarez said. "It overthrew a tyrannical regime. We got our national sovereignty. We got our pride. We survived aggression by the most powerful country in the world for fifty years. We preserved the essence of what Fidel fought for."

But did he really wage guerrilla war in the Sierra Maestra mountains so that countless talented Cubans might sit idle, plotting means to get out?

The challenges were great, Álvarez said, but Cuba would again prove Miami wrong. She pointed to joint-venture oil exploration off the northern coast and a growing "knowledge economy" that has produced patented vaccines and medicines sold throughout the world. Cuba would now export services, like that of the thirty thousand medical personnel it sent to Venezuela in an innovative barter deal bringing in ninety thousand barrels of oil daily.

"We are an example to others," she said, "an example to all those looking for an alternative to capitalism."

I did sense something hard to quantify, a kind of socialist conscience, particularly among doctors. When I met Dr. Verena Muzio, the head of the vaccine division at the Center for Genetic Engineering and Biotechnology — another official stop — she said her commitment to the revolution's achievements outweighed the knowledge "that I could go to Chicago and earn three hundred thousand dollars a year." Her salary is forty dollars a month.

At the Latin American School of Medicine, founded a decade ago to educate doctors unable to afford school in other countries in the Americas, Dr. Juan Carrizo, the rector, spoke of the universal right to health as the new humanist banner of the Cuban revolution: out with Angolan guerrillas, in with the medical brigade. Among the students are more than one hundred U.S. citizens. Pasha Jackson, twenty-six, an African-American from South Central Los Angeles, told me: "I came here because I could get an education for free for just being me. I feel more valued here than where I grew up. And when I finish, I'm going to go back to my community and bring that same philosophy."

These young U.S. medical students have joined a growing number of foreigners, tourists, and businesspeople. Sherritt International, a Canadian natural-resources company, has made major investments in nickel mining and oil. Sol Meliá, the Spanish hotel operator, has opened a number of properties. Tour buses are a frequent sight, ferrying groups that take in Hemingway's Havana bars (La Floridita and La Bodeguita del Medio) and the Che memorial in Santa Clara before heading back to the beach. Although this invasion has brought Cubans more contact with foreigners, its impact has been limited by the fact that the Cuban government does rigorous background checks on any job seekers in the international sector. Over all, most tourists seem happy with sun, sand, rum, and cigars — and to heck with totalitarian politics.

At a time when Hugo Chávez's Venezuela has replied to Fidel's *"Patria o Muerte"* with its own *"Socialismo o Muerte";* and Evo Morales is pushing Bolivia toward socialism; and Steven Soderbergh's epic-length "Che" is about to hit American theaters, it's hard to argue the revolution has lost all its glow — especially with Wall Street bloodied. A moderate Latin left that is friendly with the Castros, most conspicuously President Lula da Silva in Brazil, has also emerged. But Fidel claimed he wanted to free Cubans from oppression. Instead, his revolution has oppressed them.

I found Héctor Palacios at his cluttered apartment in the leafy Vedado district of Havana. He was thrown in prison in 2003 along with seventy-five other dissidents charged with subversion and collaboration with the United States. Sentenced to twenty-five years, he was released in late 2006 for health reasons. But fifty-five of those arrested are still in captivity, among the more than 220 political prisoners in Cuba.

"My crime was simple: thinking that the government has to change from totalitarianism," Palacios told me.

He's a big man, and when he talked about his cramped cell and isolation, his eyes darted here and there, and he began to sweat. The memory of what was his third spell in prison was still harrowing. Palacios, the leader of the banned All United opposition group, was an organizer of the Varela Project, a petition calling for a referendum on democratic change. Orchestrated by another prominent dissident, Oswaldo Payá, the movement brought ripples of a Cuban spring before the 2003 clampdown.

Palacios, sixty-five, has traveled since his release to the United States, where, last May, he met with Obama in Miami. He asked Obama to show flexibility. He urged him to allow wealthy Cuban-Americans to send money to dissidents. "Obama is the new element," Palacios told me. "He's ready to talk to anyone. As with our aging government, the hard-line generation of Cuban-Americans is dying out. Significant change is possible within two years."

"Why do you stay here?" I asked.

"I stay because I am a patriot."

That's not the official view. Dissidents are routinely called "traitors to the homeland." Palacios showed me a copy of a congratulatory letter he sent to Obama on November 4. It ends, "With the hope that I will be heard and confidence that your mandate will bring the renewal that eliminates the obstacles preventing us from putting an end to the tyranny suffered by our people." A restoration of the battered moral authority of the United States could have a significant impact in Cuba, Palacios said.

Cuba's dissidents are marginalized. The press is muzzled. The print organ of the regime, *Granma*, named after the cabin cruiser that bore Fidel, Raúl, Che, and their followers from Mexican exile to Cuba in 1956, is a study in Orwellian officialese. State television is a turgid propaganda machine. Cuba can show *The Lives of Others* at its annual Havana Film Festival, where a few thousand people see it, but that remarkable study of the all-hearing Stasi in totalitarian East Germany would never be shown on national television. Too many Cubans might want the movie renamed *The Lives of Us*.

But of course Cuba is not totalitarian East Germany. Fidel has been nothing if not a brilliant puppet master. He once said that some revolutionary fighters "let their enthusiasm for the cause overwhelm their tactical decision-making." Not Fidel, whose training as a lawyer has been evident in his mastery of maneuver and brinkmanship, not least in his dealings with the United States. There have been hundreds of executions, especially in the early years, but he has never been a bloodthirsty dictator, a Caribbean Ceausescu. Nor has he tried, in the style of some despots, to sweep the past away; he has merely let it wither.

"There's a very intelligent repression here, a scientific repression," Yoani Sánchez, the dissident whose blog is now translated into twelve languages, told me. "They have killed us as citizens, so they do not have to kill us physically. Our own police is in our brains, censoring us before we utter a critical idea."

At thirty-three, Sánchez is half Palacios's age. She represents something new: digital dissent. The authorities seem unsure how to deal with it. Sánchez, a slight and vivacious woman, started her blog in 2006. It was, she told me, "an exorcism, a virtual catharsis."

"Who is last in line for a toaster?" she asked in one blog entry this year, noting that a ban on sales of computers and DVD players had been lifted but toasters would not be freely sold until 2010. Now her biting dissections of the woes of Cuban life have a wide international following — to the point that "the intelligence services know if they touch me there will be an explosion online."

Still, they harass her. When she won Spain's prestigious Ortega y Gasset prize for digital journalism in April, she was prevented from going to collect the award. She would like to take up an invitation from New York University, but permission has been denied without explanation.

I asked if she was optimistic about change. She said she was pessimistic in the short term because "apathy has entered our bloodstream, and a lot of people are just waiting for a bunch of leaders over seventy to die." Democracy, national reconciliation, and change demand a new civic involvement, not apathy. But she was optimistic in the long term because we "are a creative, capable people, with no religious, ethnic, or other conflict, who have developed an allergy to what we have: a totalitarian system."

Sánchez looked at me — an intense, intelligent, brown-eyed gaze with humor twinkling near its surface. We were seated in the gardens of the Hotel Nacional, looking out over the Malecón to that empty sea. Here, I thought, is Cuba's future, a Blogostroika, if only the repressive gerontocracy would let it bloom; a Blogostroika that will fill that sea with bright vessels.

"You know," Sánchez said, "when a nation gets on its knees before a man, it's all over. When a man decides how much rice I eat a month, or whether or not I can leave a country, that country is sick. This man is human. He commits errors. How can he have such power? Like a lot of people of my generation, I have willed myself to stop thinking about him, as a therapy. I think there will be relief when Fidel dies. We will breathe out. The mystical and symbolic weight of his presence is very heavy, for his opponents and even for his supporters. It's hard to right his errors while he's still there."

I think Sánchez is right. Only after Mao's death could China unshackle itself by officially determining that he was "70 percent right and 30 percent wrong." Perhaps Cuba will come down somewhere like that on Fidel — say 75–25 — and move on.

While I was in Cuba, everyone I spoke to referred to Fidel as "Comandante," even though Raúl formally became commander in chief when he assumed the presidency. Rambling, almost daily "Reflexiones del Compañero Fidel" — signed commentaries on everything from capitalism to the U.S. election — appear in *Granma,* pored over like Kremlin utterances of old.

Fidel published a book last month called *Peace in Colombia.* Its presentation, the occasion for a collective genuflection by hundreds of guests in a large hall, merited hour after hour of coverage on national TV. At the gathering, I ran into Randy Alonso, host of a TV news show and the director of the information office of the Council of State, the main governing body. I asked him where Fidel is. "He's lucid, but in a secret place," Alonso said. "If he wants to reveal it, he will."

It's hard in any circumstances for a seventy-seven-year-old to be an innovator. But for Raúl, with his far-more charismatic brother looking over his shoulder, it must be near impossible. No wonder Raúl, the former defense minister who hates the limelight, has appeared faltering. He has freed up cell phones (at a price), allowed Cubans into international hotels, and intimated that some salaries might be paid in convertible pesos or even be tied to performance. But in essence all he has done in two and a half years is tinker. Perhaps that's not surprising. He has a vested interest in the existing system: the military runs conglomerates, like Gaviota, that control most of the tourism industry.

"We are at the fading of an era, and it is fading into the unknown," Juan Carlos Espinosa, a political scientist at Florida International University, said.

In Miami, I caught up with Giselle Palacios, Héctor Palacios's twenty-three-year-old daughter, who managed to get out of Cuba a few months ago, having been thrown out of the University of Havana because of her father's activities. She told me she is still in shock. She has realized that the place she was living in is not the real world. There are things happening in Cuba, she said, that don't happen anywhere else. You carry that knowledge inside you, and you feel lonely.

"Revolution was supposed to mean equal opportunity for all, but it has become a word the Castro brothers own," she said. "Young Cubans don't believe in the Castros' version of revolution. They don't believe in a world where the Internet is forbidden and your whole world is Cuba with the rest blocked out."

"Will you stay in Miami?" I asked.

"No, I want to go back one day when other jobs are possible. I think I will always be lonely here. I want to help democracy emerge."

When I returned to Lealtad Street, I found a flurry of activity: the chicken had arrived! Rodríguez, in his green overalls, had the news up on his blackboard. He was unpacking frozen chicken legs and thighs. Chicken breast is available only on the convertible-peso market. He held up the box with a big smile. It said, "Made in U.S.A."

Since 2000, when Congress bowed to the farm lobby, it has been legal to sell food and agricultural products to Cuba. That means everything from chicken legs to telephone poles. At the Miami airport, I had run into Randal Wilson, who was just back from Havana, where he was trying to sell Alabaman wine. "They seem to prefer my blueberry wine, just loved that," he told me. "You know, Alabama is very big on trade with Cuba."

In fact, the United States is now the largest exporter of food to Cuba, earning upward of six hundred million dollars this year. It's among Cuba's five biggest trading partners. (The others are Venezuela, China, Spain, and Canada.) So much for the embargo; it's as arbitrary as the wet-foot, dry-foot policy toward Cubans trying to escape. While America took in hundreds of millions of dollars from Cuba, it sent back 2,086 sea-borne refugees in fiscal 2008. Principle has nothing to do with current Cuban policy. It's just an incoherent mess.

I asked Aguirre, the young would-be escapee working with Rodríguez, if he understood U.S. policy. "It's like the situation here, you have to understand it because it is what it is," he said. "I try not to think too much, I just talk about girls, baseball, whatever."

I looked down the street, at the kids playing, a guy selling lighter fluid, the carved doors, the extraordinary baroque flourishes on the three- and four-story buildings. A gentleness inhabits Cuba, the island that Columbus, landing in 1492, called "the most beautiful land that human eyes have ever seen." It is the gentleness of time passing very slowly.

The absence of visual clutter — no ads, no brands, no neon signs — leaves the mind at peace. Fidel's colossal stubbornness has delivered a singular aesthetic, striking in the age of globalized malls. I found myself thinking of a phrase of Pico Iyer's in the excellent *Reader's Companion to Cuba,* edited by Alan Ryan: "Cuba catches my heart and then makes me count the cost of that enchantment."

That cost is high. Fifty yards down the street, I talked to Felix Morales, forty-three, who runs another chicken-egg-fish store. I asked if there was any rivalry with Rodríguez. Morales laughed. "How can there be rivalry if we both receive and hand out the same thing?" he said. "The only difference is he's black and I'm white!"

Morales told me everyone was aching for some improvement. He said he would like to work and see the fruit of his labors. He was wearing a T-shirt saying "Canada." Did he want to go there? Two women in the store burst out laughing. Of course Morales wanted to, of course they wanted to, who wouldn't?

Not Jorge Martinez, who runs the community health center near Morales's store, a place where doctors treat everything from alcoholism to depression. "Fidel is the man of the century," he told me.

I walked into a little restaurant called Asahi, one of the so-called *paladares,* independent, family-run enterprises, usually with three or four tables. José Marticorena, its owner, told me he acquired his state license a dozen years ago, but now it's difficult to obtain such a license. His father, Miguel, fought alongside Fidel and was rewarded after 1959 with this house. Later he worked in the merchant marine. A freezer he brought back from Japan had "Asahi" inscribed on it, after the Japanese beer: hence the name.

Marticorena can charge what he wants for food, but his capacity is set at twelve people, and he pays various taxes. "We have a lot of dysfunctional things," he told me, "but nobody's dying of hunger or wanting for basic medical help. I was able to do something, and I feel fulfilled by it. My wife is a dentist, she loves to cook. We have two kids. We place a lot of hope in Obama, we believe he will free things up."

With that, he took out a little digital camera, set it to video, and started filming.

"What do you think of the food?" he asked.

"Very good," I said.

"And whom do you work for?"

"The *New York Times*."

Even on Lealtad, a half-century after the revolution, capitalist public-relations instincts are not far below the surface.

Toward the end of my stay, I traveled down to Santiago de Cuba in the southeast of the island. This is mythical territory: the land of the 1860s uprising against the Spanish; the site of the decisive U.S. intervention in 1898 that stole the fruits of that uprising; the city where Fidel and a band of followers attacked the Moncada Barracks on July 26, 1953 (sixty-one dead among more than one hundred insurgents); the home of the Sierra Maestra, where Fidel and Che waged guerrilla war between 1956 and 1958. It is here that the fiftieth anniversary will be formally celebrated on January 1, although the precise location in Santiago is still secret. Whether Fidel will appear is also unknown. Most people say no.

A historian, Octavio Ambruster, showed me around the Moncada museum. The mustard yellow barracks were converted into a school after the revolution. The museum occupies a few rooms. Gruesome photographs abound of the slain in the July 26 attack. Most were tortured before execution. A front-page headline the following day in the Batista-era paper, *Ataya,* got it wrong: "Fidel Castro is dead."

In fact he slipped away, only to be captured a few days later in the mountains. He was brought to trial and imprisoned, but not before he made a now legendary declaration: "Condemn me, it has no importance. History will absolve me."

Will it? I don't think so, but it may be gentler on him than the ruinous state of Cuba would suggest. Fidel is a brilliant, romantic, and towering figure; as such, like his country, he tends to enchant even as the cost of that enchantment mounts. Ambruster told me that Fidel always called José Martí, the hero of the independence struggle against Spain, "the intellectual author of the Moncada assault." Framing his revolution as being about independence — *patria* more than *socialismo* — and casting that independence as being above all from the United States, has been one of Fidel's most ingenious ideas.

And how will history judge U.S. policy toward Fidel's Cuba? Badly, I think, especially since the end of the Cold War. If the embargo had come down then, back in 1989, I doubt the regime would have survived. But the grudges were too deep, and a mistake was made. Today the policy makes little sense. The United States dislikes Chávez but maintains diplomatic relations with Venezuela. I think Obama should add to the measures he has already announced by offering to open full diplomatic relations with Cuba immediately.

That would put pressure on Cuba and, if the offer were accepted, allow face-to-face negotiations to begin at a senior level. At these talks, Obama should not belabor democratic principles, at least not immediately, but should insist on the freeing of all political prisoners as a first step toward beginning to lift the embargo. The United States is not the European Union, which just normalized relations with Havana, although hundreds are still held in Cuban prisons for what they think.

Progress will not be easy. Representative Lincoln Diaz-Balart, one of the reelected Miami Republicans, told me, "We are very united, we will win the fights in Congress, and we will stop any moves to open commercial relations, trade financing, or tourism with Cuba." But Tony Lake, a senior foreign-policy adviser to Obama during the campaign, said, "With the new Democratic majority in Congress, and some clear Cuban gestures on human rights, you could get changes to Helms-Burton," the legislation that has determined the shape of Cuban policy since 1996. Then the ball would be rolling with a momentum that the passing of generations should sustain.

Cuba is some way down Obama's priority list. But early in his presidency, another Democratic president, Jimmy Carter, did something that changed views of him in the hemisphere: he negotiated, against all the odds, the transfer of sovereignty over the Panama Canal to Panama. It seems clear enough that a breakthrough of similar proportions with Cuba would bring a major reconciliation with Latin America.

From Santiago, I drove out to the town of Guantánamo. There were no road signs and no road markings. Cubans say they are waiting for Obama to send paint. I passed tractor-trailers crammed with people: Chinese buses imported by Raúl have not yet met needs. At Guantánamo slogans abounded: "Our duty is to be victorious" and "This is the first trench in the anti-imperialist war." From a hill, I could see the control tower of the U.S. naval base glimmering in the distance.

The land before me, and this farther stretch of empty sea, had been carved from Cuba at its independence. And now Guantánamo had become synonymous with some of the most egregious acts of Bush's war on terror, acts that have tarnished America's name. There have been other moments of American dishonor over the years in Latin America, from Chile to Argentina, where the United States told generals it would look the other way.

Yes, Fidel's communist revolution, at fifty, has carried a terrible price for his people, dividing the Cuban nation, imprisoning part of it, and bringing economic catastrophe. But as I gazed from Cuban hills at Guantánamo, and considered Obama's incoming administration, I thought the wages of guilt might just have found a fine enough balance for good sense at last to prevail.

CALVIN TRILLIN

By Meat Alone

FROM *The New Yorker*

I APPROACHED *Texas Monthly*'s cover story on "The Top 50 BBQ
Joints in Texas" this summer the way a regular reader of *People*
might approach that magazine's annual "Sexiest Man Alive" feature — with the expectation of seeing some familiar names. There
was no reason to think that the list's top tier — the five restaurants
judged to be the best in the state — would look much different
than it had the last time a survey was published, in 2003. In recent
years, Hollywood may have seen some advances in physical training
and cosmetic surgery, but barbecue restaurants still tend to retain
their luster much longer than male heartthrobs do. In fact, I've
heard it argued that absent some slippage in management, a barbecue restaurant can only get better over time: many Texas barbecue
fanatics have a strong belief in the beneficial properties of accumulated grease.

In discussions of Texas barbecue, the equivalent of Matt Damon
and George Clooney and Brad Pitt would be establishments like
Kreuz Market and Smitty's Market, in Lockhart; City Market, in
Luling; and Louie Mueller Barbecue, in Taylor — places that reflect the barbecue tradition that developed during the nineteenth
century out of German and Czech meat markets in the Hill Country of central Texas. (In fact, the title of *Texas Monthly*'s first article
on barbecue — it was published in 1973, shortly after the magazine's founding — was "The World's Best Barbecue Is in Taylor,
Texas. Or Is It Lockhart?") Those restaurants, all of which had
been in the top tier in 2003, were indeed there again in this summer's survey. For the first time, though, a No. 1 had been named,

and it was not one of the old familiars. "The best barbecue in Texas," the article said, "is currently being served at Snow's BBQ, in Lexington."

I had never heard of Snow's. That surprised me. Although I grew up in Kansas City, which has a completely different style of barbecue, I have always kept more or less au courant of Texas barbecue, like a sports fan who is almost monomaniacally obsessed with basketball but glances over at the NHL standings now and then just to see how things are going. Reading that the best barbecue in Texas was at Snow's, in Lexington, I felt like a *People* subscriber who had picked up the "Sexiest Man Alive" issue and discovered that the sexiest man alive was Sheldon Ludnick, an insurance adjuster from Terre Haute, Indiana, with Clooney as the runner-up.

An accompanying story on how a Numero Uno had emerged, from 341 spots visited by the staff, revealed that before work began on the 2008 survey nobody at *Texas Monthly* had heard of Snow's, either. Lexington, a trading town of twelve hundred people in Lee County, is only about fifty miles from Austin, where *Texas Monthly* is published, and Texans think nothing of driving that far for lunch — particularly if the lunch consists of brisket that has been subjected to slow heat since the early hours of the morning. *Texas Monthly* has had a strong posse of barbecue enthusiasts since its early days. Griffin Smith, who wrote the 1973 barbecue article and is now the executive editor of the *Arkansas Democrat-Gazette*, in Little Rock, was known for keeping a map of the state on his wall with pushpins marking barbecue joints he had been to, the way General Patton might have kept a map marked with spots where night patrols had probed the German line. I could imagine the staffers not knowing about a superior barbecue restaurant in East Texas; the Southern style of barbecue served there, often on a bun, has never held much interest for Austin connoisseurs. But their being unaware of a top-tier establishment less than an hour's drive away astonished me.

I know some of the *Texas Monthly* crowd. In fact, I once joined Greg Curtis, the former editor, and Steve Harrigan, a novelist who's had a long association with the magazine, on a pilgrimage to Lockhart, which some barbecue fans visit the way the devout of another sort walk the Camino de Santiago. I know Evan Smith, who was the editor of the magazine when this latest barbecue survey was published and has since been promoted to a position that might be described as boss of bosses. I couldn't imagine Smith jiggering the results for nefarious purposes — say, telling his staff to declare a totally unknown barbecue place the best in Texas simply as a way of doing what some magazine editors call "juicing up the story." I took him at his word when, a few months after the list was published, he told me how Snow's had been found. His staff had gone through the letters written after the 2003 survey complaining about the neglect of a superior specialist in pork ribs or the inclusion of a place whose smoked sausage wasn't fit for pets — what Smith, who's from Queens, refers to as "Dear Schmuck letters."

He did acknowledge that his decision to name a No. 1 — rather than just a top tier, as in the previous barbecue surveys — came about partly because everyone was so enthusiastic about Snow's product but partly because its story was so compelling. Smith himself was not in a position to confirm the quality of the product. Being from Queens is not the only handicap he has had to surmount in his rise through the ranks of Texas journalism: he has been a vegetarian for nearly twenty-five years. (The fact that he is able to resist the temptation presented by the aroma of Texas pit barbecue, he has said, is a strong indication that he will never "return to the dark side.") As a longtime editor, though, he knew a Cinderella story when he saw one. It wasn't just that Snow's had been unknown to a Texas barbecue fancy that is notably mobile. Snow's proprietor, Kerry Bexley, was a former rodeo clown who worked as a blending-facility operator at a coal mine. Snow's pit master, Tootsie Tomanetz, was a woman in her early seventies who worked as the custodian of the middle school in Giddings, Texas — the Lee County seat, eighteen miles to the south. After five years of operating Snow's, both of them still had their day jobs. Also, Snow's was open only on Saturday mornings, from eight until the meat ran out.

My conversation with Evan Smith took place in a Chevrolet Suburban traveling from Austin toward Lexington. I'd been picked up at my hotel at 7:20 A.M. The *Texas Monthly* rankings had attracted large crowds to Snow's, and, even four months later, we weren't taking any chances. Greg Curtis and Steve Harrigan were with Smith in the back seats. Harrigan was one of the people who, having been tipped off between the time the feature was completed and the time the magazine came out, hurried over to Snow's like inside traders in possession of material information not available to the general public. He seemed completely unrepentant. "I took my brother and brother-in-law and son-in-law and nephew," he said, smiling slyly. Next to me in the front seat, Paul Burka was doing the driving. Greg Curtis once reminded me that "all barbecue experts are self-proclaimed," but *Texas Monthly* had enough faith in Burka's expertise to send him to Snow's late in the selection process as what Smith calls "the closer." It was up to Burka to confirm or dismiss the judgment of the staffer whose assigned territory for the survey included Lexington, and of Patricia Sharpe, the editor in charge of the project, and of a second staffer sent in as a triple-check. Some people at the magazine had predicted that Burka wouldn't like Snow's barbecue simply because it bore Pat Sharpe's imprimatur. "Paul thinks Pat's judgment of restaurants is fancy and white tablecloth and Pat thinks Paul is a philistine," I heard from the back seat. "And they're both right."

When I spoke to Pat Sharpe a couple of days later, she bristled at the accusation that she is a person of elevated taste. "I'll eat barbecue in the rattiest joint there is," she said in her own defense. Burka, on the other hand, seemed unconcerned about being called a philistine. He is a large man with a white mustache and a midsection that reflects a forty-year interest in Texas barbecue. Having grown up in Galveston, which is not a barbecue center, he innocently started eating what he now describes as "'barbecue' that was one step removed from roast beef" while he was a student at Rice, in Houston; he had his true conversion experience on a trip to Lockhart with Griffin Smith in 1967, when they were both in law school at the University of Texas. Burka, who worked for five years in the Texas state legislature, writes about politics for *Texas Monthly*. Speaking to him as the Suburban rolled toward Lexington, I was reminded of the Austin brought to life in *The Gay Place*, Billy Lee Brammer's marvelous 1961 novel about an LBJ-like governor called Arthur (Goddam) Fenstermaker. That Austin was essentially a two-company town — the university and the state government — and I always pictured those connected with both companies sharing irreverent observations of the passing scene while consuming a lot of beer in the back of Scholz's beer garden.

It is an Austin that is sometimes difficult to discern in a much larger city of slick office buildings and computer-company headquarters and the mother church of Whole Foods, which actually offers barbecue in the meat department of its Austin stores. ("Organic barbecue," Burka muttered, when somebody brought that up.)

The first time Burka went to Lexington to check out Snow's, he arrived just before noon. "It looked like it had never been open," he said. "It was deserted." When he finally got there at a time when meat was still available, he was convinced. In fact, he was rhapsodic, particularly concerning the brisket ("as soft and sweet as cookie dough") and the pork butt. Smith believed that Burka's description of the latter — "the butt was tender and yielding" — was in need of some editing, but, without having to consume any critters personally, he was persuaded by Burka's report. Snow's was to be named the best barbecue in Texas, and Evan Smith never had any doubt about what would happen as soon as that designation was on the newsstands. "I basically said, 'Congratulations and I'm sorry,'" he told me, "because I knew what would happen."

"That brings up the subject of remorse," I said.

"You mean remorse on their part?" Smith asked.

"No, remorse on your part — remorse for having turned the place into an ugly scene."

"We don't publish *Best-Kept Secrets Monthly,*" Smith said, as he got out of Burka's Suburban. He sniffed confidently, presumably to reassure himself that, despite the aroma, he would have no trouble limiting himself to coleslaw and potato salad. Then he marched across the street toward Snow's BBQ.

Regular consumers of Hill Country–style Texas barbecue know what to expect when they walk into an establishment that is said to offer the real article. I had never been to Louie Mueller's, in Taylor, before this trip, but when Greg Curtis and I went there the day before the Snow's outing for what we referred to as some warm-up barbecue, the place looked familiar. At a Texas barbecue joint, you normally pick up a tray at the counter and order meat from one person and sides from another. The person doling out the meat removes it from the smoker and carves it himself. It is sold by the pound — often brisket and pork ribs and sausage and beef ribs and chicken and, in some places, clod (beef shoulder). The carver serves it on some variety of butcher paper. If, despite having worked with smoke in his eyes for many years, he is of a generous nature, as the carvers at Mueller's are known to be, he might slice off a piece of a brisket's darkened outside — what would be called in Kansas City a burnt end — and, before you've ordered anything, place it on your tray as a small gesture. (Given the quality of Mueller's brisket, it is a gesture that can make a traveler feel immensely pleased about being back in Texas.) A couple of slices of packaged white bread are also included. Usually, the only way to have a brisket sandwich in central Texas is to make your own.

A Texas barbecue joint is likely to have neon beer signs on the walls, and those walls are likely to have been darkened by years of smoke. At Mueller's, a cavernous place in a former school gym, there is a large bulletin board festooned with business cards, and most of the cards by now look like specks of brownish parchment. In a restaurant serving Hill Country barbecue, there may be bottles of sauce on the tables, but the meat does not come out of the pits slathered in sauce. I remember a sign at Kreuz Market announcing that the management provided neither sauce nor salads nor forks. In central Texas, you don't hear a lot of people talking about the piquancy of a restaurant's sauce or the tastiness of its beans; discussions are what a scholar of the culture might call meat-driven.

Geographically, Lexington is not in the Hill Country — it's in ranch land, northeast of Austin — but ethnically it is. Burka told me that a politician from Lee County once said to him, "It's the Germans against the Czechs, and the Americans are the swing vote." Snow's BBQ turned out to have the sort of layout found in a place like Kreuz Market, except in miniature. It's a small, dark red building that has room for a counter and six tables — with a few more tables outside, near the cast-iron smokers that in Texas are referred to as pits, even if they're not in the ground. A sign listed what meats were available, all for $8.45 a pound: sausage, brisket, pork, pork ribs, and chicken. The sides offered were "Mrs. Patschke's homemade coleslaw and potato salad," plus free beans. There were only a couple of people ahead of us in line. Burka stepped up to the counter to order.

"Are there five of you?" the young woman slicing the meat asked, as Burka tried to figure out how many pounds we needed.

"Well," Burka said, glancing at Evan Smith. "Four, really. One is . . . he has a big meal coming up."

"You're ashamed of your friend," I whispered to Burka. "You've abandoned him."

"I just couldn't say the V word," Burka said. He looked sheepish — not, I would guess, a normal look for him.

I had warned the *Texas Monthly* crowd that if they were looking for confirmation of their ranking by an objective outlander, someone from Kansas City was not likely to provide it. A jazz fan taken to a rock concert might admire the musical technique, but he probably wouldn't make an ecstatic rush to the stage. As we sat down at one of the outside tables, under a galvanized-tin covering, I told them that they could expect the sort of response that a proud young father I know has received during the past year or so whenever he e-mails me pictures of his firstborn: "A perfectly adequate child." Still, what Burka had ordered was good enough to make me forget that we were eating a huge meal of barbecue at a time on Saturday morning when most people were starting to wonder what they might rustle up for breakfast once they bestirred themselves. I particularly liked the brisket, although I couldn't attest that it was as soft and sweet as cookie dough. In Kansas City, it is not customary to eat cookie dough.

Although Snow's hours may seem odd to a city dweller, they seem normal in Lexington. Saturday is traditionally when farmers and ranchers from the surrounding area come into town, and at twelve-thirty every Saturday there is a cattle auction in yards that are just down the street from Snow's. From 1976 to 1996, in fact, Tootsie Tomanetz, who is known far and wide in Lee County as Miss Tootsie, served barbecue every Saturday at a meat market that she and her husband ran in Lexington. Miss Tootsie's husband is half Czech and half German. She was born Norma Frances Otto, German on both sides, and her father liked to say that when she married she went from having a last name that could be spelled backward or forward to having one that couldn't be spelled at all. Before the Tomanetzes opened their store, Miss Tootsie had put in ten years tending the pits at City Meat Market, in Giddings. In other words, Kerry Bexley, who's forty-one, could have a certainty about Miss Tootsie's gift that was based on having eaten her barbecue virtually all his life.

After lunch, if that's what you call a large meal of meat that you finish just before 9 A.M., I had a chat about Snow's origins with its management team. We talked near the pits, so Miss Tootsie could pull off sausage links now and then. "I felt like with her name and barbecue and my personality with people we could make it work," Bexley told me. He's a short, outgoing man whose résumé includes — in addition to rodeo clown — prison guard, auctioneer, real-estate agent, and shopkeeper. He already had the location — a place where he'd run a farm and ranch store in 1992. The name came from a nickname he'd had since before he was born. According to the family story, his brother, then four years old, was asked whether he was hoping for the new baby to be a boy or a girl, and he replied, not unreasonably, that he would prefer a snowman. Kerry (Snowman) Bexley and Miss Tootsie opened Snow's in March 2003 — Bexley had built the pits — and it did well from the start. "For the most part, we cooked two to three hundred pounds of meat," Bexley told me. "We sold out by noon."

In the weeks after the *Texas Monthly* feature was published, Snow's went from serving three hundred pounds of meat every Saturday to serving more than a thousand pounds. At eight in the morning — six or seven hours after Miss Tootsie had arrived to begin tending the pits — there was already a line of customers, some of whom had left home before dawn. Bexley said that one Saturday morning, when there were ninety people waiting outside, a local resident asked permission to gather signatures along the line for a petition, only to return a few minutes later with the information that there wasn't one person there from Lee County. Some locals expressed irritation at being shut out of their own barbecue joint. At times, Bexley and Miss Tootsie felt overwhelmed. There were moments, they say, when they wished that the tasters from *Texas Monthly* had never shown up. Then Bexley added three brisket pits, Miss Tootsie got some help, Snow's for a time quit taking pre-orders by phone except for locals, and the amount of meat prepared every Saturday leveled off to about eight hundred pounds.

Most of the time, Bexley and Miss Tootsie are grateful for the additional business. Not long after the survey appeared, Snow's BBQ started selling T-shirts that had on them not only VOTED #1 BBQ IN TEXAS but a motto that Bexley's wife had suggested — SMOKIN' THE GOOD STUFF. Looking around for a way to extend the newly famous Snow's brand without sacrificing the quality of the product, Bexley has hit on mail order, and is hoping to have that under way soon. Snow's already has a website. Bexley and Miss Tootsie are also pleased by the personal recognition. They've worked hard. Most people in Lee County work hard without anybody's noticing. Whether or not Kerry Bexley and Tootsie Tomanetz ever feel able to give up their day jobs, they have received the sort of pure validation that doesn't come to many people, no matter what their field of endeavor.

"Miss Tootsie gets some recognition now for what she's actually done all her life," Bexley said. "She's now" — he turned to Miss Tootsie — "seventy-four? Excuse me for asking."

"No, I'm just seventy-three," Miss Tootsie said, smiling. "You add a year every time."

"What did you do when you heard that you were No. 1?" I asked.

"When we found out we were No. 1," Bexley said, "we just set there in each other's arms and we bawled."

KARRIE JACOBS

Terminal Beauty

FROM *Travel + Leisure*

THE MOST BEAUTIFUL AIRLINE TERMINAL in the world is at
New York's John F. Kennedy International Airport. These days,
however, most of the airport's more than forty-eight million annual
passengers arrive and depart oblivious to it: the terminal in question, commissioned by TWA and completed in 1962, hasn't been
in use since 2000, not long before that pioneering airline went
bankrupt and was bought by American Airlines. Architect Eero
Saarinen's design is a lyric poem in poured concrete, all curve and
swoop, about the wonder of flight. But come September, passengers of low-cost carrier JetBlue Airways will have the option of tow-
ing their wheeled suitcases through this architectural dreamscape,
checking in at an electronic kiosk, and continuing through Saarinen's skinny tube-shaped connectors to the brand-new Terminal 5,
one of the first built in this country since 9/11.

Given that the over-the-top sensuality of Saarinen's design would
seem to have limited relevance in today's fraught air-travel environment, it's an unexpected pleasure to see TWA's contours reflected
in a new generation of airline terminals. Airports are re-embracing
the notion of beauty. Beijing's newly opened Terminal 3, designed
by Norman Foster's Foster & Partners, is a miracle of rapid-fire engineering and army ant–intensity construction; it's also the world's
largest single building, with a ceiling that is a dizzying scrim of light
and color. Madrid's Barajas Airport's 2006 Terminal 4, by Richard
Rogers of Rogers Stirk Harbour & Partners, is like an extra-long cathedral, an unending vault supported by a colorful procession of
buttresses. And Heathrow's T5, also by RSHP, which had its March

opening disrupted by a massive failure of its luggage handling system, is otherwise notable for its undulating glass roof.

By contrast, the JetBlue terminal that rubs shoulders with the historic TWA hub is conspicuously earthbound and deliberately modest. Partly, this is in deference to Saarinen: "The challenge was to lay back, if you will," says William D. Hooper, a principal architect at Gensler, the firm that designed the 650,000-square-foot building. "We never wanted to compete against Saarinen." (While the new JetBlue terminal is connected to it, the landmarked Saarinen structure is owned by the Port Authority of New York & New Jersey.) Beijing's new Terminal 3 has "a massive wow factor when you step into it," says Foster & Partners CEO Mouzhan Majidi. JetBlue didn't go for the wow — how could they? What could they have done that would have been more impressive than what Saarinen accomplished almost fifty years ago without the benefit of the computer modeling systems upon which contemporary architects rely?

According to Gensler's handout on the terminal, "glamour has been replaced by efficiency." And that's what I notice when Hooper gives me a hardhat tour of the terminal: less attention to image and more to function, and — in an era when air travel can be a trial — a refreshingly thoughtful approach to the basic needs of the passenger. Hooper leads me through the space as if I'm a departing passenger. We enter a long, gently curving hall with a sloping white corrugated-steel roof supported by metal latticework. Windows running the length of the terminal just below the roofline let in sunlight. The architecture, Hooper says, "is intended to be comfortable and generous without being overblown."

In this prototypical post-9/11 environment, the ticket counters are off to the side — JetBlue travelers tend to arrive with boarding passes already in hand — and security is front and center. The layout accommodates twenty security lanes (although there's no guarantee that the Transportation Security Administration will staff them all). I'm pleased when he points out that the floor in the security area is made of the spongy rubber that is used to cushion the pavement in playgrounds, a material friendly to shoeless feet.

But when Hooper tells me about the bench, I want to hug him. The bench, all 225 feet of it, is just beyond the security checkpoint. It's there to aid in what Hooper calls "the revesting process." In plain English, what this means is that when you pad away from the x-ray machine in your stocking feet, juggling your carry-on bags, your computer, your pocket change, your shoes, and maybe an infant or two, there will be a place to sit and put yourself back together, to revest. It's a small gesture, but a considerate one. "JetBlue is returning humanity to air travel," Hooper says.

"This terminal is the first true post-9/11 terminal, where everything is designed for a specific purpose," says Tom Kennedy, an associate principal with the engineering firm Arup, which collaborated with Gensler on the project. "There's no fat in the building whatsoever." Indeed, JetBlue's facility is intended to accommodate twenty million passengers a year via twenty-six gates, turning an aircraft around from arrival to departure in thirty minutes. On the tarmac side, there are dual taxiways, a configuration that allows a plane to zip into its arrival gate while a departing flight pulls out. Equipment to clean the aircraft between flights is stored in gateside closets, instead of at a central depot. The concourses are designed so that departing passengers will find shops and food on their right and arriving passengers will find restrooms on *their* right; the theory is that everyone will be able to move a little faster if fewer people are tempted to cut across the flow. In the economics of the low-cost carrier, seconds count and efficiency is beauty.

Functionally speaking, all the newest terminals, from majestic Beijing to understated JetBlue, share a common lineage; they are descendants of the Stansted model. This outlying London airport, designed by Foster & Partners and completed in 1991, was the first to, as Majidi puts it, "turn airport design upside-down." Mechanical systems were taken off the roof and hidden belowground, which transformed the roof into a lofty canopy. The result is an expansive, sunlight-flooded place where passengers can always pretty much see where they need to go. Foster is famous for designing Hong Kong's airport, which opened in 1998, in such a way that passengers move through the building without thinking, like water through a sieve. The terminal's billowy roof vaults work like subliminal arrows, nudging passengers in the right direction. Similarly, in Beijing, the color of the ceiling offers a clue to where in the two-mile-long structure you are and where you're going. "We use this device of color as a way of breaking down zones in the building," Majidi says. "In the processing terminal, the ceiling is all red. As you go toward the gates, the ceiling starts to turn yellow." At Madrid's Barajas, space is also marked by shifting hues, from blue to green to orange to yellow.

Embedded in the architecture of JetBlue, as in Beijing, is the notion of intuitive design. Passengers are supposed to be guided less by signage, which Gensler regards as "visual clutter," and more by cues offered by the building itself. Just beyond the security area at JetBlue, there's something Hooper refers to as the "blue glowy wall." The translucent expanse of color is, to be sure, a branding device, but it's also there to cue passengers "that there's something fun and exciting on the other side." Beyond it is a high-ceilinged hub — the Marketplace — that Hooper describes as the terminal's Times Square. "This is the nexus of this terminal," he says. "Everyone comes through this space." Actually, the terminal's one touch of glamour is the Marketplace's impressive roster of sit-down restaurants, including 5ive Steak, with a menu developed by STK's Todd Mark Miller; Piquillo, a tapas bar created by Tia Pol's Alexandra Raij; and AeroNuova, with an Italian menu by Mark Ladner of Del Posto. There will also be plenty of shopping and an enhanced selection of those crucial packaged meals (including sushi) to take on board. Travelers will be able to order meals from touchscreen monitors on tables at their gate's seating area, an airline industry first.

According to David Rockwell, an architect famous for his fanciful interiors who was hired to work on the Marketplace area, the airline wanted to avoid the anonymity of many terminals. To Rockwell, this called for a celebration of public space, and he tried to give it a New York flavor. In what's likely to be a very busy environment, he says, "If you can make movement intuitive, the density of people would be a joy to watch from above." While international passengers arriving in Beijing enter the airport on the terminal's highest level, a mezzanine where they can gaze down on the spectacle of the departing travelers, JetBlue's architecture doesn't allow that kind of sweeping gesture. Instead, Rockwell's firm created grandstand seating for the Marketplace, which will let travelers watch "the dance of public movement" from above, much as you can stand on one of Grand Central Terminal's balconies and observe the commuter pageant below. The big idea is that if the terminal is efficient enough, if you don't feel as though you are trapped in purgatory with your fellow passengers, you might actually be able to take some pleasure in their company. Which, I guess, is what Hooper means when he talks about returning humanity to air travel.

Eero Saarinen died at fifty-one, eight months before his TWA terminal opened. He never saw his vision of the "excitement of air travel" fully realized. Nor did he live to see a once magical adventure devolve into an ordeal. Now, however, the world's most ambitious new airline terminals seem designed to bring back Saarinen's brand of exuberance. Meanwhile, the Port Authority is busily stripping asbestos from Saarinen's landmark and trying to time its reopening with the inauguration of JetBlue's new facility in September. While it's not clear what the old TWA terminal's program will be — a conference center with an upscale restaurant is one possibility — JetBlue passengers will be able to use the building to infuse their travels with a little joie de vivre.

MARK SCHATZKER

A Tale of Two Crossings

FROM *Condé Nast Traveler*

ON A SUNNY AFTERNOON in Los Angeles last spring, I set out to do something relatively few people have done — I set out to cross the Pacific Ocean by boat. I know what you're thinking: lots of people ply the Pacific by ship. Sailors in the navy, for instance. Or the deckhands — lonely souls, all of them — who man the container ships that plod back and forth between China and L.A., delivering flat-screen TVs, jeans, and innumerable cheaply manufactured widgets. But hardly anybody else can be bothered.

Let's face it: crossing the Pacific Ocean hasn't been trendy since the sixteenth century, when explorers like Ferdinand Magellan and Francis Drake made it famous. But the planet's largest geographical feature never caught on with travelers, not the way traversing the Atlantic did. And yet, if you look hard enough, you can find a handful of ocean liners — maybe three a year — that make the trip. I booked my ticket. The ship was big and white. It's called the *Crystal Symphony*.

I'd never been on a cruise before and was taken with the idea of spending days on end aboard a multiton vessel designed from keel to funnel (that's what nautical types call that big chimney) with the pursuit of pleasure in mind. Which is why, right after I crossed the Pacific, I planned to cross the planet's other big ocean, the Atlantic.

Consider the geography involved. Both cruises add up to some twelve thousand miles — roughly half the planet. Half the planet, I would like to add, that no one is spending much time seeing. People have this funny habit of visiting everything but the oceans —

the deserts, the forests, the jungles, the lakes, the mountains, the rivers, the cities. So one day I decided: it's high time I saw the ocean — really saw the ocean.

Here is what I can tell you: It is vast. It is impersonal. It is wavy like you can't imagine, except for those rare moments when, miraculously, it lies still. On a bright afternoon two thousand miles south of Alaska, it looked like a magnificent indigo pile rug. A day later, under a sky blotched with clouds, it resembled the hide of a huge slumbering animal, heaving up and down as it breathed. Two days before we hit Hawaii, it struck me that an ocean swell is the ultimate in existentialism: unremitting and blind. The waves marched across the horizon like Victorian factory workers. Their movement was both vigorous and futile — as if to say, "What else you gonna do out here?"

And then, a few hundred miles later, their outlook on life changed. The waves were hulking, irritated, and crested with foam, appearing an awful lot like a bunch of young goons headed to a fight. I made a mental note: do nothing to upset the waves. And as though to stress the point, the nose of the vessel nodded up and down in exaggerated, practically patronizing concurrence.

I can gaze at water for hours. And when you stand on the deck of a 51,000-ton luxury liner, you notice the following: when the hull plunges into the ocean after being raised by a swell, it drags down a big pocket of air that explodes into billions of tiny bubbles that get caught in a slow-motion journey to the surface. To serious seafarers, this phenomenon has a name: spume. A trail of spume stretched out behind the ship for miles. It was frothy and turquoise and had the look of a rare substance. As I stared at it, I had a fantasy of collecting it in buckets — like a grape picker in Burgundy — and then selling it in fancy boutiques all over town. But as I emerged from my dream state, I realized that those little bubbles would pop and all that would be left would be saltwater. To enjoy the wonders of spume, you have to be on the ocean.

The precise moment of departure wasn't something I'd thought about even once, but it turned out to be quietly thrilling. I was seated in a roomy lounge at the front of the *Crystal Symphony* called the Palm Court, about to tuck into a scone piled with whipped cream and strawberries. There was movement, but it was movement unlike any I'd ever known. The transition from rest to motion was borderless. The swish of the two eighteen-foot propellers left not a ripple in the milky tea in my cup. The land outside began to go by.

I walked out on deck. We were making our way down a channel leading to the open sea. On one side, a crane was carefully dismantling a stack of containers on board the *Xin Yan Tian,* a cargo ship from Shanghai. On the other, more cranes and what looked like an oil refinery, punctuated by the odd palm tree. The *Symphony,* immaculate and white, must have seemed to the other boats like a fat cat in a leisure suit.

An hour later, the continent of North America had all but receded. Los Angeles and its five and a half million automobiles — five million of them stuck in traffic — had been reduced to an absurd concept just over the horizon. Ahead of us, the ocean was empty as far as the eye could see. We were traveling twenty-two miles per hour, headed for China, with nothing to do.

That's not quite true. There was lots to do. I could go to the gym or for a swim. I could take a line-dancing lesson, bid on a painting at auction, nurse a cappuccino next to the two-story fountain in the main "plaza," go to a movie, play a hand of blackjack or bridge. Where does a person start?

I started by standing on deck and staring over the side. For a long time, I was stricken by a fear of going overboard. The Pacific Ocean is an awfully big place to go for a swim. You would be nothing — a bobbing head between the waves, a tiny pinprick of individuality in a literal sea of gray. But as I stared, the sun came out and I inhaled the warm, salty breeze. Eventually, I no longer pictured myself swimming helplessly as the ship sailed away. Instead, I noticed the spume.

From this, I progressed to wandering the halls. Halls that were surprisingly empty. Crystal bills itself as a six-star cruise line, and that sixth star is due to the fact that no one ever has to line up for anything. If you want to take the galley tour, take it. No employee will greet you ten minutes beforehand to say, "I'm sorry, sir, but the tour is full." Similarly, if you become seized with the desire to soak in the hot tub, well, climb on in, because there will be room. There are no queues in front of the dining room at 6:30 P.M.; there is always an available Lifecycle in the gym; and the elevator doors never open to reveal a compartment too crowded for one more. Simply put, on Crystal the ratio of ship to passenger is a lot higher than on other vessels. There is an unintended consequence to this: even when the *Symphony* is full, it feels half empty. You can stand in a hallway for minutes and not see another soul. This, you might say, is the price of luxury.

Then there is the actual price of luxury, namely, what the cruise costs. In this case it was a bargain: $3,635 for seventeen days. The voyage from Los Angeles to Hong Kong is what's known in the industry as a repositioning cruise. This is what happens when a cruise line needs to get a ship from one continent to another. The ticket is a good deal, but the trip is not without its drawbacks. It offers hardly anything in the way of ports of call — our single stop was Honolulu, and only for a day. The median age shoots up; I was one of a handful of non-grayhairs. And more than one seasoned cruiser warned me that it's difficult to secure decent entertainment for a seventeen-day itinerary. (On day twelve, I took in a magic show that included shadow puppets set to music and realized that the warnings were accurate.)

The first organized activity I participated in was a shave — the best of my life. My face radiating smoothness, I sauntered into the casino, lost forty dollars at blackjack, returned to my cabin and donned my swimsuit, and rode the elevator to the sixth floor. The pool area was a study in relaxation: couples reclined in chaise longues on the teak deck, reading Tami Hoag novels and contemplating a plunge in the pool.

Before long, a rhythm took hold, one as lulling and constant as the ocean swells — and centered around eating. I'd wake up, have breakfast, play bridge or do Pilates or go to a wine tasting. Then it was time for lunch. After lunch I'd do something else, and before I knew it, it was time for dinner. After dinner I'd hit a show, maybe cap the evening with a drink at the nightclub Luxe. Soon enough it was time for bed — that period of prolonged rest that allows the staff to prepare the breakfast buffet.

What no one could see coming — not me, not my mother, not even my high school guidance counselor — is that I would turn out to be a sucker for the lectures. There were four a day, and I enjoyed them all. I was riveted during the one on diamonds (did you know that in Mumbai, the industry employs no fewer than seven hun-

dred fifty thousand people?). I was transfixed by the one on gas tur-
bines (the world's smallest is two inches in diameter and produces
seven pounds of thrust). And my attention did not waver once during the series on American foreign policy, delivered by Edward
Peck, a former U.S. ambassador to Iraq.

The best lecture wasn't actually a lecture. It was the kitchen tour.
It had all the informative horsepower of a lecture, but instead of
sitting there passively, you get to walk through a stainless steel
wonderland while being privy to some mind-blowing stats. In the
course of a single day, the *Symphony* goes through one ton of vegetables. During dinner alone, it takes twenty-two individuals to transfer the prepared food from the pots and pans onto plates. The
meat freezer, which can hold up to two thousand pounds, is large
enough to play tennis in. On this never-ending expanse of seawater, perhaps the most precious commodity is fresh water: the galley
uses one hundred tons a day. And over the course of the cruise, the
966 passengers consume some 1,600 pounds of iceberg lettuce.
That works out to 1.7 pounds per person — I'm quite sure someone else ate my share.

The scale of culinary activity may suggest that the *Crystal Symphony*
is a kind of floating smorgasbord, but it's much more than that.
The ship has all the earthly delights and amenities a person could
hope for — from a small hospital and a library to a business center
and a putting green — in the place you'd least expect to find them:
the middle of the ocean.

To conquer the sea, we build ships that look and feel like land.
Indeed, the *Symphony* seems to be in a state of denial over the fact
that it's on the water at all. Everywhere there are ornamental flourishes reminiscent of place. The Italian restaurant has barbershop
poles made famous by Venice. The Asian restaurant sports Chinese scrolls. And the Crystal Plaza — site of the two-story fountain
— flaunts Corinthian columns (along with smoked-crystal sconces
and a piano made of Plexiglas). The designers have succeeded
wildly: it's only from the exterior that the *Symphony* actually looks
like a ship. But when it comes to smoked crystal, polished brass,
and mirrored surfaces, more isn't always more. With its relentless
ornamentation, themed rooms, and unending schedule of activities — cards, bingo, handwriting analysis — the *Symphony* feels at
times like a suburban fantasy of the afterlife.

The result was that despite being on the ocean, I found myself craving it. When one of the staff told me of a disastrous Antarctic cruise, during which a wave crashed through one of the windows and drenched passengers in their beds with frigid water, I kind of wished the same would happen to me. Each morning, the captain would come on the loudspeaker to tell us the day's forecast and our present depth, and I would be seized by thoughts of what lay suspended between the hull and the earth's crust so many miles below. Were there schools of tuna? Blue whales? Swordfish?

The food was beginning to get to me. There was a lot of it — fish, lamb, lobster, pork, and steak at breakfast, lunch, and dinner — but every dish tended to taste the same. Sauces were either too salty, too sweet, or both. At an event called the Gala Buffet, which seemed like an informal eating contest, there were seven food sculptures on display, including a chocolate pirate and a parrot made of butter. I counted almost a hundred separate dishes, not one of which I would describe as delicious. I looked out at the ocean and fantasized about the crew throwing lines baited with mackerel off the stern and hauling in big tuna, and one of the Filipino crew slicing into its smooth hide to reveal delicious dark-red flesh. That night at dinner, I ordered grouper. During the galley tour, the chef had boasted that all the fish served on board was fresh. He assured us that seafood could last up to six days in a cold fridge. That's just how it tasted.

On day thirteen, the sea delivered. We were somewhere north of the Mariana Islands, eating breakfast in the Lido Café, when the German man who conducted the seminar on diamonds yelled, "Look! A ship!" Amazingly, this was our first such sighting, aside from a smattering of fishing vessels and private yachts near Honolulu. I walked to the bow, where I was joined by a man named Bob. Bob and I spent the next several hours looking, wishing we had binoculars. "It's an oil tanker," Bob said, "on its way from the Persian Gulf to Asia. Probably Japan." Here was a glimpse of globalism's circulatory system, conveying the blood that keeps the world economy alive and kicking.

An hour later, the ship had disappeared over the horizon. We still stood there, now watching a seabird hovering near the *Symphony*'s bridge and scanning the ocean below. More birds appeared and took similar positions near the bow. They were gannets, white and black, like seagulls but with much more style. Every now and again, one would spot a flying fish skipping over the surface. At this, the bird would turn ninety degrees in a fraction of a second and accelerate toward the water. Sometimes, the gannets would snatch the flying fish while they were in midair. Other times, they would tuck back their wings, bring their legs up landing-gear style, and torpedo beak-first into the sea at full speed. Even from several hundred yards away, you could see the trail of spume left as the birds knifed through the water. Seconds later, they would break the surface quite a distance from where they'd entered and bob like rubber duckies while they swallowed their lunch. The fish never had a chance.

Pacific means peaceful, and it was so dubbed by the first European ever to sail it, Ferdinand Magellan. (Magellan's flagship, the *Trinidad,* was one-four-hundred-fiftieth the size of the *Crystal Symphony;* it did not have an indoor pool.) It seemed pacific to me, too: there were perhaps ten minutes of rain during the seventeen-day voyage, and even though the waves occasionally struck me as big, the North Atlantic taught me that they were anything but.

The North Atlantic is not what you would call a friendly place. When I boarded Cunard's *Queen Mary* 2 in Southampton on a blustery day in late May, the wind up on the bow deck was strong enough to give anyone who didn't cover his ears a pounding headache. We all stood there, waving at the group of well-wishers back on the pier, until the wind forced us inside, where everybody headed straight for the bar.

For the next six days, the wind would not stop howling. At one point, it made an eerie whistling noise as the ship sounded its basso foghorn and plowed through fog as thick as wallpaper paste. The wind relented only when we crossed beneath the Verrazano-Narrows Bridge and chugged into New York Harbor. It was what you'd call a steady breeze.

The route out of England is pleasingly rife with geography. You begin by navigating your way down a tongue of saltwater dotted with sailboats, yachts, and ferries known as Southampton Water. Then you hit the English Channel and turn right for America. That evening, as I sat down to dinner in the spacious dining room, there was a speck of land visible in the far distance. It was the western tip of Cornwall.

Whereas the *Crystal Symphony* serves about 500 meals at a typical seating, the *QM2* serves 1,200. There are 1,250 staff, as many as 2,592 passengers, nine bars, and ten restaurants. On the fifth floor, there's a warehouse-like area where workers ferry entire pallets of supplies — celery, toilet paper, soap, Bordeaux — on forklifts. When it was christened five years ago, the *QM2* was the longest, widest, tallest ocean liner ever built; to this day, it is still the heaviest. At nine hundred million dollars, the cost of building it equals the yearly economic output of Grenada and Vanuatu combined.

That's a lot of money for a nearly extinct form of transportation. There was a time, it's true, when virtually every newcomer to North America — save the ancient natives who wandered across the land bridge from Kamchatka — arrived by boat: the passengers aboard the *Mayflower,* the throngs of newcomers who were processed at Ellis Island, and my father, to name just a few. In the first part of the last century, it all culminated in an era considered the golden age of ocean liners, when the gilded set booked passage aboard a Cunard or White Star vessel bound for America. They wore tuxedos, and they paid through the nose.

But then commercial airliners began taking to the skies between Europe and North America, and almost overnight the age of the ocean liner — which, in truth, had been in decline for a few decades — came to an abrupt end. The idea of traversing the Atlantic by ship is as outmoded today as crossing the Rockies in a covered wagon, a quaint relic of a bygone era. A berth on the *QM2* costs twice as much as an airline ticket and takes roughly twenty times as long. Like fountain pens and watches that need to be wound, the ocean liner would have no business in the here and now were it not imbued with so much romanticism.

There's a lot to be said for romanticism. And there's a lot of romanticism to be found on the *QM2*. It's hard to take ten steps without being confronted with some misty-eyed depiction of Cunard's storied past. There are oil paintings of the *Caronia* and the original *Queen Mary* sailing during the heady blue-sky moments of yestercentury. Adorning the walls on deck five are ancient menus. (They served calf's brains and roast Long Island duckling for a dinner on July 5, 1953; it is my belief that passengers had higher culinary standards half a century ago.) All over the ship, you find bits of

Cunard trivia and photo after black-and-white photo of fabulously
dressed celebrities from days gone by, including Cary Grant, David
Niven, and Douglas Fairbanks Jr. It is impossible to visit deck five
without concluding that back then all men were well versed in the
art of tying one's own bow tie.

Accordingly, every second night or so, we passengers — the male
ones, at least — donned tuxedos and headed to the dining room
for dinner. (The folks who paid more got to eat in an exclusive dining room known as the Princess Grill.) Afterward, we would retire
to the Royal Court Theatre, or dance to big band music from an actual eight-piece big band in the Queen's Room.

It's all a finely orchestrated charade. Celebrities may have sailed
Cunard ships across the Atlantic a hundred years ago and dressed
in tuxedos, but now they fly in Gulf Streams and wear five-hundred-
dollar jeans. I'd wager that you could count on one hand the number of guests who tie their own bow tie today. But movies and TV
shows are also make-believe. So are expensive dive watches worn by
nondivers, and SUVs that never leave the city. If you look closely at
the Art Deco wall moldings on the QM2, you can see that they
aren't made of plaster and appear to be some kind of preformed
plastic. But that's only if you look very closely. The point is, it
doesn't feel make-believe.

Take the following typical day: I was traveling with my brother,
and after breakfast we visited the Illuminations Theatre to take
in a lecture on the Concorde — another bygone mode of luxurious transatlantic transportation. For lunch, we headed to the pub,
where we ordered fish and chips and pints of ale and settled in for a
long and hilarious afternoon of darts (and more ale). That evening
the attire was formal, and we had dinner at the Todd English restaurant, where I had the best meal I have ever eaten while not on
land. Following dessert, we took in an Alan Ayckbourn play. The
cast consisted of actual working actors from London's Royal Court
Theatre, and the level of talent was starkly superior to that of the B-
list entertainers who usually wash up on the cruise ship circuit. And
then it was time for one last game of darts.

That day, you'll notice, was spent almost entirely indoors. And
that's because it was freezing and windy outside — not what you
would call prime tanning weather, unless windburn qualifies as a
tan. But the truth is that the positively English weather made the

ship feel that much more cozy. It's thrilling, in fact, to stand in a pub and hit a triple twenty, take a sip of ale, and then look out the window at the North Atlantic, dark green and roiling, its waves crested with spume.

Every cruise must come to an end, and it's the ending that sets apart the transoceanic sailing from all others. On most cruises, you return after your week at sea to the same place you started out (usually Florida), at which point the whole thing feels like it took place in your head. Planting your feet on a different continent after days and days at sea is considerably more memorable.

The evening before docking in Hong Kong, we spent the night slowly navigating past a series of illuminated buoys. By first light, we were in our berth and the harbor was already alive with ferries shuttling back and forth. Across the water stood Hong Kong's gleaming towers of commerce. Next to us, a little motorized junk was tootling around the harbor. It would stop and the driver would extend a fishing net into the water and pick up bits of trash. I walked off the ship onto Chinese soil, took a taxi to my hotel, and then went out for dim sum.

As we approached New York, the *QM2*'s funnel looked like it was going to bring down the Verrazano-Narrows. But it cleared the bridge with all of nine feet to spare. The vessel turned its nose to the right and all of New York lay in front of us — Manhattan dead ahead, New Jersey to port, and Brooklyn to starboard. I nodded hello to Lady Liberty.

When I stepped onto land after so many days at sea, it didn't feel like land at all. It felt like the ocean, as the ground seemed to rise up under a relentless swell and then sink down again, dropping me so suddenly that I actually stumbled. The wave wasn't big — maybe fifteen feet. After crossing this planet's two biggest oceans, I knew it was nothing I couldn't handle.

DIMITER KENAROV

Game Over, Perseverance, All I Want Is Everything

FROM *The Virginia Quarterly Review*

STOYAN IS THE MAYOR of Hope. He is also its doctor, social worker, psychologist, marriage counselor, teacher, judge.

At ten o'clock on a sweltering June morning, I find myself in Stoyan's office, a tiny room in a one-story, derelict house with barred windows. The walls have been recently painted bright pink, like a nursery for a baby girl. But instead of a crib, there is a bulky wooden desk, bare but for a rotary phone left over from the bureaucracy of a former era. Two flags — the Bulgarian white-green-red and the European Union's snake of stars biting its own tail — flank an oil painting of a lonesome landscape dotted with birches. A fly ribbon speckled with dead insects hangs from a pendant light in the ceiling, twisting with every breath of wind like a perverse crib toy.

Sitting on a shabby couch, Stoyan is a human-size fly. His checkered cotton shirt and gray pants are neatly pressed; his shoes have been polished to a maddening shine; a pair of sunglasses, like compound eyes, rests on his dark forehead. To the casual observer, Stoyan might appear as a minor public servant on summer holiday. He is, in fact, directly responsible for running the affairs of twenty thousand Roma in what is arguably the worst ghetto in twenty-first-century Europe: the Bulgarian town of Sliven's quarter known as Nadezhda — literally, "Hope."

Being the mayor of Nadezhda is not exactly like being a mayor. Stoyan prefers "sheriff," though he does not brandish a badge or carry a gun, and his position cannot be called official because official positions come with official responsibilities. He is more of a middleman, bridging his community and the municipal government of Sliven. Since he is allowed no annual budget but has intimate knowledge of the needs of the people, he puts together proposals on how to distribute public funds in Nadezhda. If a water pipe breaks, he tells the authorities to fix it; if the ambulance refuses to respond to a call from the ghetto, he reports the incident. Today, people knock on the door of his office every few minutes: a man wants help with filing documents; a woman has had an argument with her husband and needs advice; another man demands to know when the sewage truck will arrive.

I ask Stoyan what is the biggest problem that Bulgarian Roma face. "You can't define just one single problem because everything is related to everything else," he says. His Bulgarian is flawless, without a whiff of the accent usually associated with Roma — rowdy vowels amid crowded consonants. "The problem of segregation begins at birth and ends only with death. Romani women deliver their babies in a segregated maternity ward. Romani children attend segregated schools. They live in a segregated neighborhood. The Bulgarian government simply has no need for well-educated, intelligent Roma." He speaks carefully, methodically. "Out of twenty thousand who live in Nadezhda, less than one-tenth are literate. We have no more than twenty people with a high-school diploma. That's one in a thousand. Out of twenty thousand residents, we only have four with a college degree. We live in the Stone Age here in Nadezhda. What is there to change?"

Tucked in the southern slope of the eastern Balkans — the scenic mountain range that literally bisects Bulgaria and gives the peninsula its name — Sliven presents to visitors a quaint mixture of rural and urban architecture, concrete Soviet-style housing projects towering over brick houses. In the mornings, the clank of horse-drawn buggies syncopates with the roar of automobiles and buses. Roosters have not been completely outmoded by alarm clocks. Tourists, probably en route to a glitzy resort on the Black Sea coast a hundred kilometers away, recite platitudes about the unpretentious beauty of the place, unaware of Sliven's hidden deformity.

Stoyan leads me toward the first houses of Nadezhda. We pass by

a field of grass strewn with discarded cash-register receipts. Two
horses are grazing among the refuse. Soon we enter a narrow,
paved road lined with squat brick houses with or without stucco,
with or without windows, with or without doors. A few fancier
buildings are painted in vivid orange or green, marble balustrades
gracing the balconies, the double-hung windows framed in gleaming aluminum. Some of the façades are covered with bathroom
tiles. Clotheslines crisscross overhead. Satellite dishes spring out of
almost every rooftop. Countless other neighborhoods in Bulgaria
look exactly the same, except for one haunting detail: a three-
meter iron wall, topped by rows of barbed wire, surrounds all of
Nadezhda. Its resemblance to those other ghetto walls from another era is blood-chilling.

Farther down the road, a few vendors are peddling cheap mer-
chandise — shoes and vegetables, mostly — from cardboard boxes.
Three children play cards with the utmost concentration, one of
them taking furtive peeks at another's hand. In front of the barbershop, teenagers in trendy clothes wait their turns to have their hair
highlighted or leopard-spotted (a popular style among Roma); the
barber is no more than fifteen. The decoration in the barbershop
consists of fake sunflowers, U.S. dollar bills taped to the mirror,
and a large poster of a naked woman. Nadezhda is not as hopeless
as I thought.

"Are you ready to leave now?" Stoyan asks suddenly. He looks
anxious, distracted, like a man who has just remembered he has
left the stove on. He tells me it is not a good idea to walk around
the poorer parts of Nadezhda because of a problem with the sewage system that has not been fixed. Many people are upset, he says,
and might not be too fond of visitors. Last week they tried to break
the camera of a crew from Germany's ZDF television channel.
Stoyan's attempt to scare me off seems perplexing, considering his
previous eagerness to show me around; is he really worried about
me (the neighborhood seems quite safe) or uneasy about what I
might discover? I ask that we go on. He finally acquiesces but requests that I refrain from shooting pictures. Deal.

The Nadezhda quarter of Sliven is like Dante's inferno. It has circles, even if at first glance it looks like one big square. It is not a simple slum, where everyone shares poverty on equal terms. Roma

may be excluded from taking part in the workings of Bulgarian society, but that does not keep them from practicing exclusion among themselves. Hierarchies, whether religious (Christian versus Muslim), tribal, or familial, do exist, and they are rigorous and complex. Economic differences are the most obvious. Nadezhda boasts its own millionaires, proletariat, and beggars. The ghetto has its own ghetto.

The primitiveness of Stoyan's promised Stone Age is largely spatial. The portly houses are the first to disappear, then the street pavements, then clothing. The smell of animal and human excrement is terrible. No running water, no electricity. In this surreal place, flies have superseded bees, pollinating the fields of trash. The rats are better known as *pis pis* — kitty-kitty — because they can reach the size of tomcats. Instead of playing games, children huddle in large groups, emaciated and naked, by their child-age mothers. Their derisive neighbors have dubbed them the *Goli tzigani* — naked Gypsies. But nobody in this part of Nadezhda can truly be called Gypsy. The hundreds of years of wandering, of survival, of traditions have been wiped out. The only memory left is the bodily memory of hunger, then sleep. For what sins are these people being punished?

I am not allowed to talk to anyone in the ninth circle of Nadezhda. Tugging at my sleeve, Stoyan, my Virgil, leads me back to the light. Protestations are futile. We cannot stay, he insists. Enough is enough. I have noticed, of course, the way hollow eyes follow me. I know what they see: an outsider, come to document their misfortunes. I understand I am not welcome. I have become a Gypsy.

In truth, I am a *gadjo* — the term Roma apply to anyone who is not Roma. Jews are *gadje* to Roma, Roma are goyim to Jews. I am both a *gadjo* and a goy.

I was born in Sofia, Bulgaria, where I lived for nineteen years, before attending college in the United States. Between college and grad school, I squandered two more years trying to work as a freelance journalist at home. That makes twenty-one years in a country where Roma make up between 5 and 10 percent of the population — as many as eight hundred thousand out of eight million. But in those twenty-one years I got to know only one family of Roma —

280 DIMITER KENAROV

our next-door neighbors in another Nadezhda, the working-class section of Sofia. The paths of ethnic Bulgarians and Bulgarian Roma rarely cross.

But, of course, Roma can be seen everywhere, anytime: those in rags scavenging the dumpsters for leftover food or marketable salvage; those in front of Sofia's central train station sniffing glue from grimy plastic bags; those collecting scrap metal with horse-drawn carts; those with missing legs or horrendous deformities — or feigning disability — begging in downtown Sofia; bedraggled children washing windshields on the main thoroughfares; low-end hookers by the Lion Bridge after 9 P.M.; musicians with chained dancing bears or monkeys. Not only are Roma not invisible in Bulgaria — they are the favorite glass-slide specimens for the media's distorted microscope. They steal, kill, rape; they are dirty, lazy, uneducated, and exhibit no propensity for learning; they breed like rabbits and sell their babies or abandon them to orphanages; they drain social security funds; and they never pay their electricity bills. Rampant government corruption is not a very interesting story; crimes committed by Gypsies make the headlines.

Local prejudices are revealed in the language: a botched job is "Gypsy work"; a despicable person is "a dirty Gypsy"; a swindler is said to be "thieving like a Gypsy." And so on. Under pressure from human-rights organizations, *Rom* (Roma) is now accepted as the politically correct name for *tsiganin* (Gypsy), but the connotation has remained the same: *lowlife*. When I was younger, my grandmother would gently but firmly warn me to eat all the food on my plate, "lest you marry a Gypsy." My second cousin's dating "one of them" was a shameful secret whispered only at family reunions. Behind the bureaucratic veneer of tolerance, many Bulgarians — many Europeans — consider Roma an inferior, homogeneous ("they all look alike") people, better avoided, and every Roma knows it.

I am lucky to find Vassil Chaprazov. Vassil is a famous poet in the local Romani community, as well as the publisher of the monthly newspaper *Drom Dromendar* (*A Road to Roads*, roughly) and the magazine *O Roma*. Balding, somewhat overweight, with a well-trimmed, grizzled goatee, he could be any sixty-two-year-old literatus. While we drink beer at a café in downtown Sofia, he quizzes me on Roma trivia. Did I know that Charlie Chaplin had Gypsy blood? What about Elvis Presley? Vassil's attitude toward his own tribe seems to oscillate between pride in accomplished individuals and distaste for the illiterate masses. Self-esteem mingled with self-loathing. In his view, Roma's public image suffers because many talented people refuse to acknowledge their origins. The color divide is insignificant, at times nonexistent, thus successful Roma — artists, scientists, musicians, sports stars — can pass for Bulgarians, while Bulgarians are only too eager to claim celebrities as their own. As a result, only the most underprivileged, the most stigmatized — the dregs — remain "Roma."

After we finish our beers, Vassil takes me to the editorial office of *Drom Dromendar* to introduce me to his son. My namesake, Dimiter is also about my age, my height and weight; he could be my brother, my doppelgänger. A deep scar over his left eyebrow is perhaps the only significant difference between us. Dimiter is preparing the layout for the next issue of the newspaper. He flips through the copy of *VQR* that I hand him. "Nobody in Bulgaria would bother to read such a thick magazine," he says with a note of disparagement, but his careful attention to the pages betrays approval. He agrees to act as my personal guide around the Romani neighborhoods in the country. Yes, he'll be able to help me; he'll escort me to areas where tensions are too high for an outsider to travel alone. He'll be my inside man.

Because I'm a friend of Dimiter's, Peyo Peev Dimitrov welcomes me in. It is the end of the workday, but he turns on the lights in the warehouse, sets the machines roaring: mighty pneumatic hammers that unleash two hundred tons of anger on innocent anvils; giant steel cutters like guillotines. The shaking earthen floor is strewn with metal parts and razor-sharp shavings; the air has a sour, galvanized smell, a heady mixture of hot machine oil and sulfur. The few incandescent bulbs seem to absorb light rather than give it off, so that the whole warehouse remains shrouded in perpetual gloom.

In reality, this small industrial unit, near Sliven, produces plowshares. Peyo is the owner. In the early '90s, when indiscriminate privatization was in full swing, he bought all the machines from a state cooperative (known as an agrarian-industrial complex) and set up his workshop. His friends ridiculed him for his temerity, but he persevered. Now, he supplies Bulgarian tractor factories with spare parts; he even signed an export contract with an Albanian company.

Peyo's success is palpable. Next to a heap of plowshares gleams a silver Mercedes S350. To Peyo, however, the car is nothing compared to plain iron. He lifts two plowshares in his coarse hands. "This one," he says, extending the blade in his left hand, "is made by the competition. And this one," he announces, offering up the other, "is my own production." In this posture his body resembles a pair of scales weighing man's conduct in life. His good deeds, Peyo believes, outweigh someone else's bad ones. "Whatever you do," Peyo tells me with pride, "you have to put your heart into it. Nothing else matters."

His heart metaphor is more than figurative. His unbuttoned shirt reveals a long, hideous scar on his chest: four bypasses. But surgery has not dulled his passion for metalwork. With a pair of hefty pliers he picks up an iron sheet and places it under the pneumatic hammer. *Bang.* My pulse begins to race. "And this is the steel cutter." *Slash.* A festive pandemonium.

According to Bulgarian legend, Gypsies were the first blacksmiths. They worked in the armories of kings, outfitting their armies, building fortifications for their cities. After Khan Krum defeated the Byzantine Nikephoros I in the ninth century, Gypsy smiths lined the vanquished emperor's skull with silver, so the Khan could drink from it. I do not doubt that Peyo, given adequate time, could forge the shield of Achilles.

Among Bulgarians another myth persists: when no one else would do the job, it was a Gypsy who pounded out the nails to crucify Jesus.

Romanticized or demonized as fortune-tellers, charming vagabonds, or thieving nomads, Gypsies populate literature and film — from Cervantes's *The Little Gypsy* and Defoe's *Moll Flanders* to Emir Kusturica's *Time of the Gypsies* and Brad Pitt's impersonation of a pikey boxer in *Snatch*. To the west of Budapest, the word *Gypsy* conjures fanciful caravans and hot-blooded guitars; to the east, it is a swearword. Everywhere else, Gypsies are still Egyptians.

Roma were always named by outsiders, and never correctly. When ancestors of Roma arrived from India and settled in the Balkans around the eleventh century, the Byzantines called them *atsinganoi*, a name that might or might not owe its etymology to *athinganoi*, a heretical ninth-century sect that did or did not practice magic. The Bulgarian *tsigani*, the Hungarian *cigány*, the German *Zigeuner* are all derivative of that term. Whatever the case, when the *gadjo* failed to secure facts about the *tsigani*, he made things up. Few good books have been written on their history, and most of those have been relegated to the ghetto of scholarship.

Romani culture is so diverse that it may be more accurate to speak of *cultures*. The common Indian origin has collapsed into Babylonian exile. A Serbian Rom has little to say to his Finnish kinsman; someone from northern Bulgaria performs different rituals from his southern counterpart. There are more than sixty dialects of Romany in Europe, at least eighteen in Bulgaria alone — the only universal language being perhaps the language of exclusion. Theories arise in the library only to wither in the first village. None of the stereotypes are untrue, and all of them are completely false.

In the Bulgarian unconscious, Gypsies are sometimes seen as Turks in disguise. The conflation is neither new nor limited to Bulgaria. Because the arrival of the Gypsies in western Europe between the fifteenth and sixteenth centuries coincided with the most vigorous expansion of the Ottoman Empire, Roma were oftentimes taken for Turkish spies. Mass persecution resulted from, or coincided with, the mass hysteria generated by the Turkish threat. In consequence, many countries in Europe created legislation that dealt harshly with anyone suspected of being Gypsy — or even pretending to be Gypsy. Accusations of espionage were commonly evoked as justification for penal sanctions and became the basis for three edicts — among so many others — of the Imperial Diet (in 1497, 1498, and 1500), which advocated the expulsion of Gypsies from the territories of the Holy Roman Empire. Some other customary charges included theft, nomadism, witchcraft, even cannibalism.

Perhaps the most exhaustive list of hatred — an evil mirror of the time — was complied by Aventius (Johann Thurmaier) in his *Bavarian Chronicle*, written about 1522:

At this time [1439], that thievish race of men, the dregs and bilge-water of various peoples, who live on the borders of the Turkish empire and of

Hungary (we call them *Zigeni*), began to wander through our provinces under their king Zindelo, and by dint of theft, robbery, and fortune-telling they seek their sustenance with impunity. They relate falsely that they are from Egypt and are constrained by the gods to exile, and they shamelessly feign to be expiating, by a seven-year banishment, the sins of their forefathers who turned away the Blessed Virgin with the child Jesus. I have learned by experience that they use the Wendish language and are traitors and spies.

During the subsequent ages, prejudice did not loosen its hold on the European imagination. At the pinnacle of Western rationalist thought, Denis Diderot's *Encyclopédie* records: "[Gypsies are] vagabonds who profess to tell fortunes by examining hands. Their talent is to sing, dance, and steal."

Far from being the savages of legend, the conquering Turks exhibited measured tolerance toward the conquered minorities, including Bulgarians and Roma. Those who wished to pay lower taxes could abandon their Christianity and convert to Islam. Some availed themselves; the majority did not. In the nineteenth century, the dying Ottoman Empire committed a number of desperate atrocities on Bulgarian territory, but normally its policy favored noninterference in the religious and social affairs of its subjects. Gypsies were ostracized, to be sure, yet they were never forced to undergo the systematic punishment that was the norm in western Europe. Except for the kingdoms of Wallachia and Moldavia (present-day Romania and Moldova), where Gypsies were brutally enslaved up until 1864, the Balkan Peninsula was not such a bad place to be different. If India was the first home of the Gypsies, the Balkans became their second.

After the liberation of Bulgaria in 1878 from five centuries of Ottoman rule, the status of Gypsies did not improve significantly — they were still the conquered ones, though the government had changed hands. The situation was analogous in other Balkan countries with large Gypsy populations, including Romania, the former Yugoslavia, and Greece. Before any talk of discrimination, however, it should be noted that Bulgaria was the only country in Europe (along with Denmark) to save its Jewish and Romani populations during the World War II by refusing their deportation. In response, Hitler's ambassador to Sofia, Adolph-Heinz Beckerle, filed the following report: "The mentality of the Bulgarian people lacks the ideological enlightenment which our people enjoy. Having spent their entire lives with Armenians, Greeks, and Gypsies, the Bulgarians see no harm in the Jew to justify special measures against him." Sometimes backwardness could be the most enlightened attitude.

It was neither the Turks nor the Germans that did the greatest damage but the pseudocommunist regime foisted on Bulgaria by the Soviet Union in 1944. Even though the first several years were marked by promise, with Gypsies allowed their own cultural institutions, soon the party began to tighten its grip until it refused to acknowledge even the existence of minorities. Officially, there were no Gypsies in Bulgaria. Policies swung back and forth between assimilation and segregation, with no clear results. The tendency of functionaries to adopt grand-scale, arbitrary strategies without respect for cultural sensitivities doomed everything to failure. The special housing projects lay abandoned or vandalized; unemployment was crudely concealed behind the reality that many Gypsies were forced to work as either janitors or street-sweepers. When the regime was toppled in 1989 and Bulgaria entered a painful period of democratization and market liberalization, Gypsies were the first to fall through the cracks of freedom. What used to be segregated neighborhoods now turned into ghettos.

Bulgaria's 2007 accession into the European Union was beneficial to the Roma. European Union laws require the implementation of provisions that guarantee the rights of minorities and the fair distribution of public funds. Numerous government and NGO programs have been created in order to speed up the process of desegregation and integration. Most significantly, several countries, including Bulgaria, have initiated the Decade of Roma Inclusion 2005–2015, a comprehensive project intended to improve the socioeconomic status of Roma minorities in the central and southeastern European countries with sizable Roma populations (Bulgaria, Croatia, the Czech Republic, Hungary, Macedonia, Montenegro, Romania, Serbia, and Slovakia). Housing, health, education, and employment are the main fields of action. Offices throughout the continent simmer with volunteers. Enthusiasm is nearing a boil.

Stella Kostova is a major enthusiast. A member of the municipal council in Sliven, she practically exudes revolution. Authoritative

and amiable by turns, solemn and bantering, she is one of the chief
agents of the Roma civil rights movement. Like many young, well-
educated Roma activists, she seems as familiar with Budapest and
New York as she is with her own town. Having seen other worlds,
she knows what she wants for her own.

We meet in a restaurant in downtown Sliven; she has just been to
her gym. Before we start talking, she opens her cell phone to call
her English-language teacher and explain why she won't be at class
today. Then she starts a Marlboro Light, her lipstick reddening the
filter.

"The policies of the Bulgarian administration toward the Roma
have been absolutely outrageous," she says before I ask a question.
"Somebody writes documents, votes on legislation, but there hasn't
been any change. Nothing. Everything is one big theater performance, a complete sham. Of course, the Communists made the
mess in the first place, but things have only been getting worse
since."

Stella concedes that EU funds and NGO sponsors have done a
lot to ameliorate the urgent problems facing Roma, yet most of the
money, she claims, is wasted on administrative costs. "What goes
down to the people is just a trickle. More funds should be spent on
monitoring, so that we can make certain that those in need can be
given real help."

As the head of Sliven's desegregation program, Stella is responsible for ensuring that Romani children are given a fair chance at education. Currently, there are Roma-only schools in almost every
Romani neighborhood, which are nothing more than institutions
for perpetuating social inequality. Most teachers are underquali-
fied and indifferent toward their students. Sometimes the fifth
grade has classes with the fourth and third grades. The condition
of the facilities is also dreadful — windows are missing glass, during
the winter the heating does not work. Attendance is very low: out of
approximately 1,500 Romani students in the Nadezhda schools,
perhaps only two hundred go to classes with any regularity. The net
result is that oftentimes even the ones who receive primary education end up illiterate.

The goal of the program is to enroll Romani children in integrated schools and provide them with coordinators to supervise
their progress and attendance. If there is a discrimination com-

plaint, the coordinator has to take action and file a report; when a student needs additional help with schoolwork, the coordinator must arrange for it. The objective is to slowly, gradually, close down all the segregated schools and have Romani kids attend classes with ethnic Bulgarians.

Angel, one of the program coordinators in Sliven, brings along for our interview a dog-eared notebook he has titled "The Bulgarian Engineer of the Nadezhda Quarter and the Country." On each page he has diligently outlined problem issues. How can we decrease crime rates in the Romani community? How can we stop early marriage and pregnancy? There is also a picture-diagram colored with crayons. A boy and a girl are holding hands; "pupas" says the caption underneath. An arrow leads to a houselike structure identified as "school." Another arrow leads out of "school" to the already grown-up man and woman. "Butterflies."

At the office of the organization, where Stella takes me afterward, I sit through a meeting with the coordinators. The Romani flag — a red wheel rolling over an equally divided blue (sky) and green (earth) background — hangs on the wall. Computers buzz everywhere. In one corner there is a guitar missing four strings. When the meeting begins, Stella asks every coordinator for a thorough report. She is in a solemn mood; no bantering allowed. Smoking is prohibited. To those who have not done their duty, Stella raises her voice. Everybody cowers. There are five Romani kids enrolled in one of the integrated schools; six enrolled in another. Numbers in the reports never rise above single digits. Stella knows well that whatever the benefits of her efforts, the Romani hungry will go to bed hungry.

"God ordained that they go to bed hungry," says Bobby, a Roma from the Kosharnik quarter of Montana, a town in northwestern Bulgaria. "God ordained their fate. They need to go to bed hungry once or twice to learn the value of work, and stop begging. Give them ten loaves, a hundred — it'll never be enough if they don't earn what they eat. They have to start helping themselves."

"They" are Bobby's less-fortunate neighbors in Kosharnik. Dimiter and I have been sitting in Bobby's house for an hour, waiting for the afternoon heat to cease its crazy hammering. Bobby is shirtless, his potbelly a bit smaller than the fancy potbelly stove in the corner. While he is talking, he flips through TV channels: music, movies, advertisements offering work abroad. He finally settles on a sitcom.

Like so many other Roma, Bobby supplements the income of his family by traveling. He buys cheap used cars in Austria and sells them in Bulgaria; he trades in diesel fuel, sometimes illegally. Business is good: his house is spacious and clean, furnished with expensive-looking couches; there are flowerpots on the windowsills. The yard is littered with his children's bright toys. Bobby's mother, who is at a spa-resort at the moment, runs her own little café adjacent to the house. At 6 A.M. it bustles with customers drinking coffee before work; by 6 P.M. the same customers are back, daily earnings in hand, ready for a couple of beers.

Once the scorched earth cools down, we head out into the neighborhood. The café is almost full. A few men, none of them older than thirty, chatter at a table by the sidewalk, smoking cigarettes and drinking. Their hands are covered with dirt; they have just returned from work. Digging the fields. Picking strawberries at a nearby farm. Looking for scrap. Anything. Day labor is the main occupation in Kosharnik. Most Roma have no secondary education or professional training. Because state companies are more prejudiced hirers, private employment is preferable, though Roma are paid less than anyone else. Wages are around ten leva (approximately US$7) per day.

"Life was better under Todor Zhivkov," says an older man whom I meet in the street; many share his nostalgia for the former Communist dictator. "We didn't have rights back then, but we had work. Now we have rights, but you can't feed your family on freedom."

You can't feed your family on religion, either, but it's the principal diet here. Almost everyone I meet in Kosharnik is a Protestant Christian. Daily conversation is freighted with Biblical quotations or stock phrases — "Our brother stands firm in the faith" — translated literally from missionary English. Children are taught the Bible orally before they learn to read. The Turkish proverb about there being seventy-seven and a half religions in the world — the extra half being whatever the Gypsies believe — is not without a grain of truth. Whether Christian or Muslim, Roma prefer a syncretic approach to the divine. Families are known to celebrate both Christmas and Ramadan. Protestantism has hardly changed that;

rather, it is the Roma who have changed Protestantism to suit their tastes. "The family over there are Adventists, but I am a Baptist," a plump woman in her fifties brags to me. "Adventists don't allow pork, but Baptists are fine with it. And I love pork."

By reputation, Bulgarians are not very fond of God, even though Orthodox Christianity is the official religion, and Muslims (Bulgarian Turks) make up about 10 percent of the population. It was the lifting of the Iron Curtain that opened the stage for the religious drama. Hundreds of American missionaries, eager to regain souls from the communists, embarked on a transatlantic crusade. (I still have, somewhere in my library, a copy of the Bulgarian translation of the Book of Mormon.) And, naturally, it was among the most downtrodden, the Roma, that American evangelicals reaped their greatest rewards. Promises of a happier afterlife, and a few packages of salt and sugar, were enough to lure many Roma away from the penniless gods of the past. In addition, Protestant churches offered a new sort of congregation untainted by local bigotry. Religion seemed like the ready and easy way to integrate into Bulgarian society. There was a catch, however: Bulgarian Protestants were themselves a tiny minority, frequently objects of ridicule and spite. The Roma who turned to Protestantism exchanged one marginal community for another.

Like Sliven's Nadezhda quarter, Montana's Kosharnik has squares and circles, surfaces and depths. Set on a hill at the edge of town, the neighborhood has a social geometry all its own. Bobby's house is in the more affluent section — streets here have a fresh coat of asphalt, sidewalks are swept clean. Some of the other houses are equally sturdy, trellises with creeping vines throwing cool shade in the yards. Well-dressed children play tag or ride new bicycles. This is the presentable section of Kosharnik, where everyone works from Monday through Saturday and attends church on Sunday. These are Bulgaria's isolated Roma bourgeoisie, but it is hard to determine what keeps people of economic means living in the ghetto. Is the color of one's face more important than the color of money? Or is it that the outside world has been refused entry?

The bad part of Kosharnik — "the jungle," as the locals refer to it — is not, as one would expect, at the bottom, but at the very top of the arid, treeless hill. It's a million-dollar view: the gargantuan apartment buildings of Montana on one horizon; on the other, the plains of northern Bulgaria, carpeted with sunflowers, sprawling toward the invisible Danube River. Scattered across the field, like a chance gathering of misanthropes, most houses — hovels, really — are rickety and unkempt, hastily put together from corrugated iron, plywood, and cardboard; some mud-and-brick edifices look as if they might melt under the force of the next rain. Unauthorized power cables run from one building to the next. Water bottles, canisters, buckets, washtubs, and drum barrels lie empty amid mounds of refuse; there is no running water here. Everything has a vague frontier aura, dislocated only by the odd satellite dish.

The transformation of the landscape is so sudden that it takes me a while to recognize that I have crossed the threshold to another world. I realize it finally when I see a man with three English non sequiturs written across his T-shirt: GAME OVER, PERSEVERANCE, ALL I WANT IS EVERYTHING. Bobby, my guide around Kosharnik, wants us to turn back. Like Stoyan earlier, he seems hesitant to show me the less-respectable part of the community. It's clear Bobby doesn't like the people here, even if they are fellow Roma; he would never have come up here on his own. But this time, I don't budge. I want to speak with them.

Forty-seven Kamchia Street: this is the only postal address of the squatter families in Kosharnik. My reception is warm, certainly because Bobby and Dimiter stand by my side. People discuss their problems, take me around their homes. "I live here with my six children," a middle-aged woman tells me, gesturing toward one of the makeshift hovels. It is a pitiful structure with cardboard walls and tattered blankets for windows. But inside there is no trace of filth. The iron beds are covered, a quilt has been spread out on the floor, framed photographs decorate the walls. When I raise my camera, she asks that I wait until she clothes her children. There is such tenderness in her motions, such maternal care, belying all that I have heard about Romani disregard for their children. The woman lifts her cherubic baby, a girl, in her hands and poses for the camera. Renaissance artists would have found them a fitting subject.

Children are the essence of Romani culture, the alpha and the omega. Childhood might be very short — ending at ten or eleven

— but it is not solitary, nasty, or brutish. Boys and girls are loved equally. Wherever I go in Kosharnik, people ask me to photograph their young ones first, lining them up in front of their dilapidated homes. The swaddled baby raised high over the parent's head is a kind of triumph of life over adversity. Everything else might be a source of shame, but not the children.

Soon, I am surrounded. "Boy, can you help us?" The question comes from all sides, sometimes desperate, sometimes peremptory. Twenty, perhaps thirty men and women, three times as many children. The juggernaut of their complaints gathers force. Will I go to see the mayor of Montana and ask him to provide garbage collection? What documents does one need to apply for legal housing? "If we're not part of the city plan, does it mean we are dogs?" a woman asks me. Why isn't there clean water? Water, water, water, water. The water is yellow, useless. It carries dysentery. Babies die every day. "Can you help us?" the question comes up again. Here, I am not a journalist; I am only a *gadjo*, and the *gadje* run the country, the town, the village. Aren't the *gadje* one big family, like the Gypsies? Surely I know, or know somebody who knows, the president.

Keeping his distance from me, a tall, broad-shouldered, shirtless man stands in the shade of a stablelike structure. When his children gather for a photograph, he gives me a stare that conveys something between condescension and disgust. After a couple of minutes, he finally approaches. "You are from the university, right? Don't say no, I can tell by your looks. You come here asking questions, so that you can write your dissertation after that. Right? You ask for percentages, numbers, you take pictures. You just want to watch and then go home. You want to make money out of us. You want to rob us."

He is sick of people coming to his home, recording the story of his life for others to read. Narratives don't cure tuberculosis. By the time the painter completes the portrait, the model has died. The letter killeth. "Are we monkeys or bears," he asks me, "that you should come here to watch us dance, so that others can laugh at us? This is sinful, you know."

Because I have nowhere to go for the night, a Romani man, Tano, invites me to stay at his apartment in downtown Montana. In the evening he asks over several friends, piles food and drinks on the kitchen table, and the party begins. We are getting drunk — seven Roma and two ethnic Bulgarians — the talk swinging from sexual exploits to travel. Tano dated a Bulgarian woman, but she wanted to break up because her parents didn't approve of "a Gypsy in the house." Dian tells the story of his time in western Mexico as an extra in the movie *Troy*. He is a judo champion with a master's degree from the National Sports Academy. He even taught martial arts at Sofia's police academy, but when he applied for a job as an officer, he was turned down. "Look at all my credentials!" he says, handing me his wallet full of ID cards. "I just wanted to become a cop, not a very high position, you know, and they didn't accept me. Why? Because I am a Gypsy."

"To prove their worth," Tano joins in, "Roma need to be ten times better than the average Bulgarian. It's a lot of pressure, if you know what I mean." Tano used to be a representative with the European Commission in Brussels. Two years ago, he delivered a talk on the issue of Romani identity before the United States Congress.

The conversation rambles on through the night. Tano's laptop blasts traditional Romani music, Bulgarian hip-hop, drum and bass, pop. Some of us go out on the apartment's balcony to smoke up. The joint goes from hand to hand, slowly. It's our peace pipe.

PATRICK SYMMES

The Cabin of My Dreams

FROM *Outside*

COMEDY IS TRAGEDY plus time, and I'm telling you, not enough time has passed. Two years now and my friends automatically start cracking up when anyone says, "How's your cabin?"

I just get mad. I don't get the joke, presumably because I am the joke. All I wanted to do was stop talking about, and finally build, a cabin. Yet when you reach the end of this story, I won't have driven one nail.

It's not really my fault, this boondoggle. Real estate is more or less the male biological clock. There is some hardwired imperative that kicks in at a certain point, the way caribou migrate and birds sing. Around the start of their fifth decade, men suddenly discover gardening. They plant trees. They lay down fence lines. They construct and hold. Like a spoiled child, we say, This is mine. Mine, mine, mine.

Building a cabin in the wilderness is a nearly universal dream. Honestly, if you haven't had it at some point, there's something wrong with you. In college, I wasted hours with my buddy Tim arguing over where we would build our dream shack. Montana? Oregon? Hawaii? Years later, he came back from New Zealand, raving about how we could build it there.

Reality intrudes on such plans. Tim went into finance and worked long hours to support his five kids. I spent those years wandering everywhere without coming to roost anywhere. I never found that piece of peace and quiet I'd been imagining.

And then the clock started ticking. In my late thirties, my only assets — a tiny Manhattan sublet and a rusting motorcycle — came to feel inadequate. The dream cabin, with its imaginary forest, grew slowly into a compulsion. Certainly, it was an inversion of the real life I was leading with a press card in my pocket, working in war zones and Third World quagmires. Whenever something went wrong, which was often, I would catch myself dreaming about the cabin again. A cozy little bolthole. Some gentle spot where no one would point a gun at me. A "crucible of calm," as Teddy Roosevelt's place in the Badlands was called.

I started skimming from paychecks. The worse the place or the experience, the more I set aside: one thousand dollars after a nasty brush with the guerrillas in Colombia; two thousand dollars for walking into a minefield in Afghanistan; a drug gang in Brazil; teenage muggers in Havana; several Asian insurgencies. All I wanted was the basics: some running water — as in a trout stream — and a star-strewn sky. But after five years, I'd saved a mere twenty thousand dollars, which wouldn't buy a garden shed in Montana's Paradise Valley.

I looked elsewhere, out of necessity. Oregon had been bid up by Californians; West Virginia colonized by D.C. weekenders; the Adirondacks cheap only in their boggiest, northernmost reaches, five or six hours from New York City. Since anything I could afford was beyond the reach of weekend use anyway, I began to accept what my heart had been screaming all along: Go south, young man!

As in way south. Just short of my fortieth birthday, I told my wife, Beth, I was going to build us a little weekend place in . . . well, in the, uh, Southern Hemisphere. The deep Southern Hemisphere, actually. New Zealand, maybe. Or Argentina. Possibly Chile. She suggested medication.

I knew this was insane. My friends scoffed. My father-in-law called it "the most ridiculous thing I have ever heard."

But for me, the cabin was as necessary as it was preposterous. Enormously far away, these wide-open lands, which share a lonely vigil in the deepest realms of the world's emptiest hemisphere, had long ago infused me with their clean skies, eerily pure water, and deep forests. I ruled out Chile, which had too much rain and, with apologies, too many Chileans. New Zealand seemed ideal, but a visit on my honeymoon showed me how much the *Lord of the Rings* effect had changed the country, with every millionaire priced out of Napa planting grapes in Nelson.

Like at all good parties, I was left with my original date: Argentina. A lovely, unstable land, it had dug hooks into me during a hitchhiking trip in 1991. With its dry flatlands and green mountains, cowboys, rambling old cars, and lack of fences, Patagonia seemed at times like Wyoming in 1950. When the Argentine economy collapsed in 2002, the prices also retreated by a few decades. Though far away (two flights, totaling fourteen hours, plus a drive), it was still a lot closer than New Zealand, and the time zone — two hours ahead of EST — was close, close enough to stay in touch by telephone and come and go without jet lag. Despite an old-fashioned attachment to crime and the occasional run of five presidents in two weeks, Argentina had infrastructure, people, and wines that were all decent and getting better.

I was looking at northern Patagonia, a far gentler land than Tierra del Fuego, some seven hundred miles to the south. I wasn't alone in this interest: everything from Bariloche, an alpine gateway to the forests and parks of the region, south to Esquel was enjoying a real estate boom. My predecessors were Ted Turner, Sylvester Stallone, and Sharon Stone. The Benetton family owned a huge spread outside of Esquel. The flag bearers in this foreign invasion, the conservationists Kris and Douglas Tompkins, now have some two million acres in Argentina and Chile.

Big names created big expectations. "I have the perfect place for you," one broker told me over a crackling connection: "Fifteen thousand acres, fourteen buildings, and five hundred head of cattle already on the land." It was "priced to move" at seven million dollars. I couldn't bear to tell him I'd be happy with half an acre.

In the end, I made the search the old-fashioned way, mano a mano. I flew to Bariloche with Beth, and we worked our way southward in a rental car, poking up gravel roads in the mountains, following tips from hitchhikers or small signs that read LOT FOR SALE. Near the town of El Bolsón, we saw a fifty-acre place — too big for us but considered puny in Patagonia — while another lot, near the sensitive border with Chile, was forbidden to foreigners. Price depended on amenities. A hundred acres in the dry, windswept flatlands where the Benettons grazed sheep came cheap. But two acres on a trout-packed river, lined with willows, in a perfect

green valley near Cholila were offered up at a price that made even
the toothless old cowboy saying it giggle. May Ted Turner find and
bless him.

Finally, we ran out of pavement in Trevelín, a kind of Argentine
Bozeman near Los Alerces National Park. We sat beside a gray-
haired Argentine couple at dinner. At the mention of the word
cabin, they looked up.

"We have more land than we can farm," the woman said. Successful in the fruit and alfalfa business, they had picked up neighboring plots cheap over the years. With prices for land and everything
else rising, they were looking to raise some cash. "Come have a look
tomorrow," the husband said.

We drove two miles up a dirt road, into the foothills of the Andes, and walked the parcel. It was on a mild slope overlooking a valley, thickly forested with young ponderosa and Oregon pines, with
deep grass in the clearings, a few apple trees, and a flock of colorful
Patagonian parakeets bursting through the trees. It was miles from
electricity. The only water was a rivulet, fouled by cows. At ten acres,
it was twice the size I wanted, and at forty thousand dollars, it was
twice what I had in the bank.

My wife is tolerant, in a long-range way. The plan was absurd, she
reminded me. But Beth knew there was something deeper than the
rational at work in me. She loved the view over the valley. And the
Argentines were fun, she agreed: "The joie de vivre you only get in
a place that survived military dictatorship."

"Just buy it," she finally said, shaking her head.

Easier said than done, alas. I had only half the money I needed. I
called up Tim, my old colleague in cabin dreams. New Zealand was
now in Patagonia, I told him. Before I could even spit out a plan to
go fifty-fifty, he blurted out "Yes." As long as there was room to store
his kayak, he didn't care about design — and became my silent
partner when matching funds arrived a week later.

The actual purchase was held up nine months by paperwork, bi-
lingual wrangling, and lost wire transfers. All of which was merely
prologue. Eventually, when I was high in the mountains of Lebanon, interviewing a warlord, the fax in my old Ottoman hotel
ground out the news that a small piece of quiet was mine.

You can buy books on the tribulations and techniques of building a
cabin, the benefits of feng shui, and the sublime pleasures of Nor-

wegian framing techniques. I checked one on basic framing out of the New York Public Library, bought some graph paper, and headed south.

This kind of overconfidence is occasionally useful. Since I had helped build a house once before — sort of, partly, briefly, a long time ago — I figured I was qualified. In Argentina, I hired a local carpenter named Flaco ("Skinny"), who outlined glorious plans and then quit a few weeks before the start; he'd met a woman in Chile and simultaneously discovered I wasn't Ted Turner. His replacement was a disturbingly young carpenter called Julito ("Little Julio"). He'd never actually built a house before, but Julito looked over my amateurish sketches for a five-hundred-square-foot one-room cabin with a shed roof. "Fast and easy to build," he assured me. He told me that it could be framed up in thirty days of hard work. He promised to bring the tools, the expertise, and extra hands. We shook on it.

I'd be bringing my own "toolbox" to the site — a band of volunteers who'd cleared two weeks of vacation and paid their own way to Patagonia for some romantic labor. Along with my wife came her twin sister, Amy, who'd built refugee camps for Doctors Without Borders. Even better, her husband, Simon, was a civil engineer and former house builder. My side of the aisle contained more enthusiasts than engineers: my sister, Deebie, and a friend from Buenos Aires, Colin. These were the people I cruelly (and secretly) referred to as Team Sawyer, since they would paint my picket fence for me. Meanwhile I expected to engage in more executive-level pursuits, like Tom himself — supervising, translating, doodling on graph paper. There was no architect, of course, or even a genuine blueprint. We would buy everything locally and use what architects call "vernacular" methods. I called it Taoist nonplanning and actually thought it would work.

Three Argentines, all named Charley, agreed to give me advice, if not labor. The first was the owner of Casa Verde ("Green House"), a local hostel where Team Sawyer and I would all be sleeping, so I called him Green Charley. Then there was the farmer who'd sold me the lot; he was Welsh Charley, after his heritage. Gaucho Charley was a sinewy little cowboy in his sixties who ran cattle on the hillside and had the hard-won insights gained by actually living there.

I had spent ten years dreaming, three years shopping for land,

and now almost two years arranging the construction, which I planned to spend thirty days supervising. Months before the planned January 2007 start, I flew down for ten days to line up a sawmill, open accounts at hardware stores, and coordinate a tight schedule of just-in-time deliveries. Julito vowed to have the site prepped and the foundation built before I returned with Team Sawyer in January, the height of Patagonian summer. We would go straight to the barn-raising scene in *Witness* where Harrison Ford is clambering all over the roof beams.

Cut to reality. In January, Beth and I found the site green and lovely — and completely undisturbed. Not a single board, beam, nail, tile, or bolt had arrived, not a clod of dirt had been moved, and Julito and his crew were nowhere to be found — and wouldn't show up until a week later. Team Sawyer drifted in over the next few days. At sunset every night, we marveled at Trevelín's view of the Andes and toasted the coming endeavor. Mornings, we stood around the grassy clearing scuffing our heels. Right away an argument broke out over where to put the hot tub.

Who said anything about a hot tub? But building, I soon realized, is about ambition. Flee to the simple life if you want. Your dreams, friends, and family will still have their say. Deebie insisted on relocating the cabin to the highest point, for the view. Beth argued for a lower point, where a large meadow could accommodate the family house she imagined. ("One room?" she whispered accusingly. "What were you thinking?") Amy and Simon urged me to add a second story so I wouldn't have to expand later.

I gave speeches on Thoreauvian self-sufficiency, which were ignored, and then conceded several points. We would build where we were, in the small upper clearing, but expand the floor plan to 850 square feet, making space for a separate bedroom, a larger deck, and other bourgeois sellouts. Each change meant more graph-paper calculations, more wood, more delays, more costs, and more hours of carpentry.

My dream was entering the spiral of geometric expansion, and the design suggestions came pouring in. Amy came back from a rafting detour in Chile and said, hopefully, "I saw these nice railings at the camp there, made from stripped and seasoned saplings."

"Recycled barn doors," my wife suggested.

"Mapuche carvings would look nice," Colin offered.

Walls stuffed with hay bales? Why not a $1,300 propane refriger-ator shipped down from California? Green Charley visited the site one morning and waved his hands in the air as he described a pas-sive water heater made from black hoses and old wine bottles, al-though he admitted he'd never actually seen such a thing. Julito suggested energy-efficient sawdust insulation, until I pointed out that in a forest fire the cabin would go up like a Roman candle. Hadn't I heard about the new double-paned, helium-filled, nano-coated, electricity-generating windows my sister knew about? "You could make a windmill," Amy offered; she'd seen a Peace Corps de-sign on the Internet. I swatted down as many of these ideas as I could, but Team Sawyer continued to fight a quiet insurgency, and one morning I found the stakes for the outhouse moved to a new location.

Necessity is the mother of compromise. A wind turbine was im-practical, water power absurd, but in the bright Andean summer months of December through February, I often had twelve hours of sunshine on site. In Afghanistan a few years ago, I'd seen the Special Forces carrying solar panels that folded up like a map. I'd brought one, which charged my cell phone in forty-five minutes (I could get a weak signal on the highest bump of my land) and my laptop in an afternoon. Green Charley lent me a car battery, Julito wired up some twelve-volt light bulbs, and suddenly we had illumi-nation. Propane tanks would run a standard kitchen range and even a hot-water tank. For less than a thousand dollars, I soon owned all modern conveniences, though I still had no cabin to put them in.

Water was the issue that made my wife groan in frustration. A Californian, Beth expected to die of thirst on the hillside, given that the trickling stream seemed to be 50 percent cow urine. On an almost daily basis, I scrounged in the supply shops of local towns, until I came up with 420 meters of black hose to bear the water from the stream's source, a spring buried in a cleft of the hill above my land, to the cabin. After twelve days of constant promises, none of the wood for the cabin had yet arrived, so the appearance of a delivery truck carrying the hose, on the day scheduled, was such a shock that everyone pulled out their cameras.

We rolled the coiled hose uphill, to the spring. Julito built an improvised filter, and we jammed the hose into a point where no cow
could reach; pure, icy spring water now gushed through the hose at
one liter per second. Back home, we'd have run a Ditch Witch
down to the cabin, digging a trench to bury the hose. Here, Gaucho Charley turned up at dawn with a pair of bellowing oxen,
which dragged an ancient iron plow up the hill and back down,
drooling.

Meanwhile, Julito's camp was getting nicer and nicer. He and his
three assistants had built an outdoor shower, a barbecue pit, and a
huge earthen larder filled with sausages, noodles, and wine. They
dammed a bend in my little stream with logs, making a plunge pool
for the ninety-degree afternoons.

The only things missing were beams, boards, nails, brackets, and
a roof.

There was work, actually. We cleared the ground, felling a single
Oregon pine to free up space for the theoretical cabin. We leveled
hillocks and pruned branches to create an entry for the lumber
truck, which was due any minute. We designed a tower for the water tank and then abandoned the idea. We argued over different
spots for the cabin. We feuded over how to build a gate, and then
built it, but Gaucho Charley was so appalled by the result that he remade the whole thing with a pair of pliers. I made a courtesy call on
the crusty old cowboy, to thank him, but instead of hot tea he offered a cold shoulder. I wanted a buddy; he wanted a patron.

Temperatures, and tempers, were rising. Team Sawyer was burning vacation time with nothing to show for it but a blank meadow.
Delays, disagreements, and confusion ruled the site; my hardware-
store accounts sat unused. Julito would drive into town and return
hours later beaming with confidence: *"Ciao, problema!"* he'd call
out. Whatever the problem was, he'd fixed it, solved it, or arranged
it. The foundation materials were definitely coming tomorrow. The
framing lumber would arrive on Friday, for sure. We'd start building any minute.

Guido at the sawmill failed to deliver boards on yet another
deadline. Julito's own support beams, supposedly ready weeks ago,
disappeared. The hardware stores promised me everything and delivered nothing. Julito threw his hands up. Guido at the sawmill

threw his hands up. "This is the reality of a subdeveloped country," he said fatalistically, pouring me another shot of bitter tea. Julito tried yelling at him — and also pleading and begging. This produced no boards.

But Argentines know how to take a break. With summer light running from 6 A.M. to 10 P.M., it was possible to get two days of work out of one. We'd start early, at least by Argentine standards, and call it quits at two, before rousing ourselves at four or five for another three hours of work on the outhouse, or the fencing, anything but the nonexistent cabin. In the sunstruck heat of those early afternoons, I'd retreat to a hammock I'd strung between two ponderosas. Here, I'd engage in Big Picture Thinking, with a cowboy hat over my face. The boys would spend the siesta eating, drinking red wine, gossiping, sleeping hard, debating soccer, or bird watching. With a series of squawks and whistles, Julito could summon the Patagonian parakeets, which perched in the very top branches of the pines, aloof.

My father could make such birdcalls, and I'd lie in the hammock recalling the way he'd taken us one summer from Virginia to New Hampshire to build his dream cabin in the woods. I was sixteen. A couple of months of building walls, laying floors, putting up paneling, and then wiring and plumbing had given us a ski house. It also gave me a bad case of resentment. I thought him a fool for wanting a cabin so far away that we would use it only once a year, at most.

So this splendid idiocy was a family tradition, which I could now repeat board for board.

It is important to have some failures in life, so this one was working out great. And as everything unraveled, my wife never once said, "I told you so," God bless her.

By aiming my hammer at a hillside in one of the most remote regions on earth, I'd simplified my tasks in some ways — no building codes! no disapproving neighbors! — but complicated almost everything else. This was no *A Year in Provence*, in which Peter Mayle drank his way to the keyboard every day, lifting no tool heavier than a corkscrew while contractors rebuilt his house around him. Mayle, for all his famous quibbling with French stonemasons, admitted that he'd never been happier. My mood was blacker than a coal mine, preoccupied by the missing lumber, money problems, and the growing frustration of friends and family, who, two weeks in, somehow stayed sweaty and dirty yet never got to build the cabin they'd been promised. The wheels were coming off, our weeks in Patagonia expiring as a busted play.

Mayle's architect compared building to trench warfare, with long periods of boredom interrupted by sudden fits of violence. The Latin sense of time, he said, was elastic. A "quarter of an hour" really meant "today." "Tomorrow" meant "this week." Any estimate of time preceded by the word *normally*, or followed by a hand gesture that involved fluttering the palm, was real trouble. Julito spoke this language. On at least half of the thirty days I was to spend on the hillside, he promised me something that turned out not to be true — the wood was coming today or being cut to the right lengths today or delivered to the sawmill today or chopped down today. The roofing materials were coming. The telephone poles for the foundation were coming. The cement or gravel or tools or provisions were coming. Tomorrow. Definitely. *Ciao, problema.*

In America, these same delays were completely normal, according to Simon, the engineer. Builders divided all delays into three categories. First was "mobilization," which covered everyone showing up late or a lack of supplies. "Contingencies" meant any setback or unexpected development, like snow. And then there was "mañana," meaning any day in the future.

The mañanas and contingencies mounted. The sawmill truck broke down. The guy who was going to fix the sawmill truck ("Monday!") had a breakdown himself, and two Mondays later it still hadn't been fixed. (Indeed, the sawmill truck was never fixed and, to this day, sits rusting in the lumberyard.) Wire transfers from America wandered off, lost in various Patagonian banks. Every male in Argentina fell in love with my sister-in-law, Amy, and if I looked away for a moment I'd turn back to find the three assistant carpenters offering her advice in a rustic mixture of Spanish, Italian, English, and hand gestures. She meanwhile dug a giant latrine, lined it with bricks, then reinforced it with concrete. It was more like a bomb shelter than a crapper, surpassed National Park Service requirements, and could serve three thousand Boy Scouts.

At the height of summer, it snowed. It was only a light dusting before dawn, and melted quickly, but my carpenters declared the road to be endangered, descended to town, and didn't return for days. I stalked around, fuming and bitter, practicing my tirades in Spanish. I didn't fire them, only because hiring someone else would put me a year behind schedule.

Only while peering into the carpenters' larder of sausages and noodles, their tent packed with cheese and Cruz de Malta mate tea, did I finally appreciate their utter lack of urgency. I'd never understood why they'd set up a tent camp when their homes, with hot showers, were just half an hour away. Only after studying the careful construction of their fire pit — a two-day job — did I realize their true agenda: they were on vacation.

I wasn't paying them by the day, the week, or the month. They were paid the same amount whether they finished the job in three weeks or three years. From the Argentine point of view, this was not an incentive to hurry but an opportunity to linger — employment was essentially guaranteed for as long as they stayed on the hillside. Why not enjoy it? They would rhapsodize about the stars at night, the red sunsets, the jagged peaks of the Andes. They were, I realized with a shudder, hiding. Hiding from wives, girlfriends, bills, obligations. In that sense, they were like me; the cabin had become their refuge, too. They weren't building a house in the woods; they were on a camping trip that happened to involve a little digging.

Everything I loved about Argentina — the willingness to linger over a meal, the care brought to a cup of coffee, the enthusiasm for new ventures — was doubling back to haunt me. These men were talented, skilled, and hardworking when they needed to be, and happy, even when they needed to be unhappy. The cabin existed only in an idealized, future condition; the best had become the enemy of the good.

After filling another page of graph paper with scratch calculations of my mounting bills, I moved out of the Green House and pitched my tent next to Julito's camp. One member of Team Sawyer blew up and walked off the job. Two marriages went rocky for a few minutes. I was denying reality, becoming irrational, yelling at the locals. Family dysfunction, broken promises, missed deadlines — all darkened the mood.

"You could write an article about this cabin for *Psychology Today*," Julito volunteered at one point. That same night, Oscar, the cheeriest of the assistants, openly compared our doomed encampment to *"El Projecto Blair Witch."*

*

Time ran out, and we began a set of runs to the airport. Day by day, Team Sawyer broke up. They departed smiling, rapt by the Andes and, from the safety of the departure lounge, amused by the fiasco back on the hillside. There was not one board in place. Not even a foundation.

It took Mark Twain only a few pages to tell the story of Tom Sawyer's picket fence and the crew that assembled to paint it. I had interpreted that tale as a challenge, an invitation to let others build my house for me. Now, at the end of my designated thirty days, I looked at the barren hillside and saw I had been not Tom but one of his victims. I bought a bottle of *vino tinto* that day and, near midnight, drove back to my tent on the hillside, where the carpenters were snoring away; forty-eight hours later I was back in the United States.

Twain would say that in attempting you get things done, that small failures do eventually add up to something. So here's the bottom line: I did get my cabin built, sort of. Just not by me or by Team Sawyer. In the end, long after I'd gone home and dried out my soul, boards from the sawmill began trickling up the hillside. The boys spent the entire summer up there and, gradually, at their own happy pace, built the floor, the walls, and the roof. Like every other yuppie, I paid someone else to take my splinters for me.

They did a shockingly good job, though. A year after the month-long folly, I rolled up the hill again and found the trees swaying in the breeze just as I remembered, the parakeets still flitting overhead, and a beautiful cabin, standing by itself, utterly quiet. It is filled with Julito's skilled detailing and Oscar's thoughtful little adaptations of my design. The modern conveniences worked out better than expected — there's even a flush toilet leading to Amy's massive septic bunker. The price got a little out of hand, but not by too much. I don't have any furniture yet, so I ate and slept on the floor. I didn't drive a single nail, but it still felt like my refuge, the place where absolutely nothing could go wrong. Peace, at last!

There was, of course, a huge forest fire raging right then, and it barely missed my land. And a couple of months after I left, a volcano over in Chile blew up, scattering a rain of hot ash on the little building. But other than that, it all worked out perfectly.

JAY COWAN

Tracking Down James Bond

FROM *Ski*

THE SCENE REMAINS one of the most famous opening sequences in film — ever. James Bond wakes up in a mountain cabin in bed with a beautiful woman, receives a phone call, dresses quickly, and skis off. He's immediately pursued down the slopes and, at one point, spins backward on his boards to fend off attackers with a ski-pole rocket gun as he's racing down the mountain. The helicopter camera pans back wide on Bond as he straight-lines for a cliff. And then he launches.

Bond flies off the cliff, releasing his skis, which tumble into the abyss. And then he falls. And falls. Finally he deploys his chute — and there's a big Union Jack across it. Freeze-frame and cue the Bond music.

This is in 1977. The film is *The Spy Who Loved Me.* BASE jumping is still in its infancy, and Bond freefalls on skis well before the rest of the world has even contemplated such a move. Nobody does it better — and it isn't a special effect.

In the film's opening at the summit, Bond is the stunt-skier Ed Lincoln being chased down glaciers above Pontresina, Switzerland. Then Rick Sylvester takes over, ripping down the slopes into the open on Canada's Baffin Island as the camera shot widens. Skilled alpinist, stunt skier, and all-around madman, Sylvester simply skis off the 3,500-foot-high rock wall and gets as far as possible away from the cliff before he pulls cords to release his skis, and then his chute.

You didn't have to be a skier to love this stuff. But as a skier I was totally wowed. The same way I'd been when I started reading

the James Bond novels ten years earlier. The man knows how to
live. And Sylvester's real-life jump was as mind-blowing as any of
Bond's antics. It foreshadowed a new era of extreme sports, and
confirmed that skiing was still sexy, fashionable, and exhilarating.
Why else would they keep putting ski sequences in the Bond movies?

Bond is an English hero, created by the very English Ian Fleming
and adapted for the big screen by an English company, Eon Pro-
ductions. As such, the films have always possessed a European sen-
sibility. They have mostly taken place away from America, in glamorous and exotic locales. And the Bond film oeuvre is filled with
dashing ski scenes, which reflects Europeans' traditional love of
both the sport and the beau monde.

I figured if anyone could have a good time skiing, it was James
Bond. So I set off to retrace the ski tracks of the world's most famous secret agent.

For both of us, it started in Mürren, Switzerland, where they
filmed *On Her Majesty's Secret Service (OHMSS)* in 1969. I've been
there several times, and always with Bond in the back of my mind
— in part because Mürren doesn't let you forget about him. At
nearly ten thousand feet in the Bernese Alps, on top of a ragged
and windswept summit called the Schilthorn, the Piz Gloria "James
Bond" revolving restaurant commands sweeping views that include
the famous trinity of the Eiger, the Monch, and the Jungfrau.

In 1968, producers were looking for a location to film *OHMSS*,
one of Fleming's most popular novels. They found a lift company
in Mürren that needed funds to complete a cable car to the top of
the Schilthorn and a restaurant they were building there. The film
company helped with the financing in return for the right to be the
first to use the complex, which took on the name of Piz Gloria,
Fleming's moniker for Blofeld's mountaintop hideout. As kitschy
as it is — spinning around in a sky-high café eating "James Bond
spaghetti" — it's also a stunning location for anything: a movie,
lunch, sightseeing, and, especially, skiing.

The revolving restaurant housed a bevy of beauties in the film,
along with then-unknown Telly Savalas as Ernst Stavro Blofeld,
Bond's archenemy. Reminders of the building's storied history are
everywhere. The souvenir shop sells pins, patches, coffee mugs,
caps, lighters, and watches with James Bond logos. Downstairs is a

hallway decorated with large stills from the movie. And outside is the viewing deck where helicopters landed in the film. When Bond escapes from Blofeld, it's supposedly night, made so by blue filters on the cameras. Bond, played by George Lazenby and stunt-doubled by the former German ski-racing star Ludwig Leitner and the Swiss Olympic champion Bernhard Russi, drops from the tramway terminal onto the summit run at Mürren.

Thus commences a frenzied tour of the spectacular Mürren slopes, as well as the Lauterbrunnen Valley, one of the most beautiful waterfall-and-glacier-studded box canyons on earth. In the movie, several bad guys plummet off the sheer 2,500-foot cliffs into the valley. In the real world, people pay to do that in tandem paragliders. Or they just stick to the skiing, a big, rangy experience that can cover more than seven thousand vertical feet when the snow is right. Stop-and-stare views of the surrounding peaks — huge, hovering massifs constantly sloughing spindrift into the blue skies — are everywhere. The long runs have some of the best pitches in the Jungfrau region (which includes nearby Wengen and Grindelwald) and can wander into lovely off-piste routes, like the ones Bond and his leading lady, played by Diana Rigg, get to rip prior to being trapped by an avalanche.

Even today, with its high-tech lifts and vehicle-free design, Mürren has a retro buzz. The Lauterbrunnen Valley feels as though it hasn't been fully discovered, a vibe underscored by trappings from skiing's golden age: cable cars rising up icy cliffs, chic people enjoying a day of sport in the mountains, small villages with horse-drawn sleighs, and tall stucco church steeples. One day I even spot a vintage Aston Martin DB5 (the racing model mentioned in *Goldfinger*) that could have been waiting for Bond to jump in.

I load my gear into a Volvo and cruise along the serpentine mountain roads of the Jungfrau region and up to the front door of Interlaken's five-star Grand Victoria-Jungfrau Hotel, the perfect Bond layover. An elegant casino is next door, and the hotel and spa are among the finest in the Alps, ideal for meeting a Bond man such as Stefan Zurcher. He was born and still lives in nearby Wengen and has worked on more than forty films — nine of them Bond flicks — including the latest Bond adventure, *Quantum of Solace*, which is scheduled for release in November. Zurcher started his career as a stunt actor in *OHMSS* when he was twenty-three.

"When you're young you don't think about getting hurt," he says. "We always sent Ludwig Leitner off first, sometimes still a bit drunk. I worked on that film for five months. They completely remade the bobsled run for it." I remark that the avalanche scene seemed realistic, especially for 1969. "We blasted off a whole cornice to create a real avalanche. It was huge." He grins. "Then for close-ups we built ramps and dumped snow off them and had people tumbling. It was difficult."

Zurcher also worked with the famed ski cinematographer and fashion designer Willy Bogner Jr. on ski scenes in Switzerland for *The Spy Who Loved Me* (1977) and *A View to a Kill* (1985). In typical movie protocol, Switzerland stood in for Austria in the former and Siberia in the latter.

In *View*, Roger Moore's Bond doubles are the six-time world champion freestyle skier John Eaves and the snowboarding pioneer Tom Sims. Suzy Chaffee even does some of the ballet skiing behind the opening title silhouette sequence.

In one scene, Eaves is down to a single ski when he commandeers a moving snowmobile by jumping on it, kicking off his ski in the process. Stefan Zurcher was driving the snowmobile, which blows up just as Eaves jumps off. Then Tom Sims takes over as Bond, grabbing the remnant of one of the snowmobile's metal ski tips and riding it away like a snowboard. It was only 1985, but snowboarding had made its major motion picture debut.

The famous freeheeler and renowned ski guide John Falkiner played skiing bad guys in several Bond films, including *View*. "It was filmed mainly in the Diavolezza glacier area," he recalls. "We did a lot of chase sequences at high speed along the edge of crevasses and jumped off a lot of different things, falling and losing control down big ice walls as we chased Bond. All in all, a fantastic time."

I skied some of the same *View* terrain by hiking up the Morteratsch Glacier from the top of the Diavolezza ski area, and it's as raw and fun as it looks. You can check it out as you ski to the open-air Glacier Bar and down to the Engadine Valley on one of skiing's most legendary backcountry runs.

In between *View* and *The Spy Who Loved Me*, Bogner and Zurcher also worked on *For Your Eyes Only*'s thirty-five-minute ski sequence in 1981, the second longest in Bond history, behind *OHMSS*. While the skiing in *OHMSS* was based on the novel, it was completely invented by the filmmakers for *Eyes,* offering an exciting tour of Cortina, Italy, which is where I head next.

"The snow this year is better in Innsbruck," a fellow spy says to Bond on top of Cortina's signature Tofana ski mountain. "But not in St. Moritz," replies Bond. After getting briefed, he begins what, even for Bond, is a long day in the mountains. It involves the beautiful daughter of an Italian gangster, a lovely ice skater, Cortina's Olympic ice stadium, a chase featuring bad guys on motorcycles with wickedly studded tires, and an East German biathlete who keeps trying to shoot Bond during a competition instead of his targets. And this is all before lunch.

The Cortina backdrop is busy and glamorous. A former Winter Olympics host (1956) and one of the most gorgeous resorts in the world, Cortina is perched in the heart of the spellbinding Ampezzo Dolomites. Magnificent towering buttresses of rose-colored stone are stacked on every side of the resort, lending it an otherworldly brightness and buoyancy.

The village — routinely adorned with expansive public art displays — is compelling in its own right, with architecture that pays tribute to its Mediterranean heritage with lots of pastel stuccos and iron railings. Cortina is so bursting with *la dolce vita* — elegant dining, beautiful people, fast cars — that it seems even when the cameras aren't rolling they should be. And they have rolled a lot here, with more than thirty movies and shows shot at the resort. The luxe Miramonti Grand Hotel, where Bond bivouacs in room 300, has hosted generations of stars.

A popular, if frenzied, tour will introduce you to all five of Cortina's exceptional ski areas in the same day. That's the way Bond's day feels in *For Your Eyes Only* as he flees down Cortina's ninety-meter Olympic ski jump, fighting two villains on the way — on what look to be standard Olin Mark VIs, no less.

"I jumped on Olin 205 slaloms, to be exact," Eaves tells me. "You'll notice I have my own jump, allowing me to gain altitude over the Nordic jumper immediately, then I would slowly lose altitude as he went ahead, blocking me from the sights of the sniper below. Olin was so stoked about me being Bond, they manufactured my skis for the film with serial numbers starting with 007. Roger Moore did me an incredible favor by holding the skis so you could see who made them."

After the ski-jump scene, Bond is chased yet again by the fiendish motorcyclists, forcing Eaves to jump onto and off of a restaurant deck before ending up on a bobsled track — another famous Bond stunt. Still on skis, Eaves is bracketed by a bobsled in front and motorbikes behind as he races down the ribbon of ice before finally bailing and escaping. "I trained in the St. Moritz bob run over Christmas in 1980, with Willy Bogner filming me," Eaves says. "I could go on for hours about how wild it was. Being laid out horizontally on an ice wall at sixty miles per hour, held there by the force of gravity, almost defies the laws of nature."

The Olympic bobsled run is still used for competitions. You can pay for a ride, piloted by drivers who treat your two-minute run as a personal challenge to scare any good sense out of you.

For 1987's *The Living Daylights,* the producers didn't revisit a bobsled run, instead settling for cello-case sledding near Weissensee, Austria. "We did a ski sequence in a specially built sled that held the actors plus the cameraman. Stefan Zurcher and I controlled the sled with its valuable cargo," says John Falkiner.

The most recent Bond ski sequence was in 1999's *The World Is Not Enough,* in which the mountains around Les Grands Montets near Chamonix, France, stood in for Azerbaijan. Chamonix and Verbier skiers worked on the film crews and doubled for Pierce Brosnan's Bond, who tangles with motorized ultralight planes called parahawks, which land and become fan-powered snowmobiles. Bond survives an avalanche — with a girl, naturally — by using a ski jacket Q gave him that inflates into a huge bubble.

"We had Brosnan on a big toboggan for close-ups," Zurcher says. "We would prepare a nice piste by the trees, then ski with a camera and toboggan about fifty miles an hour down to an easy run-out." *World's* ski scenes are brief but attention-grabbing, presenting a spectacular show of some of the colossal backcountry skiing available around Les Grands Montets. And Chamonix is a town Bond would have been at home in, with its legendary extreme-sports culture, intense beauty, and colorful characters.

All over the Alps last winter, word spread that Daniel Craig, the latest Bond, was taking ski lessons and that Marc Forster, the Swiss director of *Quantum,* wanted to shoot in his home country and include a lot of ski scenes. The same rumors even surfaced in the London tabloids, though they turned out to be false.

No worries. Inevitably, there will be more Bond films, and they will most certainly continue to feature the glamour and inherent danger of sliding down a mountain. Even though Fleming's novels only put Bond on the slopes one time, in *On Her Majesty's Secret Service*, skiing stunts and exotic mountain resorts have become part of the Bond lexicon. When M debriefs Bond near the end of that novel, he says, "Well, you were pretty lucky to get out of that one, James. Didn't know you could ski."

"I only just managed to stay upright, sir," James answers with typical Bondian aplomb. "Wouldn't like to try it again."

ELISABETH EAVES

Ecotouring in Honduras

FROM *Slate.com*

Island Dreams

COLONIA BALFATE and Colonia Policarpo Galindo are not in the guidebooks, and for good reason. They are conjoined shantytowns that spill upward along two steep tropical gullies into the green jungle above. A few of the twenty-three hundred residents have homes made of cinder block or cement, but the rest make do with scavenged wood planks, corrugated tin, or sheets of plastic. Tawny dirt roads, raw as open wounds and lined with garbage, climb sharply from the entrance to the settlement. Water delivery to the community is sporadic, residents lack a sewage system or a health clinic, and neighbors complain that the *colonias* are crime-ridden. In March, the owner of a nearby botanical garden called them "a haven for thieves and robbers" in the local press after two hikers were robbed on his grounds.

Balfate and Policarpo Galindo are among the faces of modern tourism. These fast-growing slums are located not on the outskirts of some Third World city but on a resort-dotted island in the Caribbean — one peddling sun, sea, and piña colada dreams to a richer, colder world. Here on Roatán, one of the Bay Islands of Honduras, direct flights from the United States are on the rise, a new ferryboat speeds crossings to the mainland, and cruise-ship traffic is ramping up. A terminal slated to open in 2009 will be able to handle seven thousand cruise-ship passengers a day. Cement trucks, feeding a construction boom in new hotels, rumble along the two-lane jungle road that serves as the island's main thoroughfare. As tourism grows, though, the island is killing off the flora and fauna that lured the foreigners in the first place, while failing to enrich many Hondurans. From cruise shipper to backpacker, every traveler who sets foot on the island, including me, is contributing to this process.

I came to Honduras hoping to unravel some of the effects of travel — because I travel and don't intend to stop and because, as a child of my time, I'm cursed with the burden of knowing I live in a planet-sized web of cause and effect. I can't abstain from this web anymore than a butterfly can refrain from moving its wings, but I feel drawn, nevertheless, to follow a few of its strands.

We hear a lot about ecotourism these days, a term rendered nearly meaningless by travel-industry hype, but which the International Ecotourism Society defines as "responsible travel to natural areas that conserves the environment and improves the welfare of local peoples." That's the kind of definition that begs more questions: Improves how much? Which local people? But it's safe to say that the businesses and well-meaning organizations promoting ecotourism agree on one thing: if developing countries conserve their natural areas, revenue from tourism can make up for foregone income from other uses of the same land, such as logging, fishing, and farming. That income, in turn, will reinforce the will to conserve.

Often, though, this theory isn't borne out in real life. Consider Ecuador's Galápagos Islands, long the poster child for eco-travel, now turning into an eco-disaster. Between 1999 and 2005, the islands' GDP grew by a stunning 78 percent, two-thirds of which was due to tourism, according to a new study by J. Edward Taylor of the University of California, Davis. But individual welfare barely improved. GDP per head grew by a paltry 1.8 percent in the same period because the islands' population — drawn by the business engine of ecotourism — grew by 60 percent. That ballooning population is taking an ever-higher toll on the fragile ecosystem.

In addition to being endowed with fertile jungle and turquoise sea, Honduras is a good testing ground for ecotourism's central proposition. It's poor. It wants tourism, or indeed anything that will supplement an economy based on remittance payments, *maquiladoras,* and fruit. There appears to be an official will to conserve: the government has designated, at least on paper, 107 protected areas in which hunting and development are either limited or banned outright. Together, they make up an impressive 24 percent of Honduran territory and are home to endangered creatures, like the howler monkey and the manatee, and spectacular ones, like the scarlet macaw. My plan was to visit several of the national parks, meeting up with my parents along the way and ending our trip at the ancient Mayan ruins of Copán.

On a map published by the government-affiliated Honduras Institute of Tourism, nearly the entire eighty-square-mile island of Roatán is part of a national marine park. But a staffer at a local conservation organization told me that while that was the plan, it wasn't actually the case. At the moment, only eight miles of shoreline, stretching little more than a mile out to sea, are officially protected.

Diving in that area earlier in the day, I had seen a hawksbill turtle, two and a half feet long, beating its flippers as it glided by like a prehistoric shadow. The hawksbill — locally called *carey* — is critically endangered, still hunted for its dark-and-light patterned shell. Some locals make jewelry out of it — a barefoot man had already tried to sell me a *carey* necklace on the beach. "One of the sad side effects of the tourism and cruise-ship industry is that it has generated a lot of illegal activity," said James Foley, director of research and development for Roatán Marine Park, which maintains a tiny beachfront office in the village of West End.

The *colonias,* a handful of which are scattered around the island, are another disturbing side effect.

"See those houses?" Rosa Danelia Hendrix asked me, gesturing to some fifteen shacks scattered high on the hills, the latest expansions to Balfate and Policarpo Galindo. We were standing in the yard of the three-room yellow schoolhouse where she is principal.

"Three months ago, they weren't there. They don't have septic tanks. When the rains come, the waste will run down the hill and cause diseases," she said. The human waste, garbage, and sediment from the torn-up jungle also wash into the sea and onto nearby coral reefs, which are inside the supposed eight-mile protected area and which are home to hawksbills, bottlenose dolphins, and myriad fish. The sediment reduces the amount of sunlight that reaches the coral, killing it, which, in turn, slowly kills the fish that live there.

The residents of the *colonias* come to the island from mainland Honduras because the tourism boom shimmers with the illusion of plentiful, well-paid jobs. "The island dream," mainlanders call it. "They confront reality when they realize they don't speak English, or don't have construction skills, and they can't get good jobs," Hendrix said.

To leave the *colonias*, I hopped in a minibus, and in ten minutes I was back in West End, which is far from swanky but still a world away. It was my own island dream: a single dirt road running along a palm-fringed waterfront, lined with low-key restaurants, hotels, and dive shops. I stepped into an open-air beach bar called Sundowners and ordered a piña colada, and in no time the man on the next stool was telling me he hadn't paid federal taxes since 1967. The bar filled up, and as the sun moved closer to the sea, everyone turned to watch. It slipped over the edge of the earth, streaks of orange and pink filled the sky, and the black silhouette of a cruise ship sailed across the horizon.

Beware, Shark

Not so much swimming as hovering, I slipped into the school of sharks. There were eighteen of them, some as long as eight feet. "These are big girls," the dive master had warned us; many were pregnant and thicker than usual. They swam above, below, and around me, so close I could have reached out and touched them. The dive master had advised us not to, a warning that had struck me as bizarre. I mean, really. What idiot would do such a thing?

But now I saw the problem. These Caribbean reef sharks had skin like velvet, dark and rich in the shadows, shiny and pale when it caught the light. They shimmered hypnotically as they moved. I noticed scars, dark healed gashes on their sides and around their jaws, telling stories I couldn't read — of feeding frenzies, mating rituals, and fishermen. I wanted to touch. The sharks, meanwhile, seemed to register me as an uninteresting object. They came disquietingly close but always turned away from me at the last second. As they swerved, I found myself wishing one would shimmy along my body as she did, gliding in tandem with me for a few moments.

The sharks gave me butterflies, but the truth was that I was probably more of a danger to them than they were to me. For one thing,

I was with fourteen other humans, some of them fatter and slower than me, giving the sharks considerable choice should they choose to nibble. For another, as sharks go, the Caribbean reef shark is not especially threatening. Just four species of the 410 or so known to science account for most shark attacks on humans, and this wasn't one of them.

The sharks, on the other hand, would have had a lot to worry about had they been half as anxiety-prone as humans. Our group was shark baiting, one of the most controversial ecotourism practices in the Caribbean. Sharks, being wild animals, are difficult to procure on command. So many of the hundreds of shark-dive operators around the world tempt the animals with food. At Waihuka Diving, Roatán's sole shark operation, the dive master took a plastic bucket with holes punctured in the lid and filled it with a small amount of chopped-up fish. The dive master planted the bucket in the sand twenty feet from the coral wall where we kneeled, and the sweet smell of fish guts lured the sharks to school right in front of us. They kept schooling as, at the dive master's signal, we moved into the fray. My excitement was pure, more real and visceral than I had expected. And, fortunately, immune to the presence of other humans and the artificiality of the setup.

Which brings me back to the bait. In 2001, Florida banned shark feeding in its waters, a move hailed by public-safety officials but also by conservationists. Feeding sharks lowers their natural fear of humans, which makes them easier prey for fishermen. And repeatedly luring them to the same spot makes them easy for fishermen to find.

This is a problem, because more than one hundred million sharks are killed by humans every year. Several species are critically endangered, and some have gone extinct within specific regions. Sharks are frequently killed as collateral damage — for instance, by tuna boats in the Pacific. (Your dolphin-safe tuna is not necessarily shark-safe.) Sharks are also a direct target of fishermen, especially for their fins, with escalating demand for shark-fin soup in China and Taiwan. The fins are so valuable that fishermen often cut them off and throw the shark back into the ocean, where it bleeds and sinks to its death.

We humans returned to our places in front of the coral wall, and the dive master, wearing a chain-mail gauntlet, ripped the lid off the bucket of chopped fish. The effect was instantaneous. These lazily graceful creatures were suddenly bullets of muscle. In a matter of seconds, they became a writhing, food-focused mass. A single thrash by a single shark looked powerful enough to knock me out.

As the melee ended, the sharks dispersed, trolling the area in wider and wider curves until a few disappeared into the blue. The divers reluctantly began to swim up the anchor line. At fifteen feet below the surface, I paused and hung onto the line, floating like a windsock in the current while the nitrogen left my body. For a few minutes, I was able to watch the sharks from above, now just gray silhouettes but still recognizable by the S-curve of their swim.

A fisherman on Roatán can get about $40 for one of these sharks, or $720 for eighteen. Waihuka gets about $80 per diver, so $960 on this twelve-customer dive. They can charge $960 for those same sharks again and again, and the sharks don't have to die: the resource is renewable. Assuming similar overhead (a boat, an outboard engine, gasoline), shark-watching is more profitable for the locals than shark-fishing, and it conserves nature rather than decimating it.

Doesn't that make shark diving a good thing? The rosy view of ecotourism would say we should exploit shark viewing to stop shark fishing. Hire the fishermen as dive masters, and you've got a win-win-win for locals, tourists, and sharks. Shark-watch businesses further argue that the more people have happy encounters with the animal, the more public support there will be for researching and protecting it. (The whale-watching industry plausibly advances a similar argument.)

Unfortunately, ecology is a little more complicated. The day before my dive, I had asked James Foley of Roatán Marine Park what he thought about shark baiting. "If you feed sharks, you're interfering with their natural feeding cycle," he said. Since they're the top predators, that messes with the entire food chain. If they eat less of their usual prey, the prey population balloons and eats more of the creatures below it, and so on and so forth. "It sends shock waves through the whole ecosystem," Foley said. Masses of data and very sophisticated computing are required to get an idea of the ultimate impact, but the point is this: feed wild beasts with utmost caution, not because of some selfish concern over getting your hand bitten off, but for their sake.

Even knowing what Foley had told me about the food chain, I wanted, post-dive, to side with proponents of shark diving, the ones who say that such *cara-a-cara* encounters will teach man to love the beast. After I surfaced, and for some time afterward, I would close my eyes and try to reimagine myself back down to the reef, envisioning their skin and their scars and retasting the frisson. Not many experiences in adult life make me want to do that.

Signs of Civilization

Parks, reserves, and wildlife refuges dot the northern coast of Honduras like a string of emeralds, starting in the west at the Barra del Rio Motagua National Park, tucked away on the Guatemalan border, and reaching the vast expanse of the Rio Plátano Biosphere Reserve in the east. The reserve cuts off the easternmost province of Gracias a Dios from the rest of the country and is covered with the largest remaining expanse of virgin tropical jungle in Central America.

I approached the north coast of mainland Honduras by ferryboat from Roatán, thinking of two antecedents: Christopher Columbus, who was real, and Allie Fox, who was not. Columbus passed this way by ship in 1502 and claimed the shore for Spain. The existing human residents, the Tolupan, Pech, and Tawahka, lived in hidden jungle settlements, so Columbus would have seen an unbroken wall of green rising from the sandy beach up to the eight-thousand-foot peak of Pico Bonito. As my ferryboat approached, the peak loomed over the coast, first hazy in the bright morning sun, then greener as we got closer to the shore.

As the wilderness has become a place that humans visit by choice rather than necessity, the "leave no trace" credo has evolved into a mantra for outdoor enthusiasts. In my case, it's been ingrained since grade-school day hikes. So it's odd to think just how new this philosophy is to Western thinking. Columbus, I'm guessing, would have considered the idea of leaving no trace incomprehensible. Every Spanish name, every cathedral, every empty silver mine in Central America is testament to the belief that the bigger the trace, the better. Or consider the Babylonians, the Romans, the Mayans — the entire history of civilization is one of bending the earth to the needs and wants of humans. Today, we might worship at the altar of low-impact living, but I'll wager that our brains have not yet adapted. On a purely psychological level, impact is good. Who wants to be forgotten? We have families, make art, and build McMansions precisely so that we leave a trace.

Allie Fox and his family also approached the north coast by ship in *The Mosquito Coast,* a novel by Paul Theroux, who seems to have chosen the region as a metaphor for the opposite of civilization. Fox wants to escape a corrupt and materialistic modern United States, and he has notions that the Mosquito Coast savages, as he sees them, are a purer version of mankind. But once in the jungle, he is desperate to civilize it. He plants neat rows of beans and builds a giant ice machine.

My parents met me at the ferry terminal with Mark, a guide from a local company that specializes in *aventuras ecológicas.* The outfit is called Garífuna Tours, after an African-Indian ethnic group that lives along the north coast. This was supposed to be a group tour, but we were the only customers. We felt a bit decadent.

We drove through the modern, low-rise city of La Ceiba, which, despite its banks and restaurants and grid-patterned streets, looked bleached and weathered, as though it were still trying to assert itself against nature. The impact of humans on the north coast accelerated considerably after 1502, culminating in today's cultural peak, which comes complete with Dunkin' Donuts and KFC. Mark whisked us west of the city, turned off the paved road, and drove through a field of pineapples. A mechanical conveyor with a green-painted metal boom sat idle in the field.

The low, spiky pineapple plants grew right up to the edge of Pico Bonito National Park, 414 square miles of mountain and jungle encompassing Pico Bonito itself, the jutting peak I had seen from the sea. Entering the jungle was like stepping into a yawning palace, one made of ceiba and mahogany and rosewood trees, lit only by a few sunbeams that penetrated a latticework high above. Up there — thirty or forty yards up in the trees — existed a whole world of insects and animals that never deigned to touch the ground. The trail began to climb, and small unseen creatures rustled and were gone before I could get a look. When we came upon a termite nest, Mark urged me to eat one of the insects, and when I refused, he told me that at least I knew now that they were edible, in case I got lost in the forest. We passed a sign that banned venturing off-trail into the pathless woods beyond. Mark said a group of Spaniards had recently headed thataway, gotten lost for six days, and had to be rescued.

In an hour, we arrived at a waterfall. A foamy white feather spewed out of the jungle, down vine-covered rock, and eddied and churned its way to the deep, calm pool that spread out at our feet.

Outside the air-conditioned rooms, the heat had been constant since I arrived in Honduras. It was the kind that pressed on your body like a physical force, barely lessened by an evening breeze or a dip in the bath-water sea. During our short jungle climb, it seemed to have grown even thicker. Now here was a chance to be cool. I dove under the water and felt the blood rush to the surface of my skin.

As I was drying off, a troop of teenagers from the town of Tela arrived at the fall. They were on a Sunday hike with a lone American friend, a redheaded Peace Corps volunteer from Texas. Honduras is host to 192 volunteers — the Peace Corps' second-largest deployment in the world (only Ukraine has more) — who are scattered around the country on their vague but benign mission to be of use. Jonathan was at the end of his two-year tour, which he had spent advising the Tela mayor's office on business development. "The Peace Corps has been in Honduras for forty years," he told us. "So you might well ask, just how much good are we doing?"

Perhaps not much. But the urge to leave a trace is irrepressible.

Pineapple Fields Forever

The American short-story writer O. Henry, exiled to Honduras in the 1890s, coined a term to describe the country that was so perfectly evocative of colonial horrors, bad government, tropical weather, ripe fruit, and lush bougainvillea vines creeping up the patio railing that it's in wide circulation more than a century later. The term was *banana republic*. That piece of poetry conjures an entire period of history. For the first half of the twentieth century, large swaths of Honduras were more or less run by the Standard Fruit Company (now Dole) and the United Fruit Company (now Chiquita). They bribed the politicians and summoned the U.S. military when things got out of hand. They built and owned the railways, which tended to run from the fields to the ports but not to anywhere useful to Hondurans, such as the capital.

Of course, the country has come a long way since then. Or has it? During my visit, *Honduras This Week* ran the front-page headline PRESIDENT ZELAYA ADDRESSES MELON CRISIS. The photographic evidence showed the mustachioed president sitting at his desk, Honduran flag visible to one side, biting into a juicy cantaloupe. The power of big fruit has diminished in recent decades, but pineapples, bananas, and melons are still export staples. A relatively minor U.S. Food and Drug Administration warning — that melons from a particular Honduran farm might contain salmonella — can become a flash point for a fragile economy.

Now a lot of people are hitching hopes for Honduras's economy to tourism. Plans for at least two new resorts are under way on the north coast, one of them adjacent to a national park. Signs in the protected areas I visited bore the logos of donor organizations — USAID, WWF, the Honduras-Canada Fund for Environmental Management. Even the Peace Corps was onboard. Since running into Jonathan at the waterfall, I had met a second Peace Corps volunteer, Nicole, who was visiting the Cuero y Salado wildlife reserve with her father. Nicole was stationed in the south, in a small town in the department of Valle. I asked her what went on there, economically speaking. She furrowed her brow and thought for a minute. Finally, she said that there were a lot of armed security guards. She was working with a women's cooperative, trying to come up with things its members could sell to foreigners. They made attractive pottery, but it didn't ship well. Nicole had hit upon the idea of making small, bright-colored purses woven from old potato-chip bags, an item she had seen for sale in other parts of Central America. There were no tourists where she lived to buy such things, but she thought that maybe the townsfolk could lure travelers from the Pan-American Highway, which passed nearby.

Tourism was clearly a popular cause, but was it smart? Does it make sense, in the long term, to sell natural charms that will be steadily worn down by the buyers? A city can renew itself with man-made attractions. I wasn't sure that jungles and coral reefs had that kind of staying power.

On our last day on the coast, I floated face-down in the Caribbean, toting up my sins. I had flown in an airplane, taken taxis instead of buses, requested air-conditioning, run the air-conditioning even after I realized I couldn't shut one of my windows, and bought small plastic bottles of water. That was all before sundown on my first day. Subsequently, I had participated in the feeding of wild animals, been driven around in gasoline-powered cars and boats, eaten conch (I didn't know it was threatened), and — this one hadn't even occurred to me until I read it in a guidebook — worn sunscreen and DEET-laden bug repellent while swimming above the delicate corals. But I had no idea how to weigh all that against whatever minuscule economic benefit I might have been bringing to Honduras.

We were in Cayos Cochinos Marine National Park, a collection of cays northeast of La Ceiba. That morning, snorkeling off a deserted cay, I had seen parrotfish, jacks, schools of blue tang, and one fat, lazy barracuda, motionless except for its snapping jaw. The reef life was more vivid and abundant than anything I had seen off Roatán, probably because of all the diving and development there.

Now I was floating off Cayo Chachauate, a coral cay just a few hundred feet long that was home to a Garífuna village of about thirty families. The Garífuna, who descend from escaped slaves and Carib Indians, lived on the island of St. Vincent until 1797, when the British deported the entire population to Honduras, where they established fishing villages. Chachauate's wooden huts were strung out along the sand just yards above the high-water mark. An assortment of canoes, makeshift sailboats, and outboards sat on the beach. The big news in the village was that it had recently acquired a diesel generator, which ran every evening from six to eight. Any villager who invested in his own power line was free to share. Until the generator, only one ambitious family had had electricity, provided by a solar panel on their roof.

I watched a purple fan coral sway with the movement of the tide. The sea stretched away turquoise in three directions and grew pale where it rose up to the beach. Up there, a woman in a hut was making me fried chicken for lunch. I swam in closer to shore, gliding over sea grass and rippled sand. I saw a few tiny fish and a corroded soda can. And then I saw the bearded face of José Trinidad Cabañas, a long-ago president of Honduras. He was decorating a ten-lempira bill, which lay flat and motionless on the sand. Struck by this oddity, I dove for the bottom, but when I picked up the money, it felt so slippery and fragile that I thought it would disintegrate in my hand, so I let it flutter back down to the seabed again.

Mel Gibson and the Demise of Civilization

"Forget about the movie," Gustavo told Denise.

She ignored him.

"They took the heart out, and it was still beating," she said. "And they held it up like this!" She raised one pale, triumphant arm above her head.

"Let the movie go," we said in chorus, my mother and I now joining Gustavo. He was our portly, scholarly guide to the ancient Mayan city of Copán, an urban center of twenty-four thousand people during its heyday, which was sometime between A.D. 400 and 800. He carried a stick with a bird feather attached to one end to point out archeological details, and he had the slightly aggrieved air of a man who had to be patient a lot.

Gustavo was unhappy with Mel Gibson and, in particular, with what he referred to as "that stupid movie," *Apocalypto.* In case you missed it, the 2006 film was a revisionist and gruesomely violent retelling of history. No surprise there, but this movie happened to be set among the ancient Maya. There were beheadings, impalings, and human sacrifices performed by drug-addled priests. Not that the real Mayans didn't perform the odd human sacrifice. But Gustavo was at pains to contextualize.

At the entrance to Copán, my parents and I had teamed up with Diane and Denise, two middle-aged women from New York City, both with strong Brooklyn accents. Denise, who had short black hair and wore bright red lipstick, was a Gibson fan. To Gustavo's consternation, she kept asking where the sacrifices were performed.

And now, finally, we were in the middle of the Grand Plaza, once quite a hub, open to all members of the ancient Copán public, and used for both commerce and worship. There was a small pyramid at the center of the plaza, and steles scattered around, each one intricately carved in honor of one king or another. And there, right in front of us, was a large stone object made for the express purpose of sacrificing humans.

It was dome-shaped, about four feet wide and three feet tall, with a depression hollowed out of the top just big enough to cup a human head. Two channels ran down the sides to drain the blood away. Gustavo grabbed my arm and told me to lean backward over the dome with my head in the depression — kind of comfy, if you must be sacrificed — and made as though to cut off my head with his feather-stick. That was when Denise got excited and started recounting the *Apocalypto* sacrifice scene, thrusting her hand into the air as though holding a beating heart. "And the people were still alive!" she said.

She reluctantly followed as the rest of us moved away across the plaza to the city's ball court. Relief-carved macaw heads decorated the walls. Mayan ball courts, it turns out, were not for playing ball in the Western sense of a game, as an earlier generation of archeologists believed. "The idea of the ball ceremony was not to please a human audience, but to please the gods," Gustavo explained. Performed correctly, the ball "game," conducted by specially trained young men, was believed to make the sun and moon come up on time.

Today, though much of ancient Copán still lies buried, you can wander among its carvings and pyramids, tombs and temples, halls of government and homes, visualizing the bright-colored stucco that once adorned them. Until the nineteenth century, however, they were completely invisible. Some time in the 800s, the civilization of the Classic Maya period began a collapse so complete that by the time the Spaniards began to arrive, there was no trace of it. Descendants of the ancient Maya scattered and survived, but the great painted cities, with their pyramids and temples, were gone, swallowed whole by the jungle. The last date found on a Mayan monument corresponds to the year 909, as though time just stopped one day.

Archeologists still debate what happened. It's clear, though, that environmental degradation played a role in the collapse. In the Copán valley in particular, studies show that as the population grew, the people stripped the hillsides of trees. Major soil erosion preceded the city's downfall. Copán also suffered droughts, which may have been partly brought on by the deforestation. The Mayans cut down the trees to plant corn, and for firewood to burn limestone, a key ingredient in their bright pigments. Why didn't they pull themselves out of this ecological tailspin? Presumably they could see the trees disappearing and the mud running down the hills. In *Collapse: How Societies Choose To Fail or Succeed,* Jared Diamond suggests that the elites who might have led the way out of this mess had insulated themselves from the problems of the people. So as the poor began to suffer — infant mortality was probably 50 percent toward the end — the kings kept demanding tribute.

We stood in front of the hieroglyphic stairway, an inscription covering seventy-two steps that make up one face of the acropolis. It's the longest hieroglyphic inscription found in the Americas, and no one has completely deciphered it. Archeologists know that it tells a history of ancient Copán and that it was created by a ruler named Smoke Shell in 753, when the city was already in decline. When the staircase is eventually decoded, maybe Smoke Shell will have something more to tell us about his doomed metropolis.

In the meantime, Honduras is still being deforested. Central America has lost more than 70 percent of its forest cover since 1960, mostly to make way for cattle ranches, sugar-cane fields, and coffee plantations. Between 1990 and 2005, Honduras lost 10,567 square miles of forest — an area about the size of Massachusetts. But that's just another scary environmental statistic. Taken together, all the bad news is enough to make you turn to irrational beliefs about planetary control. Or to mindless entertainment.

Gustavo began to tell us the story of the Mayan codices, manuscripts that could help decode the hieroglyphics. Denise cut in.

"Did they sacrifice people up there?"

Gustavo sighed. "Yes, and then they let the head roll down the steps and gave it to the victim's son," he said. "Too much Mel Gibson for you."

DANIEL ALARCÓN

You Do Not Represent the Government of the United States of America

FROM *The Virginia Quarterly Review*

WE WERE LATE arriving in Damascus, though I can't remember exactly why. There was traffic coming out of Aleppo, or perhaps we got lost in Damascus, or perhaps the stop for strong, bitter coffee along the way — our driver's eyes kept fluttering closed — took longer than it should have. In any case, our group of seven American poets, novelists, and journalists was well behind schedule, and there was nothing we could do about it. We drove: desert, scrub-brush hills, then Damascus, a city, with all the requisite noise and chaos. Our two guides, the preternaturally calm Hassan, a teacher, and Fatih, a pharmacist with reddish-brown hair and a broad, welcoming smile, were both from Aleppo, and they didn't know their way around. It was such a helpless feeling: any corner might represent the correct turn, or the absolute wrong one, and we had no way of knowing the difference. There were no street signs we Americans could read and no one we could ask; between the seven of us, we spoke maybe a half-dozen words of Arabic, and none had ever been to Syria.

We finally made it to the University of Damascus and were wandering around the campus, looking for the right classroom, when some students recognized us — not as individuals, naturally, but as foreigners, likely Americans, possibly the writers they'd been told would be arriving that day. They'd been looking forward to our lecture. They led us to the right building and into a classroom, where we found a handful of students waiting patiently. Everything about it was strange — the harried morning leaving Aleppo, the long meandering drive, the teeming streets of Damascus, even the limpid quality of the sunlight in Syria, golden, unlike any I'd ever seen. Like my colleagues, I was still trying to figure out what I was supposed to be doing here. Another class was about to get started, and so a brief discussion began around us, Fatih and Hassan explaining our situation, apologizing for our tardiness, while some of us milled about, trying to appear professional. Eventually, the professor ceded us the floor, and just like that we had a classroom to ourselves, just us and the students.

The next four hours will rank, I'm certain, among the most moving experiences of my life. We sat on a raised stage in a large lecture room, as the wine-red desks gradually filled. Eventually, there were about seventy students, an even mix of men and women, though many faces changed in the course of the afternoon. Students filed in and out, or clustered at the door, peeking in at the American writers. Each of us read — poems, fragments of stories — and they listened very politely, and then they spared us nothing. Your stories are very nice, they said, but why are you here? How do you explain what the United States has done? Why was Bush reelected? What if your brother were asked to bomb us? What did Islam do to you? We're scared, they said. We're nervous. My brother and sister are dying. Israel will attack us. America will attack us. This university won't exist. This city. We'll be dead. I once lived in Baghdad, and I know I'll never go back. There are refugees everywhere, even in this room, and we don't know what the future holds. So tell us, who has power in your country? And why should we believe you? Who let the war happen?

It went on like this for hours.

Finally we left the classroom, and the conversation simply moved with us into the hallway. Women and men, politics and religion — the students wanted us to hear all of it. Students clustered around us, each eager to share his or her opinion, to clarify something that had been said, or to expand upon it. It was impossible not to be impressed by their openness, their excitement and eagerness to share. One young man — a boy, really — brought up women drivers, a relatively new development in Syria, which he considered dangerous, and it was amazing to watch his female classmates pounce on him. These women were fiercely intelligent, and they made mincemeat of that poor boy. He shrank away, and the conversation turned once again: 9/11, Israel, the troubling weight of history, and the war, the war, the war. By the end, I was exhausted. We all were. Our trip had only just begun, and already it felt like we'd been gone for weeks. That night I fell ill and nearly threw up in front of the Minister of Education.

The not-so-simple idea was to take a group of American writers to the Middle East. We were to speak at various universities in the region, meeting with local writers, poets, journalists, and intellectuals along the way. This, I suppose, is what they call person-to-person diplomacy. There is a small office within the Byzantine bureaucracy of the U.S. State Department that sponsors these sorts of things, though the logistics of our road trip through Syria, Jordan, Israel, and Palestine were left to the staff of the University of Iowa's International Writing Program. In nearly every city we visited, either the local American diplomat or one of our hosts would remind us that we were not representatives of the United States government. This was meant to reassure us, but the point was made so often and so consistently that it became a little unnerving. Try explaining the distinction to the students of the University of Damascus. We were representatives of the United States — having attended a few antiwar rallies in 2003 did not absolve us of responsibility.

I knew when I signed up for it that this wasn't going to be a normal trip. There wouldn't be a lot of free time. It would be work. It's a trade-off. On the one hand, you give up a certain amount of independence. On the other, you get access you might not otherwise have, and of course, all of it is happening on America's tab. I knew (and know) essentially nothing about the region. I speak no Arabic beyond *God bless you* and *Thank you,* and I felt that my being invited was a mistake, that I should accept quickly and enthusiastically before someone had the good sense to reconsider.

What the State Department hoped to accomplish was less clear to me. One can't help but wonder how bleak must things be if Washington has no better ideas than to send a bunch of writers out to Damascus and Amman and Ramallah. I have a very high opinion of the utility of art and literature, but there are some problems that cannot be smoothed over with a well-written short story. Imagine: Secretary of State Condoleezza Rice briefing the president on the grim news from these sundry nations he had hoped to invade someday. They are alone in the Oval Office at the end of another long week, and the president is gripped by a sense of despair. All his plans have gone awry. The Surge is a failure. Iran continues its relentless push toward nuclear weapons. President Bush stares blankly out the window.

"Goddamn it, Condi," he shouts suddenly. "Get me some novelists! Get me some poets!"

The day after falling ill, I walked to the Old City of Damascus, slipping easily into the rhythm of those who hurried along its warren of narrow streets and alleys. Now and then I stopped to admire the texture of the place: the curve of a cobblestone path, gradations of conservatism in women's dress, layers of history stacked, often gracelessly, one atop the other. A letter box painted red — BOÎTE AUX LETRE read the French; the Arabic below — affixed to the grim face of a blackened stone wall that has stood since the Ottomans. The Internet café housed within those walls, and the knock-off perfume sold ten paces away. The crowds that stream by — a boy in a Ronaldinho jersey, a woman in a black chador, a grizzled man in a baseball cap selling pistachios, or toy soldiers, or AA batteries — and the sound of Arab pop music leaking from a passing car. Damascus (or Aleppo, depending on whom you ask) is the oldest continuously inhabited urban center in the world, a fact that is easy to believe when you are face-to-face with it. It is suffused with history, even as it is completely entangled with today's messiest predicaments. If a cradle of civilization can be said to exist, this city is it.

I made my way to the door of the Grand Mosque and then to its courtyard's marble patio, where I sat to appreciate the antique dignity of the holy site. There were children playing chase, sliding in their socks across the polished stone, entire families sprawled out in the sun, and a constant, pleasing din. The muezzin's call came, and some of the gathered crowd rose and disappeared into the hall, but many stayed. The day was warm and bright. I took out the microphone a friend had lent me for my trip and recorded the wash of sounds — the call to prayer, the shouting children, the chatter of stray conversation, the shuffling of feet.

I'd been there for a few minutes when a man approached. He

glanced at the microphone and offered me his hand. Was I journalist? I explained I was a writer. He asked where I was from, and I told
him. I introduced myself, and he said his name was Murat. He was a
Kurd, he said proudly.

"From Syria?" I asked.

"Iraq," Murat said, and then frowned. My microphone had been
on the entire time, and he leaned in now and spoke directly into it:
"Don't. Ever. Go. There."

Murat's words hung in the air. Even the mosque seemed eerily
quiet as I considered what he'd said. He held his severe expression
for a moment, and then another, until it was almost unbearable.
Then he broke into a smile. No, no, really, he assured me, everything is fine in Kurdistan, no problems at all. It's the rest of the
country that's a nightmare. Ha-ha-ha. He thought he had scared
me. He had. There are at least one million Iraqi refugees in Syria.
They have fled the catastrophe next door and huddle in Damascus,
waiting, praying, hoping that the violence back home will somehow
end. Iraq is a scary place, and the physical and emotional hangover
from the previous day — from the long conversation with students
at the University of Damascus — was real.

We chatted some more, and Murat tried to reassure me: he
spoke about the beauty of his part of Iraq, the warmth of the people. Saddam is dead, and there will be peace so long as the problems of the south do not migrate to the north. He asked me about
the United States, about Peru. He told me he'd worked for the
United Nations Food and Agriculture Organization, as an interpreter, but, of course, that work no longer existed. He showed me
his green Iraqi passport, lately one of the world's more useless
travel documents, and pointed out how he had lied about his occupation: he hadn't written *interpreter,* but a word that did not imply
any collaboration or dealings with foreigners: *worker.* We rose and
wandered around the mosque, chatting, following the crowds that
flowed between the various rooms. We passed a group of women all
in black. "These are Shiites," he whispered to me, in the low, dis-
creet tone that one might use in a museum.

I nodded and felt myself blush. It seemed inappropriate to me,
this kind of talk, but Murat carried on, unperturbed, and so I followed along as quietly, unobtrusively as I could.

He posed before the green glass tomb of Saladin, the great

Kurdish sultan who battled the Crusaders, and I took Murat's photo with his cell phone. Afterward, as we sat once again at the patio, I asked him why he had come to Syria. He sighed. Tourism, he said, at first, but his heart wasn't in it. He was quiet for a moment, and then explained that he'd come to register his family on the United Nations refugee list. "If I put my name down now, *inshallah,* I'll get an interview next year."

He'd spent the last hour assuring me everything in Kurdistan was fine, lovely, calm. The people are affectionate, the countryside is breathtakingly beautiful, and there is no war to speak of. They are rid of the homicidal dictator who threatened their culture, their language, their very lives. And he wanted to leave?

"Yes," Murat said, when asked about the contradiction. He had a wife and two daughters to look out for. He'd shown me pictures. "Now things are all right. But in two years, in three, who knows?"

"Where will you go?" I asked.

He shrugged. Sweden, Australia, Canada, England. Wherever. The world is a big place, no matter that war has a way of shrinking it to the size of a fist, or a stone, or a gun.

"Of course, my first choice is the United States," Murat said, smiling.

I could do nothing but smile back.

We both knew that wasn't going to happen.

If there was any purpose to the trip, it was to hear these sorts of things. To feel just a bit of this tension. To meet this man and have nothing to say. To read our little stories, our little poems in a room full of Syrian students and feel helpless and a bit ashamed in the face of their fear. The war's American death toll has exceeded four thousand — but in the Middle East the effects are multiplicative. A cataclysm is underway, exploding outward in waves across the region. People's voices here crack when they speak of it. The dead can be tallied up, of course, however politically inconvenient it may be to do so: this many American soldiers, that many Iraqi insurgents, this many civilians. This many Sunni, and that many Shia. The refugees, the internally displaced, the millions of ordinary citizens driven from their homes — these, too, can be counted. But the psychic toll is impossible to assess, is not confined within any borders, and there is no comprehensive way to measure fear.

We went out with some local writers that night, to a cavern of a restaurant hidden (or so it seemed to me) somewhere in the Christian quarter of the Old City. The war was on my mind. How strange then to find, inside the restaurant, a celebration underway, with music and shouting and smoke, such that my sour mood seemed misplaced, even selfish. It was early yet, but folks were already dancing and singing, and so when a glass of liquor was offered, although I still wasn't feeling well, I accepted.

One of the local writers asked if we'd heard the news. *The news,* he said, with a cherubic smile, raising a glass of *araq* in a toast. Syrian television was reporting that President Bush had been caught with a prostitute and that she was going to testify against him. She was young, beautiful, fearless. Our friend beamed.

The American writers clinked glasses, all of us a little stunned. This was undoubtedly good news. Thrilling news. The cabal's last justification vanishes: their claims to piety and moral superiority disappear, the façade crumbles, and we are free. I'll admit the news excited me, that I longed to see President Bush quaver, stammer an excuse, that I longed to see him subjected to the humiliating spectacle of sex scandal. Not out of prurient interest, but out of pure spite. The man's general incompetence should be scandal enough, but, unfortunately, it often takes a salacious accusation to crystallize public opinion.

Our mood had changed dramatically, and I felt buoyed. The writer sitting across from me was like a dozen people I know in Lima: ridiculous, charming, brilliant. He smoked without pause, kept my glass full, and when I turned down a bite of some kind of spicy raw meat, he looked genuinely disappointed. I tried to explain that I'd had the same appetizer the night before and it had nearly killed me, but there was no convincing him. "Are you novelist?" he asked.

I nodded.

"If you are novelist, then you must eat this."

He leaned in to explain. "Daniel," he said, choosing his words very carefully, "a novelist is like God, but *against* God. Every day in my life I have twenty mistake. And is good. I love mistake. I want to drink the life!"

From across the table, Fatih shot me a look, part maternal worry, part implicit reprimand. *Don't eat that,* she seemed to say.

As I hesitated, the writer laughed maniacally, then ate the raw meat himself.

The music got louder, everyone shouting, and the entire place seemed drunk and thrilled to be alive. I got up to record the music — lovely, beguiling music — and when I returned, Fatih informed me that the singer was in fact, quite mediocre. Appallingly so. And it did not matter. We kept drinking, offering toasts to prostitutes who testify against presidents. The restaurant sang in one voice.

Later, another table called me over. They were a mixed group of male and female doctors, celebrating a birthday or something. A table of men in suits, their ties loosely knotted, and women in glamorous, sparkling dresses — everyone glassy-eyed, beautiful, happy.

"What are you doing here?" one of the men asked. He pointed to my microphone.

I tried to explain — American writers, reading tour, goodwill, etc. — but of course, it all sounded a little preposterous.

"Will you tell the Americans we are not bad people?" he asked.

"Sure," I said.

He smiled laconically, as if the very notion sounded cute to him. He taught me a few "Syrian greetings," which I repeated loudly to the table, hoping to spread some goodwill. Naturally, these turned out to be coarse Arabic come-ons, and the table erupted in laughter.

"You've heard the news," he said, suddenly serious. "About your president?"

I nodded. He slapped me on the back. "Very good," he said.

"We're going to see the mufti tomorrow," I said after a while. We'd just been told that the mufti, something like the bishop of Syria, had agreed to receive us the next day. We'd been told to expect a solemn encounter with a spiritual man.

"The mufti? Really?" The man was drunk and happy. I had to lean in close to hear what he said next. "Very good. He's a nice man. You can ask the mufti anything," he said. "Even about fucking."

Back at the hotel, Tony, one of the writers in our group, ran to his laptop to verify the news. I don't think I've ever been so hopeful waiting for a Web page to load. We checked CNN, the *New York Times*, the *Guardian*. Nothing. We despaired. Finally, at the *Washington Post* we found a small note, and we began connecting the dots:

some midlevel administration official had preemptively resigned,
so as to avoid publicity surrounding the D.C. madam case. This was
all. No sex scandal that would bring down President Bush. No
Monica-gate 2007. It had seemed too good to be true, and it was.

We slumped in the couches, deflated. To cheer us all up, Tony
played an MP3 of his son's band playing a song the boy had written. It was a catchy number called "Bush Sucks." We laughed and
congratulated Tony, while Fatih sat with us, listening, shaking her
head. When it was finished, she said, "If you write a song like that
here . . ." and she trailed off. Then she dragged a long, elegant
finger very slowly across her throat.

One of the sadder consequences of the Iraq catastrophe is how it
has undermined the legitimacy of those who were pushing for
democratic reforms in countries such as Syria. Try selling democracy if the only regional example is a country breaking up along
sectarian lines, a place where each day's news begins with a death
toll. Autocracy starts to look pretty good by comparison. The U.S.
decision to isolate the countries we don't get along with seems especially misguided; in the case of Syria, we have a lot to talk about.
The Democratic presidential contender Barack Obama was attacked by members of his own party for the mere suggestion that it
might be a good idea to talk to these countries. I find this baffling.
How much worse do things need to get before it becomes accept-
able to offer an alternative approach?

Still, Syria is hardly a model of openness. There are periodic
crackdowns on writers, journalists, and folks who fit in the broad
category "dissidents"; just a few weeks after our visit some democratic activists were imprisoned. There's a hefty cult of personality
being constructed around President Bashar al-Assad, whose ubiquitous portrait frowned at us in virtually every office, reception area,
public park, traffic circle, or government building we visited. Most
of our public appearances, and even our private meetings with
government representatives, were recorded, presumably for Syrian
state television, and who knows how these images were manipu-
lated, or exactly what spin our visit was given. We took the risk —
better that than the alternatives: silence and isolation.

Ahmad Badr al-Din Hassoun, the grand mufti of Syria, met us in his
elegantly decorated sitting room the following morning. He was in

his forties, with a neatly trimmed beard, dressed in a pearly white head wrap, a nicely tailored slate gray robe, and matching socks. Not long before our visit, he'd sat in the same room with Speaker of the House Nancy Pelosi, during her allegedly controversial trip to Syria. He exuded warmth, sat smiling and nodding while his attendants served us tea. I did not ask him about fucking.

Already in the course of our trip, for reasons of protocol, we'd been subjected to a few harangues from bureaucrats, university administrators, and representatives of various religious communities. Given all that, I wasn't exactly hopeful about the mufti, but my fears were completely unfounded. Speaking through an interpreter, al-Din Hassoun offered his vision of Islam, politics, and the future of the region. He was funny, engaging, hopeful, and humanist. "People of faith and intellectuals," he said at one point, "let us agree that if tomorrow we destroy Jerusalem's Al-Aqsa Mosque and the Wailing Wall, or Bethlehem's Church of the Nativity, God will not be as angry as when we kill a single child playing outside his home. In the eyes of God, this child is more important."

He described the letter he had sent President Bush in the days before the bombing of Iraq began in 2003: "The Middle East gave the world its great prophets — is our compensation for this gift of light only fire?" He spoke warmly of an American rabbi who had been his guest in Syria not too long ago — and joked that he'd had to send a video of the rabbi's speech at a Damascus mosque to the United States, proving to the rabbi's friends that it actually happened. No one in the U.S. believed Jews were welcome in Syria.

I liked the mufti, and I thought of him then as a fundamentally good man. I still do. His vision served as an antidote to the fear we'd witnessed at the university; he articulated hope with conviction. He had the winning smile and polite bearing of a diplomat, though later it struck me that nearly everything he'd said sounded as if it had been scripted by a politically correct ecumenical council in Santa Fe. Nearly everything, but not all. When he was finished speaking, he invited us to ask him questions. I thought about Murat, the Sunni and Shia worshipers mingling effortlessly at the Grand Mosque, and the dread I'd heard the university students express. It all seemed related somehow. I asked the mufti if there was any chance that the Sunni-Shia violence engulfing Iraq could spread to Syria.

"As soon as the occupying forces leave, the different groups in

Iraq will reconcile, because they are a single family," he said. I would love to believe this, but it is self-evidently untrue. All that blood being spilled in Iraq — it will stop the very moment the American soldiers leave? *Inshallah.* The mufti invoked 1948 — the year of the founding of Israel — as the beginning of the region's troubles, a constant refrain in the Middle East that does not accept any measure of Arab responsibility for the current situation. It recalled for me the kind of thinking I've heard so often in Latin America among the unreconstructed radical Left: every political crisis, every economic injustice, every pothole in every street, and every sick child languishing in the hospital is the fault of American imperialism. It's such a seductive line of thought because it provides such an obvious solution. At my first question, the mufti's clear thinking became a little muddled. Suddenly he was invoking the twenty-five thousand mercenaries brought by the Americans to destabilize Iraq, the ten al Qaeda operatives who had confessed to being trained in Tel Aviv by the Mossad, the conspiracy to murder Princess Diana because her boyfriend was Egyptian. He had veered off — though the calm tone of his voice never wavered, the content of his speech was suddenly quite different. Nor was this the only contradiction in his discourse: al-Din Hassoun, for all his stress on the importance of separating religion and the state, was himself a government appointee.

Our conversation lasted about an hour, and when we were done, we posed for a few photos. Grand Mufti al-Din Hassoun stood flanked by a few American poets and writers, beaming like a proud father. We said our goodbyes and went out to the van waiting to take us to Jordan.

Fatih pulled me aside as we walked. She would accompany us to Amman, then leave us. She had a special favor to ask me, she said, and it was very important. Would I do it?

"Of course," I said.

"Write about Tel Aviv. I want you to tell me what it's like. The city — what does it look like? The people — how are they? How do they talk?"

Tel Aviv, she explained, is rarely mentioned in Syrian media, and the city itself is never shown. As if it didn't exist at all. An interior shot might appear on television now and then, but she longed to know more than that.

I told her I'd do my best.

"Good," she said. "Write me an e-mail, but when you do, don't mention Tel Aviv by name. Just say *the city.*"

We arrived in Tel Aviv on a night when a million people gathered in the center of the city to demand that Prime Minister Ehud Olmert resign. A report on the 2006 war with Hezbollah had just been released, and this firestorm was the predictable result. I was raised to support demonstrations, to respect the powers of masses who take to the streets, but this was one protest I found difficult to get behind. From talking to people, this was the message of the march, as I understood it: *We need a new prime minister — soon — because there is a war around the corner with Syria or Iran or Hezbollah or perhaps even all of them at once and we can't have this incompetent running the show when the shit hits the fan.* It was impressive, I suppose, in that one rarely sees such bald expressions of realpolitik coming from the masses, but the underlying assumptions — war, war, war — were disheartening and sad.

The next morning, I awoke in a seaside hotel that looked out over a boardwalk and a beach and the Mediterranean, a sheet of electric, eye-popping blue. Though it was Friday — the Jewish and Muslim holy day — you wouldn't have guessed it. Couples strolled along boardwalk hand in hand, there were joggers and roller-bladers wearing iPods, and I spent the morning walking up and down the stretch of beach wondering how I ended up in Miami.

Away from the boardwalk, Tel Aviv reminded me of Lima, and this is what I wrote Fatih in my letter: no dominant architectural style, a curious, often unsightly mishmash — Art Deco, modernist, classical, here and there a nod to the Middle East. Visual cacophony. A city built facing the sea. The Israeli writer and film director Etgar Keret explained the eclectic nature of Tel Aviv to me this way: the city, as it is today, was built by Jews that came from many dozens of nations. Think about that diversity of linguistic traditions, cultural mores, and visual cultures. They arrived here and made a city. And, Keret added, it was not built with posterity in mind, but came of age under the constant threat of annihilation. Why bother with city planning if in five years the city, the country, and the Jews themselves might not exist?

In the afternoon, I walked around Jaffa, the old Arab city that Tel

Aviv has since overwhelmed, on a tour of sorts with Antonio Ungar,
a Colombian writer who had married a Palestinian woman. He
showed me the old houses, refurbished and transformed into con-
dos for rich Israelis as the area is slowly gentrified. He explained
the slow encroachment of Jewish settlement on what had previously been a thriving Arab port and described the orange groves
that once stood, the stands of olive trees razed by the Israelis. This
is the way love works, I suppose: the stories of each become the
story of both, and it was astonishing to hear this tragic Palestinian
tale recounted in the elegantly accented Spanish of a Bogotano. "It
was such a beautiful place," Antonio said, with such conviction
you'd think he'd seen it himself.

The image I had of Ramallah was from Arafat's last days, when the
Palestinian leader was holed up in his compound, under siege
from the Israelis. I thought the entire city would be bombed out,
demolished, but of course this wasn't the case at all. The day we visited, there was a movie being filmed in the central part of the city.
A few young men sat on the tiled roof of a two-story building, bak-
ing beneath the sun, while a curious crowd gathered below to
watch the actors. The streets were full of people, and traffic inched
along. There were bookstores, gaudy billboards for cell phones,
and a Starbucks — though upon closer inspection, it was a knock-
off called Stars and Bucks. Later, as we drove to our reading at
Birzeit University, our host pointed out Arafat's compound. It had
been rebuilt.
    I was surprised by the extent to which a Middle Eastern daily life
resembled most other lives. People hurry to work or to school, to
see friends or lovers. They negotiate the extraordinary circumstances they live with, and in doing so, make them ordinary. At our
reading, a student named Laila described her daily commute from
East Jerusalem to the West Bank. Were it not for the checkpoints,
Ramallah would be less than thirty minutes from Jerusalem, but depending on the mood of the soldiers on any given day, the trip can
take anywhere from two to six hours. I wonder how many American
students would overcome similar hardships to get to class. But Laila
didn't want to talk about checkpoints. She felt great sympathy for
the Israeli soldiers, she told us. They were so afraid, and the milita-
rized interaction between Israelis and Palestinians seemed almost

perfectly designed to drive both sides insane. In any case, those would not be the memories she would carry with her from Birzeit. She was just like any twenty-year-old student, and she would re- member her friends, the good times, laughter.

After our reading, we were supposed to have lunch with a few local journalists and writers. In most places, organizing a lunch wouldn't be such a big deal, but in the West Bank, in the Palestin- ian territories, everything is complicated. The problem was that one of the invited guests worked for the Ministry of Culture of the Palestinian National Authority, which, since 2006's democratic elections (and until Mahmoud Abbas dissolved the government following the civil war in Gaza) had been run by Hamas — a group on the U.S. State Department list of terrorist organizations. So our potential lunch guest was, by the transitive property of myopic dip- lomatic fiat, a terrorist. We did not represent the United States, and yet here we were, having our dialogue hampered by the govern- ment's rules.

All week long the International Writing Program had been at- tempting to resolve the issue. This man was precisely the kind of person we felt we should be talking to, but we'd been put in the awkward position of having to rescind his invitation. That hadn't sat well with anyone. E-mails went back and forth, some hostile, some hopeful, and as we left Birzeit, we were optimistic that at least some of the people we'd invited might show up. The restaurant was on the outskirts of town, and we drove through the bustling center of Ramallah and then along hillside roads through the stark beauty of high desert landscape — the bare rock glowing in the sun, a glaze of dust along the horizon. We could see the Israeli security fence — a wall, actually — a thick, concrete scar on the land or, more precisely, a perverse memorial to those on both sides who have attempted to make peace and failed. I understand why some people would rather not think about this region and its endless complexity, why some would just wish it away. We forget, even here on the ground, that there is life outside of politics, a Holy Land be- yond one thousand years of bad decisions. We forget about the people.

At the restaurant, we were led to a large, tented, and airy dining room where, in anticipation of our event, the waiters had set up a very long table with flowers in the middle; there were two plastic

flags — the American and the Palestinian — crossed in a symbol of
friendship. It was just our group and a few administrators from the
university, and so the flags in particular looked rather sad. There
were about ten seats too many. After a few words from our hosts,
the waiters began dismantling the spread. A much smaller table
was prepared, and everyone stood uncomfortably around it, not really knowing what to do. They removed the flags, and we sat.

    We kept expecting someone else to show, but no one ever did.
    The food was delicious, and we ate it alone.

Contributors' Notes

Notable Travel Writing of 2008

Contributors' Notes

André Aciman is the author of *Out of Egypt: A Memoir* and the collection of essays *False Papers: Essays on Exile and Memory*. He has also coauthored and edited *The Proust Project* and *Letters of Transit*, and most recently has written a novel, *Call Me By Your Name*. Born in Alexandria, he lived in Italy and France. He received his PhD from Harvard University and has taught at Princeton University and Bard College, and is currently the chair of the Graduate Center's doctoral program in comparative literature and the director of the Writers' Institute. He is the recipient of a Whiting Writers' Award, a Guggenheim Fellowship, and a fellowship from the New York Public Library's Cullman Center for Scholars and Writers. He has written for the *New York Times*, *The New Yorker*, the *New York Review of Books*, the *Paris Review*, and the *New Republic*.

Daniel Alarcón is associate editor of *Etiqueta Negra*, an award-winning monthly magazine published in his native Lima, Peru. His novel *Lost City Radio* won the 2008 PEN USA award for fiction, and his most recent book, a story collection entitled *El rey siempre está por encima del pueblo*, was recently published in Mexico.

Caroline Alexander is the author of *The Endurance* and *The Bounty* and is working on a book on the Iliad. Her articles have appeared in *The New Yorker*, *Granta*, and *National Geographic*, among other publications.

Frank Bures is a contributing editor at *WorldHum.com*, and his work has appeared in *Esquire*, *Outside*, *Mother Jones*, and other publications. He writes frequently about Africa, and his stories have won several awards and been selected for *The Best American Travel Writing 2004*.

Roger Cohen joined the *New York Times* in 1990. He was a foreign correspondent for more than a decade before becoming acting foreign editor on September 11, 2001, and foreign editor six months later. Since 2004, he has written a column for the Times-owned *International Herald Tribune*, first for the news pages and then, since 2007, for the op-ed page. In 2009, he was named a columnist of the *New York Times*. Cohen has written *Hearts Grown Brutal: Sagas of Sarajevo* (1998), an account of the wars of Yugoslavia's destruction, and *Soldiers and Slaves: American POWs Trapped by the Nazis' Final Gamble* (2005). He has also cowritten a biography of General Norman Schwarzkopf, *In the Eye of the Storm* (1991).

Jay Cowan is the editor in chief of the Maggie-winning *Aspen Sojourner* magazine and a longtime contributing editor at *Ski* magazine. Cowan writes regularly for *Snow, Mountain Gazette, Cowboys & Indians*, and *Big Sky Journal*, among other publications. The North American Snowsports Journalists Association has selected him for four Harold Hirsch awards for feature magazine writing, and he has received a Lowell Thomas Award for Print Journalism from Colorado Ski Country USA. His most recent book is *Hunter S. Thompson: An Insider's View of Deranged, Depraved, Drugged Out Brilliance* (2009), about his longtime friend. Cowan also wrote and photographed *The Best of the Alps* (1999). He is currently at work on an adventure travel book about Indonesia called *In the Land of Living Dangerously*.

Lynne Cox has set records all over the world for open-water swimming. She was named a *Los Angeles Times* Woman of the Year and inducted into the International Swimming Hall of Fame. Her other honors include a lifetime achievement award from the University of California, Santa Barbara, and the Susan B. Anthony Center for Women's Leadership. *Outside* has named her an Adventure Icon. She is the author of *Swimming to Antarctica*, which won an Alex Award, and the best-selling book *Grayson*. She lives in Los Alamitos, California.

Kiran Desai is the author of *Hullabaloo in the Guava Orchard*, for which she won the Betty Trask Award, and *The Inheritance of Loss*, for which she won the National Book Critics Circle Award and the Man Booker Prize.

Bronwen Dickey's essays and journalism have appeared in *Newsweek, The Oxford American, WorldHum.com, ISLANDS, Sport Diver,* the *San Francisco Chronicle,* and the *Independent Weekly,* among others. She holds a BA in history from Duke University and an MFA in nonfiction writing from Columbia University. She lives in North Carolina.

Elisabeth Eaves is a deputy editor at *Forbes* and the author of *Bare: The Naked Truth About Stripping*. She has written for many publications, including *Foreign Policy, Harper's Magazine,* the *New York Times, Slate.com, Sport Diver,* the *Wall Street Journal,* and *WorldHum.com.* Her *Slate* series on flamenco in Seville won a silver Lowell Thomas Travel Journalism award. Born in Vancouver, Elisabeth lives in New York City.

Alma Guillermoprieto, a Mexican-born journalist, writes frequently about Latin America for *The New Yorker,* the *New York Review of Books,* and *National Geographic.* Her most recent book is *Dancing with Cuba* (2004).

Karrie Jacobs, a Brooklyn-based critic and essayist, is a contributing editor at *Travel* + *Leisure, Metropolis Magazine,* and *Metropolitan Home.* She is the author of an architectural road trip book, *The Perfect $100,000 House: A Trip Across America and Back in Pursuit of a Place to Call Home* (2007), and was the founding editor in chief of *Dwell* magazine.

Dimiter Kenarov is a freelance journalist and contributing editor to *The Virginia Quarterly Review.* His work has appeared in various Bulgarian and U.S. publications, including *The Nation* and *Boston Review.* He is currently a PhD candidate in English at the University of California, Berkeley.

Jay Kirk's nonfiction has been previously anthologized, most recently in *Submersion Journalism: Reporting in the Radical First Person from Harper's Magazine.* He was awarded a Pew Fellowship in the Arts in 2005 and teaches in the Creative Writing Program at the University of Pennsylvania. He is currently finishing a book, *Kingdom Under Glass,* about the adventures of the museum taxidermist Carl Akeley, which will be published by HarperCollins next year.

Chuck Klosterman is the *New York Times* best-selling author of *Eating the Dinosaur; Downtown Owl; Chuck Klosterman IV; Killing Yourself to Live; Sex, Drugs, and Cocoa Puffs;* and *Fargo Rock City,* winner of the ASCAP-Deems Taylor Award. He is a featured columnist for *Esquire* and a contributor to the *New York Times Magazine,* and has also written for *Spin,* the *Washington Post,* the *Guardian,* the *Believer,* and ESPN. His work has been selected for the *Da Capo Best Music Writing* and the *Best American Nonrequired Reading* anthologies. Klosterman grew up on a farm near Wyndmere, North Dakota. After graduating from the University of North Dakota, he wrote for the *Fargo Forum* and the *Akron Beacon Journal.* His work is published in eight territories and seven languages. In 2008, Klosterman was the Picador

Guest Professor for Literature at the University of Leipzig's Institute for American Studies in Leipzig, Germany. He lives in New York.

A specialist in offbeat historical travel, **Tony Perrottet** is the author of four books, including *Pagan Holiday: On the Trail of Ancient Roman Tourists* and Napoleon's *Privates: 2500 Years of History Unzipped*. Raised in Sydney, Australia, he has commuted in recent years from his home in the East Village of Manhattan to Tierra del Fuego, Zanzibar, Iceland, backwoods Wyoming, and Capri. He is a regular contributor to the *New York Times, Smithsonian, Condé Nast Traveler, Islands,* and the London *Sunday Times,* among other publications, and has appeared on the History Channel commenting on everything from the crusades to the birth of disco. He is currently working on a book based on "The Pervert's Grand Tour," to be published in 2010. This is his fourth story for the *Best American Travel Writing* series. His website is www.tonyperrottet.com.

Matthew Power has reported from post-tsunami Thailand and post-Taliban Afghanistan, documented the lives of dump scavengers in Manila, ridden motorcycles through the Kashmir Himalaya and the Bolivian Andes, and hopped freight trains across Canada and Mexico, none of which adequately prepared him to spend a month drifting down the Mississippi on a raft made of scavenged materials, despite having read everything Mark Twain had to say on the subject. Power is a contributing editor at *Harper's Magazine* and *National Geographic Adventure,* and his writing has also appeared in the *New York Times, Men's Journal, Wired, GQ, Discover, The Virginia Quarterly Review, Granta, Slate.com, The Best American Spiritual Writing 2006,* and *The Best American Travel Writing 2007.* He grew up in Vermont and lives in Brooklyn, New York.

Paul Salopek is a journalist based in Johannesburg, South Africa. He has won two Pulitzer Prizes for his work with the *Chicago Tribune.*

Mark Schatzker is a travel, food, and humor writer and a frequent contributor to *Condé Nast Traveler.* He is presently at work on his first book, *Steak: One Man's Quest for the World's Tastiest Piece of Beef,* which will be published next year. He lives in Toronto, Canada, with his wife and three children.

Tom Sleigh's most recent book of poetry, *Space Walk,* won the Kingsley Tufts Award in 2008. His book of essays, *Interview with a Ghost,* was published in 2006. He has also published *After One, Waking, The Chain, The Dreamhouse, Far Side of the Earth, Bula Matari/Smasher of Rocks,* and a translation of Euripides' *Herakles*. He has won the Shelley Prize from the Poetry Society of America and grants from the Lila Wallace Fund, the American Academy of Arts and Letters, the Guggenheim, and the National Endowment for the Arts. He teaches in the MFA program at Hunter College. His new book, *Orders of Daylight*, is forthcoming in the fall of 2010.

Seth Stevenson is a contributing writer for *Slate.com*. His work has also appeared in the *New York Times*, the *Washington Post, New York Magazine, Newsweek*, and *Rolling Stone*. His first book, *Grounded* — a travel memoir about circumnavigating the globe using only surface transportation — will be published in 2010. Stevenson grew up in Brookline, Massachusetts, graduated from Brown University, and currently lives in Washington, D.C.

Patrick Symmes is an author, war correspondent, and travel writer specializing in Third World conflicts, global environmental problems, travel, and geopolitics. He has been a contributing editor at *Harper's Magazine* and *Outside* for many years and also publishes in *Newsweek, GQ, Condé Nast Traveler, Mother Jones*, the *New York Times Magazine*, and the *Telegraph* in London. He is the author of two books on Cuba, *Chasing Che* (2000) and *The Boys from Dolores* (2007).

Calvin Trillin has been a staff writer for *The New Yorker* since 1963. His most recent books are *Deciding the Next Decider: The 2008 Presidential Race in Rhyme* and the best-selling memoir *About Alice*. His novels include *Tepper Isn't Going Out* (2001), which he claims is the first parking novel, *Runestruck* (1977), and *Floater* (1980). His other books include two books of verse on the Bush administration, a collection of reportage on murders, three books on eating that were republished as *The Tummy Trilogy*, and a travel book called *Travels with Alice*. He lives in New York.

Eric Weiner, a former correspondent for National Public Radio, is the best-selling author of *The Geography of Bliss: One Grump's Search for the Happiest Places in the World*. His work has appeared in the *New York Times Magazine*, the *New Republic*, the *Washington Post, Foreign Policy, Slate.com*, and other publications. He lives in Washington, D.C.

Notable Travel Writing of 2008

SELECTED BY JASON WILSON

CHARLES BOWDEN
  Mexico's Red Days. *GQ*, August.

BRYAN CURTIS
  Baseball, Dominican-Style. *Slate.com*, May 9.

KEVIN FEDARKO
  They Call Me Groover Boy. *Outside*, July.
GEORGE MICHELSEN FOY
  Bollywood Shuffle. *Harper's Magazine*, October.
JONATHAN FRANZEN
  The Way of the Puffin. *The New Yorker*, April 21.
DEVIN FRIEDMAN
  Powder Keg. *GQ*, May.
STEVE FRIEDMAN
  Sick of the Lies. *Bicycling*, November.
  I Will Survive. *Backpacker*, October.
  I'm Hiking with Stupid. *Backpacker*, November.

J. MALCOLM GARCIA
  All the Country Will Be Shaking. *The Virginia Quarterly Review*, Winter.
PATRICK GRAHAM
  Go Before You Die. *Harper's Magazine*, February.

TOM HAINES
  Continental Shift. *Boston Globe*, March 30.
  A Wondrous View. *Boston Globe*, May 18.
JOSHUA HAMMER
  Landscape After Battle. *Condé Nast Traveler*, February.
  Paradise Regained. *The Atlantic Monthly*, April.

LEIGH ANN HENION
  Wings and a Prayer. *Washington Post Magazine,* March 30.
PETER HESSLER
  The Home Team. *The New Yorker,* September 15.
  Inside the Dragon. *National Geographic,* May.
  The Wonder Years. *The New Yorker,* March 31.

KATIE KREUGER
  My Senegalese Cousin, the Rice-Loving Pig. *WorldHum.com,* July 15.
JOSHUA KURLANTZICK
  Thai Noon. *The Atlantic Monthly,* June.

MATT LABASH
  The City Where the Sirens Never Sleep. *The Weekly Standard,* December 29.
FRANCIS LAM
  Getting to Know Him. *Gourmet,* December.
JEANNE MARIE LASKAS
  Empire of Ice. *GQ,* October.

EMILY MALONEY
  Miss Venezuela. *The Smart Set,* December 9.
  Stretch Pants. *The Smart Set,* March 11.
LEEANN MARHEVSKY
  The Wrath of Khan. *The Smart Set,* November 7.
PATRICIA MARX
  Buy Shanghai! *The New Yorker,* June 21.
BUCKY MCMAHON
  Down the Monkey Hole. *Men's Journal,* May.
  Where the Walking Shark Lives. *Outside,* July.
BRYAN PATRICK MILLER
  Return of Glavin. *New York Times Magazine,* March 16.

KRISTIN OHLSON
  Watching TV in Kabul. *New York Times Magazine,* July 20.
LAWRENCE OSBORNE
  I'll Have a Glass of Fresh Snake Blood, Please. *Men's Journal,* June.
DAVID OWEN
  My Airline. *The New Yorker,* July 7 & 14.

MATTHEW POWER
  Charlie Don't Surf. *The Virginia Quarterly Review,* Spring.

EDWARD READICKER-HENDERSON
  How the Last White Rhino in Zambia Wins at Strip Passport. *Perceptive Travel,*
  May.

FRANCIS X. ROCCA
The Caudillo's Cloister. *The Atlantic Monthly,* March.
RICHARD RODRIQUEZ
The God of the Desert. *Harper's Magazine,* January.
JULIA ROSS
Six Degrees of Vietnam. *WorldHum.com,* November 18.
STEVE RUSHIN
One Nation in Need of a Vacation. *Via,* May/June.

PETER SAVODNIK
Ghosts of the White Nights. *Condé Nast Traveler,* June.
GARY SHTEYNGART
Bangkok Nights. *Travel + Leisure,* July.
EMILY STONE
On the Occasional Importance of a Ceiling Fan. *WorldHum.com,* May.
THOMAS SWICK
Pilgrim's Progress. *The Weekly Standard,* September 8.
PATRICK SYMMES
Day of Ascension. *T Magazine: New York Times,* September 21.
The Battle of Ideas. *Harper's Magazine,* May.
Red Is the New Green. *Outside,* March.

AMY TAN
Village on the Edge of Time. *National Geographic,* May.
JEFFREY TAYLER
Feasting in Lyon. *WorldHum.com,* September.
PAUL THEROUX
Ghosts in the Machine. *Condé Nast Traveler,* August.
NATASHA TRETHEWEY
The Gulf. *The Virginia Quarterly Review,* Summer.

DANA VACHON
My Lunch at Bear Stearns. *Slate.com,* March 21.

SIMON WINCHESTER
The Hills of Serendipity. *Condé Nast Traveler,* November.
The Secret of Caves. *Condé Nast Traveler,* April.
GRAEME WOOD
Mengele in Paraguay. *The Smart Set,* Feburary 5.